Also by Calvin Trillin

Messages from My Father (1996)
Too Soon to Tell (1995)
Deadline Poet (1994)
Remembering Denny (1993)
American Stories (1991)
Enough's Enough (1990)
Travels with Alice (1989)
If You Can't Say Something Nice (1987)
With All Disrespect (1985)
Killings (1984)
Uncivil Liberties (1982)
Floater (1980)
Runestruck (1977)
U.S. Journal (1971)
Barnett Frummer Is an Unbloomed Flower (1969)
An Education in Georgia (1964)

THE TUMMY TRILOGY

THE TUMMY TRILOGY

CALVIN

TRILLIN

Farrar, Straus and Giroux

New York

THE
TUMMY
TRILOGY

AMERICAN FRIED

ALICE, LET'S EAT

THIRD HELPINGS

WITH A NEW FOREWORD

Farrar, Straus and Giroux
18 West 18th Street, New York 10011

Printed in the United States of America
First edition, 1994

American Fried *was first published by Doubleday,* Alice, Let's Eat *by
Random House, and* Third Helpings *by Ticknor & Fields. Portions of
this material originally appeared, in somewhat different form, in* The
New Yorker *and other magazines.*

The Library of Congress has cataloged the hardcover edition as follows:
Trillin, Calvin.
    The tummy trilogy : with a new foreword / Calvin Trillin.— 1st ed.
        p.   cm.
    Contents: American fried—Alice, let's eat—Third helpings.
    ISBN-13: 978-0-374-27950-9
    ISBN-10: 0-374-27950-0
    1. Dinners and dining—United States.   2. Restaurants—
United States.   3. Food—Humor.   4. Gastronomy—Humor.
5. Cookery—Humor.   I. Title.

TX737 .T76 1994
641'.01'3—dc20

                                                94-6651 CIP

Paperback ISBN-13: 978-0-374-52417-3
Paperback ISBN-10: 0-374-52417-3

Designed by Cynthia Krupat

www.fsgbooks.com

25   27   29   30   28   26

To Alice and Abigail and Sarah

—the same old crowd

(CONTENTS)

THIRD HELPINGS (1983)

HAVE I REFORMED? All and all, is it now less likely that a member of my own family who was asked to describe me would come up with a phrase like "sausage-eating crank"?

In other words, have I stopped sniffing around perfectly respectable American cities for the aroma of ribs being barbecued over authentic hickory wood? Have I reached the point of declining to attend the sort of symposium that is devoted to searching out the most stunning grocery-store boudin in southwestern Louisiana—or at least the point of not insisting that it be held someplace that can keep the panelists supplied with superior crawfish? Does health food no longer make me sick? Have the two little girls who are seen scampering through the pages of *American Fried* and *Alice, Let's Eat* and *Third Helpings*, frozen fish sticks in hand, stopped saying, "Daddy likes to pig out"?

What can I say? It's complicated. There is no question that, in 1982, when I ended fifteen years of traveling around the country for a *New Yorker* series called "U.S. Journal," I more or less quit writing about barbecue-divining and boudin-hunting and, well, pigging out. Not writing about it, of course, is hardly the same as not doing it, but as my wife, Alice, said at the time, "It's a start."

For the "U.S. Journal" series, which was an attempt to write about America without concentrating on its government or politics,

I did an article somewhere in the United States every three weeks
—a schedule that would have enhanced anyone's interest in how
a traveling man in a strange city goes about finding something decent
to eat. In 1972, around the time that I was beginning to feel a bit
overburdened by the weight of the subjects I was dealing with, I
realized that a series about America could accommodate a light
story now and then about Americans eating—a sort of change-up
that rested the arm, even at risk to the midsection. The realization
came at the Breaux Bridge Crawfish Festival, and it came as a great
relief. The relief turned to pure joy after I tasted the crawfish.

I had neither the credentials for nor any interest in inspecting,
say, a serving of veal Orloff for the purpose of announcing to the
world how it measured up to what dog-show types call the standards
of the breed. I wrote about eating rather than food, and I wrote as
a reporter who was enjoying his work rather than as an expert. If
there was a unifying proposition in what I wrote on the subject, it
was that Americans should celebrate rather than apologize for the
local specialties that they actually enjoyed—a selfish proposition,
I'll admit, since it was an argument for directing an out-of-town
visitor toward a legendary fried-chicken place or a sublime crab joint
rather than subjecting him to the rooftop dining palace that I had
begun to call La Maison de la Casa House, Continental Cuisine.
One thing led to another—a phrase I often used in those days, it
now occurs to me, when Alice asked how my friend Jaffe and I
could have gone into Buster Holmes's red-beans-and-rice emporium
on Burgundy Street for lunch at twelve-thirty and not emerged until
twilight—and by the time I called a halt to life on the road I had
published three books on eating. All of them followed the theme
announced by the subtitle of the first—"Adventures of a Happy
Eater."

By 1982, of course, the lot of a traveling man who valued his
victuals had improved considerably. The shake-up of American
society that began in the late sixties had thrown some middle-class
young people into close proximity with ingredients that were not
surrounded by a can; some of those young people came to the
realization that there was not, as it turned out, a natural law pro-
hibiting the son of a tax lawyer from becoming a chef. In larger

American cities, it became conceivable that a business leader who wanted to show an out-of-town visitor some sophistication would skip the rooftop Continental cuisine palace for a ground-floor restaurant whose menu not only didn't trouble itself with French that the waiters couldn't pronounce but boasted that the mushrooms came from Oregon.

The business leader might even—praise God!—take the visitor to the local barbecue joint. At some point in the late seventies, a lot of Americans came to the realization that their local customs—playing bluegrass music, say, or growing corn or eating enchiladas—were not as shameful as they had once been led to believe. On the road, it became rarer for me to contemplate the possibility that, in my desperation, I might be forced to sidle over to the clerk at the motel, as if I were going to make some innocent inquiry about checkout time, grab him by his necktie, pull him over the counter, and say, in a voice that signified I meant business, "Not the place you took your parents on their twenty-fifth wedding anniversary. The place you went the night you came home after thirteen months in Korea."

Just why Americans began to accept the legitimacy of their home territory involves a combination of historical factors that still have not been completely sorted out. But the event that had an even greater impact on American restaurants during my travels can be isolated easily: the reform of the immigration laws in 1965. From the point of view of a traveling man with a strong interest in immigrants being able to get a toehold in this country by starting family restaurants, the pre-1965 immigration policy was a matter of simple madness: we were basically shutting out the Chinese while letting in as many Englishmen as wanted to come, even if they were dragging their overcooked vegetables behind them. The change in the number and composition of the immigrant population was accelerated by the end of the war in Vietnam, and, I have previously acknowledged, when helicopters were snatching people from the grounds of the American embassy compound during the panic of the final Vietcong push into Saigon, I was sitting in front of the television set shouting, "Get the chefs! Get the chefs!"

By 1982, then, hungry travelers were no longer in the desperate shape they had been in in 1967, and I, having brought the "U.S. Journal" series to an end, was no longer in need of an occasional change-up. Also, I might as well admit, I was growing increasingly uncomfortable with the assumption that I actually did know or care about what was or what wasn't a proper veal Orloff—an assumption that could be taken as a lesson in how easy it is to be considered an expert in this country. Without the benefit of any formal swearing-off, I began to avoid the subject of eating. Except for a couple of pieces of backsliding in the middle eighties, I have since pretty much confined my food writing to an occasional travel piece abroad, separated by one ocean or another from the aroma of smoking hickory wood.

So these books are set within a ten-year period, ending in 1982. They do not reflect the changes that have taken place since then in American eating and in the restaurants mentioned and in my companions at table. Americans obviously tend to have a more serious interest these days in avoiding foods that are palpably ruinous to their health, for instance, and those two little girls who were clutching frozen fish sticks have insisted on growing up and moving out of our house. But have I changed my eating habits personally? Have I reformed? Have I become a traveler who is happy to eat in the hotel? When I had to reread these books, did I shudder a bit at how often I came across the phrase "cooked in pure lard"? Am I no longer the sort of person who daydreams of taking Chairman Mao Tse-tung on an eating tour of New York? Of course, the Chairman is dead now. On the other hand, he was dead when I originally wrote about the daydream. As I said, it's complicated.

AMERICAN

FRIED

ADVENTURES OF

A HAPPY EATER

(1 9 7 4)

(1)

The Traveling Man's
Burden

THE BEST RESTAURANTS in the world are, of course, in Kansas City. Not all of them; only the top four or five. Anyone who has visited Kansas City and still doubts that statement has my sympathy: He never made it to the right places. Being in a traveling trade myself, I know the problem of asking someone in a strange city for the best restaurant in town and being led to some purple palace that serves "Continental cuisine" and has as its chief creative employee a menu-writer rather than a chef. I have sat in those places, an innocent wayfarer, reading a three-paragraph description of what the trout is wrapped in, how long it has been sautéed, what province its sauce comes from, and what it is likely to sound like sizzling on my platter—a description lacking only the information that before the poor beast went through that process it had been frozen for eight and a half months.

In American cities the size of Kansas City, a careful traveling man has to observe the rule that any restaurant the executive secretary of the Chamber of Commerce is particularly proud of is almost certainly not worth eating in. Its name will be something like La Maison de la Casa House, Continental Cuisine; its food will sound European but taste as if the continent they had in mind was Australia. Lately, a loyal chamber man in practically any city is likely to recommend one of those restaurants that have sprouted in the past several years on the tops of bank buildings, all of them encased in glass and some of them revolving—offering the diner not only Continental cuisine and a twenty-thousand-word menu but a spectacular view of other restaurants spinning around on the top of other bank buildings. "No, thank you," I finally said to the twelfth gracious host who invited me to one of those. "I never eat in a restaurant that's over a hundred feet off the ground and won't stand still."

What is saddest about a visitor's sitting in the Continental cuisine palace chewing on what an honest menu would have identified as Frozen Duck à l'Orange Soda Pop is that he is likely to have passed a spectacular restaurant on the way over. Despite the best efforts of forward-looking bankers and mad-dog franchisers, there is still great food all over the country, but the struggle to wring information from the locals about where it is served can sometimes leave a traveler too exhausted to eat. I often manage to press on with a seemingly hopeless interrogation only because of my certain knowledge that the information is available—discussed openly by the residents in their own homes, the way that French villagers might have discussed what they really thought of the occupation troops they had been polite to in the shops. As it happens, I grew up in Kansas City and spent hours of my youth talking about where a person could find the best fried chicken in the world or the best barbecued ribs in the world or the best hamburgers in the world— all, by chance, available at that time within the city limits of Kansas City, Missouri. I grew up among the kind of people whose response some years later to a preposterous claim about Little Rock's having a place that served better spareribs than the ones served by Arthur Bryant's Barbecue at Eighteenth and Brooklyn was to fly to Little Rock, sample the ribs, sneer, and fly back to Kansas City.

Knowing that the information exists does make me impatient if some civic booster in, say, one of the middle-sized cities of the Southwest is keeping me from dinner by answering my simple questions about restaurants with a lot of talk about the wine cellar of some palace that has inlaid wallpaper chosen personally by a man who is supposed to be the third-best interior decorator in San Francisco. As the booster goes on about the onion soup with croutons and the sophisticated headwaiter named Jean-Pierre, my mind sometimes wanders off into a fantasy in which my interrogation of the booster is taking place in the presence of one of those ominous blond Germans from the World War II films—the ones with the steel-blue eyes and the small scars who sat silently in the corner while the relatively civilized German line officer asked the downed Allied flyer for military information. "I do hope you will now agree to tell me if there's any Mexican food worth eating around here and quit talking about the glories to be found in La Maison de la Casa House, Continental Cuisine," I tell the booster. "If not, I'm afraid Herr Mueller here has his methods."

It is common for an American city to be vaguely embarrassed about its true delights. In the fifties, a European visitor to New Orleans who insisted on hearing some jazz was routinely taken to hear a group of very respectable-looking white businessmen play Dixieland. A few years ago, I suspect, an Eastern visitor to Nashville who asked a local banker if there was any interesting music in town might have been taken—by a circuitous route, in order to avoid overhearing any of the crude twanging coming out of the Grand Ole Opry or the country recording studios—to the home of a prominent dermatologist who had some friends around every Friday night for chamber music. In most American cities, a booster is likely to insist on defending the place to outsiders in terms of what he thinks of as the sophisticated standards of New York—a city, he makes clear at the start, he would not consider living in even if the alternative were moving with his family and belongings to Yakutsk, Siberia, U.S.S.R. A visitor, particularly a visitor from the East, is invariably subjected to a thirty-minute commercial about the improvement in the local philharmonic, a list of Broadway plays (well, musicals) that have been through in the past year, and some comment like "We happen to have an *excellent* French restaurant here now." The short answer to that one, of course, would be "No you don't." An American city's supply of even competent French restaurants is limited by the number of residents willing to patronize them steadily, and, given the difficulty of finding or importing ingredients and capturing a serious chef and attracting a clientele sufficiently critical to keep the chef from spending most of his time playing the commodities market out of boredom, "an *excellent*

French restaurant" will arrive in Tulsa or Omaha at about the time those places near the waterfront in Marseilles start turning out quality pan-fried chicken. In New York, where I live now, the few restaurants that even pretend to serve French food comparable to the food available in the best restaurants in France are maintained at a cost so high that dinner at any one of them seems bound, sooner or later, to face competition from the round-trip airfare to Paris or Lyon.

"I don't suppose your friends took you to Mary-Mac's on Ponce de Leon for a bowl of pot likker, did they?" I once said to a friend of mine who had just returned from her first visit to Atlanta. Naturally not. No civic-minded residents of Atlanta—which advertises itself as the World's Next Great City—would take an out-of-town guest to Mary-Mac's. Their idea of a regional eating attraction is more likely to be someplace built to look like one of the charming antebellum houses that Atlanta once had practically none of—having been, before Sherman got there, an almost new railroad terminus that had all the antebellum charm of Parsons, Kansas. Pot likker, I told my friend, is the liquid left in the bottom of the greens pot, is eaten like a soup, after crumbling some corn bread into it, and is what a Great City would advertise instead of a lot of golf courses.

"They took me to a very nice French restaurant," she said, gamely claiming that it was almost as good as the one she can go to for lunch on days she doesn't feel like walking far enough to get to the decent places.

Since "No you don't" would be considered an impolite reply to the usual boast about a city's having a three-star French restaurant, I have, in the past, stooped to such responses as "French food makes me break out." I love French food. (In fairness, I should say that I can't think of a nation whose food I don't love, although in Ethiopia I was put off a bit by the appearance of the bread, which looks like a material that has dozens of practical uses, not including being eaten as food.) But who wants to hear a skin doctor saw away at the cello when Johnny Cash is right down the street? Lately, when the local booster informs me—as the city ordinance apparently requires him to do within ten minutes of meeting anyone who lives in New

York—that he would never live in New York himself, I say something like "Well, it's not easy, of course. There's no barbecue to speak of. That's because of a shortage of hickory wood, I think, although I haven't checked out that theory with Arthur Bryant. We don't really have any Mexican restaurants—I mean the kind you find in Texas, say. Oh, we have Mexican restaurants run by maybe a guy from the East Side who picked up a few recipes while he was down in San Miguel de Allende thinking about becoming a painter, but no Mexican family restaurants. No señora in the kitchen. No Coors beer. No Lone Star. I wouldn't claim that you can live in New York and expect to drink Lone Star. There's a shortage of Chicago-style pizza south of Fourteenth Street. They don't know much about boiling crabs in New York. It's only since the soul-food places opened that we've been able to get any fried chicken, and we still don't have those family-style fried-chicken places with the fresh vegetables and the pickled watermelon rind on the table. Sure we've got problems. Grits are a problem. I'd be the last one to say living in New York is easy."

Somehow, people have listened to my entire speech and then suggested that I forget my troubles with some fine Continental cuisine at La Maison de la Casa House. I'm then forced into playing the restaurant section of the Yellow Pages—trying one system after another, like a thoroughly addicted horseplayer who would rather take his chances with a palpably bad system than give up the game altogether. I go with small listings for a while—no place that says anything like "See Advertisement Page 253 of this section." Then places called by someone's first name. Then places not called by someone's first name. For a while, I tried a complicated formula having to do with the number of specialties claimed in relation to the size of the entry, but I could never remember whether the formula called for me to multiply or divide. Constant traveling has provided me with some information on some cities, of course, but the discovery process remains a strain. Who would have ever guessed, for instance, that the old Mexican street near downtown Los Angeles that looks as if it was restored by the MGM set department and stocked by one of the less tasteful wholesalers in Tijuana would have one place that served delicious hand-patted soft

tacos packed with *picadillo* or *chicharrón*? How can an innocent
traveler be expected to guess that he is going to be subjected to the
old Hollywood mystery-film trick of hiding the real jewel in a case
full of paste imitations?

There are some types of food that do lend themselves to sophisticated techniques of interrogation. When an Italian restaurant
is suggested, for instance, I always say, "Who controls the city
council here?" I suppose a good Italian restaurant could exist in a
city that doesn't have enough Italians to constitute at least a powerful
minority in city politics, but a man in town for only two or three
meals has to go with the percentages. It is axiomatic that good
barbecue is almost never served in an obviously redecorated
restaurant—the reason being, according to my favorite theory on
the subject, that walls covered with that slick precut paneling let
the flavor slide away.

Some time ago, I found myself in Muskogee, Oklahoma, with
dinnertime approaching, and I asked some people I was having a
drink with if they knew of any good barbecue places. Through a
system of what amounted to ethnic elimination, I had arrived at
barbecue as the food most likely to see me through the evening.
There is, I am relieved to say, no Continental cuisine in Muskogee,
Oklahoma. The people I was having a drink with were trying to be
helpful, perhaps because the liquor laws of Oklahoma see to it that
citizens who are taking a bourbon in public feel so much like
criminals—having skulked in through an unmarked back door and
flashed some patently phony membership cards—that we had developed the closeness of conspirators. (Even states that allow grownups to drink in public with comparative ease expect a traveler to
observe some bizarre liquor laws, of course, including at least one
I approve of—the Vermont statute that makes it illegal for a customer to carry a drink from one table to another. I have found that
a man who picks up his drink and moves to your table is invariably
a man who is going to talk at length about how many miles his car
gets to the gallon.) One barbecue place was mentioned, but something about the way it was mentioned made me suspicious.

"They have plates there?" I asked.

"What do you mean 'plates'?" one of my fellow criminal booz-
ers asked me.

"You know—plates you eat off of," I said.

"Of course they have plates," he said.

"You have any other barbecue restaurants around here?" I asked. I have eaten fine barbecue on plates—Arthur Bryant, in fact, uses plates—but I would hesitate to eat barbecue in a place that has plates "of course" or "naturally" or "certainly." The next piece of information an outsider is likely to extract about such a place is that it also serves steaks and chicken and maybe even a stray lobster tail.

"Well," my partner in crime began, "there's an old colored fellow out on the highway who—"

"Tell me how to get there," I said.

It turned out to be a small diner, and if it had been a half mile closer I might have been able to locate it unassisted by following the perfume of burning hickory logs. There were, as it happened, no plates. The proprietor's version of the formal restaurant custom of including a dinner plate on top of a larger plate at each place setting was to put down a piece of butcher paper and then a piece of waxed paper and then the barbecue—first-class barbecue. It would have been a thoroughly satisfying meal except that my success in finding the place caused me to ponder all through dinner on how much happier traveling would be if only I could think of a workable formula for finding fried-chicken restaurants.

(2)

Hometown Boy

I KNOW A RADICAL from Texas who holds the stock market in contempt but refuses to give up his seven shares of Dr Pepper, Dallas's answer to Beaujolais. He says that Dr Pepper, like the late President Eisenhower, is above politics. I have personally acted as a courier in bringing desperately craved burnt-almond chocolate ice cream from Will Wright's in Los Angeles to a friend who survived a Beverly Hills childhood and now lives in New York—living like a Spanish Civil War refugee who hates the regime but would give his arm for a decent bowl of gazpacho. I have also, in the dark of night, slipped into a sophisticated apartment in upper Manhattan and left an unmarked paper bag containing a powdered substance called Ranch Dressing—available, my client believes, only in certain supermarkets in the state of Oklahoma. I once knew someone from Alabama who, in moments of melancholy or stress or drunkenness, would gain strength merely by staring up at some imaginary storekeeper and saying, in the accent of an Alabama road-gang worker on his five-minute morning break, "Jes gimme an R.C. and a moon pah."

Because I happened to grow up in Kansas City and now live in New York, there may be, I realize, a temptation to confuse my assessment of Kansas City restaurants with the hallucinations people all over the country suffer when gripped by the fever of Hometown

Food Nostalgia. I am aware of the theory held by Bill Vaughan, the humor columnist of the Kansas City *Star*, that millions of pounds of hometown goodies are constantly crisscrossing the country by U.S. mail in search of desperate expatriates—a theory he developed, I believe, while standing in the post office line in Kansas City holding a package of Wolferman's buns that he was about to send off to his son in Virginia. I do not have to be told that there is a tendency among a lot of otherwise sensible adults to believe that the best hamburgers in the world are served in the hamburger stands of their childhood. A friend of mine named William Edgett Smith, after all, a man of good judgment in most matters, clings to the bizarre notion that the best hamburgers in the world are served at Bob's Big Boy—Glendale, California, branch—rather than at Winstead's Drive-in in Kansas City. He has, over the years, stubbornly rejected my acute analysis of the Big Boy as a gimmick burger with a redundant middle bun, a run-of-the-mill triple-decker that is not easily distinguishable from a Howard Johnson's 3-D.

"It has a sesame-seed bun," Smith would say, as we sat in some midtown Manhattan bar eating second-rate cheeseburgers at a dollar seventy-five a throw—two expatriates from the land of serious hamburger eaters.

"Don't talk to me about seeds on buns," I'd say to Smith. "I had a Big Boy in Phoenix and it is not in any way a class burger."

"Phoenix is not Glendale," Smith would say, full of blind stubbornness.

Smith has never been to Winstead's, although he often flies to California to visit his family (in Glendale, it goes without saying) and I have reminded him that he could lay over in Kansas City for a couple of hours for little extra fare. He has never been able to understand the monumental purity of the Winstead's hamburger—no seeds planted on the buns, no strong sauce that might keep the exquisite flavor of the meat from dominating, no showy meat-thickness that is the downfall of most hamburgers. Winstead's has concentrated so hard on hamburgers that for a number of years it served just about nothing else. Its policy is stated plainly on the menu I have framed on the kitchen wall for inspiration: "We grind U.S. Graded Choice Steak daily for the sandwich and broil on a greaseless grill." That is the only claim Winstead's makes, except "Your drinks are served in sterilized glasses."

I can end any suspicion of hometown bias on my part by recounting the kind of conversation I used to have with my wife, Alice, an Easterner, before I took her back to Kansas City to meet my family and get her something decent to eat. Imagine that we are sitting at some glossy road stop on the Long Island Expressway, pausing for a bite to eat on our way to a fashionable traffic jam:

ME: Anybody who served a milkshake like this in Kansas City would be put in jail.

ALICE: You promised not to indulge in any of that hometown nostalgia while I'm eating. You know it gives me indigestion.

ME: What nostalgia? Facts are facts. The kind of milkshake that I personally consumed six hundred gallons of at the Country Club Dairy is an historical fact in three flavors. Your indigestion is not from listening to my fair-minded remarks on the food of a particular American city. It's from drinking that gray skim milk this bandit is trying to pass off as a milkshake.

ALICE: I suppose it wasn't you who told me that anybody who didn't think the best hamburger place in the world was in his hometown is a sissy.

ME: But don't you see that one of those places actually *is* the best hamburger place in the world? Somebody has to be telling the truth, and it happens to be me.

Alice has now been to Kansas City many times. If she is asked where the best hamburgers in the world are served, she will unhesitatingly answer, from the results of her own extensive quality testing, that they are served at Winstead's. By the time our first child was three, she had already been to Winstead's a few times, and as an assessor of hamburgers, she is, I'm proud to say, her father's daughter. Once, I asked her what I could bring her from a trip to Kansas City. "Bring me a hamburger," she said. I did. I now realize what kind of satisfaction it must have given my father when

I, at about the age of ten, finally agreed with him that *Gunga Din* was the greatest movie ever made.

•

I once went to Kansas City for the express purpose of making a grand tour of its great restaurants. Almost by coincidence, I found myself on the same plane with Fats Goldberg, the New York pizza baron, who grew up in Kansas City and was going back to visit his family and get something decent to eat. Fats, whose real name is Larry, got his nickname when he weighed about three hundred pounds. Some years ago, he got thin, and he has managed to remain at less than one hundred sixty ever since by subjecting himself to a horrifyingly rigid eating schedule. In New York, Fats eats virtually the same thing every day of his life. But he knows that even a man with his legendary willpower—a man who can spend every evening of the week in a Goldberg's Pizzeria without tasting—could never diet in Kansas City, so he lets himself go a couple of times a year while he is within the city limits. For Fats, Kansas City is the DMZ. He currently holds the world's record for getting from the airport to Winstead's.

Fats seemed a bit nervous about what we would find at Winstead's. For as long as I can remember, everyone in Kansas City has been saying that Winstead's is going downhill. Even in New York, where there has always been obsessive discussion of Winstead's among people from Kansas City, the Cassandras in our ranks have often talked as if the next double-with-everything-and-grilled-onions I order at Winstead's will come out tasting like something a drugstore counterman has produced by peeling some morbid-looking patty from waxed paper and tossing it on some grease-caked grill—a prophecy that has always proved absolutely false. I can hardly blame a Kansas City émigré for being pessimistic. We have all received letters about Winstead's decline for years—in the way people who grew up in other parts of the country receive letters telling them that the fresh trout they used to love to eat now tastes like turpentine because of the lumber mill upstream or that their favorite picnic meadow has become a trailer park. When Winstead's began serving French-fried potatoes several years ago, there was talk of defection in New York. The price of purity is purists. The French fries did turn out to be unspectacular—a lesson, I thought, that craftsmen should stick to their craft. The going-downhill talk was strong a few years later when Winstead's introduced something called an eggburger. My sister has actually eaten an eggburger—she has always had rather exotic tastes—but I found the idea so embarrassing that I avoided William Edgett Smith for days, until I realized he had no way of knowing about it. Fats told me on the plane that there had been a lot of going-downhill talk since Winstead's sold out to a larger company. He seemed personally hurt by the rumors.

"How can people talk that way?" he said, as we were about to land in Kansas City.

"Don't let it bother you, Fats," I said. "People in Paris are probably always going around saying the Louvre doesn't have any decent pictures anymore. It's human nature for the locals to bad-mouth the nearest national monument."

"You'll go to Zarda's Dairy for the banana split, of course," Fats said, apparently trying to cheer himself up by pitching in with some advice for the grand tour. "Also the Toddle House for hash browns. Then you'll have to go to Kresge's for a chili dog."

"Hold it, Fats," I said. "Get control of yourself." He was beginning to look wild. "I'm not sure a grand tour would include Kresge's chili dogs. Naturally, I'll try to get to the Toddle House for the hash browns; they're renowned."

I gave Fats a ride from the airport. As we started out, I told him I was supposed to meet my sister and my grandfather at Mario's—a place that had opened a few years before featuring a special sandwich my sister wanted me to try. Mario cuts off the end of a small Italian loaf, gouges out the bread in the middle, puts in meatballs or sausages and cheese, closes everything in by turning around the end he had cut off and using it as a plug, and bakes the whole thing. He says the patent is applied for.

"Mario's!" Fats said. "What Mario's? When I come into town, I go to Winstead's from the airport."

"My grandfather is waiting, Fats," I said. "He's eighty-eight years old. My sister will scream at me if we're late."

"We could go by the North Kansas City Winstead's branch

from here, get a couple to go, and eat them on the *way* to what-sisname's," Fats said. He looked desperate. I realized he had been looking forward to a Winstead's hamburger since his last trip to Kansas City five or six months before—five or six months he had endured without eating anything worth talking about.

That is how Fats and I came to start the grand tour riding toward Mario's clutching Winstead's hamburgers that we would release only long enough to snatch up our Winstead's Frosty Malts ("The Drink You Eat with a Spoon"), and discussing the quality of the top-meat, no-gimmick burger that Winstead's continued to put out. By the time we approached Mario's, I felt that nothing could spoil my day, even if my sister screamed at me for being late.

"There's LaMar's Do-Nuts," Fats said, pulling at the steering wheel. "They do a sugar doughnut that's dynamite."

"But my grandfather . . ." I said.

"Just pull over for a second," Fats said. "We'll split a couple."

•

I can now recount a conversation I would like to have had with the "freelance food and travel writer" who, according to the Kansas City *Star*, spent a few days in town and then called Mario's sandwich "the single best thing I've ever had to eat in Kansas City." I mean no disrespect to Mario, whose sandwich might be good enough to be the single best thing in a lot of cities. I hope he gets his patent.

ME: I guess if that's the best thing you've ever had to eat in Kansas City you must have got lost trying to find Winstead's. Also, I'm surprised at the implication that a fancy freelance food and travel writer like you was not allowed into Arthur Bryant's Barbecue, which is only the single best restaurant in the world.

FREELANCE FOOD AND TRAVEL WRITER: I happen to like Italian food. It's very Continental.

ME: There are no Italians in Kansas City. It's one of the town's few weaknesses.

FFTW: Of course there are Italians in Kansas City. There's a huge Italian neighborhood on the northeast side.

ME: In my high school we had one guy we called Guinea Gessler, but he kept insisting he was Swiss. I finally decided he really *was* Swiss. Anyway, he's not running any restaurants. He's in the finance business.

FFTW: Your high school is not the whole city. I can show you statistics.

ME: Don't tell me about this town, buddy. I was born here.

"Actually, there probably *are* a lot of good restaurants there, because of the stockyards," New Yorkers say—swollen with condescension—when I inform them that the best restaurants in the world are in Kansas City. But, as a matter of fact, there are *not* a lot of good steak restaurants in Kansas City; American restaurants do not automatically take advantage of proximity to the ingredients, as anyone who has ever tried to find a fresh piece of fish on the Florida Coast does not need to be told. The best steak restaurant in the world, Jess & Jim's, does happen to be in Kansas City, but it gets its meat from the stockyards in St. Joe, fifty miles away. The most expensive steak on the menu is Jess & Jim's Kansas City Strip Sirloin. When I arrived on the first evening of my tour, it was selling for $6.50, including salad and the best cottage-fried potatoes in the tri-state area. They are probably also the best cottage-fried potatoes in the world, but I don't have wide enough experience in eating cottage fries to make a definitive judgment.

Jess & Jim's is a sort of roadhouse, decorated simply with bowling trophies and illuminated beer signs. But if the proprietor saw one of his waitresses emerge from the kitchen with a steak that was no better than the kind you pay twelve dollars for in New York—in one of those steak houses that also charge for the parsley and the fork and a couple of dollars extra if you want ice in your water—he would probably close up forever from the shame of it all. I thought I might be unable to manage a Jess & Jim's strip sirloin. Normally, I'm not a ferocious steak eater—a condition I trace to my memories of constant field trips to the stockyards when I was in grade school. (I distinctly remember having gone to the stockyards so many days in a row that I finally said, "Please, teacher, can we have some arithmetic?" But my sister, who went to the same school at the same time, says we never went to the stockyards— which just goes to show how a person's memory can play tricks on her.) As it turned out, I was able to finish my entire Jess & Jim's Kansas City Strip Sirloin—even though I had felt rather full when I sat down at the table. I had eaten a rather large lunch at Winstead's, Mario's, and the doughnut place. I had spent the intervening hours listening to my sister tell me about a place on Independence Avenue where the taxi drivers eat breakfast and a place called Laura's Fudge Shop, where you can buy peanut-butter fudge if you're that kind of person, and a place that serves spaghetti in a bucket. My sister has always been interested in that sort of thing—spaghetti in a bucket, chicken in a basket, pig in a blanket. She's really not an eater; she's a container freak.

●

It has long been acknowledged that the single best restaurant in the world is Arthur Bryant's Barbecue at Eighteenth and Brooklyn in Kansas City—known to practically everybody in town as Charlie Bryant's, after Arthur's brother, who left the business in 1946. The day after my Jess & Jim's Kansas City Strip Sirloin had been consumed, I went to Bryant's with Marvin Rich, an eater whose day job is practicing law. Marvin happens to number among his clients the company that bought Winstead's—the equivalent, in our circle, of a Bronx stickballer having grown up to find himself house counsel to the Yankees. Marvin eats a lot of everything—on the way to Bryant's, for instance, he brought me up-to-date on the local chili-parlor situation with great precision—but I have always thought of him as a barbecue specialist. He even attempts his own barbecue at home—dispatching his wife to buy hickory logs, picking out his own meat, and covering up any mistakes with Arthur Bryant's barbecue sauce, which he keeps in a huge jug in his garage in defiance of the local fire ordinances.

Bryant's specializes in barbecued spareribs and barbecued beef—the beef sliced from briskets of steer that have been cooked over a hickory fire for thirteen hours. When I'm away from Kansas City and in low spirits, I try to envision someone walking up to the counterman at Bryant's and ordering a beef sandwich to go—for me. The counterman tosses a couple of pieces of bread onto the counter, grabs a half pound of beef from the pile next to him, slaps it onto the bread, brushes on some sauce in almost the same motion, and then wraps it all up in two thicknesses of butcher paper in a futile attempt to keep the customer's hand dry as he carries off his prize. When I'm *in* Kansas City and in low spirits, I go to Bryant's. I get a platter full of beef and ham and short ribs. Then I get a plate full of what are undoubtedly the best French-fried potatoes in the world ("I get fresh potatoes and I cook them in pure lard," Arthur Bryant has said. "Pure lard is expensive. But if you want to do a job, you do a job"). Then I get a frozen mug full of cold beer— cold enough so that ice has begun to form on the surface. But all of those are really side dishes to me. The main course at Bryant's, as far as I'm concerned, is something that is given away free—the burned edges of the brisket. The counterman just pushes them over to the side as he slices the beef, and anyone who wants them helps himself. I dream of those burned edges. Sometimes, when I'm in some awful, overpriced restaurant in some strange town—all of my restaurant-finding techniques having failed, so that I'm left to choke down something that costs seven dollars and tastes like a medium-rare sponge—a blank look comes over my face: I have just realized that at that very moment someone in Kansas City is being given those burned edges *free*.

Marvin and I had lunch with a young lawyer in his firm. (I could tell he was a comer: he had spotted a hamburger place at Seventy-fifth and Troost that Marvin thought nobody knew about.) We had a long discussion about a breakfast place called Joe's. "I would have to say that the hash browns at Joe's are the equivalent of the Toddle browns," Marvin said judiciously. "On the other hand, the cream pie at the Toddle House far surpasses Joe's cream pie." I reassured Marvin that I wouldn't think of leaving town without having lunch at Snead's Bar-B-Q. Snead's cuts the burned edges off the brisket with a little more meat attached and puts them on the menu as "brownies." They do the same thing with ham. A mixed plate of ham and beef brownies makes a stupendous meal— particularly in conjunction with a coleslaw that is so superior to the soured confetti they serve in the East that Alice, who has been under the impression that she didn't like coleslaw, was forced to admit that she had never really tasted the true article until she showed up, at an advanced age, at Snead's. Marvin, a man who has never been able to rise above a deep and irrational prejudice against chicken, said nothing about Stroud's, although he must have been aware of local reports that the pan-fried chicken there had so moved the New York gourmet Roy Andries de Groot that he could only respond to his dinner by stopping at the cash register and giving Mrs. Stroud a kiss on the forehead.

After an hour or so of eating, the young lawyer went back to the office ("He's a nice guy," Marvin said, "but I think that theory of his about the banana-cream pie at the airport coffee shop is way off base"), and Marvin and I had a talk with Arthur Bryant himself, who is still pretty affable, even after being called Charlie for twenty-five years. When we mentioned that we had been customers since the early fifties, it occurred to me that when we first started going to Bryant's it must have been the only integrated restaurant in town. It has always been run by black people, and white people have never been able to stay away. Bryant said that was true. In fact, he said, when mixed groups of soldiers came through Kansas City in those days, they were sent to Bryant's to eat. A vision flashed through my mind:

A white soldier and a black soldier become friends at Fort Riley, Kansas. "We'll stick together when we get to Kansas City," the white soldier says. "We're buddies." They arrive in Kansas City, prepared to go with the rest of the platoon to one of the overpriced and underseasoned restaurants that line the downtown streets. But the lady at the USO tells them they'll have to go to "a little place in colored town." They troop toward Bryant's—the white soldier wondering, as the neighborhood grows less and less like the kind of neighborhood he associates with good restaurants, if what his father told him about not paying any attention to the color of a man's skin was such good advice after all. When they get to Bryant's—a storefront with five huge, dusty jugs of barbecue sauce sitting in the window as the only decoration—the white soldier flirts for a moment with the idea of deserting his friend. But they had promised to stick together. He stiffens his resolve, and walks into Bryant's with his friend. He is in THE SINGLE BEST RESTAURANT IN THE WORLD. All of the other guys in the platoon are at some all-white cafeteria eating tasteless mashed potatoes. For perhaps the only time in the history of the Republic, virtue has been rewarded.

Bryant told us that he and his brother learned everything they knew about barbecue from a man named Henry Perry, who originated barbecue in Kansas City. "He was the greatest barbecue man in the world," Bryant said, "but he was a mean outfit." Perry used to enjoy watching his customers take their first bite of a sauce that he made too hot for any human being to eat without eight or ten years of working up to it. What Bryant said about Henry Perry, the master, only corroborated my theory that a good barbecue man is likely to tend toward the sullen—a theory I had felt wilting a bit in the face of Bryant's friendliness. (A man who tends briskets over a hickory fire all night, I figure, is bound to stir up some dark thoughts by morning.) I'm certain, at least, of my theory that a good barbecue man—or a good cook of any kind, for that matter—is not likely to be a promoter or a back-slapper. Once, while my wife and I were waiting to try out the fried clams at a small diner on the Atlantic Coast, I asked the proprietor if he had any lemon. "No, but I'll just make a note of that and I'll have some by next time you come in," he said, turning on his best smile as he made the note. "You have to keep on your toes in this kind of business." We looked around and noticed, for the first time, a flashy new paint job and a wall plaque signifying some kind of good-citizen award. "Watch it," my wife whispered to me, "we're in for a stinker." We were. The redecoration job must have included reinforcing the tables so they would be able to support the weight of the fried clams.

When Arthur Bryant took over the place that had originally been called Perry's #2, he calmed the sauce down, since the sight that made him happiest was not a customer screaming but a customer returning. He eventually introduced French fries, although the barbecued sweet potatoes that Perry used to serve do not sound as if they were the source of a lot of customer complaints. Arthur Bryant is proud that he was the one who built up the business. But he still uses Perry's basic recipe for the sauce ("Twice a year I make me up about twenty-five hundred gallons of it") and Perry's method of barbecuing, and he acknowledges his debt to the master. "It's all Perry," he says. "Everything I'm doing is his." He keeps jugs of barbecue sauce in the window because that was Henry Perry's trademark. I immediately thought of a conversation I would like to have with the mayor and the city council of Kansas City one of these days:

ME: Have you ever heard of Henry Perry?

MAYOR AND CITY COUNCIL (IN UNISON): Is that Commodore Perry?

ME: No, that is Henry Perry, who brought barbecue to Kansas City from Mississippi and therefore is the man who should be recognized as the one towering figure of our culture.

MAYOR AND CITY COUNCIL: Well, we believe that all of our citizens, regardless of their color or national origin—

ME: What I can't understand is why this town is full of statues of the farmers who came out to steal land from the Indians and full of statues of the businessmen who stole the land from the farmers but doesn't even have a three-dollar plaque somewhere for Henry Perry.

MAYOR AND CITY COUNCIL: Well, we certainly think—

ME: As you politicians are always saying, we have *got* to reorder our priorities.

•

Sometime after my grand tour of Kansas City restaurants, I managed to get to the Glendale, California, branch of Bob's for a Big Boy. Since I had to be in Los Angeles anyway, I decided to take the opportunity to end the debate with Smith once and for all, and also to check out a place called Cassell's Patio, which some people in Los Angeles have claimed has the best hamburger in the world. (Mr. Cassell ostentatiously grinds his beef right in front of one's very eyes, but then he uses too much of it for each hamburger patty. I suspect that Cassell's hamburger probably is the best one available in Los Angeles, but among Kansas City specialists it would be considered a very crude burger indeed.)

"The game is just about up, Smith," I informed William Edgett Smith before I left for California. "You won't be able to get away with any of that 'Phoenix is not Glendale' stuff anymore."

"Be sure to go to the original branch, across from Bob's international headquarters on Colorado," Smith said.

The Big Boy at Bob's on Colorado Avenue tasted like the Big Boy at Bob's in Phoenix—only slightly superior, in other words, to a McDonald's Big Mac anywhere. I was not surprised. Smith knows nothing about food. He once dragged us to a kind of Women's Lib restaurant he had thought was glorious, and it only required one course for anyone except Smith to realize that the point of the restaurant was to demonstrate, at enormous damage to the customers, that women are not necessarily good cooks. I have been at family-style dinners in Szechuan Chinese restaurants with Smith when his persistence about including lobster Cantonese in the order has forced the rest of us to threaten him with exile to a table of his own. I long ago decided that the one perceptive remark he ever made about food—the observation that it is C. C. Brown's in Hollywood rather than Will Wright's that has the best hot fudge sundae in Southern California—was a fluke, an eyes-shut home run by a .200 hitter.

"It's all over, Smith," I said to him when I returned to New York. "I had one and I can tell you that Glendale is Phoenix."

"You went to the original, you're sure, on Colorado?" Smith asked.

"Right across from Bob's international headquarters," I said.

"And you did ask for extra sliced tomatoes?" he said.

I paused for a long time, trying to remain calm. "You didn't say anything about extra sliced tomatoes," I said.

"But the whole taste is dependent on extra sliced tomatoes," he said. "The waitress would have been happy to bring you some. Bob prides himself on their friendliness."

"You realize, of course," I said, "that it's only a matter of time before I get back to Glendale and ask for extra sliced tomatoes and call this shameless bluff."

"I'm surprised you didn't ask for sliced tomatoes," Smith said. "It's the sliced tomatoes that really set it off."

The Ordeal

of Fats Goldberg

MY FRIEND FATS GOLDBERG, the pizza baron, has been slim enough to be called Larry for years, of course, but I still think of him as Fats Goldberg. So does he. Although he has "been down," as he puts it, for fourteen years, after twenty-five years of exceptional fatness, he sees himself not as a man who weighs one hundred and sixty but as a man who is constantly in danger of weighing three hundred and twenty. "Inside, I'm still a fat man," he sometimes says. When Fats and I were boys in Kansas City, he was already renowned for his corpulence—though I can't say I was ever approached about posing for Refugee Relief ads in those days myself. During college, at the University of Missouri, he reached three hundred pounds and became known as both Fats Goldberg and Three Cases Goldberg—Columbia, Missouri, having been, through a derivation process that must still puzzle students of the language, the only place in the country where anybody recognized a 100-pound unit of measurement called the case. I occasionally saw him when I visited Columbia, where he was one of a number of storied eaters. According to one tale, when a restaurant near the campus instituted a policy of giving customers all they wanted to eat on Sunday nights for $1.35, a fraternity brother of Fats's called Hog Silverman, who weighed less than two and a half cases, went over one Sunday and put it out of business. Fats was known not only for that kind of single-sitting tour de force but for the fact that he never stopped eating. When he talks about those days, a lot of his sentences begin with phrases like "Then on the way to lunch I'd stop off at the Tastee-Freez . . ."

Although Fats has never cared much for salad, he used to eat just about anything else within reach. He had a catholicity of taste comparable to that of a Southern eater I once heard mentioned as being happy to eat "just about everything except Coke bottles." His specialty, though, was always junk food. "I did not get fat on *coq au vin*," he once told me. Candy bars. Lunch-meat sandwiches on white bread. Sweet rolls. Hamburgers. Chili dogs. Cake. Fats loves cake, and I suspect he likes it even better when it comes in a package. When he was visiting our house one day, long after he had forbidden himself to eat cake in New York, we wondered why he kept wandering in and out of the kitchen; then Alice remembered that there was a cake on the kitchen counter. Fats had been prowling back and forth in front of it, like a tiger circling a tethered goat. At Missouri, Fats often brightened up the late afternoon with something called a Boston sundae, which is, more or less, a milkshake with a floating sundae on top—a floating chocolate sundae with bananas if Fats happened to be the customer. I don't mean to imply that Fats was completely undiscriminating. There are good chili dogs and bad chili dogs. The only food that Fats still finds almost literally irresistible is, of course, a double cheeseburger with everything but onions at Winstead's, and our afflictions differ only in that I prefer the double hamburger with everything and grilled onions. For a number of years, Fats was in the habit of reading the latest diet book at Winstead's—holding the book in one hand and a double cheeseburger with everything but onions in the other.

I didn't see Fats for ten years after college, and when I did see him I didn't recognize him. It was a Sunday morning in New York, and I was at Ratner's on Second Avenue. I was having eggs scrambled with lox and onions, trying to ignore the scoop of mashed potatoes that Ratner's, for some reason, always includes on the plate—perhaps as a way of reminding the customer what less fortunate people may be eating in London, or wherever it's late enough for gentiles to be having dinner. I was glancing around constantly, as I tend to do at Ratner's, to see if some other table was being given a roll basket with more of my favorite kind of onion rolls than our roll basket had. Fats didn't even look familiar. In fact, if we hadn't had some intimate discussions since then about Winstead's hamburgers and Arthur Bryant's barbecued spareribs, I might even now suspect him of being an imposter. Fats later told me that on the morning of May 1, 1959, while employed as a 320-pound salesman of newspaper advertising space in Chicago, he had decided to lose weight. Naturally, he had made similar decisions several dozen times in the past, and he still doesn't know why he was finally able to stop eating. He can't remember any single incident having set him on his course—no humiliation by some secretary who called him fat stuff, no particularly embarrassing experience buying trousers or trying to tie his shoelace. He is certain that it was not fear for his health that stiffened his willpower; several years before, his reaction to a serious warning by a doctor in Kansas City was to think about it over three Winstead's cheeseburgers, a fresh-lime Coke, and a Frosty Malt. On May 1, 1959, Fats started losing weight. He didn't use pills or gimmick diets. "It was cold turkey," he says now, referring to the method rather than the food. "I suffered." In a year, Fats weighed 190. Then, gradually, he went down to 160. In other words, by the time I saw him at Ratner's, the Fats Goldberg I had known was half gone.

Fats was still selling advertising space then, but he wasn't happy in his work. He believed that his true calling was stand-up comedy. After he moved to New York, he and a young woman he knew formed a nightclub comedy act called Berkowitz and Goldberg. Their first public performance was at the Bitter End, in the Village, which has what amounts to an amateur night on Tuesdays, but they got on so late that the audience consisted of only four people, all of them grim-faced. Berkowitz later discovered that none of them spoke English. As it turned out, a knowledge of the language did not vary the audience response. I never saw the act, but I think I have a pretty good idea of what it was like from a chance remark Fats once made while we were reminiscing about our show-business careers. (At Southwest High School, I had a comedy act with a partner who specialized in foreign dialects and took great advantage,

I realized some years later, of the fact that none of the people we performed for had ever met any foreigners.) "We were called Berkowitz and Goldberg but we didn't do Jewish humor," Fats told me during that talk of lost opportunities. "That was one of the jokes."

After having inspired audiences all over town to puzzled silence, Berkowitz and Goldberg finally folded. Fortunately, Fats had one joke left; he opened a restaurant called Goldberg's Pizzeria. He was armed not only with the gimmick of having a Jewish pizza parlor but with the recipe for an excellent version of what the connoisseurs call a Chicago pizza—characterized by a thick, crisp, and particularly fattening crust. I have only an occasional craving for pizza—a craving that I used to nurture carefully, like a small trust fund, at the Spot in New Haven, Connecticut—but I have eaten enough of it to know that Fats serves superior Chicago pizza. Almost as soon as Goldberg's Pizzeria had opened, Fats had what every comic dreams of—a lot of free publicity, critical acclaim, and "exposure" on *The Tonight Show*. (Actually, it was the pizza that was exposed rather than Goldberg; one was given away to a member of the audience who named a tune the band couldn't play.) Fats himself became so celebrated that he was able to publish a pizza cookbook—a volume that may add little to the literature of food but seems at least to have provided a resting place for some old jokes from the Berkowitz and Goldberg days. (One chapter is called "The Goldberg Variations, or How to Make Johann Sebastian Roll Over on His Bach.") Within a few years, there were three Goldberg's Pizzerias, and Fats was getting feelers from conglomerates.

Although Fats enjoys the trappings of a pizza barony, he realizes that his most notable accomplishment is not having created a successful business but having stayed thin. Among his pizza customers are some experts in obesity, and they have informed him that any fat man who remains slim for fourteen years can safely consider himself a medical phenomenon. (Since all Goldberg's Pizzerias display poster-size pictures of Fats when he weighed three cases, the subject of fatness often comes up, particularly on Sunday night, a traditional time for eating pizza and making diet resolutions.) Fats has been told that specialists can always make fat people thin through a variety of hospital treatments—treatments that a layman would probably summarize as solitary confinement. But once released, the patients almost invariably become fat again—meaning that, according to any reasonable assessment of the odds, Fats really is someone constantly in danger of weighing three hundred and twenty pounds.

Someone who has gone without a relapse since 1959 is so rare that one researcher from Rockefeller University asked Fats if he would mind donating some of his fat cells for analysis. Researchers at Rockefeller and at Mt. Sinai Hospital have found that fat people who were fat as children have not only larger fat cells but more of them. When a chronically fat person loses weight, all his fat cells just shrink temporarily, remaining available for re-expansion—or, as someone who apparently enjoys taunting the fatties once put it, "screaming to be refilled." Fat-cell research has led to the depressing speculation that a person who was fat as a child faces horrifying pressure to become fat again and again, no matter how many times he sits in Goldberg's Pizzeria on a Sunday evening and vows that the diet he is going on the following morning will be different. Fats is unenthusiastic about the Rockefeller people's method of studying his fat cells, which would amount to withdrawing a section of tissue from the part of the body in which it is most accessible (or, as Fats sees it, "having three nurses stick an eight-inch needle in my *tushe*"), but he sometimes hints that he might be willing to cooperate. The more he thinks about the effort required for a fat man to stay thin, the more he thinks that he is extraordinary enough to be a boon to medical research.

•

A thin psychologist I know, Stanley Schachter, has done a lot of research at Columbia on obesity, and I once asked him if it was scientifically sound to consider Fats Goldberg truly amazing. After I had described Fats's accomplishments, Schachter seemed filled with admiration. According to Schachter's research, staying thin would be even more difficult for a pizza baron than for a run-of-the-mill fatty. The research indicates that what causes fat people to eat is not the physical sensations that go along with an empty stomach but what Schachter calls "external cues"—the sight of candy in the candy dish or the smell of hamburgers frying or the information that it is dinnertime or, in the case of poor Fats, the constant presence of delicious, aromatic pizza. One of Fats's doctor friends once told him that a remarkably high percentage of the few former fatties who have managed to stay thin had fetched up in businesses having to do with food in one way or the other—tightrope walkers who want to defy the odds a bit more by working in unsnapped galoshes.

Schachter believes that fat people are unable to recognize the physical sensation of hunger—so that they actually eat less than thin people if external cues are missing. When two Columbia doctors, Theodore Van Itallie and Sami Hashim, removed virtually all external cues—they allowed people to eat all they wanted of an almost tasteless liquid, but nothing else—the thin people ate about the same number of calories per day that they had eaten of normal food but the fat people ate so little that one of them lost more than two hundred pounds in eight months. Schachter has found that among Jewish college students with roughly the same habits of synagogue attendance, the fat ones are more likely to fast on Yom Kippur than the normal-sized ones—and that their fasting is more likely to be helped by staying in the synagogue, where there are few food cues. The normal-sized ones get hungry. Normal people given food in a laboratory will eat less if their stomachs are full or if they're frightened, but if a plate of crackers is put in front of a fat person who has just eaten or who has been led to believe he is about to receive some electric shocks, he is likely to clean the plate anyway—or, in Schachter's terms, to eat until he is out of cues. The crackers have to be decent crackers, of course; fat people tend not to be interested in food that doesn't taste good.

After listening to Schachter explain the peculiar eating habits of fat people for a while, it occurred to me that what he had really discovered was that fat people are smarter than other people. For instance, in an experiment to test the hypothesis that fat people are less willing to work for their food than ordinary people, he found that the appeal of a bowl of almonds to normal-sized people who were filling out some meaningless forms he had concocted (Schachter is a very devious researcher) was unaffected by whether or not the almonds had shells on them. But when fat people were given the same test, only one out of twenty ate almonds that had to be shelled and nineteen out of twenty ate almonds that were already shelled. That seems to me a simple matter of intelligence. Who wants to spend his time shelling almonds? Testing the same hypothesis, Schachter and some of his students loitered around Chinese restaurants and found that fat Occidentals are much less likely to try chopsticks than thin Occidentals—the difference being, Schachter assured me, too great to be accounted for by the problem of manipulation inherent in chubby little fingers.

"But the fat people behave the way any normal intelligent person would behave, Stanley," I said when I heard about that discovery.

Schachter didn't say anything. Then I began to realize that a lot of the fat-people habits he had talked about applied to me. I have always thought that anyone who sacrifices stuffing power by using chopsticks in a Chinese restaurant must be demented. I would use a tablespoon if I thought I could get away with it, but I know that the people I tend to share my Chinatown meals with, terrified that I would polish off the twice-fried pork before they had a chance to say "Pass the bean curd," would start using tablespoons themselves, and sooner or later we would be off on an escalating instruments race that might end with soup ladles or dory bailers. Although I may have talked about being hungry from the moment I learned to talk, I am still not sure precisely what physical feeling people have in mind when they describe hunger. The last piece of food I left on my plate—that was in the fall of 1958, as I remember— had a bug on it. I suppose I might be persuaded not to finish a normal helping of Grand Marnier soufflé if a reputable and eloquent person I had every reason to trust insisted that my host had poisoned it, but I really couldn't say for certain until the situation actually came up. Schachter's theories, I decided, must be incorrect.

I tried to prove it to myself the next time I saw Fats by asking him a question in what I knew was a somewhat misleading way.

"Do you ever get hungry, Fats?" I asked.

"You bet your booties I do!" Fats said.

That would show Schachter, I thought. But a few days later,

when I asked Fats for an example of a time when it was particularly hard for him to avoid eating, he said, "Tonight when I passed that pizza stand on Eighth Street that has that great frozen custard, it almost killed me." External cue.

My discussion with Fats about hunger began at the Gaiety Delicatessen on Lexington Avenue, where he goes every day for a kind of lunchtime breakfast. Having been terrified by Schachter, I ordered the tuna-fish-salad plate with double coleslaw, hold the potato salad, and a low-calorie cream soda. Fats ate two scrambled eggs, sausages, a bagel with cream cheese, and four cups of coffee with a total of eight packets of sugar. "A fat man's got to have something to look forward to," Fats said. "When I'm reading in bed late at night, I think about being able to have this bagel and cream cheese the next day." Underlying the Fats Goldberg system of weight control is more or less the same philosophy that led to the great Russian purge trials of the thirties—deviation is treason. His Gaiety meal varies daily only in how the eggs are done. In the evening, he has either a steak or half a chicken, baked in the pizza oven. (He is always careful to cut the chicken in half before baking and to put the unneeded half back in the refrigerator. "You have to preplan," he says. "A fat man always cleans his plate.") On Sunday night he permits himself a quarter of a small sausage pizza in place of the steak or chicken, but then he works at the ovens trying to sweat it off. On Monday he cheats to the extent of some bread or maybe a piece of pie. The schedule is maintained only in New York, of course. Kansas City remains a free zone for Fats. He says that in the earlier years of his thinness a week's trip to Kansas City to visit his family would mean gaining seventeen pounds. Lately, restraint has begun to creep into his Kansas City binges. The week's eating he was about to start when I saw him on the Kansas City plane cost him only ten pounds.

A few days after our meeting at the Gaiety, Fats happened to drop by my house. It had been a difficult few days for me: Schachter's theories were still fresh in my mind, and St. Anthony's, my favorite Italian street fair, was being held so close to my house that I had been able to convince myself that I could smell the patently irresistible aroma of frying sausages—Italian sausages, frying on a griddle right next to the peppers and onions that always accompany them. I have looked all over the country for a sausage I don't like, trying them all along the way. In the course of my research, I have tested country patties in Mississippi and Cuban *chorizos* in Tampa and bratwurst in Yorkville and Swedish potato sausages in Kansas (yes, Kansas) and garlic sausages in Romanian restaurants in New York and just about everything else that has ever been through a sausage grinder. So far, I love them all. I even like English bangers. I look on the bright side: with all that bread in them, they couldn't possibly cause heartburn.

Trying, I think, to keep my mind off my own problems, I mentioned to Fats that a doctor I knew had said that in order to gain even fourteen pounds a week in Kansas City it would be necessary for Fats to consume an additional seventy-two hundred calories a day—or the equivalent of fifteen or twenty Winstead's cheeseburgers.

Fats considered that for a while. He didn't seem shocked.

"Just what *did* you eat on a big day in Kansas City the week you gained seventeen pounds?" I asked. I prepared to make a list.

"Well, for breakfast I'd have two eggs, six biscuits with butter and jelly, half a quart of milk, six link sausages, six strips of bacon, and a couple of homemade cinnamon rolls," Fats said. "Then I'd hit MacLean's Bakery. They have a kind of fried cinnamon roll I love. Maybe I'd have two or three of them. Then, on the way downtown to have lunch with somebody, I might stop at Kresge's and have two chili dogs and a couple of root beers. Ever had their chili dogs?"

I shook my head.

"Greasiest chili dogs in the world," Fats said. "I love 'em. Then I'd go to lunch. What I really like for lunch is something like a hot beef sandwich or a hot turkey sandwich. Open-faced, loaded with that flour gravy. With mashed potatoes. Then Dutch apple pie. Kansas City is big on Dutch apple pie. Here they call it apple crumb or something. Then, sometimes in the afternoon, I'd pick up a pie—just an ordinary nine-inch pie—and go to my friend

Matt Flynn's house, and we'd cut the pie down the middle and put half in a bowl for each of us and then take a quart of ice cream and cut that down the middle and put it on top of the pie. We'd wash it down with Pepsi-Cola. Sometimes Matt couldn't finish his and I'd have to finish it for him. Then that would be it until I stopped at my sister's house. She's very big on crunchy peanut butter. She even has peanut butter and jelly already mixed. They didn't have that when I was a kid. Then for dinner we'd maybe go to Charlie Bryant's or one of the barbecues out on the highway. At the movies I'd always have a bag of corn and a big Coke and knock off a Payday candy bar. Payday is still my favorite candy bar. They're hard to get here, but they have a very big distribution in Kansas City. Then we'd always end up at Winstead's, of course. Two double cheeseburgers with everything but onions, a fresh-lime Coke, and a Frosty Malt. If it was before eleven, I'd stop at the Zarda Dairy for one of their 49-cent banana splits. Then when I'd get home maybe some cherry pie and a 16-ounce Pepsi."

And so to bed. I looked at the list. "To tell you the truth, Fats, I'm afraid to add it all up," I said. I looked at the list again. Something on it had reminded me of sausages. It must have been the mention of Bryant's, which used to have barbecue sausages but quit serving them before I had a chance to try them—a situation that has always made me feel like an archaeologist who arrived at the tomb just a few days after the locals began to use the best pot for a football. I decided that I would walk over to the fair later and have just one sausage sandwich with peppers and onions—saving a few calories by having a barbecued rather than a fried sausage. If things got out of hand, I figured, I could always go on one of those diets that allow you as much as you want to eat as long as you eat only Brussels sprouts, quinces, and summer squash. I had mentioned the fair to Fats, but he couldn't go. It wasn't a Monday.

"Is life worth living, Fats?" I asked.

"Well, I figure that in my first twenty-five years I ate enough for four normal lifetimes," Fats said. "So I get along. But there is a lot of pain involved. A lot of pain. I can't stress that enough."

(4)

The Dance of

the Restaurant Trotters

WHEN PEOPLE in other parts of the country ask me why I live in New York, they expect a specific answer. After all, if I asked one of them why he lives in, say, St. Paul, he wouldn't hesitate to give me a specific answer ("Well, I was born here, and we have a lot of family here, and when I got out of the Army an uncle of mine knew somebody in this window-shade firm that needed a sales representative . . ."). They often try to help me out by saying something like "The cultural life must be exciting, of course—the opera and all." The opera has nothing to do with it. I have been to the opera only once in New York, and that is when we were sent tickets by a friend in Kansas City. Early in autumn a few years ago, I finally found the short answer I had been looking for. We had spent the summer in New Mexico, and, during a brief stop in Santa Fe, we had been grilled on why we live in New York by that group of Eastern-refugee remittance men the place specializes in—people who half-retire at forty-two in order to devote themselves to talking about a novel they might write and overseeing the repairs of any cracks that might develop in the adobe walls of their house and discussing the water rights their land carries by virtue of the original Spanish land grant and raising a herd of twelve or fourteen particularly elegant goats. A week or so after our return, Alice and I happened to walk by a Chinese restaurant on Irving Place and we

realized we had forgotten about it. I don't mean we had forgotten
its name or its exact address; we had forgotten about its existence.
The previous spring, we had eaten a spectacular meal there, including a dish that came close to being the Great Dried Beef in the
Sky—an Oriental grail we had been in search of since we ate an
awesome dried-beef dish in a Chinese restaurant in London (across
the street from the Golders Green tube station) several years ago.
"This is why we live here," I said to Alice. "Where else could you
forget a restaurant like this?" Now when someone asks me why my
family and I choose to live in New York, I don't have to launch
into all sorts of complicated and fuzzy explanations. I just say,
"We're big eaters."

I once met someone who had collected information about four
hundred New York restaurants and stored it in a computer in Cu-
pertino, California. In the context of the conversation we were
having at the time, it struck me as a natural enough thing to have
done. We were eating dinner at the New York apartment of some
friends named Peter and Alessandra Wolf, where the talk often turns
to food even before the first course is served. Peter, who grew up
in New Orleans, and Alessandra, who is an immigrant from Fort
Worth, are basically regional loyalists who eat or prepare other types
of food as a kind of casual sideline—the way some tournament-
class tennis player might mop up all of the paddle tennis and table
tennis competition at the local club if it's too cold to play the real
game. Peter is such a discriminating consumer of his hometown
cooking that when a trip allows him time for only one or two meals
in New Orleans, the one American city most citizens associate with
French cuisine, he is likely to take them at Italian restaurants—
Italian restaurants that specialize in something like baked oysters
and cracked-crab salad, it's true, but still Italian restaurants. Peter
once discovered, in an Upper Broadway Szechuan restaurant, a dish
called Red Soup, which he claimed was the best Chinese dish
available in New York for those who like their Chinese food flavored
hot, but the claim turned out not to be subject to independent
confirmation, since Red Soup was so hot that only someone who
had trained on Cajun peppers or Henry Perry's barbecue sauce for
twenty or thirty years could eat enough of it to find out what it
tasted like.

Alessandra lived in France for quite a while, but she hasn't allowed that to ruin her cooking. She can turn out a first-rate French meal, of course, and she is one of the few Occidentals in New York whose Chinese cooking does not evoke sympathy for the organizers of the Boxer Rebellion. But an occasion at her house seems particularly special when she serves something called Chili Texas Party Style—a Fort Worth meat delicacy that each guest flavors to taste by adding chopped onions or sour cream or shredded lettuce or Monterey Jack cheese or, in my case, all of the above. (In such situations, I have yet to add anything less than everything. I like everything with everything, and I find people who don't impossible to fathom except as victims of the Puritan Ethic. Failing to add everything, it seems to me, demonstrates not the presence of restraint but the absence of curiosity—the kind of healthy curiosity that impels me to sample every single cheese on the cheese board no matter how many times the French waiter with the tight smile emits one of those impatient sighs he practices in the kitchen during slack hours.) I believe it was merely a delicious French meal we were being served by Alessandra when the subject of New York restaurants worked its way into the conversation and I learned that one of the other guests, an investment banker named Anthony Lamport, could summon data on four hundred of them simply by strolling over to a computer terminal he had installed in a small office one flight above his bedroom and punching a few keys—having first dialed a special number in California on the telephone and placed the receiver next to what passes for the machine's ear.

Those who consider Lamport's facilities, well, more than the situation calls for have never developed a serious interest in eating out in New York. On long winter nights, when more responsible citizens are presumably discussing foreign policy or urban mass transit, I have found myself locked in intent conversation about restaurants. Perhaps a fifteen-year-old Spanish restaurant on Staten Island has been rediscovered, like an elderly black blues singer who is plucked out of the Mississippi Delta and brought to New York for a well-received appearance at Town Hall at least once every twenty years. Or there is a new Chinese restaurant on Doyers Street specializing in the dishes of a remote province whose cuisine is so exquisite that those of its residents who have to travel to Szechuan

or Hunan traditionally never leave home without packing a lunch.
Or there is new word on a chef who moves constantly from restaurant
to restaurant, carrying with him not only a grudge against all restaurant proprietors but the Ancient Greek secret of spinach pie.

By eating out I don't mean dining out—showing up at the
kind of East Side restaurants that are often mentioned in gossip
columns and expense accounts, restaurants that prosper or languish
for reasons other than how the food tastes. There is, of course,
always plenty of that going on in Manhattan, and there is also plenty
of business for the fast-food operators. McDonald's, which got a
late start in the city, is now doing the kind of volume restaurant
people speak of in the tones that theater people reserve for discussions
of Neil Simon's box office, and lately there has been a spreading
rash of Steak 'n Brew outlets, Steak 'n Brew being a chain that has
done for steaks what Astroturf did for outfields. (If I ever captured
control of City Hall, the first law promulgated would require all of
the merchants running establishments with names like Steak 'n Brew
or Doodads 'n Things or Birds 'n Bees to spell out all words or be
put in the stocks.) Fats Goldberg believes that, the appeal of limited-
menu, fast-service operations being what it is in New York, a restaurant entrepreneur could enrich himself by creating a midtown
restaurant based on a two-way conveyor belt moving within a building between, say, Forty-fifth and Forty-sixth Streets. The customer
who entered on Forty-fifth would pay for one of three or four set
lunches, sit down at a table on a slow-moving conveyor belt, and,
after eating his fill and perusing some discreet advertising displays
on the wall and nodding to a few acquaintances who have passed
slowly in the other direction, be dumped out on Forty-sixth Street.

People who are serious about eating out in New York have to
work a territory way beyond the expense-account joints or fast-food
operations. There are in the five boroughs something like twenty-
three thousand establishments that serve food of one kind or another,
and the devout restaurant trotter has to consider every single one
of them. He might find out, after all, that what looks like an expanded lunch counter actually functions in the evenings as a Syrian
family restaurant featuring a minced-lamb dish so fantastic it would
tempt a Zionist to change sides. The lunch counter then becomes

not merely an enjoyable place to eat but a discovery, almost a personal possession. Although young couples in films set in New York have always seemed very fond of fatherly old Enrico, the man who runs the little red-and-white-checkered-tablecloth Italian restaurant they frequent, there is a limit to the kind of success real New Yorkers would wish for old Enrico. What they dread more than rubbery fettuccine is a write-up in the *Times*. They believe, of course, that keeping information about Enrico's place on what the Army calls a strict need-to-know basis is all for Enrico's own good. Ever since Craig Claiborne established the restaurant column in the *Times* as the first item of morning business for a confirmed restaurant trotter, an out-of-the-way place praised by the *Times* can be instantly Claibornized—swollen and perhaps even burst by a sudden infusion of temporary loyalists. If Enrico reacts to a favorable notice in the *Times* by trying to run the kind of place he operated before, he is likely to find the regulars driven away forever as a horde of fickle review followers manage to turn the chef into a short-order cook before they move on to the West Side Spanish seafood house that has just had its *mariscos* extolled at length. If Enrico proves adaptable enough to exploit the publicity, he will redecorate and raise the prices and eventually open a fancy place in midtown, where his encounters with the waiters' union and the real-estate sharks will drive him into the life insurance business. Who would wish such alternatives on a pal? Shortly after John Hess took over as restaurant critic of the *Times*, he wrote a piece about a modest upstairs trattoria called the Eldorado, which had been in the garment district for years but was about to close. "I would never tell you about the Eldorado if it weren't doomed," Hess's informant said to him. With only a few weeks to go, in other words, the place might as well be Hessed.

A New York restaurant trotter who remains wary of the *Times* restaurant column because of some rough handling in the past by a band of Claibornites or a horde of Hessians can now get his restaurant tips from a restaurant newsletter. The premise of a newsletter—the premise that its subscribers will pay well for information not shared with the entire population—is the kind of openly selfish notion easily appreciated by the serious eater in New York.

Reading restaurant reviews of any kind, of course, carries the risk of being lectured to about how the texture of the *crème anglaise* in question deviates from the texture *crème anglaise* is supposed to have—an experience that always makes me feel the way a man who takes great joy in his pet basset hound might feel if he found himself trapped in a room with a couple of dog-show types who want to discuss only whether the poor beast has the prescribed depth of chest or the classic markings. When a reviewer starts explaining how the preparation of a quiche Lorraine at the restaurant he has visited differs from the way one prepares a *true* quiche Lorraine, I always want to interrupt. "But did you like it?" I want to shout. "Did it make you happy? Did you clean your plate?" Any chance that I might someday acquire a serious interest in how closely what I ate resembled the true article disappeared one day at a block party near our house while I was eating some homemade gazpacho and talking about how it differed from the authentic gazpacho one got in Seville. The more I talked about the difference, the faster I wolfed down the gazpacho—until I realized that one way what I was eating differed from authentic gazpacho was that it tasted better.

I now realize, though, that before restaurant newsletters came along we were in the position of people who had to argue about the latest film without having a collection of film critics to cite with approval or dismiss with contempt. Just after one newsletter, *The Restaurant Reporter*, had criticized the prices and service at the Palm steak house, for instance, some zealous *palmistes* I know took Alice and me there and presented an impassioned two-hour defense over dinner—a defense that did not, in fact, include everything they wanted to say on the subject, since their mouths were often too full of steak or home-fried potatoes to permit articulation. At the end of the evening, they remained unpersuaded by my argument that a diner who is presented a bill at a restaurant—such as the Palm—that has no menu and therefore no announced prices has no choice but to negotiate. I still think that if a man tells you for the first time that the lobster you just ate costs eighteen dollars, the only sensible response is to offer him six.

I am now so accustomed to *The Restaurant Reporter* that I would probably subscribe even if I lived in Kansas City, just on the chance that I might fall into a conversation with a visiting machine-tools drummer about Japanese restaurants on the Upper West Side. (The other New York newsletter I have seen, *The Craig Claiborne Journal*, devotes more space to recipes than to restaurants and is therefore of less use to me, since my cooking skill does not extend past a special way of preparing scrambled eggs so that they always stick to the pan. I do enjoy Claiborne's use of the editorial we, such as "We remember the first time we ever dined at Le Pavilion . . ." It has the effect of making me think that he is eating double portions of everything.) I like *The Restaurant Reporter* for the writing as well as for the tips. The ordinary restaurant reviewer might express his displeasure over a dish of spinach by saying that it was limp or tasteless or not in conformity with the classic dish of spinach. *The Restaurant Reporter* described the spinach served at one midtown restaurant as tasting like "new-mown artificial lawn." Reviewing Mr. & Mrs. Foster's Place, a small, expensive restaurant on the East Side, *The Restaurant Reporter* said, "After overcharging 25 patrons twice a night, six nights a week, for a couple of years, Mrs. Foster, the sole proprietor, apparently still cannot afford larger quarters for her establishment, or the elimination of a couple of tables, so that the remaining diners could eat comfortably." Talking about a steak restaurant that had every characteristic of those out-of-the-way, informal little places New York restaurant samplers are always touting except good food, *The Restaurant Reporter* said, "You have heard of a tourist trap? This restaurant is a New Yorker trap."

•

One spring evening in New York, I happened to run across a friend of mine who was on his way to Chinatown but seemed to lack the look of gleeful anticipation I associate with the beginning of such a journey. What concerned him, I quickly learned, was that an excellent new restaurant he had been patronizing for a while had just been reviewed in the *Times*. We were both familiar with an uptown Chinese restaurant that had been Sokoloved a year or so before—having transformed itself within a few days of being praised in the *Times* by Hess's predecessor, Raymond Sokolov, into an approximation of what might have happened during the more antic phases of the Cultural Revolution if someone had tested out his new authority by ordering every single soldier in the People's Army to eat at the same mess hall.

"It was a very good notice," my friend said glumly. It had even mentioned the cold-kidney appetizer, his favorite dish. He admitted that complete lack of publicity also had its perils: he said he had once managed to keep a perfect Chinese restaurant pretty much to himself for six months, until it closed, apparently having maintained an exclusivity that was inconsistent with paying the rent. But as he started off toward his first post-review dinner, I could tell he was haunted by expectations of having a harried waiter bob up from a shoving mass of new customers after a forty-minute delay only to announce that the chef had been forced to turn to canned shrimp for the Shrimp with Brown Sauce and had, regrettably, given up trying to make the cold kidneys altogether.

"Cheer up," I wanted to say. "Maybe they'll be listed in the *Times* tomorrow for a health-code violation." But he seemed inconsolable.

•

For a chronic restaurant sampler, one of the rewards of success is being able to take a friend to the new discovery and smile knowingly as he tastes the kind of bouillabaisse he thought did not exist more than two hundred yards from the Mediterranean. That kind of moment seems particularly savored by the specialists—New Yorkers who make themselves lay experts in a particular cuisine the way some securities analysts concentrate on keeping completely up-to-date on all aspects of, say, copper mining or the toy industry. Zero Mostel—the actor, painter, and eater—is, for instance, widely known in New York as a specialist in Jewish food, although, like Alessandra Wolf, he is creative about wandering effortlessly from his specialty. During a tour of the Lower East Side I once took with him to observe him in action—I did it in the medieval spirit of an eager novice apprenticing himself to a master glutton—he described an experience of taking an acquaintance of his to a kosher dairy restaurant that used to exist on Upper Broadway. At the time, we were standing on Houston Street, having just emerged from the back room of Russ & Daughters appetizer store, where a counterman friend of Mostel's named Herbie Federman had created for us some stupendous sandwiches of Nova Scotia salmon, cream cheese with vegetables in it, sliced onions, and Russ & Daughters' ineffable sturgeon. Mostel, who can speak with talmudic subtlety for ten minutes on, say, the soured milk with fresh chives that Yonah Shimmel used to serve in the spring, said he had prepared the acquaintance for his first trip to the dairy restaurant by describing some of its specialties, and I could imagine a cab ride to Upper Broadway fragrant with Mostel descriptions of *kasha varnishke* and potato *latkes*. "The guy ordered angel-food cake and a glass of milk," Mostel said. He paused to let that sink in. His eyes opened wide, and he seemed to expand. I thought he was going to begin shouting. But he lowered his voice nearly to a whisper. "Angel-food cake and a glass of milk," he repeated, very calmly. "He went into a restaurant like that and ordered angel-food cake and a glass of milk. It's like going into this store and Herbie asks you what he can get you and you say, 'Herbele, open me up a can tuna.' I said, 'You sure you want angel-food cake and a glass of milk?' He said he wasn't very hungry." Mostel paused again. Suddenly he flung out his arm to point dramatically straight in front of him. "I said, 'GET OUT OF HERE! GET OUT OF THIS RESTAURANT!' " he said, in a voice that caused some motorists on Houston Street to slow down and look in our direction. "ANGEL-FOOD CAKE AND A GLASS OF MILK! THE NERVE!"

Mostel seems to enjoy talking about the restaurants he goes to; the real masters have never been stingy about sharing trade secrets with apprentices. But there are, of course, some people in New York who enjoy knowing about little-known restaurants for the same reason that some people in the White House enjoy knowing national secrets—it makes them feel superior to people who only know what they read in the newspapers. Some people in New York concerned with rank and station attach as much importance to the answer to "Where do you usually go in Chinatown?" as some people in other parts of the country attach to the answer to "Whadaya drive?" When two restaurant trotters meet, the conversation is often tense. "We happened to run across a little Italian place at Eighteenth and Ninth

Avenue last month," one competitor will say. "The sign, for some reason, says something like Mantucci's Bolt & Nut Supply, and you have to call in advance, of course, and the owner doesn't know much English, but he has a dish that starts with these little dumplings—"

"Oh," his opponent will say, in the tone of someone doing his best to be polite while listening to the plot summary of a film he happens to have written. "Is that place still good?"

•

I admit to having been intrigued by the idea of storing restaurant information in a computer. I could think of a few useful ways to arrange New York restaurants into the kinds of subgroups computers are always providing—those restaurants that use actual potatoes for their French fries and those that merely fry the icy fingers found in bags of precut Idahos, for instance. I phoned Anthony Lamport and arranged to come around one evening to investigate the computer. I ate first, just in case.

Lamport, as it turned out, is a director of a computer-time-sharing company in California, and had figured that it would be to the company's advantage if he learned to write and use programs such as his restaurant-selection program. I wouldn't argue with that; directors are obviously less likely to cause management a lot of trouble if they're well fed. Lamport finds a number of uses for the computer in his business, and while he was in the market for a brownstone or a co-op apartment, he fed into it all sorts of figures like yearly maintenance and tax-deductible operating expenses in order to determine the real cost of each piece of property—another confirmation of the axiom that computers have no intelligence of their own, since a machine with any brains would have taken one look at a collection of New York real-estate figures and typed out, "MOVE TO ST. PAUL."

Now that Lamport has the restaurant program, if he happens to want to eat, say, medium-priced Italian food within ten blocks of Sixtieth and Third on a Monday, the machine will provide him with a list that varies according to such matters as whether or not he is interested in a place that has live music. I could see from the variables Lamport had included that his machine was of limited use. There was no provision for schmaltz. Nothing was said about French fries. Some variables that he had included—live music or atmosphere or outdoor dining—were of no interest to me. As far as I'm concerned, a place that serves perfect gnocchi or soft-clam bellies that taste like the bellies of soft clams can feature a quartet of female tuba players if that's what makes the chef happy. If a New York restaurant figured out how to serve crawfish bisque or the kind of *sopapaillas* available in, say, Española, New Mexico—a *sopapailla* being a sort of pastry that tastes like what might result if some little old lady in New England were inspired by the devil himself to fry her popovers in oil and pour honey on them—I would be happy to eat the special of the day in a small, dark closet. People who attach great importance to the bright lights ought just to go to Radio City Music Hall and pack some sandwiches.

I decided to give the machine at least one try. "Tell the thing to type out the name of a three-star French restaurant with moderate prices and a headwaiter who believes that accepting tips is unethical," I said. Lamport said the computer was not programmed to do that. I hadn't really thought it would be. If Lamport found such a place, he would know better than to say anything about it to a machine.

(5)

A Sunday Morning

Tale

HAVING HEARD a number of people discuss the Last Straw that drove them from the city, I realize that if I didn't leave when Ben's Dairy started closing Sundays I'm probably in New York for good. It was an awful blow. It happened four years ago, and I still remember the details of the morning I discovered it, the way some people remember what they were wearing when they learned of the attack on Pearl Harbor—which also, as I remember it, took place on a Sunday morning. (I mention that without trying to imply any mystic pattern governing catastrophes. I understand that the Spanish Inquisition began late on a Tuesday afternoon.) At about nine-thirty, I had parked brilliantly on Houston Street itself—as the ex-co-editor of a one-issue journal called *Beautiful Spot: A Magazine of Parking*, I find that a perfect spot on Houston Street on Sunday morning can give me almost as much pleasure as a freshly baked bialy—and found myself in front of Yonah Shimmel's Knishery. Restraining myself from having one of Shimmel's legendary potato knishes at that hour of the morning, I had settled for a cheese bagel, figuring a little extra energy might be useful when I faced the counter crowds down the street. At Russ & Daughters, ordinarily my first stop, I was hardly in the door before someone was expertly removing from a succulent-looking Nova Scotia salmon some slices that were going to be my very own. My next move had been established years before.

Leaving Russ & Daughters, I would take a quick look into Ben's Dairy, next door, and a quick look into Tanenbaum's Bakery, next door to Ben's—both tiny stores with barely enough room between the counter and the wall for a customer to elbow aside more than one other customer at a time. In either place, there could be an occasional lull in the crowd, the way there is a lull when a group of large men who are breaking down a door with a battering ram back up to get some running room. Making a quick, hard decision about which crowd looked less lethal at the moment, I would plunge into Ben's or Tanenbaum's, stagger back out to Houston Street, and plunge into the other one—emerging at the end carrying Ben's homemade cream cheese with scallions and Tanenbaum's fresh pumpernickel bagels, both of which would be combined with my Russ & Daughters' Nova Scotia to create the single perfect Nova Scotia and cream cheese on bagel available in today's depleted market. Whenever I put the final ingredient in my shopping bag, I felt ecstatic in the way I have always imagined a Manhattan real-estate speculator must feel ecstatic when he finally gets his hands on the last historic brownstone he needs to make up an entire block that can be torn down for a luxury high-rise. That Sunday, I shot my customary glance toward Ben's as I moved toward Tanenbaum's, and I saw a steel gate across the storefront. Closed.

I remained calm. In the past, I had often found Ben closed when I expected him to be open. Although his official policy had always been to close only on Saturdays and Jewish holidays, it had long seemed to me that Ben knew about Jewish holidays that had escaped the notice of other observant Jews. Finding Ben closed on Sundays when knishes were pouring out of Yonah Shimmel's and customers were four deep at Russ & Daughters and the open-air discount cubbyholes on Orchard Street, around the corner, were booming, I had got the impression that Ben might sometimes observe, say, the anniversary of the death of some wise and scholarly rabbi whose wisdom did not happen to spread much beyond the boundaries of one small neighborhood in Vitebsk. But my assumption that Ben was closed for religious reasons was destroyed when I looked into Tanenbaum's. Tanenbaum was known on Houston Street to be at least as strict about such matters as Ben. I had always suspected, in fact, that Tanenbaum observed the anniversary of the death of not only great rabbis but maybe cantors as well and maybe some secular heroes and perhaps an ecumenical Methodist or two. Tanenbaum was in his store, dealing out bagels with both hands. I raced back into Russ & Daughters to find out what had happened, and my worst fears were confirmed: Ben had decided to close Sundays.

I had never objected to Tanenbaum and Ben closing on Saturdays. After all, freedom of religion is guaranteed in the Constitution, and besides, I'm usually busy on Saturday shopping for Italian food. On a Saturday morning, I'm likely to be walking down Bleecker Street making last-minute adjustments to the intricate timing that sometimes allows me to start by buying a pound of prosciuttini at Mario Bosco's, get to Zito's just as the fresh-baked bread is coming up from the basement, and still arrive at the mozzarella store on Sullivan Street before it has been snatched clean of cheese-in-the-basket. (I go to the mozzarella store mainly to buy mozzarella, of course—mozzarella soaked in milk and salt, smoked mozzarella, any kind of mozzarella they are willing to sell me. But I often eat all of it before I've gone two blocks from the store, so if I fail to get cheese-in-the-basket I can arrive home with nothing to show for the trip.) Sometimes I stop in at the bakery on Carmine Street that, on Saturdays only, creates a ring-shaped loaf of bread containing small pieces of cheese and sausage, both of which snuggle into the dough when the loaf is heated. On Saturdays I have things to do. I had never even objected to closings on Jewish holidays that I suspected were known only to two or three senior professors at the Jewish Theological Seminary. But Sundays!

I took it personally. My Sundays had been ruined. The satisfaction of capturing each of the ingredients for the perfect Nova Scotia and cream cheese on bagel was no more. The pleasure of a late breakfast that could be extended to include picking at the small bits of Nova Scotia left on the platter at three-thirty or four was gone. I felt like a baseball manager who, having finally polished a double-play combination to such brilliance that it provided the inspiration for the entire team, learns that the second baseman has decided to retire so that he can devote full time to his franchise estate-planning business.

It seemed to me that the reasons for the decision I had heard on Houston Street—that Ben was tired, that Ben had found it impossible to prepare enough cheese for the Sunday rush, that Ben could no longer take the crowds—were unpersuasive. Sunday is by far the busiest day on Houston Street. Closing on the busiest day is the kind of thing I might expect from some stationer in Surrey but not from a cheese merchant on the Lower East Side. I was not myself, of course. I became convinced that Ben, realizing how much I depended on him, had decided to close on Sundays as a display of independence. I knew, after all, that he was a strong-minded man. A year or two before, at a time when France had placed an embargo on spare parts for Israeli jets, Ben had put up a sign in his store that said something like UNTIL GENERAL DE GAULLE CHANGES HIS POLICY TOWARD ISRAEL, BEN SELLS NO MORE FRENCH CHEESE.

"He's trying to drive me from the city," I said to Alice when I arrived home, bearing a half pound of cream cheese that I had finally managed to find after a forty-minute traffic-and-parking struggle in the southern reaches of the Lower East Side—a dry, bland, half pound of cream cheese that tasted as if it might have been made by a Presbyterian missionary rigidly following directions from the Camp Fire Girls recipe book.

"He doesn't even know you," Alice said.

"He didn't know de Gaulle either," I said. But I decided to remain in the city. Out of the city, I wouldn't even be able to get decent cream cheese during the week.

•

I tried to look on the bright side. I told myself I could always make an extra trip on Friday to Ben's and then return on Sunday for fresh bagels and Nova Scotia; two routinely caught pop-ups may not provide as much beauty as a perfectly executed double play, but they provide precisely as many outs. I reminded myself that the ingredients for the perfect Nova Scotia and cream cheese on bagel were only part of my usual haul on Houston Street. As it happened, Ben's specialty was not even cream cheese but baked farmer cheese—a product I had learned about, years after I started going to Ben's, only because a lady from Scarsdale who shoved in front of me at the counter one morning ordered a baked farmer cheese

with caraway seeds and then included an eloquent description of
its taste in the speech she delivered to me about being double-parked
and in a terrible hurry. (Baked farmer cheese can be eaten cold,
which, out of ignorance, is the way I wolfed it down for three or
four years, until I heard Ben say that reheating it makes it taste "like
a soufflé or a *crêpe suzette* or whatever you want"—a description
I found to be completely accurate.) How could I begrudge Ben an
additional day of rest, I asked myself, when I could come in any
weekday and have my choice of baked farmer cheese with scallions
or baked farmer cheese with vegetables or even baked farmer cheese
with pineapple? Who was I to complain about a little break in my
Houston Street routine when there were millions of people all over
the world who would never taste Russ & Daughters' chopped
herring?

There were, I reminded myself, even non-food reasons to come
to Houston Street on Sunday. Whenever I begin to feel oppressed
by being shoved ahead of in the various lines I'm forced to stand
in around New York, I spend part of a Sunday at Katz's Delicatessen,
a block or two east of my combination stores, where the sandwich
makers at the counter always maintain rigid queue discipline while
hand-slicing a high-quality pastrami on rye. Fathoming line behavior in various cities requires, I have found, serious research. It
was only after I took sample measurings of neighborhood cinema
queues in London at a time when the press was printing statistics
on the imminent demise of the film industry that I realized why
there seem to be so many lines in England: English people apparently queue up as a sort of hobby. A family man might pass a mild
autumn evening by taking the wife and kids to stand in the cinema
queue for a while and then leading them over for a few minutes in
the sweetshop queue and then, as a special treat for the kids, saying,
"Perhaps we've time to have a look at the Number 31 bus queue
before we turn in." New York line behavior can be explained only
by assuming that just about everyone in the line believes himself
to be in possession of what the Wall Street people call inside information. Someone has convinced the people in the subway-token
line that the next person to the booth is likely to receive not just a
subway token but a special golden subway token, the recipient of

which will never have to ride the subways again. The people about to board a Madison Avenue bus at five-thirty in the afternoon have somehow permitted themselves to be convinced by a shady-looking little tout that what they are trying to board is not actually a Madison Avenue bus but the last boat from Dunkirk. Some out-of-towner without inside information has no way of knowing that what he is being shoved off of is not merely one of a number of buses going to Sixty-fourth Street but the last chance of escaping the Huns, so he naturally finds the behavior of his fellow citizens excessive.

After a week or two of being badly dealt with by elderly women half my size, I'm always reassured by my first sight of those Katz countermen standing there. They seem to loom over the crowd—casually piling on corned beef, keeping a strict eye on the line in front of them, and passing the time by arguing with each other in Yiddish about what I have always preferred to think was anarchosyndicalism. I stand there happily while some woman—undoubtedly the wife of the gentleman who elbowed past me in the potato-salad line at the P.S. 3 fair—tries to sneak in for a quick tongue on rye and receives from the counterman a devastating look and some comment like "And who are you—a movie star maybe?" Katz's is the place in which a counterman who was told by a customer that a particularly lean corned-beef sandwich would earn a commendation to the boss replied, "The boss! May the boss's nose fall off!" I find it a great comfort.

A couple of years after my first daughter was born, I realized that I was going to Houston Street on Sunday partly to have her properly appreciated. At that time, a check of the census statistics for Manhattan had confirmed a suspicion that had been growing in my mind: at least half the people who saw her on the street were neither Jewish nor Italian, and were therefore culturally handicapped in trying to demonstrate their appreciation of her in a way I considered appropriate. At Russ & Daughters, people pay some attention to a two-year-old. I don't mean quick smiles or routine "Isn't she cute?"s. I mean Notice Is Taken. Lox lies unsliced. Strategic places at the counter are abandoned. Candy fish are pressed into hands. I always thought that Russ & Daughters could get away with charging admission to new parents.

After Ben started closing on Sundays, in fact, I faced the simple truth that I could never give up Sunday mornings at Russ & Daughters completely, even if the entire Nova Scotia supply were lost to the Russian fishing fleet. (I will admit that when I stumble across one of those late-night philosophical discussions about whether war is ever justifiable, the question of how much of the Nova Scotia supply the Soviets can be allowed to swallow up leaps to my mind.) I have always thought that anyone who wants to open up a retail business in New York—a candy store or a Manhattan branch of Harrods—ought to be required to observe Russ & Daughters in action for a week. Russ & Daughters is a splendid refutation of the false teaching that a store selling pickled herring cannot have character and a clean display case at the same time. The daughters of the late founder are particularly warm and cheerful women, and a customer who enters the store having just stormed the counter at Tanenbaum's or subjected himself to the discipline of a Katz counterman could get the impression he has wandered into the Fourth of July outing of a large family. The salesperson—a daughter, a husband of a daughter, lately even a daughter of a daughter—is likely to be friendly enough to disarm even an experienced tormentor of Lower East Side countermen.

"A nice piece of whitefish," a customer says.

"A piece of whitefish," the counterman says cheerfully, moving toward the riches of the smoked fish section.

"A *nice* piece of whitefish," the customer repeats.

"Right, I'll get you a very nice piece," the counterman says.

The customer waits until the chosen piece is weighed and wrapped—four or five previous pieces having been rejected—and then, looking suddenly indecisive, says, "Is the whitefish *good?*"

"Very good," the counterman says.

"Is it *excellent?*" the customer asks.

"You're going to love it," the counterman says.

The potential licensee can then step forward, sample the whitefish, and learn the most important lesson of his week's observation: he loves it.

•

Three years after Ben started closing Sundays, I went to the Lower East Side one Sunday morning partly to take a look at the city's experiment of turning Orchard Street into a "mall" on Sunday by forbidding automobile traffic from Delancey to Houston. I found that the absence of cars did make Orchard Street much less crowded and chaotic, which would have been all to the good except that Orchard Street is *supposed* to be crowded and chaotic. Looking down poor, barren Orchard Street, I realized that it is only a matter of time before the city officials of Addis Ababa find themselves approving an avant-garde plan for banning traffic in the city market—a plan proposed by one of those jazzy American urban-design specialists who flourished in Great Society times by knowing how to outfit an office-building complex in a way that qualified it for federal aid under a Department of Housing program to improve drainage facilities in low-rent residential areas. "We'll get a marvelous sweep of space here and a great flow of movement over here," he'll explain, stepping over four or five vegetable peddlers and wedging himself into a three-foot alley. "Naturally, we'll have designated off-street parking for all these donkeys."

I don't mean that I'm opposed to change. Tanenbaum sold his bakery a year or two ago, and I have always spoken approvingly of the transition, once I satisfied myself that the young man who bought it was not going to do anything foolish like closing on Sunday or cutting back on his supply of a favorite pastry of mine called *rugelach*. The mozzarella store on Sullivan Street, Frank's Dairy, changed hands a year or so after Tanenbaum's, and the new proprietor turned out to be a student of the craft—the kind of young man who would answer a customer's question about an interesting-looking kind of cheese not merely by saying that it was used in cooking a special Sicilian dish of liver and onions and cheese but tossing in the information that the one restaurant still serving that dish was a lunch counter on First Avenue. For stores as well as for governments, a stable transition is the test of the system. After rattling around Orchard Street for a few minutes that Sunday, I dropped into Russ & Daughters, and the subject of the stores next door came up.

"Ben's retiring," one of the daughters said.

"Retiring!" I said. I had spent three years making extra trips or making do with inferior cream cheese. Could he now plan, as the final blow, cutting off my supply completely?

"He's training someone to take his place," the daughter said.

Greatly relieved, I went to Ben's the next day to investigate the switchover. The man being trained in the art of farmer cheese, it turned out, was taking over in partnership with the young man who ran what had been Tanenbaum's Bakery. They were even considering the possibility of knocking down the wall in between, creating one store in a space almost as vast as a Checker cab. Despite their youth, the partners are traditionalists in such matters as observing the Sabbath—they are Hasidim from Brooklyn—but they believe in progressive business techniques. I noticed that they had erected a brightly painted double sign between the stores announcing Ben's Cheese Shop and Moishe's Bakery. The bakery had even acquired a motto: "Keep This Place in Mind/A Better One Is Hard to Find." Having a motto is not unknown on Houston Street (the Russ & Daughters' shopping bags say "Queens of Lake Sturgeon"), but it was hardly Tanenbaum's style. Ben's Dairy, where the presence of baked farmer cheese was a secret Ben managed to keep from me for years, now had a sign in the window that not only announced the cheese but listed the varieties on individual slats hanging from the sign, in the way some ice-cream parlors announce their flavors.

"Will the place be run the same way?" I asked Ben and his successor.

"He's going to be closed on Saturdays and Jewish holidays," Ben said firmly.

"Of course. Naturally," I said, trying to control my excitement. "And, uh, the other days?"

"This week," the young man said, "we start opening on Sundays."

6

Table Morals

ALTHOUGH THERE ARE restaurant reviewers in New York who go to some lengths to preserve their independence, I have never run across one as militantly uncompromising as Jack Shelton, publisher of *Jack Shelton's Private Guide to Restaurants* in San Francisco, who has written so convincingly of how he avoids being recognized at restaurants he plans to review that I always picture him eating in disguise—doing his best to sniff the bouquet of a Burgundy through a putty nose, trying to figure out whether the odd texture of the vichyssoise is due to improper pureeing or its trip through his false mustache, standing nervously at the door of some old hangout like the Tadich Grill wondering if the waiters will greet him warmly by name despite the pains he has taken to disguise himself as the Korean consul general. I can appreciate the necessity of taking an absolute position on such matters, since, in moments of being candid with myself, I realize that I could be tempted to betray my principles for a handful of burned edges from Arthur Bryant's or an extra helping of bread pudding at the Bon Ton in New Orleans (in a special away-from-home issue on New Orleans, Shelton once printed the recipe for that marvel of a dessert, a service for which I stand, somewhat fattened, in his debt) or between eight and ten fried dumplings at any good Chinese restaurant. I once asked a fanatic gourmet—a man who exists quietly in the Midwest between annual eating tours of the French provinces, like a python dozing in the sun until another smallish antelope happens along— when he first realized he had a serious interest in food. At the age of twelve, he told me, he had spent some time with his grandmother, and she had said, upon returning him to his mother, "He would kill for his stomach."

I often remember his remark when I am thinking about the connection between eating and morality—a subject that occasionally floats into my mind when I realize that I am coveting the ice cream being eaten by one of my small and defenseless daughters or that I had been tempted to shove aside a kindly-looking old couple rather than miss the last bowl of seafood chowder at a Nova Scotia church supper. The subject was brought to my mind again not long ago by an article I read in one of those magazines that every airline now publishes and distributes free to the passengers—apparently as a desperate attempt to keep their minds off the lunch tray they are being served. The article, written by Stanley Jacobs for the TWA magazine, said, "Increasingly, doctors, psychiatrists, educators and personnel men are scrutinizing what we eat, seeking additional clues to our mental ability, character, hostilities, ambition, defeatism and other traits." Most of the research has apparently amounted to analyzing food preferences in order to arrive at such findings as "If you're extra fond of starchy foods (breads and potatoes), it could mean you are on the complacent side and averse to solving problems or making judgments"—or, in another way of looking at it, too fat to care.

Research on eating preferences causes me no concern. It says right in the article, after all, that people who "like everything"—a description, in its mildest form, of me—are fortunate. "Studies at the University of Maryland," it says, "indicate that the person who has few or no food hangups tends to have a mature outlook, a balanced personality and a logical mind." (So much for people who do not like Beef Wellington *and* barbecued spareribs!) It seems to me only a step or two from that finding to a refutation of the proposition that a person is displaying maturity if he is able to order what he wants in a restaurant without being haunted by the thought that several other items on the menu are almost certain to be worth tasting as well—a proposition that Nora Ephron once expressed in a different context (she was writing about people searching for kinky sex) by saying, "I am no longer interested in thirty-one flavors; I stick with English toffee." I long ago decided that among the flavors of ice cream sold at Baskin-Robbins I liked English toffee best, but I find myself trying a different flavor every time I walk in—a result, I now realize, of my balanced personality and logical mind.

What disturbs me is that any encouragement of people like psychiatrists and personnel men to poke around in everybody's dinner plate can eventually make eating about as satisfying as playing basketball with New York intellectuals who always follow the game with a few hours of analyzing each player's entire character in terms of how often he passes or whether he is willing to risk a hook shot with his left hand. ("You can't tell me that somebody who elbows that much under the basket is in poverty law strictly to help poor people.") That kind of approach can only lead to judging people by whether they happen to covet their neighbor's Peking duck or whether they would betray their friends for a perfectly sautéed soft-shell crab. Where would that leave me?

It should be obvious even to a personnel man that modern society has brought decisions that are much more complicated than they were in the days when a moral man could face up to the simple question of whether or not it would be hypocritical for him to perform small acts of kindness for a particularly nasty neighbor lady who happened to make the best apple pie in the territory. An example is provided by Martha's Vineyard, an island off Cape Cod on which many writers and academics and liberal intellectuals spend the summers employing their creative energy to compose NO TRESPASSING signs. It is an island on which beaches are guarded so fiercely against the non-property-owning public that a common business transaction is the sale of a share in an access road to the beach. Simple moralists would say that a person who disapproves of such arrangements should merely avoid Martha's Vineyard—at least until he is able to buy some beachfront property himself and begin talking about the necessity of protecting the shore for the generations to come. But what if the person in question has eaten the fried clams at Nick's Lighthouse in Oak Bluff, Martha's Vineyard, and has found them to be the finest fried clams on the continent? Still a simple choice, the moralists say. But what if that person—the same person who has tasted the clams—happens to have a wife who would commit armed robbery for the right piece of chocolate cake and that wife has found the chocolate cake served in a restaurant in Edgartown, Martha's Vineyard, to be necessary to her continued happiness? There are no easy answers these days.

People in simpler times—a nineteenth-century apple-pie freak, for instance—had to face nothing comparable to the strike at Nathan's in New York. The origins of the strike apparently had to do with a jurisdictional dispute between a pizza baker and a pizza slicer, although I have never done enough research to be absolutely certain of that, pizza at Nathan's not being a great interest of mine. The strikers, mostly Puerto Rican countermen, turned out to be raucous, old-fashioned picketers who shouted at people on the street to pass Nathan's by—in a chant that came out sounding something like "Possumby, possumby, possumby." What was a responsible person to do? Launch a citizens' inquiry to ascertain where justice lay between Nathan's and its pizza slicers? Cross the picket line but only eat hot dogs and French fries, which happen to be the best things at Nathan's anyway? Not go in but, in fairness, explain to the pickets that the decision had been based on cholesterol rather than political considerations? Is an eater being fair to the family he supports if he substitutes for Nathan's hot dogs some inferior lunch that so depresses him he performs badly at his daily task? But what if the son he supports grows up to be a radical professor of Latin American Studies and says one day, "Father, did you break the picket line of the *possumbyistas?*" In a simple world, Nathan's fried clams would be as good as Nick's fried clams, combining with Nathan's hot dogs and Nathan's French fries to create an eating place so palpably irresistible that a picket-line breaker would be rendered blameless.

Psychiatrists and personnel people would never understand about how one is forced to act in a Chinese restaurant when ordering must be done family-style for six or eight people. As the government has always told us when discussing some of the foreign regimes it supports, there are some places where democracy is simply not applicable. Democracy in a Chinese restaurant means inflicting lobster Cantonese on a lot of innocents merely because William Edgett Smith, the man with the Naugahyde palate, is carrying on about proper representation. In my vision of purgatory, the Devil tells me that I am about to eat eternally in the best Chinese restaurant that has ever existed—with, of course, a couple of qualifications. My dining partners will be seven of those baseball players who always used to be described in the sports magazines as "strictly meat-and-potatoes men." They will do all the ordering for the table. I will not be allowed to indicate my preferences by word or gesture. "Maybe we should have some of that chop-suey stuff," one of them says, as I see an entire carp being carried by, floating in a sauce whose aroma alone makes me weak.

"That stuff's too gooey," a large first baseman says. "You think they have any plain chicken?"

•

On the chance that the eating analyzers ever do come to power, I have been taking notes on my behavior at the Tri-County Relief Sale held by the Mennonites every spring at Morgantown, Pennsylvania—putting together my defense like a cautious bureaucrat covering himself with a memo for the record. I happen to love eating in that part of Pennsylvania. An early riser can drive down any Saturday morning from New York to, say, the weekly farmers' market at Lebanon, stock up on Lebanon bologna and sweet bologna and cheese and chow-chow and bean salad and shoofly pie and pumpkin custard, and then stage a banquet in the public park of Lebanon. Sometimes, in warmish weather, the man behind the meat counter at the market tells me that the scrapple I want will not keep quite all the way to New York—as if the Almighty did not intend anyone to eat anything that tasted like country scrapple in a wicked city of eight million people—but on cool days it can be carried home, where, with luck, it will all fall apart in the frying pan and come out like some crisp, mystical hash.

It's not that I eat less at the Tri-County Relief Sale. I eat more—but in a good cause. I suppose there must be some other worthy causes in the United States, but the Mennonite relief operation is the only one I'm sure of. In a number of places that have suffered, say, a tornado or a hurricane, I have been told by the residents that the Mennonites showed up the morning after the disaster as if they had a contract. Anyone with any lingering doubts about the strength of the Mennonite tradition to do the right thing need only inspect the quilts donated for the quilt auction at the Tri-County Sale—an inspection that makes it obvious that every quilt maker routinely forks over her best quilt.

There I am, in other words, among certifiably good people who are selling food in order to get money for their good works and who also happen to be able to make a chicken-and-corn soup that I would walk through a tornado to eat. There I am in a place where a man with any decent instincts at all would buy a few sausage sandwiches. I am standing in front of the strawberry-pie counter behind which live people are actually cutting up strawberries that have been picked by human hands and are arranging them in pie-crusts that just emerged from the oven. I have just come from the apple-fritter booth, where I observed actual apples being made into the kind of fritters I was forced to have six of—having remembered, after finishing off my first order of three, the remarkable job the Mennonites did on the Gulf Coast of Mississippi after Hurricane Camille.

"You're not going to have another piece of strawberry pie, are you?" Alice is saying.

"My friend Paul Bates told me that when he lived in Assaria, Kansas, he walked out of his house the morning after a tornado and found Mennonites all over," I say, pushing my money toward a kindly-looking lady who is in charge of the pie. "They didn't say much more than a friendly hello to him because they were too busy cleaning up his yard."

"I thought you were saving room for some funnel cake," Alice says. Funnel cake is a sort of dough fried in oil to crispness and sprinkled with powdered sugar—a Pennsylvania Dutch version of the dessert pastry I have eaten pounds of in New York Italian restaurants whose proprietors have never even been to Assaria, Kansas.

"I'll have room," I say. "I've decided to have only one order of sausage and pancakes."

"Sausage and pancakes!" Alice says.

"Sausage and pancakes," I say. "Anything for a good cause."

7

Buckeye Gourmet

I ARRIVED FOR DINNER at the home of one of the leading gourmets in Columbus with high expectations, despite the fact that Columbus is not known as the gourmet center of Ohio. Ordinarily, anyone in Columbus who wants to take a fling at *haute cuisine* goes to Cincinnati. I have met people in Columbus who regularly drive the two hours to Cincinnati for dinner, stay the night, find some way to occupy themselves until lunchtime the next day, eat lunch, and return to Columbus—fortified against another five or six weeks of deprivation. Cincinnati's reputation for French cuisine extends beyond the borders of the state: of the eleven restaurants in the country awarded five stars by the *Mobil Travel Guide* the year I visited Columbus, three were in Cincinnati. Anyone familiar with a couple of the New York restaurants given five stars by the *Mobil Guide* may have the impression that its restaurant critic was promoted to that position as a reward for the initiative and efficiency he demonstrated as a service-station attendant. But just the presence of three serious French restaurants, however many stars they deserve, is likely to make a *béarnaise*-sauce addict in Columbus look toward Cincinnati with the kind of envious expression that a shameless profligate trapped in some particularly pious Judean village must have worn when discussing life in Sodom. Columbus has a chapter of the International Wine & Food Society—my hosts, Joseph and

Jane Cooper, were among the founders—but the supply of suitable restaurants for dinner meetings being what it is, the society once responded to a special occasion by flying in a cook from the East, more or less the way a community of pioneer families with a backlog of unconsecrated marriages and unbaptized babies might have pooled its money to bring in a proper preacher. Apparently having been thoroughly briefed by telephone on the marketing situation, the cook arrived from Boston bearing her own *Ballottine de Pigeons à la Périgourdine.*

One reason I expected an excellent meal at the Coopers' is that I knew Joe Cooper's standards are high enough to keep him from eating anywhere else. Other Wine & Food Society members risk Columbus restaurants regularly, but Cooper has boycotted the entire city. If someone tells Cooper that Columbus has an *"excellent French restaurant,"* he doesn't bother to claim that French food makes him break out; he just shudders. Sitting at his own dinner table, he often says, "This is the only decent restaurant in town." There is one restaurant in Akron he rather likes, but he hasn't been there for a while. I went to Columbus partly to find out how someone who thinks of himself as a gourmet survives in a city that is not the gourmet center of Ohio, and the simple answer in Cooper's case is that he stays home—a man put under house arrest by his own palate. The Coopers probably come closer than anyone else in Columbus to living off the land. Joe Cooper raises just about every vegetable the climate will allow, allocating the garden space to various crops in the manner of the ranking officer on a lifeboat handing out drinking water. Jane Cooper bakes all of their bread. Once off his own property, Cooper has the wariness that one might expect to find in an Arab peddler who works rural Alabama in the full knowledge that anyone who invites him to stay for a meal is unlikely to put anything on the table without frying it in pork fat first. Cooper does not assume that the home of a fellow member of the International Wine & Food Society is a safe harbor. "I went over there for dinner once," he told me when discussing one member, "and they served Sara Lee cake."

Cooper had invited me to lunch to discuss dinner. Jane Cooper was not at home—she teaches school—but we were joined by Bruce

Campbell, a Columbus lawyer who happens to believe that there is no food on earth superior to a properly prepared bowl of chili. Campbell grew up in Dayton, where, when he became a certain age, his father started taking him to a chili parlor named Mike's— in the way my father started taking me to a chili parlor named Dixon's in Kansas City, and in the way, I suppose, that fathers in some other parts of the country take sons of a certain age out in the marshes and start teaching them how to point a shotgun at a duck. Campbell is the kind of eating enthusiast I grew up with in Kansas City—what is known in some parts of the country as a "big hungry boy"—and is therefore less likely to find himself in a serious discussion about where to find a perfect terrine than about where to find the best hash-brown potatoes in the world. (Some big hungry boys include a sophisticated taste for French food and wine in their eating repertoire—others may look on people who talk about the bouquet of a wine or the perfection of a soufflé the way they look on members of a narrow, mildly loony religious sect—but those who do have a favorite French restaurant tend to praise it with restrained phrases like "one of the better French restaurants west of New York" or "very good under the circumstances." A man who is defending his favorite fried-chicken restaurant never qualifies his superlatives. When I told some people at the Coopers' that there must be a decent restaurant in Columbus if they would settle for something other than French food, they finally acknowledged the presence of one good barbecue place and, as a matter of course, described its specialty as "the best spareribs in the world.") Campbell's culinary pilgrimages to Cincinnati are made to eat chili. Among serious eaters in the Midwest, in fact, Cincinnati is as well known for its chili parlors—particularly the Empress and Skyline chains—as it is for the French restaurants that have been anointed by the *Mobil Guide*. The chili served is so singular that a chili parlor may describe its product as "authentic Cincinnati chili."

Because I had told Cooper that I have some interest in chili myself, he had decided to serve me some of his homemade chili for lunch and to have Campbell present as a sort of expert witness. Cooper serves chili to people like Campbell and me with only the barest touch of the mood the New York Philharmonic might affect while playing "Jingle Bells" at a special Christmas concert. Being a man who knows a purist when he sees one, Cooper seemed particularly interested in Campbell's opinion of his homemade version. Campbell had tasted Cooper's chili before. When the subject came up, just before lunch, Campbell appeared to spend a few moments gathering up his enthusiasm, and then acknowledged that he had found Cooper's chili to be "very passable." I thought it was very passable indeed. Cooper made a few remarks about the wine during lunch, but Campbell and I were too busy eating to offer any appropriate replies.

The bread was spectacular—baked by Jane Cooper from flour the Coopers get from a woman who imports it from Texas in the kernel and grinds it herself. The Coopers manage to get their hands on some of the Texas flour by granting the woman who grinds it every other picking of the red raspberries in their garden—bartering being the normal method of commerce practiced by settlers in remote areas. As it turns out, the Coopers not only cultivate fruits and vegetables but also cultivate people who cultivate fruits and vegetables. The same woman has been providing them with strawberries for seventeen years. Cooper told me that he once found an elderly man who grew perfect asparagus and was willing to have Cooper snap off the stalks at the precise moment that suited him, but the elderly man had to leave town after a dalliance with a young girl—leaving behind a mild scandal in Columbus and near-despair at the Coopers'. Joe Cooper now grows his own asparagus.

•

Although many people who have an intense interest in French cooking would sooner eat TV dinners than use the word "gourmet," I could tell that the guests at the Coopers' for dinner that evening were gourmets from the way they referred to the prominent figures of American *haute cuisine* by their first names—not to give the impression they were personally acquainted but merely to use a form of respectfully affectionate address, just as a Cuban cane cutter might refer to the leader of his country as Fidel. "I got that recipe from Julia," one of them might say, or "Craig said it was superb." The meal was delicious—a fish stew, pork with *sauce diable*, carrots and parsnips that Cooper had wrenched from his icy garden the day before in eleven-degree temperature—but Cooper did not discuss it with great enthusiasm. He is, I had learned, as quick to criticize the food at his own house as he is to criticize what some particularly brave hostess in the Wine & Food Society brings herself to put in front of him. When Campbell and I had complimented him on the salad at lunch—a salad that he had been forced to make with store-bought escarole and scallions, since he had nothing available from his garden—he said, "It's decent, but compared to what it should have been, it's straw." I liked the *sauce diable*, but when Cooper wrote me later to discuss the meal he said he had been disappointed in it. "At best, it was inoffensive," he wrote. "It lacked the balanced intensity which should have made us exclaim with delight."

The dinner guests and Cooper seemed much more interested in talking about wine than about food. It may be that an almost pedantic interest in wine is what separates a Midwesterner who thinks of himself as a gourmet from one who thinks of himself as merely a serious eater, or it may be that a Columbus gourmet tends to concentrate his attention on wine because it is the one ingredient on which he does not have to compromise, assuming he likes to settle down every evening in his easy chair with a good wine cat-alogue. The Coopers make their own sausage and ferment their own vinegar and barter for their own hand-ground flour, but there is still a limit to the ingredients they can acquire for cooking. As Cooper regularly laments, he is not in a position to raise his own livestock.

Finally, around coffee time, the conversation turned to the traditional topic—which of the Cincinnati French restaurants serves the finest food between coasts, and how the memory of all of them fades with the first meal at Bocuse in Lyon or Troisgros in Roanne. (A gourmet who lives in Columbus, like a concert pianist who lives in Cheyenne, cannot be afraid to travel.) The eating experiences put forward to support claims and counterclaims began to revive an appetite that I thought had perhaps been permanently satisfied by a huge portion of Cooper's chocolate mousse. I was leaving for Cincinnati in the morning myself, and I realized that before noon I could be sitting in a Skyline chili parlor.

(8)

Harry Garrison

HARRY GARRISON, the eater who had agreed to serve as my consultant in Cincinnati, had been recommended by my friend Marshall J. Dodge III—a fact that gave me pause, particularly after Marshall described him as a calliope restorer by trade. I don't mean that I harbor any prejudice against calliope restorers or that I think Marshall would make a frivolous recommendation. Marshall is a practical man. He has a practicality so pure, in fact, that it sometimes makes him appear eccentric. He is an uncompromising bicyclist—partly because bicycling is the most practical way to get around New York—and when he travels to, say, Cincinnati, he merely removes the wheels of one of his bicycles, stuffs the parts into something that resembles a swollen Harvard bookbag, and checks the mysterious bundle along with his luggage. If the ticket agent asks what the bag contains, Marshall looks at him solemnly —Marshall can manage an awesomely solemn look when the occasion calls for one—and says that the bag contains his grandmother's wheelchair. Like New York's most photographed bicyclist, John V. Lindsay—a tall man who was once the mayor—Marshall attended Buckley and St. Paul's and Yale, and it is implicit in his appearance and manner that he takes the presence of many generations of Dodges at those institutions before him and after him as a matter of course. But if it is practical to take along a knapsack while riding his bicycle, Marshall takes along a knapsack. Then if someone happens to ask him, say, if he knows the address of a good calliope restorer in Cincinnati, he can reach into the knapsack, pull out a small file of three-by-five cards, and thumb through it until he finds the answer.

What concerned me about depending on Marshall's recommendation for a guide to Cincinnati is that the knapsack is much more likely to produce the address of an expert on antique piano rolls or a supplier of Cajun-dialect phonograph albums than a specialist in French-fried onion rings or barbecue—a natural outgrowth of Marshall's own specialty, which is regional humor. (He has made an album of Down East stories called *Bert and I* and he has presented his monologues before groups in various parts of the country, always arriving by plane and bike.) I hinted about my concern to Marshall, but he assured me that Garrison would be the perfect guide to Cincinnati and environs. He was not certain if it had been Garrison who put him on to a small restaurant in Rabbit Hash, Kentucky, that served what Marshall remembered as the best fried chicken in the world, but he was certain that it was Garrison who had introduced him to Professor Harry L. Suter, an elderly musicologist who was able to play the piano and the violin simultaneously by means of an invention the professor called the viola-pan.

Garrison, I found out, not only restores calliopes but also restores and sells player pianos, appears professionally around the state as Uncle Sam the Magician, delivers an occasional lecture on how to detect crooked gambling devices, and in the midst of all those activities manages to spend more than the ordinary amount of time at table. He was not going to be able to meet me until a few hours after I arrived in Cincinnati, but he had suggested on the phone that for my first taste of authentic Cincinnati chili, at lunch, I might want to try the unadorned product and therefore should start with what is known locally as a "bowl of plain." He had no way of knowing, of course, that I have never eaten the unadorned version of anything in my life and that I once threatened to place a Denver counterman under citizen's arrest for leaving the mayonnaise off my California burger.

"What should I order if I don't want to start with the plain?" I asked.

"Try a four-way," Garrison said.

In Cincinnati, everyone knows that a four-way is chili on spaghetti with cheese and onions added. I never saw any numbers on menus in Cincinnati, but it is accepted that a customer can walk into any chili parlor—an Empress or a Skyline or any of the independent neighborhood parlors—and say "One three-way" and be assured of getting chili on spaghetti with cheese. Cincinnati eaters take it for granted that the basic way to serve chili is on spaghetti, just as they take it for granted that the other ways to serve it go up to a five-way (chili, spaghetti, onions, cheese, and beans) and that the people who do the serving are Greeks. When the Kiradjieff family, which introduced authentic Cincinnati chili at the Empress in 1922, was sued several years ago by a manager who alleged that he had been fired unfairly, one of his claims amounted to the contention that anyone fired under suspicious circumstances from a chili parlor with Empress's prestige was all through in the Greek community. There are probably people in Cincinnati who reach maturity without realizing that Mexicans eat anything called chili, in the same way that there are probably young men from Nevada who have to be drafted and sent to an out-of-state Army camp before they realize that all laundromats are not equipped with slot machines.

What is called chili in America, of course, has less similarity to the Mexican dish than American football has to the game known as football just about everywhere else in the world. Like American football, though, it long ago became the accepted version within the borders, and anyone in, say, northern New Mexico who wanted to claim that the version served there (green or red chili peppers sliced up and cooked into a kind of stew) is the only one entitled to the name would have no more chance of being listened to than a soccer enthusiast who made a claim to the television networks for equal time with the NFL. As American chili goes, what is served in Cincinnati is sweeter than what I used to have at Dixon's and what I still have occasionally at the Alamo—a Tex-Mex chili parlor in Manhattan that offers eight or ten combination plates, all of which taste exactly alike, and is famous for a notation on the menu that says, "All combinations above without beans 25¢ extra." (I know people who have tried to work out the economics of how much the Alamo has to pay a professional bean extractor to come out ahead on that offer, but a definite figure has eluded them.) The chili in Cincinnati is less ferocious than Texas chili, but I wouldn't want to carry the comparison any further. I decided a long time ago that I like chili, but not enough to argue about it with people from Texas.

To an out-of-towner, the chili in various Cincinnati chili parlors may seem pretty much alike, but there are natives who have stayed up late at night arguing about the relative merits of Empress and Skyline or explaining that the secret of eating at the downtown Empress is to arrive when the chili is at its freshest, which happens to be at about nine in the morning. In Cincinnati, people are constantly dropping into a new neighborhood chili parlor only to find out that it serves the best chili in the world. One chili fanatic I met was a supporter of a place across the river, in Kentucky, that he claimed serves a six-way and a seven-way.

"What could possibly be in a seven-way?" I asked.

"I don't know," he said. "They won't even tell you." I later learned from Bert Workum, a serious eater who works for the Kentucky *Post* in Covington, just across the river from Cincinnati, that the Dixie chili parlor in Kentucky had once served a seven-way by including eggs (fried or scrambled) and cut-up frankfurters but is now serving only a six-way, having abandoned its egg-cooking operation.

Garrison had turned out to be a large man who wears three-piece suits and a full beard and has what used to be called an ample stomach. He appreciates good food, but even at a restaurant that he might patronize mainly because it has a pleasant atmosphere or is open late at night or charges reasonable prices he is what one of his friends described as a Clean Plate Ranger. One of his friends, a man who runs a barbecue restaurant called the Barn and Rib Pit in downtown Cincinnati, told me, "I love to see Harry eat ribs. He just inhales those ribs. You look at him and he's just glowin'."

I spent an afternoon with Garrison riding around Cincinnati, and found him to be one of those rare Americans who truly savor their city. I was still a bit concerned that he might be someone who would be more excited about finding an authentic boogie-woogie pianist or maybe a mechanical violin in perfect working order than he would about stumbling onto, say, the classic corn fritter. But he relieved my fears somewhat by describing what we were going to have for dinner at his house as "the best fried chicken in the world." At about that time, by coincidence, we passed a run-down-looking restaurant whose sign actually said, WORLD'S BEST FRIED CHICKEN. Garrison glanced at it contemptuously. "I don't see any point in considering his claim at all," he said.

There was a lot of food talk among the dinner guests at Garrison's that evening, and there was also some staggering acorn squash and the best apple pie I have ever tasted. The chicken was delicious, but I still think the best fried chicken I have ever eaten was at a sort of outdoor homecoming that Cherokee County, Georgia, held for Dean Rusk, a native son, shortly after he was named Secretary of State—fried chicken so good that I still nurture a hope, against long odds, that Cherokee County will someday produce another Secretary of State and throw another homecoming.

Garrison finished off the meal by handing around made-in-Cincinnati cigars and treating the entire company to a display of smoke-ring blowing. Garrison's smoke-ring technique includes a remarkable motion by which he more or less nudges the ring along by pushing at the air a few inches behind it—a variation of the assistance that curlers offer a curling stone by sweeping away at the ice in its path. Between rings, Garrison announces his performance with the kind of grandiloquence he must use on the magic stage, and he is as irritable as a matador about the threat of air movement that could mar his artistry. Just when everyone at the table expects a ring to emerge, Garrison is likely to pause, glance around sternly, and say, in a majestic voice, "I detect human breathing in this room." Even after having stopped eating for a while to watch the smoke-ring blowing, none of us felt up to the late-night visit to the Barn and Rib Pit Garrison had contemplated. The fact that I knew the proprietor was white made me less disappointed at missing the Barn and Rib Pit than I might have been. Going to a white-run barbecue is, I think, like going to a gentile internist: it might turn out all right, but you haven't made any attempt to take advantage of the percentages.

•

Garrison had promised me a special treat for my last night in Ohio—a treat to be found in a restaurant near Oxford—but even as we drove to the restaurant he insisted that precisely what the treat was would have to be a surprise. After the day I had spent, I figured it might require more than a surprise treat to induce me to take any food on my fork. At about eleven, I had stopped at the downtown Empress to see what it looked like and, deciding that it might be rude to leave without eating (particularly so early in the freshness cycle), had polished off a three-way. For lunch, Garrison had led me to a splendid place called Stenger's Café, which he described as the last of the old-fashioned workingmen's bars left in what had been the old German section of Cincinnati known as Over the Rhine. At Stenger's I cleaned a plate on which the counterman had piled mettwurst, two potato pancakes, a helping of beans, some beets, bread and butter, and, at the last minute, a piece of beef from a tray I had spotted being carried across the room. For that, I had parted with one dollar and twenty-eight cents. My appetite was returning as we drove, though, and Garrison helped it along by describing what we might have eaten at a few of the places he had considered taking me to before he decided on the restaurant in Oxford—including a place in Kentucky that specialized in farm food like ham with gravy.

"Red-eye gravy?" I asked.

"Red-eye gravy," Garrison said.

We drove along for a few miles while I thought that over.

"Is it too late to turn back toward Kentucky?" I asked.

"You'll love the place we're going," Garrison said. "It's going to have a fine surprise for you."

The place he had picked out was a restaurant outside Oxford called the Shady Nook. It turned out to be a normal-looking suburban restaurant with a sign in four or five colors of neon in the parking lot. Garrison insisted that we sit at the bar for a while to have shrimp cocktails and some wine. Behind the bar there was a stage that went completely around the room, and in front of the stage was a covered square that looked as if it might be a small orchestra pit. I was beginning to wonder what the surprise was. I didn't see anything amazing about the shrimp except how many of them Garrison was eating. Between bites he managed to say hello to a man he identified as the owner of the Shady Nook and to explain how Professor Harry L. Suter happened to design the viola-pan as he whiled away the time on the top floor of his house in Moscow, Ohio, during the great flood of 1913. Garrison told me that he had hired Professor Suter to play a Christmas party in 1959, and had the pleasure of being able to say in the introduction that it was the Professor's first Cincinnati appearance since the summer of 1917, when he played the Bell Telephone picnic. I couldn't spot anything extraordinary on the plates of the people already eating, but somehow I got it in my mind that the surprise was going to be either The Great Cherry Cobbler or maybe even The Classic Onion Ring. Suddenly the recorded music that I had been listening to without realizing it was turned off. From deep within what I had thought was an orchestra pit came a rumbling noise. Before my eyes there arose a gigantic gold, intricately carved, four-keyboard, three-ton Wurlitzer Theater Organ. The owner of the Shady Nook climbed up on the stool, high above the bar, and—by playing at least all four keyboards at once and flicking on and off several dozen switches at the same time—transformed the Shady Nook into Radio City Music Hall. I was indeed surprised. Harry Garrison looked at the theater organ and looked at me and beamed.

9

Idea Man

MY FATHER OWNED a restaurant for a few years in Kansas City, although I always suspected he thought of it mainly as an outlet for his poetry. He wrote a two-line poem every day on the lunch menu. At dinner, the restaurant drew mainly a family trade, and the diners had to eat their turkey or breaded veal cutlet or Swiss steak without benefit of rhyme. (I can't remember much about the taste of the food; I suppose that in itself amounts to a description of it.) Although the restaurant was in the residential district, quite a few businessmen came in for lunch—a crowd from an insurance company building not far away, some merchants from a shopping district, salesmen who happened to find themselves in the neighborhood—and they were accustomed to seeing on the menu, in a space between the luncheon specials and the desserts, a poem like "Try Mrs. Trillin's pie, I'm sure one piece'll/Give your motor more power than a diesel." A lot of them came back regularly anyway.

As quick as he was about using the restaurant for his poetic ends, my father never seemed interested in turning it into a platform for his own ideas on what was good to eat. That would have been a true test of the regulars' loyalty. My father had absolute ideas about food—as well as about a number of other subjects—and once he made up his mind he was about as flexible as Fats Goldberg's eating schedule. More than once he told me, "The best thing in the world to eat is a good ear of corn"—in the matter-of-fact tone of someone announcing the date of the Battle of the Boyne.

"If you were blindfolded, you couldn't tell whether there was cream in your coffee or not," he said to me one night at dinner, after I had declined the cream.

I told him I thought that he was probably not in the best position to speak authoritatively on the subject, since, as it happened, he had never tasted coffee, with or without cream, in his life. (I was never certain why his avoidance of coffee had to be absolute, except that he tended to be an all-or-nothing man. I have since come to believe that people who pride themselves on their willpower might sometimes swear off things just to stay in practice—looking at themselves in the mirror on a quiet morning and saying, for no particular reason, "My friend, you have eaten your last scrambled egg.")

When it came to poetry, my father was not an absolutist. Pie was his favorite subject for a couplet, but every three or four weeks he would write about something else—perhaps a couplet like " 'Eat your food,' gently said Mom to little son Roddy/'If you don't, I will break every bone in your body.' " The next day he would be back to pies—"Mrs. Trillin's pecan pie, so nutritious and delicious/Will make a wild man mild and a mild man vicious" or "A woman shot her husband in our place last July/He started talking while she was enjoying her pie." He made a strong case in the poems for the pies being completely free of calories. "Don't blame your weight/On the pie you ate," he would write, or "So you love the sound of the soft-lowing cattle/Then eat lots of pie and be lighter in the saddle." He often returned to the theme of pie being good for one's general health, like mineral water or brisk walks. "A piece of pie baked by Mrs. Trillin," he would write of a pie baked, of course, by a black woman named Thelma, "will do you more good than penicillin." He rhymed pie with "eye" and "goodbye" and "fry" (" 'Let's go, warden, I'm ready to fry/My last request was Mrs. Trillin's pie' ") and "evening is nigh." His shortest poem, as far as I can tell, was "Don't sigh/Eat pie."

My cousin Nardy owns a restaurant too, and he uses it as an excuse to publish a newsletter about the customers. Nardy, I believe, graduated from the University of Missouri School of Journalism, the same institution that produced Fats Goldberg, the pizza baron, and, I can only assume, dozens of other successful restaurant men, all of whom are more prosperous than the night city editors turned out by other journalism schools. Nardy sees the newsletter as an opportunity to express himself; I see the same opportunity for me in the restaurant business. I don't mean I actually want to own a restaurant, any more than Nardy actually wants to cover City Hall for the Wichita *Eagle*. I see myself more as a consultant—an idea man. An amazing number of people do want to own a restaurant. They know a couple of remarkable recipes and they like to meet people and it all seems so easy that the failure rate for new restaurants in New York is 65 percent the first year. On Sunday evenings in Goldberg's Pizzeria, a lot of the people who don't talk to Fats about going on a diet the next morning talk to him about their ideas for starting a restaurant. Once, a woman told him that she wanted to start a restaurant on the strength of a secret recipe for coleslaw. Fats, being a man who started a restaurant on the strength of a pizza recipe and a small joke, did not feel that he was in a position to discourage her. He gave her the same advice he gives all other aspiring restaurant owners—run the place yourself. "People have a funny idea about what owning a restaurant is like," Fats says. "Their idea of running a restaurant is naming it after themselves and then coming in to buy a round of drinks before they go to the theater."

Once, Fats, who has a lot of ideas himself, called me to ask what I would think of putting in a sandwich at his pizzerias. Fats figures he loses a lot of groups of people just because of not offering one item for a non-pizza eater to eat. When business is slow at the pizzeria and Fats is in a worrying mood, he finds himself imagining two prosperous young couples who are about to step into a cab and come to Goldberg's. As they enter the cab, one of the wives says, "I hate pizza." Her husband sighs, and the other couple tries to be polite, and they're all lost to some East Side bar with sawdust on the floor and overpriced hamburgers and a spinach-and-bacon salad that has been in the refrigerator so long that the discerning palate cannot tell the spinach from the bacon. Fats and I spend a lot of time on the phone talking about what his non-pizza item should be. When I spoke to him about sandwiches, he had just returned from Kansas City, where he had sampled some of the local sandwiches, as well as just about everything else that was edible and for sale. Fats had gained so much weight in Kansas City that, upon returning, he had even given up his Monday treats. Before he had gone to Kansas City, he spent six months or so watching television advertisements for a new Sara Lee breakfast roll—the kind called a pull-apart—without being able to eat one. When he arrived in Kansas City, one of his first acts was to drive to the A&P and buy a container of pull-aparts. "I ate them all before I got out of the parking lot," he told me. "I think one of them was still frozen."

Fats was complaining about the constant food temptations facing someone walking along the street in New York—the frozen-custard stands, the Greek *souvlaki* joints, the places that sell Sicilian pizza by the slice. "In the suburbs, you have to make a decision to get in the car and go get something to eat," Fats said. "You're not always passing right in front of it."

"Anybody can diet in Mamaroneck, Fats," I said, trying to cheer him up. "This is the Big Apple."

"What do you think about a hamburger called a Goldburger?" Fats asked.

"Not a Goldburger, Fats," I said, "a Pure Goldburger."

Fats drifted toward other possibilities—a way, I suppose, of not having to admit that my Pure Goldburger idea was worth thousands. We discussed Mario's grinder and a sandwich of grilled cheese with jalapeño peppers I had eaten in New Mexico and a variety of the New Jersey hoagie and even a Nu-way (a Nu-way, the specialty of a place with the same name that used to exist in Kansas City, is loose ground beef on a bun. My sister and I were the only people I ever knew who would eat them, but Nu-way managed to stay in business for years—on the strength, I have always thought, of an eerie appeal it had for women in hair curlers. There were always so many women in hair curlers at Nu-way that for years I thought it just happened to be near a hairdressers' college). I spent a long time talking about the possibilities of a sandwich that would have, as its main ingredients, Swiss cheese and the kind of prosciuttini I buy at Mario Bosco's.

Suddenly there was a gasp on the other end of the line. "Oh my God!" Fats said. "I just got so hungry I almost fainted."

•

When my next-door neighbor, the ferociously named Zohar Ben Dov, took over the Riviera Bar, on Sheridan Square, I naturally assumed he would turn to me for advice about French-fried potatoes. People are always coming around to talk French fries with me. I'm constantly under pressure from the McDonald's fancy to acknowledge that frozen French fries can be delicious if fried to the proper crispness. At a party one night, a respectable-looking mother of three told me that Nathan's French fries (at the original Coney Island branch, it goes without saying) are at their finest just after the corn oil is first poured into the Pitman Frialators, before nine-thirty in the morning—at about the time, in other words, allowing for the difference in time zones, that the chili diehards in Cincinnati are drifting into the downtown branch of Empress. I told her that I have never touched a French fry before eleven in the morning and that I never intend to. There is a difference between an authority and a fanatic.

Anticipating Zohar's request for help, I started eating French fries all over town to refresh my palate—having left the field for a few months to look after a well-deserved case of fatness. I made a list of the great French fries I have eaten—the ones that used to be served with fried shrimp on the wharf in Santa Monica, the crude fat ones with parts of the potato skin still visible that I have run across at steak restaurants now and then. I even interviewed Murray Handwerker, the president of Nathan's. Zohar seemed to be taking his time about coming around for a consultation. I realized, of course, that he was busy renovating the building. The Riv, which is just a couple of blocks from where Zohar and I live, is one of those Greenwich Village bars that people who live in the Village count on to remain more or less the same, so Zohar was faced with the problem of making sure the walls would stay up without making the place look as if someone had made sure the walls would stay up. I revised my great French fries list again and polished my notes from the Handwerker interview, but Zohar never did come around.

On quiet afternoons, when my mind wanders, I still see myself as Zohar's French-fry consultant. Zohar and I meet on the street, just after the Riviera deal has been closed. "I know," I say. "You want to tap my know-how on what kind of French fries to serve. You'll want to start by sampling the little wonders at Arthur Bryant's barbecue, just to give you something to shoot at. It's only a two-and-a-half-hour flight to Kansas City."

"I'm kind of busy," Zohar says. "We're renovating."

"I have already stated in public that Arthur Bryant's is to the smooth kind of French fries what Nathan's Coney Island branch is to the fat kind with krinkly edges," I say. I tell Zohar a true story to illustrate the point that the French fries at Nathan's and at Bryant's are interchangeably delicious: An acquaintance of mine who grew up in Kansas City but now lives in New York once stopped in Kansas City on a flight back from California, went to Arthur Bryant's, picked up twenty-eight orders of ribs and some sauce, and got on the next plane to New York. That night he threw a magnificent banquet—a gathering of expatriate Midwesterners coming together in the way British colonial officials might have gathered in the clearing of some steamy African jungle during imperial times for a proper Christmas dinner, complimenting the cook on how close she had come to cooking a true Christmas goose in the makeshift oven and pointing out the significance of the sixpence in the pudding to the few specially favored native civil servants who had been invited. Realizing that even Bryant's fries would not travel, he substituted Nathan's krinkly-cuts—hot from the Eighth Street branch. I completely approved of his decision. I was sorry he neglected to bring along any burned edges of brisket from Kansas City, but if a man delivers twenty-eight orders of Bryant's ribs to within walking distance of my house in New York, I do not feel in a position to quibble with him.

"Excuse me," Zohar says, turning in the direction of the Riv, "I think I hear a ceiling crumbling."

I go on eating French fries, crossing off the ones that anyone would consider dipping in ketchup. Within a week, I manage to wangle the appointment with Murray Handwerker, and hurry back to the Riviera with an intelligence report. I find Zohar, looking harried, trying to hire some waiters for the Riviera's reopening.

"Nathan's prefers Maine potatoes, Zohar," I say. "I got that from the top man."

"How come everybody in the Village who wants to work as a waiter says he's really an actor?" Zohar says.

"Mr. Handwerker says Idahos are fine for baking—the people in Idaho shouldn't be mad—but too mealy for a firm French fry. Long Island potatoes have too much water in them for French fries. He says Long Islands are good for chowder. I guess they float well."

"What do I want with actors?" Zohar says. "This is not a play about a bar. It's a bar."

I continue testing French fries, although Alice tries to persuade me that enough research has been done. I realize I made a mistake in letting her know that the public-relations man for Nathan's gained thirty-one pounds after joining the firm.

"I must press on," I say to her. "Zohar needs me."

I go right over to the Riv to talk about Suzy-Q's—the skinny but soft kind of French fries that are served all tangled up, usually in a basket. They are as rare in New York as a superior taco. I find Zohar trying to get rid of a sinister-looking man who had offered to put in a coin-operated skittle machine in return for a 75 percent interest in the business—all moneys to be exchanged in cash. "I'm going to Thomforde's in Harlem to check out their Suzy-Q's," I say to Zohar.

"I've got to make a decision among two hundred and thirty-eight brands of draft beer," Zohar says, staring at a table full of beer samples with a look of anticipated nausea.

"Life is not all beer and skittles," I say, getting in a line that can be set up properly only in daydreams on quiet afternoons. "There are French-fried potatoes to be considered."

"Please stop," Zohar says. "Enough. No more with the French fries."

Realizing that Zohar is just feeling guilty about all the help I am giving him, I persevere. I find a struggling young potato farmer near Patchogue who has learned to grow Maine potatoes on Long Island. "He's small potatoes now," I tell Zohar, "but they're not watery." The farmer is willing to grow all the potatoes needed at the Riv and have them sliced just before delivery by a group of local women who have been poor and idle since a project for making precut old-fashioned quilts was shut down by the Office of Economic Opportunity. I report this triumph to Alice.

"A sort of cottage industry, I suppose," Alice says.

"Strictly French fries," I tell her.

Zohar is grateful. People are coming in all the way from Rego Park just to have a go at the Riv's potatoes. There are rumors in the trade that Nathan's has been sending around scouts.

·

One of the best ideas I ever gave Fats Goldberg was for a diet restaurant in midtown Manhattan called Slim Pickin's. The name alone, I figure, is worth a couple of hundred thousand. I even told Fats we could call it Fats Goldberg's Slim Pickin's—with the Fats Goldberg written in script, of course—if he wanted to take the idea and run with it, but Fats was not enthusiastic. "People don't like to think about dieting when they go out to eat," I was told by the man who has thought about practically nothing else during every waking moment since May 1, 1959. "Also, you can't have enough variety." That shows how much Fats knows about the dieting habits of Americans who do not happen to use the Fats Goldberg method of eating the same thing every day of their lives except within the city limits of Kansas City, Missouri. What he was thinking of was a restaurant that would serve only those low-calorie specials that are always being offered in midtown coffee shops to guilt-ridden secretaries—broiled lean ground round, cottage cheese, and mauve Jell-O for dessert. I once found the businessman's equivalent in a book that calls itself an executive diet guide and has a list of a lot of expensive restaurants where the dieting executive can spend forty-five dollars to watch his business prospect eat pancakes stuffed with creamed chicken while he chews away at a lean piece of roast beef with no sauce.

What Fats does not seem to understand is that all of the diets these days allow the dieter to eat as much as he wants of one thing or another as long as he stays away from something else, and the forbidden type of food is different in every one of the diets. A restaurant that was set up to accommodate the followers of whichever four or five diets are selling more than a million books that week could therefore serve virtually anything. Drinks are allowed on the drinking man's diet. One diet allows anything that can be passed off as protein. I wouldn't be surprised to hear that someone has come out with an all-potato diet that would permit all the potatoes the dieter could stuff down—French-fried, cottage-fried, home-fried, mashed, shoestring, *latkes*, dumplings—as long as he puts nothing else to his lips except fourteen quarts of water a day. What could be more appealing to a New York restaurant entrepreneur than a restaurant that serves precisely what all other midtown businessmen's restaurants serve while maintaining a gimmick that leads people to believe that there is some special reason to patronize it? But somehow Fats Goldberg has resisted the idea of Slim Pickin's. He does occasionally ask me if he should put in a low-calorie salad at the pizzerias, though. Apparently, he sometimes imagines that the one person who keeps the two couples from Goldberg's Pizzeria every night not only hates pizza but is on a diet.

Not long ago, I came up with an idea that I knew Fats would find as irresistible as a double cheeseburger with everything but onions. It is the reverse of Slim Pickin's—a restaurant that would encourage people to be happy in their eating instead of making them feel like a gaggle of Methodist ministers in Las Vegas. We would call it Ah Fat! If Goldberg saw the light and came in as a managing partner, we could even call it Fats Goldberg's Ah Fat! There would be pictures on the wall of famous fatties—Winston Churchill and Babe Ruth and Santa Claus and that crowd. There would also be cheerful sayings on the wall about not watching calories—like YOU CAN ALWAYS START TOMORROW and GO AHEAD—YOU DESERVE IT and TASTES DON'T COUNT. One of the specialties would be a Fats Goldberg Kansas City Special—an exact replica of what Fats asks his mother to make him for lunch in Kansas City (fried pork tenderloin with gravy, creamed corn, French-fried potatoes, a loaf of Wonder bread). Naturally, we would make use of some of my father's menu poetry—adapting couplets like "Mrs. Trillin bakes like mad, she gets no salaries/Spends most of her time extracting the calories." A notice on the menus would say "All Dishes Cooked in Butter Unless Pure Lard Is Appropriate."

In preparation for presenting the idea to Fats, I even wrote some folktales that could be handed out with the menus—the way some restaurants patronized by businessmen hand out a synopsis of the twelve o'clock news or the latest market averages. I showed my favorite one to Alice:

Once, in Dayton, Ohio, there lived a shingle salesman named Harry Kahn. He was five feet ten inches tall and weighed two hundred and eighty-five pounds. He enjoyed eating and he despised exercise of any sort—to the point of having an electric eye installed on his refrigerator so that the door opened when he approached. Some of Harry Kahn's friends said that Harry ate constantly because he was unhappy, but Harry was, in fact, very happy, and one of the reasons he was so happy is that he ate constantly and enjoyed it. His wife, who had taken Psychology 110 at Ohio State University, always told Harry he was fat because his mother had used rich foods as a reward when he was a child, although Harry's wife knew very well that Harry had grown up in a Baptist orphanage in Lima, Ohio, where eating between meals was strictly forbidden and the dining-hall menu was dominated by Brussels sprouts.

One day, Harry's wife told him that she would divorce him if he didn't go on a diet. She thought if Harry were thinner he would sell more shingles and they could afford to join the country club. Harry could not bear the thought of losing his wife. She was a loving wife and a loyal companion and she made the best toasted peanut-butter-and-honey sandwiches in the state of Ohio. He went on a strict diet and began to lose weight. In a year, he weighed one hundred and forty-eight pounds. He was very unhappy. He sold the same number of shingles he had sold before.

One day, a foreign-looking man rang Harry Kahn's doorbell and asked him if he was the Harry Kahn who had grown up in an orphanage in Lima, Ohio. Harry said he was. "Praise Allah," the foreign-looking man said, whereupon he fell on his knees and started kissing Harry's high-school graduation ring. He explained that the orphanage had misunderstood Harry's name: It wasn't Harry Kahn but Ari Khan, and he was a member of the Khan Dring Klan, a schismatic Muslim sect. Every forty years, according to age-old custom, the sect selected one of its members, chosen by lot, weighed him, and gave him a ruby for every pound he weighed more than the weight of the average unwed maiden. Harry—or Ari—had been selected.

The foreign-looking man took Harry to Iran, where there was an elaborate ceremony that ended with Harry being weighed. By eating as much as he could on the plane, Harry had managed to get his weight up to one hundred fifty-one pounds, three pounds heavier than the average maiden of the Khan Dring Klan, which had traditionally equated fat with beauty. The three rubies he received were worth three hundred and eighty-five dollars, not quite enough to cover his fare back to Dayton.

Alice said that it would be thoughtless to show Fats a folktale that encouraged him to become fat again. "Also," she said, "it's the silliest folktale I've ever heard."

"It may be sort of silly at that," I said. "Maybe we should start with the one I've written about an Indian brave named Back Behind the Mesa who was shamed by his father into losing weight so he would be able to move through the forest as swiftly as an elk, and was then shot by another brave who mistook him for an elk."

"That one is even sillier," Alice said.

"I have one about two sisters—a fat one and a slim one—who both worked as carhops in Canoga Park, California, waiting to be discovered," I said. "The slim one is discovered and eventually becomes a movie star and then starts drinking and ends up as a dime-a-dance girl in Ocean Park, New Jersey. The fat one is left at the drive-in, and eventually she takes over the business and franchises."

Alice said that the entire idea of Ah Fat! could not possibly be brought up to Fats Goldberg, a man who has a hard enough go as it is trying to keep from weighing three hundred pounds. I finally decided she was right. She is a levelheaded person who has, on occasion, moved the basket of Ratner's onion rolls out of my reach when others at the table were too caught up in the excitement of the moment to think about sensible medical precautions. It is a shame, though. After I had already abandoned the project, I thought of one of my best ideas for Ah Fat! Instead of just giving customers their leftover meat in doggie bags the way conventional restaurants do, we would give each customer (at least each customer who had not followed the admonition on our wall plaque—CLEAN YOUR PLATE) not only a doggie bag but a sign that would help him enjoy the contents—a ready-stick sign that would be easily attached to the refrigerator door and would say ANYTHING CONSUMED WHILE YOU'RE STANDING UP HAS FEWER CALORIES IN IT THAN IT WOULD IF IT WERE CONSUMED WHILE YOU WERE SITTING DOWN.

10

Marital Bliss

WHENEVER ONE OF THE lunchtime regulars at my father's restaurant—somebody like a cheerful young salesman of plastics, say—revealed that he was going to be married, my father said, "Did you check her teeth?" He said it before he offered congratulations. He had a strong feeling that ordinary flaws of personality or looks or background could be corrected or adjusted to, but that bad teeth represented a lifelong financial drain. About the time the dentist who had been treating Alice seemed to start counting on one of her wisdom teeth as a sort of small second income—the way that someone who works in a corporate auditing office might figure on picking up some extra money doing income-tax returns on the side, or the way a mildly corrupt policeman might begin to include some free lunches in his budget—it occurred to me that I had neglected my own father's advice. I also realized, of course, that we were beyond such matters, being together for better or for worse, and all that. It would make no difference to me, I told Alice manfully while I was studying one of the wisdom-tooth bills, if she suddenly confessed a history of root-canal operations. There are more important things in a marriage than teeth, I told her, and while I was trying to put my finger on precisely what they were, I realized that the question I would ask a young man who told me he had at last found his beloved is "Does she share her food?"

The kind of scene I conjure up when I try to envision what could make a man grow to regret his youthful, romantic decision takes place at a twentieth-anniversary dinner in a French restaurant. The husband, a fellow who has a roving eye for the entrees but has managed to settle on the cassoulet, reaches over for a forkful of his wife's trout meunière, which looks delicious, and the wife says, stiffly, "There really isn't much of this, you know." The husband returns the fork to his cassoulet, troutless, and stares out into space, numbed by the vision of sharing his twilight years with a woman who is stingy with her fish.

Fortunately, Alice is so generous in such matters that she would never say to a waiter "I'll take the cannelloni, too" if she knew that the person who had just ordered the cannelloni also happened to be desperate for a few bites of fettuccine Alfredo. I don't mean we never disagree. We disagreed, for instance, about whether or not she should take advantage of having a number of immigrant Chinese students in an English class she was teaching at City College by trying to worm some restaurant information out of them. I was on the side that said she should.

"Isn't it accepted practice to let students with language problems write about their own experiences so they can gain confidence?" I asked. "It seems perfectly logical to suggest that they use their favorite restaurant as a scene for a reminiscence."

"I'm ashamed of you," she said.

"It would also be helpful if they included translations of a few of the dishes some of those Chinese restaurants always list on the wall," I said. "Remember the old writing-course motto—Individualize by Specific Detail." Some restaurants in Chinatown have, in addition to the menu they hand the simple Westerner, a series of dishes announced on signs tacked to the wall—signs that are almost invariably written in Chinese characters. For complicated reasons, the only Chinese ideogram I can recognize happens to be the one that signifies "revisionist quagmire," so I often have to sit in a Chinese restaurant helplessly while a tableful of Chinese businessmen across the room are stuffing down succulent-looking dishes that were obviously ordered off the wall. Requests to the waiter for a translation always draw unsatisfactory responses—varying, according to the proficiency in English, from "No beer, sorry" to "You no like that" to "I really haven't the time to translate the entire wall so why don't you tell me which one you want translated most?" One would think that if one's wife were in a position to correct a situation that causes one a great deal of frustration and even anger, one's wife would do so. But no marriage is perfect.

•

"Guess what Tricia Nixon Cox's favorite recipe is," Alice said one morning at breakfast as she came upon the information in the *Times*.

"I'm not sure I'm up to hearing about it," I said. As it happened, I had been daydreaming about grits—the kind of grits that a lot of restaurants in the South just assume you'll want to have nestled next to your eggs at breakfast. When I'm home, I usually have just coffee for breakfast—being full to the gills with guilt over what I consumed the night before—and my thoughts naturally turn to grits, although occasionally I muse about hash browns. My grits daydreams have greatly improved since the days when I thought there was no convenient place to find grits in my neighborhood anyway—a situation that had put me in the position of a goldminer who tries to fantasize about how he's going to spend his winter's horde even though he knows there isn't a town within a thousand miles that has facilities for a proper toot.

The brief fashion for Southern black people in the middle-sixties left Manhattan with some soul-food restaurants south of Harlem—it also produced at least one $100-a-plate soul-food benefit at the Waldorf-Astoria—but most of them are not the kind of places that open for breakfast. I used to think that the closest place to Greenwich Village a person could eat grits for breakfast was the Criminal Courts Building off Foley Square. The coffee shop in the lobby there has served them for years—the number of poor people coming to New York from the South to get in trouble being large enough to make grits a natural part of the menu, the way that American hamburgers must be a natural part of the menu by now in the London Airport. Then I discovered that a small restaurant right around the corner from my house—the Pink Teacup—serves grits all day long. When our younger daughter was born, I went straight from the hospital to the Pink Teacup, thankful that a man no longer had to go all the way to Foley Square to stage a major celebration. William Edgett Smith joined me there for breakfast, and the grits were so good that even Smith realized it—a fact that cheered those of us who were beginning to be concerned that he might be suffering from pathological hypogeusia, a serious impairment of the sense of taste.

"Tricia Nixon Cox's favorite recipe is called Chicken Divan," Alice said.

"Spare me the details, please," I said. "I'm a citizen, after all."

"I will say only that it has two cans of cream of chicken soup poured into it," Alice said. "Also, the White House told the *Times* the President doesn't eat ketchup on his cottage cheese anymore."

"It must be one of those pieces about how a man can grow in the presidency," I said. I didn't really mind if the President put ketchup on his cottage cheese—it's a personal matter—but people who pour cans of cream of chicken soup on a defenseless bird that happens to be a chicken already never eat the results quietly at their desks alone. They expect other people to eat it, on wedding-gift china. Anxious to demonstrate their versatility, they prepare some dishes with canned mushroom soup instead of canned cream of chicken soup. I have always thought that the label on canned mushroom soup should be required by statute to say, "For soup purposes only. Using the contents of this can for Beef Stroganoff or turkey casserole is thoughtless and unlawful."

A year or so after Alice interrupted my grits daydream with the news about Chicken Divan, John Hess revealed in the *Times* a Republican cookbook that featured Tricia's mushroom-soup variation (Chicken Imperial) and her mother's recipe for something called Continental Salad, which has as its active ingredients canned beets, canned grapefruit juice, and Jell-O. It occurred to me again that the women who talk most about the importance of preserving the traditional American family never seem to bring any more American enterprise to their traditional role as ma-in-the-kitchen cooks than is required to make the choice between Campbell's and H. J. Heinz. From my palate-numbing experience with William Edgett Smith at the Women's Lib restaurant, I know that there must be some feminists who have gone so far as to include a contempt for cooking along with a contempt for washing the pots. But most of the women I know who would never accept the old idea of a woman's place being in front of the stove—Alice, for instance—would also never be caught using a can of soup for purposes that the Almighty did not intend it to be used. They seem to be good cooks partly out of an inclination to become accomplished at whatever they set out to do—an inclination that leads to a loose set of skills and values that, when the histories of feminist ideology are written, may be set down as The Domestic Deviation.

Alice's ability to cook like a member of The Domestic Deviation is particularly fortunate for me because, unlike a lot of people with enthusiasm for food, I have never had any interest in learning how to cook. I'm a specialist; I just eat. Because of Alice, though, I don't even have to leave home to eat dishes—from a subtle poached salmon to a sausage concoction called Lunenberg Leftovers—that could make the average plastics salesman forget the cost of a between-the-teeth gold inlay. It is good fortune indeed, marred only by my embarrassment when a dinner guest in his middle years reacted to something Alice had done with cheese-in-the-basket, strawberries and Grand Marnier by asking if we would adopt him.

I think that some people in Kansas City at first found Alice's reputation as a cook somewhat intimidating. I have heard her identified as a gourmet cook in the same way my cousin Kenny is identified as a CPA. I have explained that she is flexible enough to have become addicted to the pig-in-the-blankets served at the Yankee Doodle in New Haven, but I must admit that I once caught her about to grind fresh Parmesan cheese onto my Kraft dinner. It happened in Georgia, while we were borrowing a friend's summer house. During a trip to the local supermarket, I had spotted the kind of macaroni-and-cheese dish that comes in a box and was always called Kraft dinner in our house when I was a child—which was the last time I could remember eating any. It didn't seem to taste right in Georgia. At first, I thought Alice might have already managed to sprinkle some fresh cheese on it before I walked into the kitchen, but the next day I tried some heated up from the refrigerator and realized that what I had been nostalgic for was not Kraft dinner but day-old Kraft dinner.

There was also a tense moment, I remember, the first time our older daughter asked for ketchup. "How did you know about ketchup?" Alice asked, after informing her that we didn't have any.

"Those wild kids down the street probably told her," I said. "Maybe we oughtn't to let her play with them anymore."

•

I have another vision of what brings second thoughts to a man who, as they say, married a pretty face and a record of no cavities. The couple has just arrived in a town they have never visited before. The man is making routine preparations for the evening—scanning the county weekly for notices of any suppers at fire halls or churches, applying his current restaurant-selection system to the Yellow Pages, engaging the desk clerk in a casual conversation that can be led around to asking him about the places he dreams of when he's out of town. "Why don't we just eat here at the motel?" the man's wife says. "It seems to be clean."

Alice has sometimes registered a complaint if, at ten-thirty or eleven, I am still circling around the barbecue places of a strange town, sniffing for the smell of hickory smoke and peeking in the windows to check for precut paneling. But she ordinarily joins in restaurant hunting with some vigor. She is particularly good at searching out Chinese restaurants—a skill that comes partly from confidence, I think, in the way that a professional hunter always seems to come up with the required water buffalo partly because he left the camp assuming he would. Alice has been confident about finding good Chinese restaurants in unlikely places ever since we ate a spectacular Chinese meal at Star Twinkles, one of the two restaurants on a remote Central Pacific island called Nauru—an island that is made of phosphate and is gradually disappearing, being more valuable as a mineral than as an island. Her confidence grew in London. Who, after all, would have ever expected to find the Great Dried Beef in the Sky (not to speak of a superb fried-seaweed dish) across from the Golders Green tube stop?

Once, in Kansas City, I was invited to a Chinese banquet in Waldo, which struck me at the time as the equivalent of being invited to sample the finest French *haute cuisine* in Uvalde, Texas. Waldo is a neighborhood that must have started out as a farm town, and what would have constituted a banquet for the Waldo folks I went to school with was an extra helping of chicken-fried steak. (The Waldo classmate I remember best from grade school had more eating experience than most grade-schoolers, having been there so long that he was said to have had a 2-S student deferment in sixth grade.) The Chinese banquet in Waldo turned out to be magnificent. When I told Alice, she seemed unsurprised—a reaction that I at first put down to her imperfect acquaintance with Waldo but that I now think was due purely to her confidence in the resourcefulness and cooking skill of the overseas Chinese. Once, in Lisbon, I tried my best to work the phone book in a way that would assuage a longing we both had for certain Chinese dishes—it was the first time my system had been applied to a phone book written in Portuguese—and I think that Alice was actually surprised when we arrived on a quiet residential street and found a darkened building that I now believe must have been the home of a man named José Mandarin.

I have absorbed some of Alice's optimism about Chinese restaurants, and I have suffered for it. In small Midwestern towns, I have sat with quiet confidence as my Chinese dinner was brought to the table by a large Occidental female whose name tag says she is Wilma Sue. Once, in El Paso, I allowed myself to be taken to a Chinese restaurant across the border in Juárez that my host claimed was the best Chinese restaurant on the continent. Would I go to a French restaurant in Juárez? What would I say to someone who offered to buy me a fried-chicken dinner in Juárez? The restaurant, I was able to inform my host at the end of the meal, might rank within the top ten Chinese restaurants in the state of Chihuahua.

When Alice and I—finding ourselves in central Kansas but crazed for moo-shu pork—unearth a Chinese restaurant that gives every indication of being awful, we are always reluctant to admit that we have been let down again. We retreat gradually. They advertise their steaks and chops, we assure each other, because a strictly Chinese restaurant could not survive in a farm town of three thousand people. Don't worry about the menu, we say when it arrives. Having only chow mein on the menu is merely a way to attract people who wouldn't understand what the chef could do if someone just asked him to go flat out. Toward the end of the meal, there are long silences. Then we decide that something might be salvaged by treating the rice with soy sauce and a bit of gravy that picked up some flavor from the scallions without permission. Occasionally, we mix those last-ditch concoctions separately, and on those occasions Alice always offers me a taste of hers.

11

Eating Festively

THE QUESTION IN MY MIND when Alice and I arrived at the
Breaux Bridge Crawfish Festival was whether to enter the official
crawfish-eating contest or content myself with acts of freelance gluttony. The idea of entering the contest came from Peter Wolf, who
had returned to Louisiana from New York to join us at the festival,
having concocted some sort of business conference in Houston to
serve as an excuse for flying in that direction. Peter was brought up
to appreciate what the entire state has to offer. His father was the
man who put the state government in perspective for me in 1960,
just after I had returned from watching the legislature in Baton
Rouge stage some particularly bizarre entertainments in anticipation
of the imminent desegregation of the New Orleans public schools.
"What you have to remember about Baton Rouge," he said, "is
that it's not Southern United States, it's northern Costa Rica."
Peter's sister, Gail, who still lives in New Orleans, has been able
to participate in a lot of serious crawfish eating in the Cajun area
of southern Louisiana since she decided that it was the most
convenient place to visit with friends who live in Houston—the
spot of precise equidistance being, as far as I can interpret Gail's
calculations, an area bounded by the Vermilion Restaurant, the
L. & L. Seafood Market (suppliers of fresh crawfish), and a racetrack
called Evangeline Downs. Gail is so accustomed to crawfish eating

that the word "crawfish" is understood rather than expressed in her discussions of restaurants. "They have a great *étouffée*," she may say of a place, or "They don't serve boiled there." Since she is isolated in New Orleans, miles away from the Atchafalaya Basin— a swampy wilderness that is to crawfish what the Serengeti is to lions—she produces her own crawfish *étouffée* after each pilgrimage to the L. & L. and stores it in the freezer, like a pioneer woman putting up preserves against the winter.

Peter had simply assumed we would enter the contest. Not entering, he told me while we were safe in New York, would be like going to the festival at Pamplona and not running with the bulls. (I once spent almost the entire week at the festival in Pamplona before I could bring myself to run with the bulls, in fact, the delay having been caused not merely by cowardice but by the fact that the running took place in the morning and I knew that if I participated I did so at the risk of arriving at my favorite café after it had run out of a type of sweet roll I adored.) My hesitation about entering the eating contest at Breaux Bridge was based on equally practical considerations. The contest is conducted with boiled crawfish, and if I had to pick my sport I would say *étouffé* or bisque rather than boiled. (Crawfish *étouffée* means smothered crawfish, and is otherwise indescribable; crawfish bisque is indescribable.) Also, I had learned in advance of the festival that, whatever a contestant's capacity, the amount of crawfish he can eat is governed by the amount of crawfish he can peel. (Only the tail of a crawfish is eaten, although people who are not under the pressure of official competition sometimes take the time to mine some fat from the rest of the shell with their index fingers.) Through geographical circumstances over which I have no control, I have little opportunity to keep in practice at peeling crawfish. There are crawfish (or crayfish, or crawdads) all over the country, but outside of Louisiana they are all but ignored—lumps of clay lacking a sculptor. People outside Louisiana, in fact, often scoff when they hear of people eating crawfish —the way an old farmer in Pennsylvania might scoff at the New York antiques dealer who paid fourteen dollars for a quilt that must be at least a hundred years old and doesn't even look very warm. A New York crawfish craver who couldn't make it to the Atchafalaya

Basin would have to settle for Paris, where crawfish are called *écrevisses*, except by people from Louisiana, who always call them inferior.

The world record at crawfish eating—the record, at least, according to Breaux Bridge, which is, by resolution of the Louisiana legislature, the Crawfish Capital of the World—was set by a local man named Andrew Thevenet, who at one Crawfish Festival ate the tails of thirty-three pounds of crawfish in two hours. My doubts about being able to peel that much crawfish in two hours—not to speak of eating it—were increased by some stories I heard about tricks contestants have used in the past. One man was said to have perfected a method of peeling a crawfish with one hand and popping it into his mouth while reaching for the next crawfish with his other hand. Somebody told me that one contestant had spent the evening before the contest "lining his stomach with red beans and rice"—although that sounds to me at least contradictory and maybe suicidal. A pharmacy student who triumphed at the Crawfish Festival two years before I arrived in Breaux Bridge (festivals are held only every other year) drank orange juice with his crawfish instead of the traditional beer, and Gail had heard that the orange juice was laced with exotic chemicals (known only to people like pharmacy students) that somehow provided the same service for crawfish in the stomach that an electric trash compacter provides for trash. In fairness, I should add that a former contestant from Lafayette told me the pharmacy student had used no tricks at all and was just a hungry boy.

I was in Breaux Bridge a few days before the festival began, and I found that a lot of people were happy to discuss the question of whether or not Peter and I should enter the crawfish-eating contest. They like to talk about crawfish in general. Once the subject came up, they were likely to spend a while talking about an evening they once spent with some particularly tasty boiled crawfish or a dish they had that was somewhere between an *étouffée* and a stew or a woman in town who used to make crawfish *beignets*. (I don't mean that we talked about nothing other than eating crawfish. I spent a lot of time, for instance, discussing a restaurant in Opelousas named Dee Dee that specializes in oyster gumbo, roast duck, and a marvel called dirty rice.) The Cajun parishes of Louisiana constitute just about the only section of the United States in which good food is taken as the norm in any kitchen, private or public. Before my first trip to Iberia Parish, I asked a serious New Orleans eater where I should eat while I was there. I prepared to take notes on secret routes to secret cafés or the names of local collaborators who might risk divulging to a hungry traveling man where the decent restaurants were. "Eat anywhere," he said.

Taking his advice, Alice and I had lunch one day during that trip in the first tacky-looking bar we came to in a small town not far from New Iberia—one of those places decorated with Jax Beer clocks and fake fishnet and a wire potato-chip dispenser. There were two ketchup bottles on the table. One held ketchup; the other one contained the best rémoulade sauce I have ever tasted. I had the blue-plate special, which happened that day to be shrimp *sauce picante*. Alice ordered boiled crawfish, and was brought a tray holding what we estimated to be about a hundred of them. I ordered some Jax, and we stayed the afternoon.

A couple of days before the Crawfish Festival, I asked a local citizen named Woody Marshall—a man who can list among his many accomplishments the invention of crawfish racing as we know it today—whether or not Peter and I could expect to face Andrew Thevenet, the world record holder, if we entered the eating contest. Marshall said that Thevenet, a man of about seventy, had been so ill that serious eating was over for him. When I expressed my sympathy, Marshall told me about having heard Thevenet, after his retirement, describe a lifetime of eating—the fresh oysters, the venison, the crawfish prepared in ways a crawfish fancier dreams about. "You know what he told me?" Marshall said. "He told me, 'There have been kings who didn't eat as well as I did.'"

Lately, the Cajun parishes have been having what people in Lafayette and Baton Rouge sometimes call a French Renaissance. It is a phenomenon that has engaged the diplomatic interest of, among others, the Republic of France, the Province of Quebec, and the Louisiana State Tourist Commission. What surprises the devout eater about an effort that is devoted to preserving the Cajun atmosphere of southwestern Louisiana is its concentration on the

French language as the basis of Cajun culture. Even with the new emphasis on teaching French in primary school and exhorting Cajuns to speak it to their children at home, the language is likely to disappear from Louisiana eventually through lack of use. (The language preservationists have to contend not only with television and Anglo newcomers but with the stigma French has always represented for Cajuns—an echo of all the bad jokes about ignorant swamp dwellers named Boudreaux who speak with comical accents.) Most of the people in Breaux Bridge who grew up before the war grew up speaking French at home and being punished if caught speaking it at school—including Woody Marshall, despite his Anglo name —but the young people rarely speak it now. When Marshall told me about Andrew Thevenet's royal history of eating, it occurred to me that those in charge of the French Renaissance might not be concentrating on the strongest element of the culture. Marshall and I were having lunch at the time—a splendid chicken *étouffée* and some French bread for me—at a tiny Breaux Bridge restaurant called Schwets. (The proprietor is not named Mr. Schwet. The restaurant was meant to be called Chouette—a pet name that means "screech owl" in French—but Marshall, who serves as the town sign painter, was, like most Cajuns of his age, raised speaking French rather than spelling it.) It occurred to me that the posters of the kind the state commission for the French Renaissance furnished for the window of Schwets should not say *"Parlez français avec vos enfants à la maison"* or *"Aidez vos enfants à parler le français"* but *"Transmettez vos recettes à vos enfants"*—"Hand down your recipes to your children."

•

I am a confirmed festival and fair attender. I like world's fairs and state fairs and county fairs and street fairs. My tolerance for fair organizers' natural inclination to rook us rubes is practically inexhaustible—the only exception I can remember having been the New York World's Fair of 1964, an overblown American industrial show masquerading as a world exhibition, like a nut-and-bolt manufacturer from Illinois wandering around the South of France wearing a beret. If I feel myself becoming irritated at someone who wants to charge me seventy-five cents for an ear of corn (butter and salt included, napkin available at the hot-dog stand on the other side of the freak show), I merely recall the words of Nate Eagle, the greatest sideshow barker and carnival promoter of them all, who often said, for publication, "It's not how much it costs them to get in but how much it costs them to get out."

I routinely drive miles out of my way for the most pedestrian county fairs. I even enjoyed the Baltimore City Fair, which is an event so infused with the city dweller's principal product, contentiousness, that I seemed to spend an entire day wandering by booths at which someone would demand that I support a petition mandating the city of Baltimore to end its discrimination against the use of plastic garbage cans or would thrust into my hands documentation of the devastation that would come from the construction of the Leakin Park Expressway or would explain to me that the Fund for Animals was a kind of Red Cross for animals—a phrase that conjured up for me visions of a kindly lady in a gray uniform offering a wallaby a hot cup of coffee at the scene of his extinction.

Fairs are good places to eat, particularly for stand-up eaters—which is one of the kinds of eaters I am, although when I eat standing up away from home I sometimes miss the familiar cool breeze coming from the open refrigerator. The Baltimore Fair, in fact, had fine Polish sausages in addition to the crab cakes that some of the city's literary figures have attempted to immortalize in sonnet form. (I was not too full to accompany a local couple of my acquaintance to a steamed-crab bout at Obrycki's—where my friends compared the crabs to those served at the crab hall in their neighborhood and at another one downtown and at one next to the market, while I nodded and ate.) The Baltimore Fair also had a Weight Watchers booth—the equivalent, it seemed to me, of a bishop, wearing full vestments and a stern expression, standing quietly at an orgy. When I spotted it, I marched right over and said to the woman who was about to offer me something like an ersatz chocolate milkshake that contained ten calories and tasted as if it had five, "You people ought to be ashamed of yourselves."

If I happened to be in the right part of the state at the appropriate time, I know I would attend, say, the North Louisiana Cotton

Festival and Fair at Bastrop, or even the Louisiana Brimstone Fiesta at Sulphur—although, as far as I know, neither of the products celebrated in those places is edible. These days, of course, the festive atmosphere is always dampened a bit by the inevitable discussion about whether the festival I am enjoying is likely to be the last of its kind ever held. The impending demise is always blamed on young people from outside—young people who seem to travel from one event to another, behaving more or less the way a horde of dropped-out fraternity boys might be expected to behave at their first rock festival. The cultural forces that produced this band of celebrants have lately included a merchandising milestone—the development of what are sometimes called "soda-pop wines." Although it was not long ago that a lot of citizens in places like Breaux Bridge would have been hard put to find anything good to say about a lot of mindless young people roaming the streets carrying beer cans, they now realize that beer is less inebriating than wine and that a gutter full of beer cans is not as dangerous as a gutter full of broken glass. From what I was told by the organizers of the Crawfish Festival—who had banned drinking from glass containers the year I arrived—I am justified in holding the idea man who developed soda-pop wines personally responsible for the fact that the Cochon de Lait Festival in Mansura, Louisiana, ended before I had a chance to sample the *cochon*. May the next belt tightening in the wine industry (or in the advertising industry, if that is where he's harbored) find him in an expendable position.

In Louisiana, where some mildly legitimate cultural basis can actually be found for some of the festivals (altogether if I were in charge at Opelousas, which holds a yam festival every year, I would celebrate Dee Dee's roast duck rather than a bunch of potatoes), there is a kind of pattern that transforms an informal local celebration into one of the stops along the route from Fort Lauderdale. The festival becomes primarily a business proposition, great efforts are made to attract the visitors who are later deplored, the local citizens lose interest or retreat to those events that are unaffected by outsiders (events ordinarily having to do with naming queens, or at least princesses), there is a lot of talk about the outside kids "taking over," and then the discussion turns to whether or not having a festival is worth the trouble after all.

The transformation of the New Orleans Mardi Gras took over a century, but Breaux Bridge managed to telescope the whole process into a dozen years. The Crawfish Festival grew out of the town's centennial, in 1959, and everyone agrees that the first few festivals were joyous occasions—townspeople costumed in old-fashioned Acadian dress, everyone dancing the fais-dodo in the streets, jollity at the crawfish races in the afternoon and at the local dance hall at night. The remarkable increase in fame and attendance seemed to be a blessing at first, except to motorists trying to get to Breaux Bridge from Lafayette, the nearest city with a motel. (Even becoming hopelessly stuck on the road could be seen as joyous: Thelma's, a restaurant between Lafayette and Breaux Bridge, is a sort of crawfish festival in itself.) Merchants in Breaux Bridge welcomed the opportunity to remove the glass from their storefronts and peddle as much beer or boiled crawfish as they could stock. The area had begun to develop a sort of crawfish industry that was enhanced by the publicity—peeling plants to service the restaurants, rice farmers "growing" crawfish in ponds to supplement the supply known as "wild" crawfish, even a modern plant whose owners believe that they have a freezing method that will make it possible for people to go into restaurants in St. Louis or Dallas and eat crawfish meat that actually tastes like crawfish meat rather than like balsa wood.

But the popularity of the festival with outsiders made it less popular with a lot of residents of Breaux Bridge, a quiet town on the Bayou Teche that has only five thousand people—a remarkable number of them named Broussard or Guidry or Hebert. The Crawfish Festival Association insisted that everyone would be happy with the festival if only it could be controlled and could eventually acquire the reputation of a "family event." It is hardly appropriate, of course, for organizers of a festival to preach sobriety. Woody Marshall, who often uses the same flourishes in speech that are necessary in sign painting, explained it to me as a matter of moderation. "We would appeal to the beautiful youths to practice a degree of restraint so that they are not wantonly drunk, if you know what I mean," he told me, a day or two before the festival. "If the youths persist in conducting themselves in such manner as they have conducted themselves, they will destroy the very festivals they like. But, as we say here, *'Laissez le bon temps rouler'*—'Let the good times roll.' "

The festival I attended was to be an experiment in control—an attempt to hold most of the events in a sort of pasture a mile or so from the business district. I told the festival organizers that I would be happy to attend the festival wherever they held it. I had not been offended by the criticism of outsiders. My wife would be at the festival, so, in a way, we were one of the families attending a family event. Also, in all the discussions about excesses—about beer cans being thrown and immoral acts being committed in the churchyard and people walking half-naked in the street—nobody had said a word about gluttony.

The day before the festival weekend began, a hard rain turned the pasture into a mudhole. The food booths and the festival events had to be moved back into town. I tried to show some sympathy for the financial burden the sudden move had put on the festival association, but I have to admit to being pleased that the festival would take place where it had always taken place. I'm a traditionalist when it comes to festivals, even when the tradition in question is only ten or twelve years old. Somehow, a festival that is known for inspiring dancing in the streets wouldn't seem quite the same if it inspired dancing in a pasture. The rain seemed to have cut down the crowd, and the festival association—staggered by the move and by the spoilage of thousands of pounds of boiled crawfish it had intended to sell—seemed to forget about the issue of raucous behavior. By the time the festival started, the sun was out.

Woody Marshall, looking spectacular in a bowler and a red vest and sleeve garters, stood next to the crawfish track he had invented, and formally entered the names of the entries in the official logbook he had made a few years before by folding over several old "Allen Ellender for Senator" posters. When he had been charged with the task of building a racetrack for the first festival, Marshall worked for days without finding a solution to the problem of how to compensate for the notorious reluctance of a crawfish to walk in the direction anyone expects it to walk. "Finally," he told me one day, when we were discussing how the track came about, "bull's-eye—I thought of it! A bull's-eye!" The final model is shaped like a target, with the starting gate in the bull's-eye and the finish line anywhere on the outer circle. Marshall keeps the contenders in the starting gate with an outsized version of the kind of device short-order cooks sometimes use to keep fried eggs in their place on a grill. Having heard previously from Marshall that a racing crawfish could be provided to a visitor in return for a small donation to the festival association kitty, I entered one in the first race. Alice thought about Scotch-taping racing colors to his back, but we finally decided that might seem ostentatious. It was pleasure enough to hear our names and hometown announced with a flourish by Marshall as he introduced Number 8, *Le Gros*.

"I didn't know y'all had any crawfish in New York," said a fraternity boy standing behind me.

"We've just got one that can race worth a damn," I said, nodding toward Number 8. "I have to bring him down here every two years to get any competition."

The fraternity boy looked impressed, but *Le Gros* ran badly, appearing to be less interested in racing than in, literally, backbiting.

"New York crawfish," the fraternity boy said in a disgusted tone. "Sheeee . . ."

•

Somehow, the fraternity boy did not impress me as a threat to my enjoyment, maybe because he did not treat ten o'clock in the morning as a time to be drinking soda-pop wine but as a time to be drinking a nice old-fashioned can of Schlitz. I was also untroubled by the displays of crawfish T-shirts, crawfish beer mugs, and crawfish aprons. Breaux Bridge could shine through almost any amount of commercialism and Lauderdale-ism as, in fact, the Crawfish Capital of the World. Breaux Bridge people are incapable of turning out the kind of leaden junk food usually peddled to tourists even when they try. Woody Marshall, for instance, invented something called a crawfish dog—he is, as I have said, a man of many accomplishments—and although that may sound pretty awful, it happens to be delicious, except for the hot-dog bun. (The recipe in the official program says, "Make roux with shortening and flour, cook until light brown, sauté onions, add crawfish and fat and water and seasoning. Cook 20 minutes and serve on an open-face hot-dog bun." If someone could figure out how to make hot dogs taste like crawfish dogs, he could bring back baseball.) The same booth that served beer and ordinary hot dogs sold, for fifty cents, something called a crawfish patty, which is also known as crawfish pie, and which if served in some expense-account French restaurant in New York would keep that restaurant jammed on rainy recession Tuesday evenings. ("Six dollars is, of course, a lot to ask for an appetizer," the review would say, "but the exquisite *Écrevisses à la Teche* at the Cajun d'Or happen to be worth every penny of it.")

A crawfish patty is what I happened to be eating when the time for the crawfish-eating contest approached. I was also drinking a glass (nonbreakable plastic) of non-soda-pop wine and reclining under an oak tree and listening to some fine music played by Celbert Cormier and His Musical Kings (a violin, an accordion, two electric guitars, and a drum) and discussing the logistics involved in timing our departure the next day in a way that would put us at a restaurant called The Yellow Bowl in Jeannerette around mealtime. Peter Wolf, who was doing all those things himself, was saying that we had waited too late to register for the contest and would be unable to participate, since only ten eaters are allowed. (Otherwise, every-one would be up there gobbling up the free crawfish.) I happened to know that only nine people had registered, but I also knew that they included such formidable eaters as the oyster-eating champion of Louisiana, who had downed fifteen and a half dozen oysters in an hour at the Oyster Festival in Galliano—a festival that was somehow kept secret from me for years. I also knew that we had been invited to dinner that evening at the home of Mrs. Harris Champagne, who, according to experts in Breaux Bridge, was the first person to serve crawfish *étouffée* in a restaurant, and I realized that sitting down to a plate of her legendary *étouffée* when already stuffed with boiled would be an act of irresponsibility. It had also occurred to me that if I did become full before approaching Mrs. Champagne's table, I would prefer to become full of patties. Boiled, after all, is not my sport. I told Peter it was a shame we hadn't registered in time.

The oyster-eating champion, a specialist away from his specialty, was the first contestant to drop out. "I'm not full. I could have a hot dog," he said when I asked him what happened. "But these things don't taste right." The first female contestant in the history of the contest, a trim secretary, dropped out sometime later. ("I'm not as hungry as I thought I was," she said.) The winner, Chester McGear, looked like one of the fraternity boys everyone had been so worried about, although he had actually graduated a couple of years before. He wore a sweatshirt emblematic of having consumed ten pitchers of beer in some tavern in Chicago, and he had a small rooting section that chanted "Go, Chester, go!" or "Allons, Chester, allons!" or "Come on, Chester, Eat That Meat!" He was on his twenty-second pound of crawfish when his final opponent dropped out. I was pleased to see that McGear acted the part of a traditional eating champion. They never admit to being full. My father always used to tell me about a boy who won a pie-eating contest in St. Joe by eating thirty-three pies and then said, "I wooda ate more but my ma was calling me for supper." When the reporters went up on the stand to interview McGear, he remained at his place, and as he answered the questions he absently reached toward the platter in front of him and peeled crawfish and popped them into his mouth, like a man working on the peanut bowl during a cocktail party.

I was relieved not to have had to face him. We all had dinner at Mrs. Champagne's, and Peter, by chance, was seated next to the French consul general from New Orleans. Peter, exhibiting his interest in Franco-American relations and the southwestern Louisiana French Renaissance and all that, spoke to the consul general immediately in excellent French, taking the opportunity to ask him why it is that a person cannot get decent shellfish in Paris.

(12)

Eating Sensibly

AT THE ANNUAL MEETING of the American Dietetic Association in New Orleans, I lived in constant fear that the dietitians would find out what I had been eating all week. The discovery would be made, I figured, by an undercover operative—some strict diet balancer who normally worked as the nutritionist in a state home for the aged but was posing as a raving glutton in order to trap me. "How were the oyster loaves at the Acme today?" she would ask casually, chewing on a Baby Ruth bar and fixing me with a look of pure food envy.

"Not bad at all," I would say, thrown off my guard by having met an apparent soulmate in an exhibition hall that included displays for such items as "textured protein granules with beeflike flavor" and some evil-looking powdered substance for which the most appetizing boast was that it was rapidly absorbed in the upper intestine. "I had to have two oyster loaves, in fact, which left room for only an ordinary-sized platter of red beans and rice and home-made sausage at Buster Holmes's place on Burgundy Street. I think if I hadn't had so much beer at the Acme, I might have been able to go a few pieces of Buster's garlic chicken, but—"

"Get him, girls!" the agent would shout, whereupon a gang of dietitians would fall upon me and hold me down while the chairman of the public-policy committee crammed carrot-and-raisin salad down my throat.

"Oysters are extremely high in cholesterol," a lecturer would say while the force-feeding was going on. "If one must eat oysters, oysters on the half shell rather than the fried oysters in the oyster loaf would be a better choice. Buster Holmes's homemade sausage defies scientific analysis."

"There were some good carbohydrates in the beer," I reply weakly between bites. Nobody is listening to me. A line is forming behind the dietitian who is dishing out the carrot-and-raisin salad —a dozen determined-looking ladies holding plates of green vegetables and gray meat. I spot the dietitian from Southwest High School in Kansas City, standing patiently with some broccoli I left on my plate in 1952.

My fears, as it turned out, were without foundation. I should have realized that on the first day of the meeting, when I was having breakfast at the Four Seasons, a pastry shop on Royal Street that has made me happy to be awake on a number of mornings in the past. I had figured that a week during which not only the dietitians but also the franchise operators of Roy Rogers Family Restaurants were meeting would be a good time for someone who is interested in both eating habits and conventions to be in New Orleans, but I had no intention of permitting an inquiry into other people's eating habits to interfere with my own. When I'm in New Orleans, my habit has always been to eat as much as I possibly can—partly, of course, as a precaution against developing some serious nutritional problem like rémoulade-sauce deficiency in the event I don't make it back to town for a while. On that first day of the dietitians' meeting, I was demonstrating my usual lack of restraint with Four Seasons croissants. After the first few bites, I was in no mood to worry about being observed by some special agent in the pay of the American Dietetic Association. The dietitians, after all, did not have the only game in town for a convention buff. The Independent Oil Compounders were having their annual meeting at the Royal Orleans, right across the street. The National Screw Machine Product Association was meeting at the Royal Sonesta and the Louisiana Nursing Home Association was meeting at the Fontainebleau. The Roosevelt was harboring a slew of narcotics-control agents. I looked around at the other breakfasters defiantly. I was astonished to find myself surrounded by women carrying the program of the annual meeting of the American Dietetic Association. Some of them were even wearing their identification badges. None of them was spying on me, because they were all too busy eating. The woman at the table next to me was attacking not merely a croissant but a croissant filled with cream and covered with chocolate. Tortes and sweet rolls were disappearing all around me. A lady across the room was wolfing down a huge piece of cheesecake. At nine o'clock in the morning! I should have known then that I had nothing to fear from the dietitians. They are obviously just folks.

•

If I had any suspicion that the Roy Rogers people might not be just folks, it should have evaporated the moment the first executive I called in their national headquarters picked up the telephone and said, "Howdy, pardner." Unfortunately, my first reaction was that I must have reached the wrong number. According to the information I had been given, Roy Rogers Family Restaurants was owned by the Marriott Corporation, with headquarters in Bethesda, Maryland, just outside Washington. "Howdy, pardner" is not my idea of how a corporation executive in Bethesda, Maryland, is likely to answer his telephone. I have to admit that I had a more serious suspicion that concerned the Marriott people—the suspicion that some of the cardboard food I have been served on airplanes had been delivered by the Marriott catering-service truck I always see pulling away from the plane just before takeoff.

Every single day, it turns out, Marriott provides the airlines with one hundred and fifty thousand meals, none of which contains anything a steady patron of Buster's would recognize as food. I have never blamed Marriott for my own absentmindedness that day between St. Louis and New York when, confusing two of those little plastic cups that are always on meal trays, I poured cream on my salad and French dressing in my coffee, but I do think it's fair to blame them for the fact that I did not become aware of the mistake until it was called to my attention *after I had eaten the entire meal.* The one hundred and fifty thousand airline meals are all prepared in one huge kitchen, the location of which Marriott would do well to keep secret, just in case a traveling salesman who also happens to be a discriminating eater is someday driven to terrorism by the breast of chicken he is served between Miami and Chicago.

Discovering that all Marriott airline meals are prepared in one kitchen intensified a fear I have had for years—that someday, by federal law or some kind of executive order, all meals eaten by everyone in the United States will be prepared in one single gigantic kitchen. Could it have been a mere coincidence that Willard Marriott, who owns what is presumably the kitchen most likely to get the contract, is a personal friend of Richard Nixon, a President who had a history of eating cottage cheese with ketchup (the "old Nixon" we've heard so much about) and has raised a daughter whose favorite recipe is made with canned soup? Is it just happenstance that the Big Boy hamburger defended by William Edgett Smith as the best hamburger in the world—a defense that remains inexplicable by any normal rules of logical argument—is produced by a company that is now a totally owned subsidiary of the Marriott Corporation?

As I see it, the process will start slowly, with agents of various local and state and federal agencies closing restaurants that could serve as rallying points for rebel eaters. Mr. Galatoire shows up one morning at his restaurant on Bourbon Street only to meet two heavies from the New Orleans Department of Maritime Engineering who tell him that his papers are not in order. The country restaurants that serve chicken dinner family-style—those shrines that decorate the table with huge bowls of creamed corn and mashed potatoes and biscuits—are visited by a deputy sheriff who says "Y'all got a license to serve them fresh vegetables?" In Iowa, a neatly dressed postal inspector informs the Meat Department of the Amana Society that it has been found guilty of using the mails to transport summer sausage. The City Council of San Francisco passes, without debate, an ordinance banning all Chinese restaurants that do not specialize in either chop suey or egg foo yung. Arthur Bryant's Barbecue and Doe's, the legendary tamale restaurant in Greenville, Mississippi, are closed by the Justice Department for premature compliance with the public accommodations section of the Civil Rights Act of 1964. In New York, Gage & Tollner, Sweets, Sloppy Louie's, and Lundy's are, within a few weeks, all turned into outlets of Arthur Treacher's Fish 'n Chips. She-crab soup is banned by authorities in Charleston,

South Carolina, supposedly as a way of avoiding an anticipated demonstration against it by feminists—although the reaction of the city's feminists to the news is puzzlement and hunger. Then, using as an excuse something like the problems created by farm surpluses or the necessities of civil-defense preparation, the government announces that all citizens will henceforth be required to eat only food provided by the One Big Kitchen. Those of us who refuse to go along will have to go underground—living in caves in the Arkansas hills with an ace barbecue man who somehow managed to escape the round-up of decent cooks, and maybe sneaking out at night to forage for fresh apples and to buy contraband chopped liver made with real schmaltz.

When I discovered that Marriott owns the Roy Rogers Family Restaurants company and the Bob's Big Boy company as well as the airline-catering operation, I became more convinced than ever that the sudden proliferation of fast-food franchises several years ago was no accident. In the fast-food industry, of course, "family" means people who spend quite a bit of money but don't wreck the furniture. The merchandising method of the industry, as far as I can gather, is based on luring the entire family by appealing to the children—a shrewd device, since even the best-brought-up children seem to like bland food, particularly if it is served by a cowgirl or wrapped in a package that is shaped like a clown. Children can now be lured into the fast-food restaurants and exposed to Styrofoam hamburgers and wood-chip French fries at an impressionable age. Then they enter school, and the dietitians take over with a gray-meat and carrot-and-raisin-salad diet that goes on through college, interrupted only by Marriott airline meals flying to and fro on Christmas vacations. By the time these kids are of voting age, their discrimination in food will amount to a preference for Burger King or McDonald's—a preference based on which one gives away the best decal with its hamburgers—and they will be easy marks for the forces intent on putting over the One Big Kitchen conspiracy.

To test this theory, I asked a friend of mine in New Orleans —Ruth Wolf, Peter's mother—where her New Orleans grandchildren like to eat when she takes them out for lunch. I conducted this bit of research during a dinner a few of us were having at

Pascal's Manale, a restaurant that specializes in a dish it calls Manale Original Barbecue Shrimp—a school of huge shrimp, still in the shell, floating in a sauce made of butter and pepper and a number of other ingredients that, put together in some other proportions, could probably power a small speedboat. I considered the children in question less vulnerable than most to the machinations of the One Big Kitchen conspirators. These children, after all, have a grandmother who appreciates Manale's shrimp and a mother who makes crawfish *étouffée* in her own kitchen while discoursing on the wonders of a Casamento oyster loaf and a father who, at the very moment of our conversation, was devouring one of Manale's crabmeat casseroles while wearing an expression of otherworldly bliss. Their uncle, of course, eats Red Soup on Upper Broadway and was nearly a participant in the contest that decided the crawfish-eating championship of the world. "We always have to go to two places for lunch when I take the kids," Ruth Wolf told me. "Stephen insists on going to Roy Rogers for a roast-beef sandwich, and then we have to go to Burger King so Nancy can have one of their hamburgers."

It was an answer that carried a bleak view of our future. I sought solace in Mr. Manale's shrimp.

•

Night after night, I would see the dietitians in New Orleans restaurants, although I don't know how those who spent much time in the exhibition section of the meeting managed to keep up their enthusiasm for eating. Before dinner at Galatoire's one evening, I made the mistake of reading a list of what various corporations were demonstrating to the dietitians in the exhibition hall, and I was put off my feed to the extent of being able to order only a dozen oysters *en brochette* and some soup—passing up the eggplant stuffed with seafood, a dish I have always believed New Orleans city authorities ought to erect a statue of in Jackson Square.

The salesmen manning the booths at the meeting used the same kind of patter one might expect to hear from salesmen at, say, an oil compounders' convention, but most of what they were selling sounded considerably less appetizing than petroleum. "This is your total diet, not a supplement," a salesman at one booth would say, holding up a tiny cardboard box. "This has your amino acids, your carbohydrates." A few booths away, a young woman would offer passersby a cracker covered with a gray substance and would say, as cheerfully as she could manage, "Have you tried our meatless chickenlike product?" Recipes were being distributed to show all the imaginative dishes that could be made from products like "modified chicken breasts" and "dinner balls" and something that comes in what looks like gallon milk cartons and is called Versa 'Taters. ("What it is is a multipurpose potato," the man at the Versa 'Taters booth said. "You just put it in a pan, fill the pan with tap water, let it sit for thirty minutes, and you have cooked potatoes.") Whenever I found a booth that was displaying something I might think about eating—Sara Lee pastries, for instance—the salesman would hand me a chart that gave a complete analysis of what, say, Sara Lee's Double Chocolate Layer Cake consisted of, *including the calories*. I cannot think of any information I want to know less than I want to know how many calories are in a piece of Sara Lee Double Chocolate Layer Cake.

Somehow, the dietitians managed to clean their plates every morning at the Four Seasons anyway—the early risers among them joining those of us who tend to show up a few minutes before nine and loiter on Royal Street until the doors are opened. One day during the meeting, I was walking from the New Orleans convention center, a flashy new building in a cluster of flashy new buildings near the riverfront, when I passed a place called Joe's Jungle Bar. Joe's Jungle, as it is also known, has the look of one of those bars that the patron saint of construction workers always makes sure are left standing in otherwise bulldozed urban-renewal areas so that the people doing the renewing have someplace to drink a beer after work or to watch the baseball game during the lunch break. It had a sign on the window that said, WELCOME, AMERICAN DIETETIC ASSOCIATION. Could it be, I wondered, that a crowd of dietitians had actually been lured into Joe's Jungle? Does justfolksism go that far? I found the prospect disturbing. I was not certain that I wanted to find the person who was in charge of balancing my diet at Southwest High School (a person who must have suffered, poor woman, from desperate efforts to fill her menus with whatever balances hamburgers) perched on a stool in Joe's Jungle Bar drinking Regal beer from a can and cussing the New Orleans Saints' backfield and maybe giving five in the mush to some loudmouth who passes a slighting remark about lima beans. I happened to be in a great hurry at the time. I was on my way to a place that is renowned for a ham-and-roast-beef po' boy sandwich, and I wanted to get there before the line formed so that I would also have time to stop at a store that sold Zatarain's Crab and Shrimp Boil, a few bottles of which I intended to take back to New York with me despite my fear that an airport baggage inspector might find it in my luggage and rule it an explosive. But I immediately went through the bar door. There were, I am relieved to say, no dietitians in Joe's Jungle.

•

Dietitians did seem more conscientious than most conventioneers about attending the lectures and panels that in most annual meetings I've seen drive the membership toward places like Joe's Jungle. Sensing that something important must have been going on, I resolved one day to attend an entire afternoon of such events myself, even if it meant hearing some balanced-diet talk that I would ordinarily go blocks out of my way to avoid. I have always had trouble following speeches at conventions and sales meetings and annual meetings and conferences—mainly, I think, because so many of the speakers use what my high-school speech teacher called "audiovisual aids." Whether the speaker is a Marriott executive telling Roy Rogers franchisers how they can put over Roy's new Double-R-Bar-Burger or a committee chairman of the American Dietetic Association explaining how dietitians can work for the passage of important federal legislation, he or she always seems to be pointing to a chart or a slide that lists Key Words. I am always left with such a strong impression of the Key Words that I can't remember what they were meant to be the key to—and the words themselves provide no clue, since they seem to be the same words no matter what the subject of the speech is. One of the Key Words is always ACTION. I can never remember if that refers to action in developing an effective advertising campaign or political action or, as might be possible at a dietitians' conference, peristaltic action.

I decided to attend the afternoon meetings anyway, right after I had lunch at Buster's. Although Buster's looks like a corner bar with a lunch counter added, it may be the finest restaurant in the world outside the city limits of Kansas City. A serious meal had been arranged there by Alvin Lambert, a friend of mine who helps run Preservation Hall—a place in which New Orleans jazz is played by some of the black musicians who are talented enough to have helped develop the form and intelligent enough to eat a lot of their meals at Buster's. We started with a huge platter of fried oysters. By the time we were halfway through, Buster's waiter had brought a bowl of spaghetti with a sauce that would probably have brought tears to the eyes of Pascal Manale (as well as to the eyes of anyone who reacts normally to pepper). We ordered a couple more quarts of beer to help with the sauce. Alvin was taking a healthy interest in the oysters and spaghetti, but I didn't feel any pressure to eat with both hands in order to get my share, the way I sometimes feel while eating with Alvin's brother-in-law, Allan Jaffe, with whom I have shared some happy Buster's lunches that lasted until dinnertime. Jaffe—who has managed Preservation Hall since it opened in the early sixties, and has played the tuba in its traveling band for the past few years—was away on a road trip. A few years after the Hall opened, the temptation to insinuate himself and his tuba in the last set of the evening had proven too much for Jaffe, the only person I ever met who attended Valley Forge Military Academy on a tuba scholarship. Eventually, he was playing funerals and church dedications with a street band, and then he was touring the country. Unfortunately, he becomes saddened on the road by hunger for Buster's cooking. Sometimes he is able to cheer himself up by steering the band's bus toward El Campo, Texas, where he treasures a barbecue place run by a Yugoslav butcher, and when the bus draws within a hundred miles of Kansas City, it detours, by unanimous consent, to Arthur Bryant's. But in some places around the country Jaffe's hunger reaches close to the point of despair. Then he phones Buster and persuades him to pack up some ingredients, climb on a plane (a particularly aromatic plane, once Buster's luggage is aboard), and spend a couple of days with the band. I used to think that Jaffe, by traveling as a member of the Preservation Hall Jazz Band, was one of the few people I knew who was living out his childhood fantasy—there, after all, is Big Jim Robinson in Carnegie Hall doing his solo, and there, behind him, is the kid from Valley Forge going bom-bom-baba-badee-bom-bom—but then I realized that his true fantasy is not traveling as a member of the Preservation Hall Jazz Band but traveling as a member of the Preservation Hall Jazz Band and having Buster Holmes along as a kind of court chef.

I could see that I might miss the first speech of the afternoon at the dietitians' conference. I knew we would have to spend at least forty minutes eating fried chicken. Buster's fried chicken tastes as if it is made from chickens that have spent their entire pampered lives strolling around the barnyard pecking contentedly at huge cloves of garlic. As we were finishing the chicken, the waiter brought out some beans and rice, along with some of Buster's hot sausage. Allan Jaffe's older son was practically raised on Buster's rice, fortunate child, and only ate rice that tested less than 80 percent garlic by volume when he traveled with the band. As soon as he was able to talk, he looked up at his mother during dinner at some Howard Johnson's or Holiday Inn in some far-off state and said, "Mommy, the rice tastes funny."

Empty quart beer bottles were all over the table by the time we finished the beans and rice. The sausage was gone. Somehow, we were still eating an hour later. Finally, knowing I had to get to the conference, I pushed back my chair and resolutely placed my third apple turnover on the table unfinished.

"My compliments to the chef," I gasped, and staggered out into the sunlight.

By the time I reached the convention center, I was puffing ominously, although I had taken a cab the entire way. I walked into the first lecture room I saw—my breath coming in gasps, my pockets rattling with Gelusil tablets. In an attempt to fight off Buster's sausage, I was eating Gelusil, chewing some gum, and sucking on a Life Saver at the same time. The lecture turned out to be on obesity. The lecturer had a slide flashed on the screen and pointed at a word. I assumed the word was ACTION, but I really couldn't see very well. My eyes were watering. The lecturer started talking about the diseases that obesity could be a factor in—gallbladder trouble, gout. A wave of heartburn passed over me. The lecturer began to discuss diabetes and hypertension. I felt slightly feverish. I broke out in a sweat. Finally, I managed to make my way out of the room and into the fresh air. I knew from previous experience what had happened to me: I had come close to going into garlic shock.

I made my way back to my hotel and resolved to become more sensible about eating. I decided that I would even forgo a trip I had planned that evening to Mosca's, a roadhouse whose baked oysters I revere. I knew it was important to begin taking care of myself right away. I had heard that Buster was serving spareribs as his special the following day, and I had no intention of having to miss them.

ALICE, LET'S EAT

FURTHER ADVENTURES OF

A HAPPY EATER

(1 9 7 8)

(1)

Alice

NOW THAT IT'S FASHIONABLE to reveal intimate details of married life, I can state publicly that my wife, Alice, has a weird predilection for limiting our family to three meals a day. I also might as well admit that the most serious threat to our marriage came in 1975, when Alice mentioned my weight just as I was about to sit down to dinner at a New Orleans restaurant named Chez Helène. I hardly need add that Chez Helène is one of my favorite restaurants in New Orleans; we do not have the sort of marriage that could come to grief over ordinary food.

Without wanting to be legalistic, I should mention that Alice brought up the weight issue during a long-distance telephone call —breaking whatever federal regulations there are against Interstate Appetite Impairment. Like many people who travel a lot on business, I'm in the habit of calling home every evening to share the little victories and defeats of the day—the triumph, for instance, of happening upon a superior tamale stand in a town I thought had long before been completely carved into spheres of influence by McDonald's and Burger King, or the misery of being escorted by some local booster past the unmistakable aroma of genuine hickory-wood barbecuing into La Maison de la Casa House, whose notion of "Continental cuisine," I finally decided, must have been derived in some arcane way from the Continental-Trailways bus company.

Having found myself on business in New Orleans—or, as it is sometimes expressed around my office, having found it my business to find business in New Orleans—I was about to settle into Chez Helène for a long evening. First, of course, I telephoned Alice in New York. I assumed it would give her great pleasure to hear that her husband was about to have enough sweet potatoes and fried oysters to make him as happy as he could manage to be outside her presence. Scholars of the art have often mentioned Chez Helène as an example of what happens when Creole blends with Soul—so that a bowl of greens comes out tasting of spices that the average greens maker in Georgia or Alabama probably associates with papists or the Devil himself.

"I'm about to have dinner at Chez Helène," I said.

"Dr. Seligmann just told me today that you weighed a hundred and eighty pounds when you were in his office last week," Alice said. "That's terrible!"

"There must be something wrong with this connection," I said. "I could swear I just told you that I was about to have dinner at Chez Helène."

"You're going to have to go on a diet. This is serious."

It occurred to me that a man telephoning his wife from a soul-food restaurant could, on the excuse of trying to provide some authentic atmosphere, say something like "Watch yo' mouth, woman!" Instead, I said, "I think there might be a better time to talk about this, Alice." Toward the end of the second or third term of the Caroline Kennedy Administration was the sort of time I had in mind.

"Well, we can talk about it when you get home," Alice said. "Have a nice dinner."

I did. It is a measure of my devotion to Alice that I forgave her, even though my second order of fried chicken was ruined by the realization that I had forgotten to tell her I had actually weighed only a hundred and sixty-six pounds. I always allow fourteen pounds for clothes.

I must say that Alice tempers her rigidity on the meals-per-day issue by having a broad view of what constitutes an hors d'oeuvre. That is not, of course, her only strong point. She is tenacious, for instance—having persisted for five or six summers in attempting to wheedle the recipe for the seafood chowder served at Gladee's Canteen, in Hirtle's Beach, Nova Scotia, out of the management. She is imaginative—a person who can turn a bucketful of clams into, on successive evenings, steamed clams, clam fritters, clams in white wine sauce, and a sort of clam billi-bi. I can testify to her restraint: on the Christmas I presented her with a Cuisinart food processor, not having realized that what she really wanted was a briefcase, she thanked me politely, the way an exceedingly courteous person might thank a process server for a subpoena. ("Well," I finally said, "I thought it might be good for mulching the Christmas tree.") She is generous—the sort of wife who would share even the tiniest order of, say, crawfish bisque with her husband, particularly if he had tears in his eyes when he asked. Alice has a lot of nice qualities, but when someone tells me, as someone often does, how fortunate I am to have her as my wife, I generally say, "Yes, she does have a broad view of what constitutes an hors d'oeuvre."

I don't mean that her views on this matter are as broad as the views held by our friend Fats Goldberg, the New York pizza baron and reformed blimp, who, in reporting on the semiannual eating binges in Kansas City he still allows himself, often begins sentences with phrases like "Then on the way to lunch I stopped at Kresge's for a chili dog." A Kresge chili dog, it seems to me, reflects a view of hors d'oeuvres that has strayed from broad to excessive. (It also reflects the fact that Fats Goldberg in binge gear will eat almost anything but green vegetables.) What I mean is that if we happen to be driving through Maine on our way to Nova Scotia, where we live in the summer, Alice does not object when, ten miles from the lobster restaurant where we plan to stop for dinner, I screech to a halt in front of a place that has the look of a spectacular fried-clam stand. "It'll make a nice hors d'oeuvre," she says.

While I'm speaking in Alice's defense, I should also say that I consider her failure with the children half my own: no one person could be responsible for engendering in two innocent little girls a preference for frozen fish sticks over fish. In fact, in Nova Scotia I have seen Alice take a halibut that was on a fishing boat an hour before, sprinkle it ever so slightly with some home-ground flour, fry it for a few seconds until it is covered with a batter whose lightness challenges the batter on a Gladee's fishball, cut it into sticklike slices, and present it to her very own little girls—only to have them pick at it for a few minutes and gaze longingly toward the freezer.

Oddly enough, both of our girls have shown, in quick, maddening flashes, indications of having been born with their taste buds intact. Once, while we were visiting my mother in Kansas City, Abigail, our older daughter, looked up at me during breakfast and said, "Daddy, how come in Kansas City the bagels just taste like round bread?" Her father's daughter, I allowed myself to hope—a connoisseur of bagels before she's five. By age nine she'll probably be able to identify any bialy she eats by borough of origin; she'll pick up some change after school working at Russ & Daughters Appetizer Store as a whitefish taster. On trips to Kansas City, her proud father's hometown, she'll appear as a child prodigy on the stage of the concert hall, lecturing on the varieties of the local barbecue sauce. Not so. At nine, offered anything that does not have the familiarity of white chicken or hamburger or Cheerios, she declines with a "No, thank you" painful in its elaborate politeness. This is the daughter who, at the age of four, reacted to a particularly satisfying dish of chocolate ice cream by saying, "My tongue is smiling." How quickly for parents do the disappointments come.

Abigail's younger sister, Sarah, has a palate so unadventurous that she refuses to mix peanut butter with jelly. I have often told her that I hope she chooses a college rather close to home—New York University, perhaps, which is in Greenwich Village, just a few blocks from where we live—so that when I show up every morning to cut the crusts off her toast I won't require a sleepover. For a couple of years, Sarah refused to enter a Chinese restaurant unless she was carrying a bagel in reserve. "Just in case," she often explained. More than once, Alice and Abigail and I, all having forgotten Sarah's special requirements, started to leave for a family dinner in Chinatown, only to hear a small, insistent voice cry, "My bagel! My bagel!"

One night, in a Chinese restaurant, Sarah became a fancier of roast squab. We were at the Phoenix Garden, a place in Chinatown that happens to have, in addition to excellent roast squab, a dish called Fried Fresh Milk with Crabmeat, which tastes considerably better than it sounds, and a shrimp dish that is one of the closest New York equivalents to the sort of shrimp served in some Italian restaurants in New Orleans. Just why she would decide to taste roast squab still puzzles historians, since it is known that three months were required for Abigail, perhaps the only human being Sarah completely trusts, to persuade her that chocolate ice cream was really something worth trying. Sarah herself has always treated her passion for a single exotic foodstuff as something that requires no explanation—like a mortgage officer who, being sober and cautious and responsible in every other way, sees nothing peculiar about practicing voodoo on alternate Thursdays. During lunch once in Nova Scotia, the subject of favorite foods was brought up by a friend of ours named Shelly Stevens, who is a year or two older than Abigail and is known among gourmets in Queens County mainly for being just about the only person anybody has ever heard of who eats banana peels as well as bananas. Sarah looked up from her peanut-butter sandwich—hold the jelly—and said, "Squab. Yes. Definitely squab."

It is not really Alice's fault that our girls are subject to bad influences. One morning, while I was preparing lunches for them to take to P.S. 3, I unwrapped some ham—some remarkably good Virginia ham that Alice had somehow managed to unearth in a store around the corner otherwise notable only for the number of hours each day the checkout counter clerk manages to spend doing her nails. Sarah said she didn't want any ham. It turned out that she had trouble eating a ham sandwich for lunch because a little girl with a name like Moira would always sit next to her and tell her how yucky ham was—Moira being a strict vegetarian, mungbean and bean-sprout division.

"The people who warned us about sending our children to public school in New York were right," I said to Alice. "Now our daughter is being harassed by a mad-dog vegetarian."

Alice was opposed to my suggestion that Sarah attempt to place Moira under citizen's arrest. At the least, I thought Sarah should tell Moira that bean sprouts are the yuckiest food of all except for

mung beans, and that carrot juice makes little girls pigeon-toed and
bad at arithmetic. As it happens, health food does disagree with
me. I tend to react to eating one of those salads with brown grass
and chopped walnuts the way some people react to eating four or
five fried Italian sausages. (I, on the other hand, react to eating four
or five fried Italian sausages with a quiet smile.) Alice claims that
what bothers me is not health food but the atmosphere of the health-
food restaurants in our neighborhood—some of which seem modeled on the last days of a particularly unsuccessful commune. It's
a neat theory, but it does not account for the time in Brunswick,
Maine, when—during a festival whose atmosphere was absolutely
splendid—I was fed something advertised as "whole foods for the
multitudes" and immediately felt as if I had taken a very long journey
in a very small boat. Fortunately, someone at the festival had mentioned hearing that a diner just outside Brunswick served chili spicy
enough to charbroil the tongue, and just a small cup of it turned
out to be an antidote that had me feeling chipper enough to order
some more. I had realized I was at the right diner even before I sat
down: a sign on the door said, WHEN YOU'RE HUNGRY AND OUT OF
WORK, EAT AN ENVIRONMENTALIST.

•

Now and then—when Alice mentions, say, the nutritional value
of brown rice—I have begun to worry that she might have fallen
under the influence of the Natural Food Fanatics or the Balanced
Diet Conspiracy. Once they learned of her fundamentalist views
on Three Meals a Day, after all, they might have figured that they
had a foot in the door. Could it be, I wonder in my most suspicious
moments, that Moira's mother has been sneaking in for missionary
work—waiting until I'm out of town, then clunking over in her
leather sandals from her food co-op meeting to talk up the health-
giving properties of organically grown figs? In calmer moments I
admit to myself that Alice's awareness of, say, the unspeakable
destruction wreaked by refined sugar is probably just another example of knowledge she seems to have absorbed from no immediately ascertainable source. Occasionally, for instance, we have
come home from a party and I have said, with my usual careful

choice of words, "What was that funny-looking thing whatsername was wearing?" Then Alice—the serious academic who teaches college students to write and explains foreign movies to her husband, the mother of two who still refers to those rich ladies who swoop through midtown stores as "grownups"—tells me who designed the funny-looking thing and how much it probably cost and which tony boutique peddled it and why some people believe it to be chic. At such moments I am always stunned—as if I had idly wondered out loud about the meaning of some inscription on a ruin in Oaxaca and Alice had responded by translating fluently from the Toltec.

I admit that Moira's mother has never been spotted coming out of our house by a reliable witness. I admit that the girls do not show the vulnerability to Natural Food propaganda they might show if their own mother were part of the conspiracy. Sarah, in fact, once left a summer nursery program in Kansas City because the snacktime included salad. "They gave me salad!" she says to this day, in the tone a countess roughly handled by the customs man might say, "They searched my gown!"

All in all, I admit that Alice is, in her own way, a pretty good eater herself. The last time she failed to order dessert, for instance, was in the spring of 1965, in a Chinese restaurant that offered only canned kumquats. I have been with her in restaurants when she exulted over the purity and simplicity of the perfectly broiled fresh sea bass she had ordered, and then finished off the meal with the house specialty of toasted pound cake covered with ice cream and chocolate sauce. I suppose her only serious weakness as an eater—other than these seemingly uncontrollable attacks of moderation—is that she sometimes lets her mind wander between meals. I first began to notice this weakness when we were traveling in Italy just after we got married. ("It all shows up on the honeymoon," the wise heads used to say when the subject of marriage came up at LeRoy's Waldo Bar in Kansas City.) There we were in Italy, and Alice was devoting a good hour and a half right in the middle of the morning to inspecting a cathedral instead of helping me to comb the Michelin guide for the lunch spot most likely to stagger us with the perfection of its fettuccine. I tried to explain to her that marriage is sharing—not merely sharing one's fettuccine with one's husband if he is gazing at it adoringly and is obviously having second thoughts about having ordered the veal, but sharing the burden of finding the fettucine restaurant in the first place.

Since then, Alice has, as they say, grown in the marriage—and so, in another way, have I. Still, there are times when, in a foreign country, she will linger in a museum in front of some legendary piece of art as the morning grows late and I become haunted by the possibility that the restaurant I have chosen for lunch will run out of garlic sausage before we get there. "Alice!" I say on those occasions, in a stage whisper that sometimes fails to get her attention even though the museum guards turn to glare in my direction. "Alice! Alice, let's eat!"

(2)

Off the Beach

AFTER ALICE AND I spent a week in Martinique one winter, I finally began to sympathize with those hard-driving business executives who are so jumpy on the beach that their wives spend the entire vacation telling them to relax: I was in a constant state of tension over such matters as whether I should have had the *crabes farcis* rather than the *calalou* as an appetizer. We all have our own sources of stress.

"Relax," Alice said. I was pacing the sand as usual, giving a pretty good imitation of a frenzied conglomerateur possessed by the fear that he had swallowed up a company that would prove to be indigestible.

"But I just realized that Le Gommier is particularly renowned for its *crabes farcis*," I said, referring to a small restaurant in Fort de France where we had eaten ourselves to distraction the previous day.

"But you said you loved the *calalou*," she said, soothingly.

True. I loved it. *Calalou* is a sort of pureed vegetable soup— a spicy marvel whose texture fuels my suspicion that buried somewhere in those gastronomic histories of how the French and African cultures came together in the French West Indies to create Creole cooking is the information that a Waring blender was introduced in the islands in 1863. On the other hand, *crabes farcis* are stuffed crabs, and chefs on Martinique tend to use as stuffing what I suspect a crab would have chosen to stuff himself with if only he had been given the opportunity.

"And you said the *blaff d'oursins* was spectacular," she said. "I'm sure you made the right choice with the *blaff d'oursins.*"

She used the tone the wife of the hard-driving conglomerateur might use to calm him down ("I'm sure it was a very nice company to have swallowed up, dear"). She was right, of course. *Blaff* is what people in Martinique call a sort of stew they make, heavy on the limes. I think I had been put off at first merely because the word *"blaff"* sounds so much like what Sarah says when presented with unfamiliar food. When I first saw it on the menu, I responded the way I might respond to being offered some French dish called, say, *yuque de champignons*. Then I realized that *blaff d'oursins* has a rather noble sound to it ("Suddenly she saw him riding out of the darkness—the Count Henri-Claude Blaff d'Oursins, a fearfully handsome man who disarmed the evil Fouchard with a casual flip of his sword"). *Oursins* are sea urchins, and while eating the version blaffed up by Le Gommier, I declared a blanket amnesty for all the sea urchins that had ever attempted to puncture my feet in those small Mediterranean resorts with high infection rates and unshaven doctors.

"You're right, of course. You're right," I said to Alice.

"Can't you just sit down and relax?" she said. "Read a book or something."

"Of course you're right," I said. "I'll do that." I reached into the beach bag and withdrew a copy of Dr. André Nègre's *The French West Indies Through Their Cookery*.

•

I had some difficulty understanding how Alice could relax on a beach whose very snack bar offered eggs mimosa and *salade niçoise*. We were not, after all, on one of those Caribbean islands where the locals spent a few centuries acquiring an English appreciation for cool gray meat. We had served our time on those islands. Once, while we were living in a rented house on Tortola, Alice asked the storekeeper she had ordered a chicken from if he would cut it up for her, and returned to find that he had taken a frozen chicken and run it through a band saw. Alice, as I remember, said something on that occasion that sounded rather like "Blaff."

How could a person who had once been handed a chicken that looked like fifteen perfectly uniform pieces of thickly sliced bologna be so casual about spending her vacation in a place that has had entire books written about its cookery? I don't mean Alice was allowing herself to become malnourished. At La Grand' Voile, a distinguished Fort de France restaurant whose proprietor is from Lyons, she had casually downed an avocado with shrimp, a steak with morels, and an order of *cèpes*—a marvelous variety of French mushroom so large that an elf coming across one in the forest could climb up on it and address the other elves, up to his ankles in garlic and oil. She had missed no desserts. Between meals, though, she appeared to be in danger of backsliding into her old interest in the peripheral issues of travel—like touring the rain forest or lying on the beach. Fortunately, I was there to put her back on the track.

"Isn't it about time we cleaned up for lunch?" I asked. I had skipped rather quickly over a section of Dr. Nègre's book that seemed to carry West Indian authenticity a bit further than I wanted to go—it referred to "a bat worthy of the plate"—and had arrived at a passage that reminded me how close we were to a restaurant reputed to have a first-rate version of *blaff de poissons*.

"It's ten o'clock in the morning," Alice said. "We just had breakfast."

"We may have already stayed out too long in sun this strong," I said.

"But you're as pale as you were when we left New York," Alice said.

"Then it must have gone right through," I said. "Because I definitely have heartburn."

•

"Food isn't everything," Alice said the next morning. She had passed up the French toast soaked in rum she normally had for breakfast at the hotel, making do with a croissant or two, and she seemed to be feeling exceedingly virtuous, like a London air raid warden during the Second World War who had refrained from taking his full meat ration as a matter of principle.

"You're absolutely right, Alice," I said. "The French have never been able to make scrambled eggs worth a damn."

"You agreed that we would see some part of this island that was not the inside of a restaurant," she said. "The rain forest. The volcano."

"Well, I thought the view of the Fort de France harbor from La Grand' Voile was quite picturesque," I said. "I suspect it seemed even more picturesque because of the way they took the avocado out of the shell, mixed it with some mysterious goodies in one of their ancient blenders, and put it back in. But I think it would have been picturesque anyway."

"Views from restaurants don't count."

I reminded her that just two days before we had stood in a quaint fishing village while the villagers hauled in their communal net—stood there for almost an hour before driving off to have some very satisfying *soupe de poissons* at the hotel in Diament les Bains. I've never minded watching fish being hauled in as long as such activity was preparatory to eating some. Was Alice implying that I had no interest in flora, fauna, and fancy buildings? Who was it who took her to Chartres, while in the neighborhood searching out a stew of local renown?

On the other hand, I wanted Alice to have a lovely vacation. It is true that I hate scenery, but hadn't I been the one who said that marriage is sharing more than just your fettuccine? "You're absolutely right, Alice," I finally said. "We should definitely take a drive around the island. We could end up in Morne-des-Esses for lunch; a lady there named Mrs. Palladino is supposed to serve spectacular crawfish." Crawfish, one of the fauna that had drawn us to Martinique, had turned out to be hard to find. I thought that the sea urchins I was gobbling down might soothe the longing for crawfish I had been nursing since my last trip to southwestern Louisiana—at one restaurant outside Fort de France I had even devoured a sea urchin soufflé—but the true cure for a crawfish longing is a crawfish.

Alice consulted the map. "That would actually be out of the way," she said.

"If there's one thing I believe, Alice," I said, "it's that no place that has spectacular crawfish is out of the way."

•

"The volcano in Martinique is really quite famous," Alice said, as we drove along the next morning. "It once erupted and killed thirty thousand people."

"All the more reason not to approach it," I said, pulling into the small mountain village of Morne-des-Esses. Both the volcano and the rain forest were a long way from Morne-des-Esses, but I had convinced Alice that we would still have time to see them if lunch turned out to be a quick snack.

Mrs. Palladino's restaurant, Le Colibri, amounted to a half-dozen tables on an open porch in the back of her house. The house appeared modest from the outside, but the porch looked out over some huge banana trees, and a mountain or two, and, a few miles away, the sea—a view that seemed picturesque to me even before Mrs. Palladino brought us some delicious *calalou des crabes*.

"I suppose we could just get some crawfish and dash off, Alice," I said. "But this is really like someone's house, and I hate to eat and run."

"I just hope you'll be able to walk," Alice said, watching me go after the second course—a torte made with minced conch. I knew she meant nothing by the remark. She wanted to protect me from overeating in the same way I wanted to protect her from a volcano that had once erupted and killed thirty thousand people.

Eventually, Mrs. Palladino returned with what she called *buisson d'écrevisses*—a bush of crawfish, formed by arranging half a dozen huge crawfish in a goblet, and accompanied by a Creole sauce for dunking. As we polished off the crawfish, I discussed with Alice the problem created by a friend having phoned ahead to make certain that Mrs. Palladino served us some of our friend's favorite dishes. "If we leave now," I explained, "we'll never know what she might have brought out next." What she did bring out next was a stuffed pigeon, resting on a nest woven out of shoestring potatoes and accompanied by a purée of *christophene*—*christophene* being something I can describe only as what vegetables would be like if they were pure white and tasted good.

We had been eating for a couple of hours when Mrs. Palladino arrived to clear away the pigeon and inform us that dessert was fresh coconut flan. Alice sighed.

"When we talk about a rain forest, what are we really talking about, Alice?" I said. "What we're talking about is a bunch of wet trees."

Alice nodded, and turned to Mrs. Palladino and said in very good French, "We'll take two."

(3)

Stalking the

Barbecued Mutton

I ONCE WRONGED the state of Kentucky, but compared with the Kentucky Fried Chicken people, I am an innocent. All I did was to pass on the information that a friend of mine named Marshall J. Dodge III—a man renowned on the East Coast for having somehow forged a successful career as a semiretired amateur folklorist—claimed that he had encountered the supreme fried chicken in a town called Rabbit Hash, Kentucky, while touring the area with a calliope restorer of his acquaintance. Local connoisseurs quickly point out that Marshall must have been thinking of a chicken restaurant in Cynthiana, Kentucky—Rabbit Hash being a place so small that the goods and services it offers the traveler probably don't extend to high-test. People I know in the state seemed satisfied with my explanation that Marshall is the sort of person who would never say Cynthiana when he could say Rabbit Hash. I pointed out, as an example, that the friend Marshall always refers to as a calliope restorer might be described by most people as a piano dealer—although I believe the friend thinks of himself mainly as an actor and a semiprofessional blower of smoke rings.

A few years after the unfortunate misidentification of Cynthiana as Rabbit Hash, I told Alice that I was thinking about making further amends by journeying to Cynthiana and sampling a platter or two of the chicken in question.

"That sort of penance seems to be one of your specialties," Alice said.

"Well, naturally, I'd like to get this thing straightened out once and for all," I said. "There's nothing like a clear conscience."

I phoned a serious eater I know in Covington, Kentucky, and he informed me, in the sort of voice a heavy investor in Mexican savings banks might have used to discuss the drop in the peso that winter, that the Cynthiana restaurant had closed its doors. I was not surprised. In recent years legendary fried-chicken places seem to have closed at about the rate that indoor shopping malls open— Mrs. Stroud's, in Kansas City, and Mrs. Kremer's, near Jefferson City, just to toss off the names of two darkened shrines in my own home state. I suppose there were serious fried-chicken eaters in Kansas City who considered emigration after Mrs. Stroud's closed, but fortunately a successor appeared—a place called R.C.'s, which serves deep-fried chicken livers, and fried chicken with a strong, peppery batter, and potatoes with a marvelous suggestion of bacon grease that has, like an old retainer, been with the family for years. Someone who composed menus for those restaurants that spin around on the top of bank buildings in places like Kansas City, endangering the superstructure with the weight of their sauces, would probably refer to R.C.'s potatoes as *pommes de terre à la bas église*, or potatoes in the Low Church manner.

Because a superior fried-chicken restaurant is often the institutional extension of a single chicken-obsessed woman, I realize that, like a good secondhand bookstore or a bad South American dictatorship, it is not easily passed down intact. Still, in sullen moments I blame these lamentable closings on the vertical integration of the broiler industry—the method by which one mass-producing corporation controls broilers from hatching to marketplace, keeping strict control on their tastelessness the entire time. In fact, in sullen moments I blame almost everything on the vertical integration of the broiler industry—the way some people trace practically any sort of mischief or natural disaster back to the Central Intelligence Agency, and some people, presumably slightly more sophisticated, blame everything on the interstate highway program. If the civilization is really about to crumble, everybody is entitled to his own idea of which is the most significant crack. Which brings us to Kentucky Fried Chicken.

Once, when I had the honor of accompanying Fats Goldberg to the Smithsonian Institution for the opening of an exhibition that included the neon sign saying GOLDBERG'S PIZZERIA as one of the artifacts assembled to remind us of the roots of our culture, both Fats and I noticed how much of the neon display was devoted to signs advertising American franchise restaurants in foreign languages. It occurred to me that Kentucky Fried Chicken is what a schoolboy in Osaka or a housewife in Brussels thinks fried chicken tastes like. The world may be growing smaller, but schoolboys in Osaka have never even heard of Mrs. Stroud. Kentucky Fried Chicken has become an international symbol of fast food, even though a chicken fried with care and respect is particularly slow food—pan-frying being a process that requires enough time to make any prospective diner begin worrying about whether he has come close to filling himself up with pickled watermelon rind and assorted relishes. It is also a symbol, I realized, of Kentucky—as if French cuisine were associated in the minds of all foreigners with the sort of frozen French fries dished out to hot-rodders in greasy drive-ins. Are the Swiss thought of as people who sit around all the time eating what high-school dining halls in the Midwest call Swiss steak? Why should Kentucky be maligned?

"It hardly seems fair," I said to Alice.

"I suppose your sense of justice requires that you stuff yourself with something," Alice said.

She understands these matters. The reputation of Kentucky could be reclaimed, I decided, only if the people who spread the word about food were tipped off to a Kentucky specialty that would blot out memories of what Colonel Sanders himself has called "nothing but a fried doughball wrapped around some chicken." I resolved to seek out the barbecued mutton of western Kentucky—a unique regional delicacy I heard about when a restaurant tout wrote me to say that the menu of her favorite restaurant in Owensboro said, "Mary Had a Little Lamb. Won't You Have Some Too?"

•

"I'm calling from Horse Cave," I told Alice on the telephone a couple of nights later.

There was a long silence. "I thought you said barbecued mutton was a specialty of *western* Kentucky," Alice finally said. "According to the map, Horse Cave is in south-central Kentucky. The specialty there wouldn't be country ham, would it?"

"As a matter of fact, it would," I admitted. "But that does not happen to be the reason I'm here."

I began to understand what one of my fellow Traveling People—a drummer in electronic software, as I remember—meant when he told me that a conscientious husband on the road gets nothing for calling home every night but suspicious questions and reports of plumbing emergencies. As a traveler who had always looked forward to nightly calls home—even after the Chez Helène Incident—I was astonished to hear suspicion in the voice of my own wife, a person I would trust with my last fried dumpling. I'll admit that I would rather say Horse Cave than Owensboro, and I'll admit that I'd rather say country ham than almost anything if the person I was saying it to happened to be a waitress. But I had stopped off at Horse Cave for the perfectly legitimate purpose of seeking the advice of Tom Chaney, a reformed English professor who runs a corn-and-tobacco farm there with his Aunt Daisie Carter. Tom happens to be a practicing specialist in the eating of Kentucky foods.

It was perfectly natural that Tom and I and his Aunt Daisie, a cheerful lady who spent fifty-one years in the Hart County school system and seems none the worse for wear, held our first meeting while eating country ham. There is nothing suspicious about that. We had driven to a nearby town called Sulphur Well around noon, and pulled up at a small brick building identified on a Coke sign as Porter's—a place that had apparently inherited the local country-ham trade from the Beula Villa, an old hotel that used to serve as headquarters for people who drink the sulfuric water of the area to clear up whatever had been bothering them. I sampled the magic spring, and, just before we went in to lunch, revealed to Chaney my suspicion that the reputation of Porter's might rest on the fact that anything would taste good after that water. But the ham turned out to be a triumph—sliced thin, and fried, and served with a bowl of red-eye gravy. In fact, while we were eating at Porter's it occurred to me that country ham rather than barbecued mutton might be the local specialty that could put soggy fried chicken out of the public mind—until Tom's Aunt Daisie informed me that the most authentic country hams are illegal.

The actual ham we were wolfing down, she assured me, was quite within the law, but the sort of country ham that local people traditionally bought from a farmer—a farmer who might kill three or four hogs a year, cure the hams to sell, and use the rest of the meat for his own table—could no longer be sold legally because such farmers were obviously not set up to meet modern government meat-inspection standards.

"You mean the country ham you cook at home has to be bought from a supermarket?" I asked.

"Well, it's sort of like bootleg whiskey," Mrs. Carter told me, making it clear from her tone that she had not been the kind of schoolteacher who spent her spare time roaming the neighborhood kicking over stills and lecturing on the evils of Demon Rum.

I suddenly had a vision of Tom and his Aunt Daisie racing from their long-time supplier with three or four bootleg hams in the back seat, the Agriculture Department's version of revenuers in hot pursuit—Tom and Aunt Daisie tearing around curves, losing the law at last on the back roads they knew so well, and arriving home with the contraband they would cook secretly at night, hoping that the succulent aroma would not draw the authorities to their door. Knowing that people in some parts of Kentucky are still sensitive about their reputation for freelance distilling, I could hardly draw attention to a product whose most authentic version was illegal. We each had two or three more pieces of ham while we talked it over. Then Tom asked me how the sulfur water had affected my health.

"I feel like a million," I said. "A little full, but like a million."

Tom was reminded of a legendary eater in Horse Cave named Miss Fannie Hiser, a large woman who used to live with his Aunt Minnie. After everybody had finished one of the huge Sunday dinners Miss Fannie prepared, Tom recalled, she used to lean back in her chair, fold her hands contentedly under her ample midsection, and say, "Thank God for capacity."

•

"Are you sure this place we're going for dinner serves decent fried chicken?" I asked Tom late that afternoon. Tom had gathered some barbecued-mutton information by phone that day from an old college friend who grew up in Sturgis, Kentucky, right in the heart of the barbecued-mutton belt. We had arranged to go over the information while eating a fried-chicken supper with Tom's father, Boots Chaney, a more or less retired insurance man who remains fully active as a chicken eater. What had aroused my suspicion was Tom's choice of the concession restaurant in Mammoth Cave National Park—the sort of restaurant I have been suspicious of since Alice and a friend of ours waited forty-five minutes in a Bryce Canyon version for some broiled brook trout, only to discover when it finally arrived it had been broiling the entire time.

I was reassured when I noticed that the menu specified native chicken and a thirty-minute wait. "It's heartening to see that a restaurant in a national park is going to take the time to pan-fry some chicken," I told Tom. "It's the sort of thing that could help restore Americans' faith in their government." A necessary assumption in serving the slow-food variety of fried chicken is that the people waiting for it in the dining room are waiting with people they don't mind waiting with. Waiting for pan-fried chicken with the Chaneys is a treat. At the time of my visit they were sharing an office in Horse Cave—a two-room affair they sometimes referred to as Bogus Enterprises Inc.—and they have always shared a fondness for anecdotes about the area. Either of them could easily fill a half-hour pan-frying wait just with stories of the methods owners of the area's limestone caves once used to snatch tourists from each other, or just with stories about the adventures undergone by sane men trying to survive in a dry county. No wonder the people who emerge from fast-food emporiums look so sour: they probably haven't heard a good story in years.

The Chaneys are such splendid hosts that even though my comment on the fried chicken was an endorsement of some restraint

("The chicken is certainly no disgrace"), they offered to let me have one of their limited supply of country hams. I was loath to take it, knowing what I did about mad chases down tricky country roads, but I agreed to accompany Tom and Boots to Bogus Enterprises Inc. so that we could at least take a look at it. When we got to the office, Boots slid a pasteboard box from underneath one of the desks and pulled a country ham out of it. The ham had been wrapped in newspapers, bits of which were still sticking to it. A country ham is not, at first glance, beautiful. Even without bits of newspaper, it is often covered by what appears to be mold and dirt. A cousin of mine who is from Kentucky had a friend who worked his way through the state college at Bowling Green uglying up ordinary hams to make them look like properly cured country hams—much the same way some ambitious young fellows in England work their way through school distressing wood to make eighteenth-century tables. (My cousin's friend, having successfully completed his degree, is now apparently working contentedly as a grave digger—a reminder that if Frank Merriwell or Dink Stover had lived in an age of downward mobility, they might have followed up their college triumphs by becoming operators of a bead-and-leather shop.)

"I hate to take one of the few you have," I said, looking at the ham.

"You owe it to yourself," Tom said. "I'll even include the family country ham recipe." He immediately sat down and typed out the recipe, using some fancy stationery he had bought for his father which said *B. T. Chaney* on top and had across the bottom the legend *Widows Tended—Lies Told—Whiskey Hauled.*

Boots Chaney assured me that the bits of newspaper sticking to the ham were the county paper of Hart County—adding to rather than detracting from the ham's authenticity.

"It's not that," I said. "I just know the trouble you go through to get one of these." Then I thought of something. "I'd be grateful to take it," I said.

I hauled the ham back to my motel and phoned Alice in New York. "I've got a gift for you, Alice," I said.

"Oh, how nice," she said. "Is it a surprise?"

"It's a surprise," I said. I had advised the software salesman that it's the little touches like surprise, no-special-occasion gifts that keep the romance in a marriage.

•

I approached Owensboro warily. Barbecue is a touchy subject all over the country. Some of the regional quibbling on the subject can become ferocious, barbecue specialists being united only in the belief that the finest barbecue place in the country is Arthur Bryant's of Kansas City. The only serious question ever raised about Bryant's food turned out, to everyone's relief, to be nothing but a misunderstanding. It came in the summer of 1974. Alice, I remember, had gone back to New York from Nova Scotia for a couple of days that summer, and she returned bearing a copy of *The New York Times Sunday Magazine*. She said the magazine contained some harsh words about Arthur Bryant's. Alice has always been fond of Bryant's, but, perhaps because she was born and raised in the suburbs of New York, I have never completely erased the suspicion in my mind that she might be playing along a bit when it comes to barbecue eating—the way someone who married a maniac trout fisherman might, all things considered, evidence more interest in the intricacies of fly-tying than she really felt. I have, after all, been with her at Bryant's when she stopped eating twenty or thirty minutes before I did, although in fairness I should say that the other people at the table stopped with her. She has been rather resistant to stories about the livestock aspect of Kansas City culture—refusing to believe, for instance, that the cow on top of the American Hereford Association building contains a heart and liver that light up at night. Sometimes, in those low hours we all have if we wake up just before dawn, I wonder if barbecue can really be appreciated by someone who can extract the heart of an artichoke as deftly as Alice can. Mixed marriages are not without their strains.

On this occasion, though, Alice seemed second to none in her loyalty to Arthur Bryant's. She turned to a piece by John and Karen Hess on American restaurants, and read out loud from their report on a visit to Arthur Bryant's: " 'To our taste the ham was very good—' "

"Well, I agree that's a rather bland response," I interrupted. "But Easterners are known for understatement."

" '—the beef poor and greasy, and the famous spareribs edible but dry and disappointing.' "

I was, I admit, taken aback. We knew the Hesses to be serious people of the sort I believe French intellectuals refer to as *premiers fressers*—a distinguished couple who . . . Suddenly I understood what had happened. I immediately sat down and wrote a letter to *The Times Magazine* which read, in part, "At Bryant's, it has always been the custom of the counterman to pick up the ribs in his right hand and toss them on the plate he pulls toward him with his left hand—a motion he has perfected in a career of some twenty-eight years. When the counter was approached by Mr. and Mrs. Hess— a distinguished-looking couple if ever there was one—the counterman obviously was sufficiently awed to serve the ribs with a pair of tongs that are used for special occasions and were last employed, I believe, during a visit to Kansas City in 1937 by Emperor Haile Selassie of Ethiopia. Alas, what everyone in Kansas City knows and someone should certainly have thought to tell Mr. and Mrs. Hess is that the taste of the ribs is partly in the counterman's hand."

•

Even with the matter of supremacy settled to everyone's satisfaction, I knew I could encounter some defensiveness in Owensboro. Americans argue not just about whose barbecue is second-best but even about what barbecue is. In the Southwest, for instance, people ordinarily barbecue ribs, but in North Carolina the word is used as a noun referring only to chopped pork that has been flavored, in a manner of speaking, with a vinegar-based sauce. It is normal for regional loyalists to be both chauvinistic and arcane when talking about the local version. Griffin Smith, who had a distinguished career as Barbecue Editor of *The Texas Monthly*, has, after research that some considered excessive, managed to divide Texas barbecue into sauce and non-sauce categories—the non-sauce people looking down on the sauce types as people who have every reason to disguise the flavor of their meat. I once talked to some North Carolina expatriates in New York about barbecue, after returning from a short visit to their home state, and found myself subjected to stern geographical probings:

"Were you east of Rocky Mount?"

"Is Goldsboro east of Rocky Mount?"

"West. There's no decent barbecue west of Rocky Mount."

"I don't know where Rocky Mount is, but it must be east of all the towns I ate barbecue in."

"I expect so."

Although I assumed that people in Owensboro would be proud of their local version—not just a different sort of pork or a different way of slicing beef but an entirely different animal—it also occurred to me that Owensboro might not want to be proclaimed "Barbecued-Mutton Capital of the World." It's a fairly sophisticated town, after all, with four distilleries, and a General Electric plant that was turning out more than half a million tubes a day before it was struck low by the Japanese transistor, and two colleges, and a river port on the Ohio, and a thirteen-story motel just as perfectly round as a good silo. Baffling as it may seem, there are residents of Cincinnati who are not pleased when I refer to their city as the Center of Greek Chili in Ohio.

In cities the size of Cincinnati and Kansas City, food like barbecue and chili remains an embarrassment to people who want to think of themselves as living in a big-league city that is sophisticated enough to have an array of Continental restaurants modeled on the continent of Antarctica, where everything starts out frozen. A friend of mine who once wandered into Kansas City on the lecture circuit asked his hosts to take him to Arthur Bryant's—expressing at the same time his thankfulness for at last having the opportunity to visit what has been identified as the single greatest restaurant in the world. His hosts refused. They were apparently among those people in Kansas City afflicted with a disease of the American provinces I have managed to isolate and identify as rubaphobia—not the fear of rubes but the fear of being thought of as a rube. Rubaphobiacs would not think of taking someone as important as an itinerant lecturer to a barbecue joint whose main dining room has no decorations beyond an eye chart. (I have always assumed that the eye chart is there to give customers some way of determining when they have had enough of Mr. Bryant's barbecue sauce. It is, at any rate, what a New York designer might call "elegant in its simplicity.") In a city that "boasts," as they always say, so many restaurants advertising Continental cuisine, how can one take an out-of-town visitor to a restaurant that identifies itself as the House of Good Eats? They took him instead to the Arrowhead Club of the Harry S Truman Sports Complex (a football stadium standing next to a baseball stadium, as if the builder couldn't get it right the first time and tried again), where, he has since testified, he ate what the menu described as "a fish of the Pacific waters."

Still, I had some reason to believe that Owensboro would not mind being the Barbecued-Mutton Capital of the World. Rubaphobia is much more prevalent in towns of a half million than in towns of fifty thousand. But it did occur to me that Owensboro might already have a slogan that it would be reluctant to part with.

"No, I think slogans for cities are trite," the executive vice president of the Chamber of Commerce told me. "We don't have one anymore."

"What did the slogan used to be?"

"Opportunity Center of the U.S.A."

"I see what you mean. But you do think that Owensboro is— in fact, if not in slogan—the barbecued-mutton capital of the world?"

"Undoubtedly," he said.

Two hours later Tom Chaney, who had been doing some further checking with specialists from Union County, informed me by telephone from Horse Cave that Waverly, Kentucky, forty-five miles west of Owensboro, might be the barbecued-mutton capital of the world. Not an hour after that, the proprietor of Posh & Pat's, a barbecue place in Henderson, on the way to Waverly, said of Owensboro, "They've got the reputation, we've got the barbecue." Meanwhile, I had been told that the premier barbecue mutton was served by a man named Woolfolk in Cairo, Kentucky, just south of Henderson, but only in the summer. I knew I had come to the right territory.

•

"How come this is the only area where mutton is barbecued?" I asked an Owensboro merchant who had been kind enough to give me change for a nickel parking meter.

"I expect because there are so many Catholics here," he said.

I didn't want to appear ignorant. "Yeah," I said. "I suppose that'd do it."

As I was searching my mind for some connection between the Roman rite and mutton consumption, the merchant told me that the large Catholic churches in town have always staged huge picnics that feature barbecue and burgoo—burgoo, another staple of Owensboro barbecue restaurants, being a soupy stew that I had always associated with southern Illinois. In the early days the church picnics apparently served barbecued goat. In fact, Owensboro might have arrived at barbecued mutton by a process of elimination, since people in the area seem willing to barbecue just about any extant mammal. In western Kentucky, barbecue restaurants normally do "custom cooking" for patrons who have the meat but not the pit, and among the animals that Posh & Pat's offers to barbecue is raccoon. The Shady Nest, one of the most distinguished barbecue joints in Owensboro ("We have people in here from all over," the waitress told me. "We had a Puerto Rican in here once"), has a sign that says, IF IT WILL FIT ON THE PIT, WE WILL BARBECUE IT. It is probably fortunate that people in western Kentucky settled on barbecued mutton as the local delicacy before they had a go at porcupine or boll weevil.

•

I started eating barbecued mutton. I tried the Moonlite, which barbecues eight hundred pounds of mutton a day, and I tried lunch counters that probably don't account for the demise of more than a sheep or two a week. I ate sliced mutton. I ate chopped mutton. I ate mutton ribs. My findings confirmed the natural law that the shape of an object has limited effect on its taste. I liked barbecued mutton, but then, I might have liked barbecued porcupine, Alice's theory being that the taste I truly crave is the taste of hickory-wood smoke.

After only six or eight meals of barbecued mutton, I had prepared the report I would give the first internationally influential eater I ran across. I tried it out on Alice when I called home that night. "They serve barbecued mutton just about every way," I said. "Sliced, chopped, ribs, hidden in burgoo."

"Is it good?" she asked.

"It's not bad at all."

"Just 'not bad at all'?" she said. "You had six or eight meals of it today, and it's just 'not bad at all'?"

"I believe I prefer it to Greek chili," I said. "Also, as far as I know, it is, unlike country ham, not illegal in its most authentic form."

Barbecued mutton is, as the saying goes, not Kansas City, but there are reasons not to apply such standards. In Posh & Pat's, after all, the restaurant gossip going on when I walked in was not about someone's secret sauce formula but about the Burger Farm franchise just down the interstate being replaced by a Wiener King. A local restaurant man who happened to be at Posh & Pat's counter downing a sliced-mutton sandwich said he was thinking of opening a new steak restaurant with an "old depot" décor. "It's all Western or Barn here now," he told me. With the franchisers and the décor-mongers closing in, any authentic local specialty obviously needed celebrating. Did I want a nice river city like Owensboro—a city that, according to my calculations, has a barbecued-mutton restaurant for every 5,188 residents—to be known as the Ex-Tube Capital of the World? Was it fair to serious eaters in Kentucky—the Chaneys, for instance—that foreigners should believe their state to be nothing but a jungle of fast-food franchises like Burger Farm and Wiener King? "Kentucky is the Barbecued-Mutton Capital of the World," I would tell the first eater of influence I could find. "Spread the word."

Not a month later, Tom Eblen, a renowned Kansas City rib eater I happened to be talking to on the telephone, said, "What's this you're spreading about barbecued mutton being unique to western Kentucky?"

"That's right," I said, delighted that the word had reached an authority of Eblen's stature so quickly. "Barbecued-Mutton Capital of the World."

"You know who serves barbecued mutton?" Eblen said. "Arthur Bryant's. They've had it on the menu for years."

I was momentarily stunned. "How would I be expected to know that?" I finally said. "I've never had occasion to look at the menu at Bryant's. I've been ordering the same thing since I was fourteen."

Since my talk with Eblen I have consciously avoided testing Bryant's barbecued mutton. If it is up to Mr. Bryant's usual standards, Kansas City would also be the Barbecued-Mutton Capital of the World, and that hardly seems fair.

(4)

To Market,

to Market

JEFFREY JOWELL, a friend of ours who teaches law at the University of London, likes to go to the Friday morning market at Barnstaple to chat about poultry and eggs. "You say a bit of peat on the floor of the coop?" he will ask a farmer's wife, staring at her with the sort of intent look that law professors must dream of finding on the faces of their students during a lecture. "How very interesting!" I have never missed an opportunity to go to the Barnstaple market with Jeffrey, although it also happens to be true that I have never missed an opportunity to go to any market with anyone at any time. I love weekly markets, even when they do not offer the added attraction of a law professor discussing chicken feed with a vendor of brown eggs. Wandering through the Friday morning market at Barnstaple—poking at fresh tomatoes or bargaining for what is purported to be an antique clipboard or munching on some Farmhouse Cheddar to keep up my strength between stalls—I occasionally pause to wonder why all the other tourists are at Buckingham Palace or the Tower of London. Alice is also enthusiastic about the Barnstaple market, although the suspicion lingers that when she seems to be completely absorbed in selecting peaches she is actually glancing over now and then to make certain that I make no overt attempt to corner the North Devon scone market.

A Friday morning at Barnstaple is definitely enhanced by the opportunity to hear Jeffrey say, "Yes, laying very well at the moment, thanks," to an egg vendor, inspecting the color of her shells rather closely as he speaks. When the university is not in session, Jeffrey and his family live near Exford, a Somerset village about an hour's drive from Barnstaple. During their first summer there, we were informed by letter that Jeffrey, whose interest in husbandry had previously escaped our notice, had finished second in the other-than-white egg division of the Exford and District Flower and Produce Show. Jeffrey did not take the victory lightly, even though, we later learned, the other-than-white egg division of the Exford and District Flower and Produce Show had only three entries. According to the reports we got from England, Jeffrey talked a lot about chickens and he talked a lot to chickens. "Good night, ladies," he would say each evening when he shut his hens into their coop, safe from marauding foxes. "Sleep well, my lovelies." Jeffrey's wife, Francie, even reported that on visits to neighbors in Somerset Jeffrey had taken to cracking eggs he found in the pantry and sneering at their yolks. I wasn't certain whether Francie was joking until we arrived in England for a visit, about a year after Jeffrey had acquired his flock, and noticed on the desk in his study, in the sort of frame some people might use for a picture of their wife and children, a five-by-seven-inch color portrait of Rudolph, his rooster.

We attended the second Exford and District Flower and Produce Show that Jeffrey entered, and I was with him when he learned, to his great dismay, that he had fallen to third place in the other-than-white egg division.

"Look on the bright side," I said, trying to cheer him up. "There were four entries this year, so in a way you did just as well as you did last time—second from last."

Francie offered some token condolences, but she does not like to encourage what she occasionally calls Jeffrey's "obsession." I can't blame her. It was presumably her picture, after all, that was on Jeffrey's desk before Rudolph came along. Also, it must be embarrassing for Francie to be sitting quietly at a neighbor's dinner table when suddenly her husband snatches an egg from the pantry, cracks it into the dish the hostess was planning to use for the custard, and begins a lecture on causes of yolk paleness. Francie has been known to make light of Jeffrey's career in poultry management. She was among those on a panel of Jeffrey's family and friends—a panel on which Alice and I also had the privilege of serving—that, after some informal calculations, priced out the cost of Jeffrey's home-grown, economical eggs at "one pound fifty per egg, plus a hundred points of cholesterol." She has neither confirmed nor denied rumors that she may have been privy to a conspiracy—a conspiracy that Alice and I had the privilege of devising and successfully carrying out—by which some London supermarket eggs were secretly substituted for the freshly gathered eggs that Jeffrey was about to serve his guests as examples of what fresh farm eggs should taste like. (Jeffrey later denied that he had been completely fooled; he has not denied that the next time we arrived in Exford from London all the eggs in his pantry had been marked with his tiny initial.) At some point, Francie began referring to Jeffrey as Chicken George.

These days, of course, there is nothing particularly unusual about a law professor being deeply involved in poultry raising. It wouldn't surprise me, in fact, to find that in some Midwestern university, professors of agricultural science, who were once thought of by the liberal arts faculty as ranking just above phys. ed. majors, are now sought as dinner guests by the chairman of the Philosophy Department, who hopes they might share some of their erudition in the area of soil preparation or slug eradication. Academics have their own way of approaching agriculture: Jeffrey, according to my last count, owns at least fourteen books and several pamphlets on poultry keeping. He has read *Starting Poultry Keeping* and he has read *The Small Commercial Poultry Flock* (Technical Bulletin #198 issued by the Ministry of Agriculture, Fisheries and Food). He sometimes says that the sight of his chickens taking their first tentative steps into the sunlight—they had been kept by their previous owner in cages, and Jeffrey decided to allow them to roam the farm as what the English call "free-range hens"—reminded him of the prisoners' chorus in *Fidelio*, an image I have never heard used by the farmers' wives who sell eggs at the Barnstaple market.

Although professors may reach for an operatic image to describe a barnyard phenomenon, it must be even more common for them to discover that what they had assumed was a metaphor is simply a fact of rural life. My own experience with the agricultural sciences in Nova Scotia is limited to a little experiment I'm carrying out on levels of production in totally neglected apple trees, but I am occasionally astonished anew to find that a neighbor who mentions the need to prime the pump is talking not about tinkering with the free-market economy but about priming the pump. People in Nova Scotia do make hay, and if at all possible, they make it while the sun shines so that it will be dry when they store it in the barn. One day in Nova Scotia Alice came home with the information that one widely used method of improving apple production was to gather up all the windfalls every autumn—gather up not unearned and sudden profit but apples that had been caused by the wind to fall. (I decided against it, on the theory that it was the sort of behavior that could invalidate the results of my experiment.)

"Rudolph, you might say, rules the roost," Jeffrey told me the first time he showed me his flock settling in for the night. Jeffrey also mentions now and then that his flock actually does have a pecking order—one that he can recite, as it happens, since he has given each chicken the name of one of his cousins. Jeffrey's barnyard observations on the matter of pecking order are, of course, buttressed by a certain amount of scholarly research. It is from reading a book—*The Chicken Book*, by Page Smith and Charles Daniel— that he knows that the phenomenon of pecking order was discovered earlier in this century by a Norwegian psychologist named T. Schjelderup-Ebbe. I sent him the book. Jeffrey once mentioned the possibility of commissioning some local potter to fashion eggcups bearing the Clarence Day quotation that it uses as an epigraph— "Oh, who that ever lived and loved can look upon an egg unmoved?"

"You will most certainly not," Francie said at the time. "This obsession has gone far enough."

Francie, I think, might make light of Jeffrey's poultry library except that she has, in addition to a doctorate in the history of art from Harvard, at least twenty-one books on gardening. She has V. *Sackville-West's Garden Book* and she has *Potatoes* (Technical Bulletin #94 issued by the Ministry of Agriculture, Fisheries and Food). She has entered the Exford and District Flower and Produce Show in as many as eleven categories at once, including such exotic competitions as Three Turnips and Four Sticks of Rhubarb. She does not bid her vegetables good night every evening, as far as I know, but I have heard her refer to store-bought provisions as "foreign vegetables" in the same tone of voice some British politicians use these days when referring to immigrants from the Indian subcontinent. In one Exford show, she won first prizes in both Heaviest Marrow and Two Matching Vegetable Marrows—a marrow being what the English call a large squash. Jeffrey occasionally refers to her as the Marrow Queen of Exford.

•

I have always been partial to market people. In England the difference between market people and shopkeepers is particularly pronounced. The grocers in Exford or Dunster or Taunton or Barnstaple strike me as the sort of correct English shopkeepers who find their greatest fulfillment in telling the customer who wants bread, "The bread's finished," and informing the customer who asks for bacon, "We don't do bacon, thank you very much." The people behind the tables that are lined up every Friday morning at Barnstaple may be rather quiet by the standards of, say, the Italian fruit-and-vegetable peddlers who appear at the Haymarket in the North End of Boston every Friday and Saturday, but compared to most English shopkeepers, they take a positively overt pleasure in selling their wares. In Barnstaple on Friday mornings, Jeffrey is not called Mr. Jowell by the vendors but "my dear" or "my love." Informal, even intimate address is the norm at markets everywhere; I suspect that the only female customers not addressed as "honey" by vendors in the Haymarket are those wearing nun's habits. Once, when Alice and I were moving slowly with a Saturday jam of people in the Haymarket, a man who looked to be in his late seventies stepped forward, kissed Alice warmly on both cheeks, and said in a heavy Italian accent, "I would like to bring you home to meet my mother."

As much as I like the atmosphere at markets, I go mainly for the food. In the United States these days, some people shop at a market on the theory that it represents their only hope of coming across fruit and vegetables that have not been bred by the agribusiness Frankensteins to have a shelf life approximately that of a mop handle. They hope, for instance, to find a tomato that does not have a bright-red skin so hard that anyone who wanted to indulge in the old-fashioned American pleasure of slinging it at a windy political stump speaker would risk being arrested for assault with intent to kill. By the time American consumers began to take serious notice of such matters, of course, 90 percent of the broilers available in grocery stores were already being produced by agribusiness corporations that had discovered the cost-effectiveness of vertical integration. The English who are always chastising themselves these days for economic stagnation and failure to adopt modern management practices fail to realize that what they have avoided is the vertical integration of the broiler industry.

A lot of vegetables sold at the Barnstaple market taste more like vegetables than shelf displays simply because they are the product of a kitchen garden rather than an assembly line. Although there are stalls at the market that sell great quantities of fruit and vegetables acquired from wholesalers, it is not unusual to come across a farmer's wife standing behind a table that holds, say, three dozen eggs, one chicken, three bunches of carrots, some beetroot, five turnips, six baby cabbages, a bunch of rhubarb, one marrow, a jar of apple chutney, and a jar of quince jelly. Barnstaple does not have the sort of customers who demand to know whether a cucumber or a radish has been grown under conditions the Natural Food Fanatics would consider "organic," but some of the eggs at the market carry prominent signs labeling them "free range." In England, consciousness of free-range eggs extends from vendors at provincial markets to gourmet stores in Knightsbridge that label eggs "free range" and leave enough grit and hay sticking to them to support the claim. A preference for free-range eggs is based partly on the theory that a chicken that spends its life roaming around a barnyard instead of being crammed into the wire cages used for what are called battery or factory or deep-litter hens is a healthier fowl that is likely to produce a better egg. But in England, where concern for dumb animals is so acute that there may well be people willing to picket beekeepers for keeping their bees in crowded conditions, part of the steam of the Free Range egg movement comes from groups with names like Chicken Lib—groups that object to hens leading a "thoroughly miserable existence." According to the brochure of an organization called Compassion in World Farming, factory farm animals "degrade the sensibilities of all who work with them," while free-range animals "through their active self-expression . . . make a valuable contribution to the countryside scene."

"Oh, you mustn't coop them up," an egg vendor at Barnstaple once told us. "With free-range hens the yolks are that much richer altogether."

"My first hens had been deep-litter hens, and I set them free," Jeffrey told her. She nodded and smiled. Jeffrey beamed. The emancipator.

•

The last time we were in Somerset, Jeffrey and Alice and I went to Barnstaple early on Friday morning for the market, leaving Francie home to tend her marrows. Francie asked us to be a restraining influence on Jeffrey, who had apparently gone off to a supermarket to do some marketing not long before and, seized by the zeal that foodstuffs bring out in him, had managed to spend seventy pounds on groceries—mumbling, in response to Francie's chastisement, something about the difficulty of coping with an inflationary economy. Jeffrey said he was interested in arranging to buy two or three chicks at the market if he could find a farmer's wife whose egg display met his standards. I didn't even have that excuse. I was interested in acquiring whatever I could to eat. I have never been to an open market that did not have something remarkable to eat. I believe it is fair to say that the West Country of England is not internationally renowned for its food, but I have always found marvelous food at the Barnstaple market—hardcakes baked by members of the Women's Institute, for instance, or a marrow we once came across that is known locally as spaghetti squash, or runner-bean chutney, or some liver dumplings called faggots, or a regional delicacy called, indelicately, hog's pudding.

Alice's response to her first look at hog's pudding had not been encouraging. "This happens to be a regional delicacy, Alice," I said. "If we don't at least try it, Jeffrey might be hurt. You know how sensitive he is."

Alice fried the hog's pudding to a crisp crust, the same way she treats country scrapple we bring back from Pennsylvania. Even she acknowledged that the results were magnificent. I like a person who can admit she was wrong, I told Alice, particularly if that person can also cook scrapple.

As Jeffrey searched for a trustworthy purveyor of chicks that Friday morning, I wandered from booth to booth with a large market basket under my arm. Jeffrey was putting a few things in a market basket himself, and Alice volunteered to make a detailed inspection of the fish and meat available in a line of shops across from the market known as Butcher's Row. We had thought we were just picking up a few odds and ends, but when we returned to Exford and unpacked our market baskets in the Jowells' kitchen—carefully observed by Francie, who was presumably guarding against infiltration by foreign vegetables—we found that we had three jars of honey, one jar of raspberry jam, two cabbages, a jar of pickled onions, some Cheshire and Caerphilly and Cheddar cheese, a half-dozen honey lollipops, a carton of raspberries, a carton of blackberries, a bunch of bananas, a jar of tomato relish, an astounding number of shortbread cookies, a package of clotted cream, some bread pudding, a few tomatoes, a pound of hog's pudding, a pound of sunflower nuts, some extra-fruit strawberry jam, a lemon cheesecake, a half-dozen rock cakes, some fresh salmon, some fresh haddock, a cooked crab, six scones, a jar of runner-bean chutney, a jar of loganberry jam, one melon, a second jar of raspberry jam, three toy horses, one toy car, a jar of olive oil, a bunch of grapes, some sunflower oil, some wine vinegar, a pineapple cheesecake, even more rock cakes, three kippers, two smoked mackerels, a knitted hat, two hundred-weights of chicken feed, a few lemons, and half a faggot—another faggot and a half having been consumed in the heat of shopping.

Francie looked at Jeffrey and then at me. "Alice was the one who bought the salmon," I said weakly.

"Well," Jeffrey said. "We needed everything."

"Yes, I suppose so," Francie said. "We couldn't have lasted another day without those sunflower nuts."

•

Alice and I went back to Barnstaple with Jeffrey the following Friday so that he could pick up his chicks and I could replenish my hog's pudding supply—perhaps picking up some more Cheddar and another jar or two of runner-bean chutney as long as I was in the neighborhood. At one of the stalls three chicks, in a pasteboard box, were waiting for Jeffrey. On the ride back to Exford, his only two concerns about them were that they might be cocks rather than pullets and that they might not be chickens of any kind. They were odd-looking little gray birds that were supposedly of the Maran variety of chicken but suggested to the untrained eye—the kind of eye Jeffrey happens to have—baby hawks, or perhaps vultures.

"Determining the sex of chicks has only been successfully done on a regular basis by the Koreans," Jeffrey said, apparently having pulled that fact out of *National Poultry Management* or *The Complete Poultry Keeper and Farmer.*

"I don't suppose you're going to be able to find any Koreans in Exford," I said. "Maybe in Taunton."

"Well, they're lovely little chicks anyway," Jeffrey said. I gathered from his remarks that he had decided to assume that the predatory-looking creatures in the back of the car were in fact chickens.

He slowed in the traffic leaving Barnstaple and pointed toward a car in front of us that was towing a trailer containing a calf. "That's my next venture," he said.

"Does Francie know about this?" Alice asked.

"Lovely thing, that," Jeffrey continued. "Lovely. I once fell in love with a Jersey cow at the Dunster Show."

Fly Frills to Miami

MY DECISION TO TAKE a rather elegant picnic along on my no-frills flight to Miami was solidly based on a theory of economics known as Alice's Law of Compensatory Cashflow, which holds that any money not spent on a luxury one considered even briefly is the equivalent of windfall income and should be spent accordingly. If you decide, for instance, that buying a five-hundred-dollar color television set would be, all things considered, an act of lunacy and the final step toward complete financial collapse, you have an extra five hundred dollars that you "saved" on the television set available to spend on something else.

I'll admit that for several years I had some difficulty grasping the fine points of Alice's Law of Compensatory Cashflow. Alice would say something like "We have that five hundred dollars we saved on the television set," and I would nod quietly, meanwhile patting various pockets in a desperate effort to find it. I was not surprised at my difficulty in catching on. My own grasp of economics and finance is so tenuous that the fantasy I have during those blank moments aboard airplanes—when the plastics salesman sitting next to me is probably having a fantasy about being pursued by a sex-starved gang of Hollywood starlets who won't take no for an answer—is that all of our family's financial transactions are handled by a first cousin I have invented, a mildly wonky but lovable financial wizard named Harvey. In my fantasies, Harvey comes over to the house now and then for dinner when we are having one of his favorites—shad roe, maybe, or blintzes donated by Alice's Aunt Sadie. He always brings Alice flowers, smiling his awkward, wonky smile when he hands them to her. Abigail loves the nonsense poems Cousin Harvey recites to her. He is patiently trying to teach Sarah to wiggle her left ear. Dinner conversation is mainly remembering old times in Kansas City—like the time my sister, Sukey, one of Harvey's favorites, tried to toss me down the laundry chute. At some point, though, Harvey may say something like "By the way, bubbele"—he has always called me bubbele—"we prepaid your New York State quarterly to take advantage of the shelter you got when we took you out of ball bearings and put you into frozen pork bellies and took care of the American Express bill you forgot to pay."

"Fine, Harv," I always say, idly. "Would you mind passing the sour cream?"

•

I began to understand the advantages of Alice's Law of Compensatory Cashflow rather suddenly one day when I realized that saving thirty-three dollars over coach fare or seventy-one dollars over first class by doing without the affliction of an airline meal on no-frills service called for spending at least thirty-three dollars and perhaps seventy-one dollars on a decent picnic lunch to see me through the flight.

"Just because you saved thirty-three dollars doesn't mean you necessarily have to spend it on food," Alice said.

"Every theory needs a corollary," I told her.

Having absorbed Alice's Law at last, I climbed on board a flight to Miami carrying, among other necessities, a small jar of fresh caviar, some smoked salmon I had picked up at a "custom smokery" in Seattle the week before, crudités with pesto dipping sauce, tomato-curry soup, butterfish with shrimp en gelée, spiced clams, lime and dill shrimp, tomatoes stuffed with guacamole, marinated mussels, an assortment of pâté, stuffed cold breast of veal, a bottle of Puligny-Montrachet, a selection of chocolate cakes, some praline cheesecake, and a dessert made from Italian cheese-in-the-basket and fresh strawberries and Grand Marnier by Alice—that rare example of an economic theorist who can also cook.

I am not among those people who have difficulty eating on airplanes because of anxieties connected with flying. As someone who travels constantly in the course of business, I naturally have no fears or superstitions brought on by being in an airplane; years ago, I discovered that I could keep the plane I was flying on from crashing by refusing to adjust my watch to the new time zone until we were on the ground, and I have used that method ever since. My only anxiety while flying off somewhere in an airplane has to do with being able to find the airport for the flight back. In a lot of American cities, the location of the airport is the final municipal secret. A traveling salesman who starts out in his rental car toward the airport, dreading the time he will have to spend in a place so purposefully designed to make human beings miserable, can take some perverse comfort in the fact that he probably won't be able to find it anyway. Occasionally, sitting in an airplane that is taking me to one city or another, I begin to have visions of what I will go through in a few days trying to get back—desperately steering my rental car in what I judge by the sun to be the right direction, switching lanes suddenly to ask guidance from a policeman who turns out to be a deaf-mute, taking dangerously sudden turns onto thruways that lead to interchanges with other thruways that eventually end abruptly at Vista Vue Estates, model home open. Will the Bob Blakely Field referred to in the sign with an arrow pointing to the right but too close to the intersection to make a turn possible be the type of field from which airplanes take off—the city airport, perhaps—or the type of field upon which nine-year-old boys try to strike each other out for the glory of their parents? Could it really be that a road-sign symbol that looks like an airplane is being used to guide travelers to the municipal water-treatment plant? In a just world, any city that did not clearly mark the way to its airport would automatically lose its major-league franchise.

Kansas City used to have an airport that was practically walking distance from downtown. Then a gang of rubaphobiacs—the sort of people who would sooner lose the fire department than the major-league franchise; the same people who hired a New York public-relations firm to persuade everyone that Kansas City was a "cow town no longer"—decided that what a "glamour city" like Kansas City could not do without was a $250 million "international airport." The city council annexed some land that seemed to be more appropriate for a suburb of Omaha—the city council's policy on accumulation of noncontiguous land having been inherited intact from the British Colonial Office of 1843—and the old airport quickly became part of our shameful cow-town past. I was outraged. I loved the old airport. I liked the name, Kansas City Municipal, which sounded like the sort of tax-free bond Cousin Harvey talks about now and then. I liked the approach over downtown Kansas City. Mostly, I loved landing so close to town that a native son who had a twenty-minute stopover before returning to the East could be met by a relief column bearing real barbecued ribs, still warm from their exposure to an authentic hickory-wood fire.

Driven to extremes by thoughts of how many pounds of Arthur Bryant's barbecue I would be deprived of over the years, I pointed out, in public print, that Kansas City International did not happen to have any flights that took off from its runways and landed on foreign soil. It was a spiteful revelation, and I regretted it almost immediately. Who wants to be in the position of knocking his own hometown—particularly such a splendid hometown, a hometown virtually flawless except for the presence of a few people who want to turn it into a bad imitation of Houston? Who wants to reveal that his own hometown lacks the savvy to cover itself in such a situation by bribing some place like Matamoros to take a flight or two? The people who so dread the thought of living in a cow town, I realized, are actually as fond of Kansas City as I am, in their own warped way. I finally even realized what they hated about the old airport: the landing approach I loved exposed the stockyard cattle pens and the cow on the top of the American Hereford Association—not to mention a line of grain elevators and a World War I monument that, by the purest chance, happens to look like a grain elevator—to any sneering sales representative from New Jersey who happened to have a window seat. I suppose the rubaphobiacs love Kansas City, but mostly they just hate cows.

•

What usually keeps me from eating on an airplane is not anxiety but the food I'm served. I cannot say I have never had a good meal off the ground. Once, just before we left New Orleans, Alice had the inspired idea of stopping at Buster Holmes's restaurant, on Burgundy Street, to pick up some garlic chicken for the flight. It occurred to me that while we were about it we might as well stop at the Acme for an oyster loaf—a half-dozen succulent oysters freshly fried and installed in buttered French bread.

"Aren't you always saying that oyster loaves won't travel more than twenty yards from the kitchen?" Alice said. "They would be awful on the plane."

"Who's talking about the plane?" I said. "Have you given any thought to what we're going to eat on the way to the airport?" Every theory needs a corollary.

Buster's chicken had been, as usual, a triumph, but a picnic as elaborate as the one I had prepared for my flight to Miami was a new departure in air-travel eating for me. I'll admit that I took some steps to conceal my treasures from my fellow passengers. I think I am as generous as the next person about sharing certain kinds of food: if trapped by an avalanche in a mountain shack, I'm sure I would split my last few pieces of, say, packaged white bread or institutional roast beef with my fellow trappees, figuring that a natural disaster was always a good opportunity to take off a pound or two. I had, however, taken pains not to include in my no-frills picnic any of the type of food I would share. For that reason I planned to carry it in a squat briefcase once given to me by a part-time peddler of home-improvement business courses—a briefcase that has always caused people on subway platforms to edge away from me, as if I were about to whip out an *Encyclopedia Americana* and tell them that they owed their children a home filled with culture and learning, suitably bound. As it turned out, though, my eyes were bigger than my briefcase. By the time everything was packed, I found myself carrying a sort of annex to the briefcase in the form of a large shopping bag from my purveyor of caviar (and, on simpler occasions, of chopped herring and smoked salmon), Russ

& Daughters—casually trying to keep my newspaper over the part of the bag that carried Russ's irresistible motto, "Queens of Lake Sturgeon."

I need not have bothered. Even when I offered the man sitting behind me some caviar—an uncharacteristic gesture prompted by his loan of a nail clipper to pry open the caviar jar—he declined. The woman in the aisle seat across from mine gazed longingly at my marinated mushrooms, but only shook her head nervously when I offered her one. I finally realized that my fellow passengers— chewing away at what people unfamiliar with Alice's Law would think of as a sensible lunch of, say, a chicken sandwich and a Tab—assumed they were in the presence of a maniac, a man who might get a kick out of slipping giggle powder into some spiced clams before he offered them to an innocent traveler. While I was eating my caviar and smoked-salmon course, the woman sitting at the window two seats away from me—the seat between us being empty except for two cartons of my food—glanced over now and then with a suspicious but not unfriendly look, the way someone might look at the fellow at the Fourth of July picnic who insists, after a few beers, that everyone form a pyramid on the table he has balanced on his stomach.

She turned out to be a good-humored lady named Mrs. Eve Infeld, who, after attending to some family business in New York, was returning to Miami Beach, where her husband was semiretired in the garment game. She did not speak to me until we became co-conspirators—the stewardess's reminder about a regulation against drinking out of one's own bottle on an airliner having forced me, after some token resistance ("Are you sure that rule is meant to apply to Puligny-Montrachet?"), to secrete the bottle between my briefcase and Mrs. Infeld's shopping bag. I had to fill my glass covertly whenever the stewardess was busy supplying coach passengers forward with balsa-wood rolls, and some gray meat that resembled cardboard left out in the rain, and whatever other delicacies they were getting for their thirty-three dollars. Mrs. Infeld could hardly help noticing my extralegal boozing, but she observed the ancient code of *omertà*.

"Do you always eat so lavish?" she finally asked me.

"Only on no-frills," I said, explaining to the best of my ability Alice's Law of Compensatory Cashflow.

"If you spent all that money on food, why didn't you go first class?" Mrs. Infeld asked.

"Because the food's no good in first class," I said.

"You're right," she said.

Mrs. Infeld seemed less suspicious after that, but a few minutes later, while I was attacking a salad of roasted peppers and eggplant that I had snared the previous evening from a restaurant in our neighborhood called Tito's, she fixed me with an accusing look and said, "You must be a gourmet eater."

I denied it, of course. The accusation made me realize, though, that I was carrying some pretty *haute* eats for a Midwestern traveling man. I explained to Mrs. Infeld that my picnic had been gathered partly by my wife, an Eastern sophisticate who knew that arugala was not a folk dance and could poach a salmon in some secret way that made it taste as good as barbecued ribs. I also pointed out that except for a mix-up the main course of my picnic would have been some cold fried chicken from the Pink Teacup—the no-frills café in our neighborhood whose way with a plate of grits had made it the site of the celebratory breakfast on the morning my younger daughter was born. How could she make such an accusation, I asked, about someone who was planning to eat, as the main course of his dessert course, a delicacy that is called a Keen's Special in our neighborhood and can only be described as the final chocolate-chip cookie?

I do think Mrs. Infeld and I gradually became allies of sorts, although all I could persuade her to share with me was something that both she and I took for a deviled egg but turned out to be what a wildcat East Village caterer named Montana Palace describes, quite accurately, as "eggs stuffed with shrimp and horseradish." I don't mean she was without criticism. When I got out Montana Palace's pesto sauce and started shoveling it onto some celery, she said, "Listen, with that garlic, they're going to throw you off the plane." And she did not, I think it's fair to say, have a natural community of interest with someone who ate tomatoes stuffed with minted mussels out of a business-course briefcase. ("If you put an egg salad sandwich in front of my husband, he's happy," she said, as I was eating some pistachio pâté.) But she did not turn me in for flouting the authority of the Federal Aviation Administration, or whichever agency it is that forbids freelance liquor on high, and she did, after all, accept from me an egg stuffed with shrimp and horseradish.

As we began our descent into Miami, I was feeling a bit like an egg stuffed with horseradish myself. I had been eating pretty steadily for an hour and a half. By prorating furiously in my head, I calculated that I had spent several dollars less on the trip than the coach passengers who were sitting only a row or two away, still looking dispirited from memories of the enlisted men's mess-hall rations they had suffered at the hands of the airline. I felt a bit guilty about that, so I had another piece of chocolate cake to revive my spirits.

Mrs. Infeld was telling me that her friends would never believe her. "I want you to know I had a very interesting trip," she said when we touched down. "Usually it's boring, but it wasn't boring."

"Thank you, Mrs. Infeld," I said. "It really is amazing how time passes when you keep busy."

(6)

Mao and Me

AS LONG AS I HAVE DECIDED to go along with the literary fashion of Total Disclosure, I might as well admit that my Cousin Harvey fantasy is not the only fantasy I have. For years, I have had the recurring fantasy that Mao Tse-tung makes an official visit to the United States and I am asked by the State Department to take him eating for a week in New York. The fantasy was not altered in the least by news of Mao's death. For a while, I did consider changing to the new leaders, but that possibility melted away within a few weeks of their ascension. They simply didn't strike me as either hearty eaters or cheerful dining companions; they reminded me of the dour Kremlin crowd that took over from Khrushchev and then bad-mouthed him for "phrasemongering" and other qualities I admired. I decided that for the purposes of my fantasy I would not recognize Mao's death. That sort of thing is permitted in fantasies; Abigail and Sarah do it all the time.

Even before Mao died, I had one sticking point in my fantasy. Why would the State Department choose me instead of one of the people Alice persists in calling "grown-up food writers"? I have no influence in the State Department. Just about everyone I have ever known who entered the Foreign Service seems to have been sent immediately to Ouagadougou, Upper Volta, which, as I understand it, is not where Foreign Service officers want to be sent. Why wouldn't the wise heads at State ask, say, Craig Claiborne or Mimi

Sheraton to show the Chairman around? Claiborne has co-authored a cookbook of Chinese recipes, so he might even be able to speak a couple of words of Mandarin to Chairman Mao—at least if the couple of words the Chairman wanted to hear happened to be words like "bamboo shoots" or "black mushrooms" or "hot and spicy."

Finally, after staring out of a lot of airplane windows with Mao on my mind, I invented a satisfactory reason for my receiving the assignment—an invention that permitted me to continue to what might be called the meat of the fantasy. I was specifically requested by the political officer of the Chinese delegation to the United Nations. He found me ideologically appealing. After some research, he had been able to ascertain that I was an enthusiast rather than an expert—"glutton" is a word that has occasionally been used by the unkind—and therefore a fine choice for anyone wanting to avoid the crimes of elitism or careerism or professionalism. The Chinese Cultural Revolution happens to be raging during my fantasy, and what, after all, would one call a teenage Red Guard who took over the directorship of a medical school during that period except an enthusiast rather than an expert? Asking someone like Mimi Sheraton to be the guide merely because she may know something about the subject would have made no more sense than having the former director of the medical school perform an operation merely because he happened to be a surgeon. The political officer asks the State Department for me, by name and address, adding, in slightly inexact English, "The Chairman sees with pleasure toward meeting that folk type which people in your Medium Western states are sometimes saying as a big hungry boy."

Alice is, of course, appalled. The power of a fantasizer to control the fantasy may extend to reincarnating the Chairman of the Central Committee of the Communist Party of the People's Republic of China, but it falls short of being able to alter Alice's inevitable reaction to my plans for some serious eating. In my fantasy Alice had, just before the word from State came through, prevailed upon me to start a diet for which I have sworn unswerving allegiance to a peck of carrots.

"But you promised to lose ten pounds," she says, when I inform her that I've received the call.

"I wish I could keep that promise, but my country comes before any personal considerations," I say. "Think of all those people who have gone off to Ouagadougou with hardly a murmur of complaint."

"I'm afraid you're going to start looking more and more like the Chairman yourself."

"A man must do what he must do," I say.

Alice pauses for a while. "You know that Mao is the one who started calling your friend Khrushchev a phrasemonger," she finally says. This, I realize, is what the marriage counselors mean by "playing dirty." I am silent. "It was Mao who said Khrushchev was in a 'revisionist quagmire,' " Alice continues.

"The people from State asked me not to talk politics," I say.

•

My Chairman Mao fantasy has to do not just with tossing aside a diet but with an old dream I have had about being able to eat a favorite dish in one restaurant and then dash off (by limousine with diplomatic license plates, if at all possible) for another favorite dish in another restaurant. It is a dining method I have always been embarrassed to employ without having the excuse of shepherding around a visiting head of state who has to sample many American dishes in the short time his busy schedule allots him. I did engage in a sort of trial run once, on a very small scale. While some friends were visiting us one day, it was decided that a friend I'll call Jones and I should pick up some food in Chinatown and bring it back to the assembled eaters. I no longer remember why we all didn't just go to Chinatown for dinner; perhaps the city was locked in a bagel bakers' strike, making it impossible for Sarah to enter a Chinese restaurant.

On the way to Chinatown it occurred to me that there was no reason to get everything at the same restaurant. We could park the car in a strategic spot, then separate and hit two or three restaurants apiece, picking up a favorite dish in each place. In my heart of hearts, of course, I have always believed that what may actually be my favorite dish in a number of Chinatown restaurants is something I have never even had the opportunity to taste, simply because of my inability to read the wall signs that announce some house specialties in Chinese. Sometime ago—many years, I should say, before such intimate family disclosures became the rage—I revealed publicly that Alice and I had been through a family disagreement concerning the signs, Alice having arbitrarily dismissed a reasonable and politely worded request that she assign some Chinese immigrant students in a class she was teaching at City College to translate the signs as a way of polishing up their English. Even without the secret dishes, though, Jones and I faced an opportunity to snatch up a spectacular variety of food within easy running distance of where we parked the car. If we planned our operation with the precision of an exquisitely plotted guerrilla raid, we could even arrive home with our booty still hot. "I don't think the flounder Fukienese-style from Foo Joy will travel, so I'll grab the cold spiced kidney from Chef Ma's while you're getting the eggplant with garlic from Szechuan Cuisine," I told Jones. I hated to give up the flounder—some texture specialists of my acquaintance have rated it "80 percent crunch"—but in these sorts of operations losses have to be cut ruthlessly and decisions made with no hesitation. If someone paused to bemoan the fact that green fish from Say Eng Look or pork dumplings from one of the *dim sum* houses might not make it from Chinatown to the Village in good order, he could ruin the entire operation. Ten minutes after Jones and I had fanned out—if two people can be said to have fanned—we were back in the car, loaded with specialties. We had taken no losses except for a slight bruise I acquired when I knocked over an elderly lady while escaping from Phoenix Garden with the Pepper and Salty Shrimp. The operation was, in other words, a remarkable success. I think it would have gone even better if Jones had not, for reasons I can't imagine, declined to make a map of the strike zone and synchronize our watches.

•

"I suppose your duty to your country requires you to spend a long Saturday evening with the Chairman at the Parkway," Alice is saying, with a touch of sarcasm that many people might consider inappropriate to inquiries about an act of patriotism. In my fantasy the Parkway, one of the last of the Romanian-Jewish restaurants in New York, is still on Allen Street, on the Lower East Side; actually, it closed and then reopened again in the Forties, but my fantasies have never worked well in midtown. Alice always said she was fond of the Parkway, but I sometimes thought I caught an undercurrent of disapproval—another hint that agents of the Balanced Diet Conspiracy may have been sneaking over to lobby with her whenever I left town. There is no question that Romanian-Jewish food is heavy. At the Parkway, a dispenser of schmaltz (liquid chicken fat) is kept on the table for those who want to improve on the chef's excesses. Following the Romanian tradition, garlic is used in excess to keep the vampires away; if the vampires get through the garlic defense, they're hit with heartburn from the garlic. The standard line about Romanian-Jewish cooking is usually credited to Zero Mostel, a great fan of the Parkway: "It's killed more Jews than Hitler."

"I've decided that the Parkway would not be appropriate," I say, in a tone of voice that makes it clear that sacrificing my own desires for the good of my country is for me an everyday occurrence. I have decided that during the Chairman's visit I will forgo places that would require him to stay for a full meal in order to savor an atmosphere that is an important part of the experience. It would have been impossible just to dash into the old Parkway on a Saturday night, wolf down a plate of chopped liver with schmaltz and chopped onion and chopped radish and greven (cracklings from rendered chicken fat), and then dash out again. What if the strolling accordion player happened to be playing *"Hava Nagilah"* and everyone in the restaurant felt like joining in? What if Teddy Southard, known to some regulars as "the *goyishe* waiter," had just reached the most dramatic verse of "If I Loved You," which he was singing while standing in the middle of the dining room holding an armful of dirty dishes? The *goyishe* waiter got his sobriquet because of being so relentlessly gentile that at the Parkway he stood out like John V. Lindsay at the dedication of a Hasidic synagogue. The G.W.'s real ambition, of course, was to be an actor, and if he had ever made it he would have undoubtedly been typecast as a sophisticate. At the Parkway he would set a huge bowl of mashed potatoes on the table, hold the schmaltz above them in one hand and the greven in the other, and say, in the tone and diction George Sanders might have used while holding a cognac bottle above the empty glass of a dinner guest, "May I?" The Parkway used to have another singing waiter, Murray Kaye, but he never started a song while he was holding dishes; he needed both hands to sing. He sometimes referred to himself as "the last of the belt-'em-out singers." I knew that the Chairman might enjoy meeting Murray and exchanging some show-biz stories, and he would certainly have liked to meet the chef of the Parkway in those days—a Puerto Rican named Florentino Salas, who, when asked once if it had been difficult for a Puerto Rican to master Romanian-Jewish cooking, said, "I learned from a colored fella who was here." But, knowing that stopping at the Parkway meant stopping for the entire evening, I reluctantly cut it from my list. What a man entrusted with the appetite of Chairman Mao needs, I explain to Alice, is restraint.

"In that case," she says, "they may end up with Craig Claiborne or Mimi Sheraton after all."

·

The Chairman has arrived. Instead of just having his chauffeur honk the limousine horn for me, he has come in to meet the entire family. Alice mumbles something to him about the role of healthy nutritional habits in building a revolutionary society, and he smiles politely. Cousin Harvey offers to put him into Costa Rican soybeans on the ground floor. Sarah, despite our entreaties, has insisted on holding a bagel while the Chairman is in the house, but he appears not to notice. "Well," I finally say cheerfully, "it's Brooklyn night tonight, Mr. Chairman." Off we go in his limousine to gobble down a Brooklyn dish here and a Brooklyn dish there.

Fifteen minutes later the limousine has pulled to a stop in front of Gage & Tollner—that testimony, in a city full of mad-dog restaurant discoverers, to the pleasures of a thoroughly discovered restaurant. "Just the soft-clam-belly appetizers here, Mr. Chairman," I say—just the bellies of succulent clams (their necks and tails having presumably been donated to The New York Times Hundred Neediest Cases), barely floured and broiled in butter. Almost before the waiter realizes that he has served the Chairman of the Central Committee of the Communist Party of the People's Republic of China—almost, in fact, before I have a chance to ask if it might be possible to get a bowl of Duxbury Stew to go—we are off to pick up some French fries at the original Coney Island Nathan's and stop for a steak at Peter Luger's. (Alice, having completely lost her aloofness in all the excitement of meeting the Chairman, had shouted out the window as we were leaving, "Remember—foreigners love steak!") The Chairman is still nodding his pleasure at Peter Luger's tomato-and-onion salad as I lead him to the limousine that will take us to Junior's for cheesecake.

The Mao fantasy often returns, I find, when I'm doing something like standing in the kitchen munching a raw zucchini, trying to concentrate on calculating whether the difference in taste between honey-vanilla yogurt and plain yogurt is worth the difference in calories. My mind starts to wander, and I find myself putting together a peripatetic meal for the Chairman and me. We are dashing around town for Italian food—stopping in Little Italy at one place for the roast-pepper appetizer and at another for fried mixed vegetables. We cut up to the Village for pasta—splitting first some *paglia e fieno* ("No, no, the larger portion is for you, Mr. Chairman—you're the guest") and then some of Tito's cannelloni stuffed with cornmeal ("Well, thanks, Mr. Chairman—maybe just another spoonful or two"). Then we head uptown to let one of the running dogs of imperialism who operate the fancy Italian places set some veal before us (side dish of escarole for me, thanks very much) before we head right back downtown to Grand Street for a cup of cappuccino and a selection of Italian pastries. While I am enjoying a particularly delicious *sfogliatelle*, the Chairman's interpreter asks the waiter for a dish of plain yogurt, and the resulting ridicule forces him to wait for us in the car.

Sometimes I don't bother to organize the meal by borough or type of food; particularly when I'm in one of my raw-vegetable periods, I daydream of random dishes that have nothing in common except how much better they taste than celery. The Chairman and I stroll through the Village to the Coach House for some black bean soup—they are sticky about whether a Mao jacket is the equivalent of a coat and tie until I point out, "This is not just a Mao jacket, this is Mao"—and then rush up to Harlem to have Suzy-Q potatoes at Thomforde's. I tell the driver that he might as well take First

Avenue up to Harlem so that we can stop on the way to pick up a few hedges against starving in the car—a stop at Kurowycky's butcher shop for Polish meatloaf, maybe, and a stop at the Foccaceria, which serves what some people I know call "the best spleen sandwich in the Borough of Manhattan."

"It would be out of the way to take First Avenue to Harlem," the driver says, in more or less the same tone Alice used to point out that Mrs. Palladino's restaurant was not on the way to the rain forest.

The Chairman gives him a look that has promises of fourteen years in a re-education camp in Yunnan, and we head up First Avenue. The Chairman loves these eclectic meals. "Let a thousand dishes be served," he says.

When it is all over, Chairman Mao is exceedingly grateful, as well as a few pounds heavier. As a going-away gift, I tell him that if he drives to LaGuardia by the Williamsburg Bridge/Brooklyn-Queens Expressway route, he practically has to pass Russ & Daughters, the appetizer store of my dreams. That means he can supply himself with some Nova Scotia salmon and a pound or two of chopped herring and maybe a nice piece whitefish, then drop into Moishe's Bakery, a couple of doors away, for the kind of pumpernickel bagels not ordinarily available in Peking, and then double back to Ben's Dairy, between Russ's and Moishe's, where he can buy a baked farmer cheese with scallions that, reheated in the People's Republic, would make him think fondly of America even if, in an idle moment, our government decided to invade.

He wants to give me the Order of the People's Struggle against Reactionary Landlords, or some such. I decline, modestly. He offers me a smallish province, internationally famous for its dumplings. I tell him no reward is necessary, the pleasure having been all mine. He insists on doing something to repay me. "Well," I finally say, "if you could just lend me your interpreter for one afternoon, Mr. Chairman. There are certain wall signs in some restaurants in Chinatown I happen to be very interested in."

(7)

Confessions

of a Crab Eater

WHEN I READ IN *The New York Times* one winter that Dungeness crabs were being caught in California almost faster than they could be eaten, I didn't rush right out there the way some crazed Wedgwood collector might have dashed off to London when the pound dropped to $1.75. I did manage, though, to make it to the West Coast on business well before the end of the season. I try to show some restraint and still get plenty to eat. On the plane to California the seat next to me—the seat I might ordinarily expect to find occupied by a regional sales manager or an itinerant shopping-center developer—was occupied instead by my own wife, Alice, who was chattering away about how beautiful the coast of Northern California must be when all the wildflowers bloom in the spring. Alice's business in California, as far as I could gather from the conversation, was to shoot me full of scenery propaganda while I was trying my best to get something decent to eat.

Someone who has a serious interest in eating Dungeness crabs cannot dally indefinitely on the East Coast; the Dungeness is a West Coast creature, named for a small town in Washington. Even on the West Coast, someone who wants to eat a Dungeness crab that was alive and crawling twenty minutes before the meal has his work cut out for him. On either coast of the United States, a lot of fish seem to leap out of the sea straight into a flash freezer. Even fish restaurants on harbors often seem to have chosen the spot more for the ambiance than the source of supply—the fish caught in the picturesque bay visible through the fishnet-covered windows having apparently found their way by truck to Boston, where they were frozen and sent back, without unseemly haste. For a long time I have had the suspicion that Alaska and Florida are providing each other's shorefront restaurants with bland frozen fish, in the way that some countries with cultural-exchange agreements provide each other with overly polite high-school students.

Alice and I once spent several days in an Alaskan seaport whose restaurants offered the traveler less chance of coming across a fresh piece of fish than he might have if he were entrapped in a farm county of Arkansas—where he might at least have the good fortune to stumble upon an only recently dispatched catfish. Alice was beginning to look desperate. I was forced to remind her that when she first expressed a longing to see the magnificent, snow-covered mountains of Alaska, I had prudently mentioned my theory that the quality of food a place offers is often in inverse proportion to the splendors of its scenery—a phenomenon I account for with the additional theory that the cooks in a spectacularly beautiful place are often outside drinking in nature's wonderments instead of standing in front of a hot stove where they belong. Alice has not had the opportunity to test out my theory thoroughly, since the business trips on which she decides I need company have never happened to be trips to middle-sized industrial cities in Ohio.

My reminder, for some reason, only made Alice look more desperate. The Alaskan seaport did have a fish plant that processed Dungeness crabs—boiling them as they came in off the boats and freezing them in brine to produce what the trade calls "brine-frozen whole cooks"—and finally I paid what I allowed myself to think of as a courtesy call on the manager.

"Nice operation you have here," I said, sidling up to one of the huge boiling pots. "A shame all of these get shipped away."

"Would you like one of these crabs?" my host said, snatching from the cooling table a crab that must have been ten inches across the shell.

I took it and ran. Back at the motel, Alice and I had already supplied ourselves with Portuguese wine and Hydrox cookies—the pick of the provisions in that seaport. I spread a newspaper on the floor to prepare the main course, only to discover that the crepe-soled shoes I was wearing were totally useless for cracking a crab shell. Fortunately, Alice had some sturdy wooden heels, which did the trick, and we settled down to the best meal we had in Alaska. "Alice," I said, when we had polished off about half the crab, "I'm certainly glad you decided to come along."

The fact that I would go to some trouble to get my hands on a Dungeness crab—the fact that I would do a little polite panhandling in Alaska, or even transport myself to California with barely seemly haste—does not mean that I prefer Dungeness crabs to all others. In New Orleans one of our favorite pastimes is eating in lakefront restaurants where boiled shellfish are served up on beer trays and the only problem left in life is whether to attack the crabs or the boiled shrimp first. I have spent some happy evenings in Baltimore in one of those restaurants where all that seems required for happiness is a pile of Maryland blue crabs on a piece of butcher paper and a wooden mallet and a supply of napkins. (My only regret about eating crabs in Baltimore is that the crab restaurants don't serve my favorite local side order, deep-fried potato skins—a dish that is available, as far as I know, only in a flashy joint otherwise notable for little more than the shine on the shoes of its headwaiter. If only the Chairman were here, I sometimes muse when I have time for only one meal in Baltimore. I do manage to down a few crabs while I try to come up with a plausible geopolitical reason for a Chinese head of state to be visiting Baltimore.) Driving through the wheat fields of Kansas or the mountains of eastern Kentucky, I have found myself daydreaming of the cracked-crab salad at Mosca's outside New Orleans, or of she-crab soup at Henry's, across from the city market in Charleston, South Carolina. The mixed blessing of an American city's maintaining a cultural identity is expressed for me in the question of whether I would be willing to endure a lecture on the authenticity of detail in the historical renovation of Charleston south of Broad Street if I were allowed to eat Charleston she-crab soup while I listened.

In a fishing town near the California-Oregon state line, where

Alice and I once stopped for a quick bite on her way to the scenic wonders of the Oregon coastline and my way to a renowned seafood restaurant in Newport called Mo's, I ate something called a crab-burger—openly, in full view of the other diners—and I loved it. It was not as good as a Maryland crab cake served on the Eastern Shore at some place like Pope's Tavern, in Oxford, but then hardly anything is. For me, the coming of spring has nothing to do with the appearance of crocuses or robins; spring is here when soft-shell crabs begin appearing on the menus of fish houses and West Side French bistros in Manhattan. When I am in Florida, I search out a stone-crab palace and tell my dining companions to quit comparing stone crabs unfavorably with blue crabs or favorably with lobsters and just enjoy themselves. When I'm in New York, I go regularly to some-place like the Yun Luck Rice Shoppe in Chinatown for crab Cantonese-style—cooked in the shell with scallions and pork and ginger, and served with a selection of hand-wiping supplies. When I'm in England, I search out the sort of crabs that are cooked on boats in the North Sea and then sold in open markets. When it comes to crabs, I'm ecumenical.

My fondness for crabs may have something to do with having suffered a crab-deprived childhood. The largest body of water near Kansas City is Lake Lotawana, a lake so small that it is said to rise a foot and a half on Fourth of July weekend, when everyone gets in at once. There are people who claim that the way boats are anchored in Lake Lotawana is to lay them across the lake, like a butterknife. When I first met Alice, I was trying to impress her, of course, and, not wanting her to think me an inlander completely ignorant of sophisticated eats, I told her that Lotawana had a species of lake crab that was remarkable for the delicacy of its taste. Then one day I told her about how I used to go down to the lake before dawn when I was a boy to buy crabs off the boats and then sit around swapping tales with the old freshes who always hung around the dock.

"Old freshes?" she said.

"Yeah, like old salts," I said. "Only fresh water."

"I don't believe old freshes," she said. "When it gets right down to it, I don't believe lake crabs."

I'm still trying to impress her. I am not always successful, of course, but the story making the rounds that I still have to have her extract the heart of my artichoke for me is completely untrue. She does sometimes extract the heart of my artichoke for me, but strictly on a volunteer basis.

•

"It was because of the crab that the Wharf became so popular," the guidebook in our San Francisco hotel room said of Fisherman's Wharf. "It is one of the world's most delectable catches, one of the most remembered treats of San Francisco. Descendants of the Italian fishermen who first cast nets into the seas off San Francisco in the 1850's began to line the Wharf with huge iron pots, cooking live crabs and selling them to passers-by." The huge iron pots were still there. So, of course, were the passersby—so many that we had difficulty passing by them on the way to the crab pots. "Dungeness-deprived couple!" I wanted to shout. "Desperate Easterners! Let 'em through, folks!"

We finally made it to a crab boiler, a cheerful fellow who once ran a small seafood restaurant just on the other side of the walkway from his crab pot but had finally decided to turn the restaurant into a souvenir stand. ("This way, you don't have to worry all the time about the clam chowder spoiling.") While we were waiting for our crab to boil, he informed me that this most remembered treat of San Francisco had been trucked in the night before from Eureka, two hundred and forty miles up the coast. The fishermen who were going out of Eureka and Crescent City for crabs may have been having a spectacular year, but San Francisco fishermen hadn't been able to catch enough crabs to supply even the Fisherman's Wharf crab pots for more than the first two or three weeks of the season. The crab hawkers on the Wharf were in the position of country farmstand operators who, having sold off too much of the farm for real-estate developments, find themselves importing fruits and vegetables from the city market in order to supply the summer people.

For reasons that are not certain to anyone, the supply of Dungeness crabs off the West Coast of the United States rises and falls dramatically in cycles of about eight to ten years. In the early sixties, though, the catch in central California—the vicinity of San Francisco Bay, which has historically acted as a nursery for crabs—leveled off, so that the low end of the cycle became a dismal norm. I suspect there are people in California who are quite certain that San Francisco had its crab supply shut off for more or less the same reason that Sodom and Gomorrah encountered their difficulties, but I learned that the California Department of Fish and Game had been investigating other possibilities. As soon as I felt full enough to travel, we drove from San Francisco to Menlo Park to talk with Dr. Harold Orcutt, the director of the Fish and Game Department's crab project. Alice said she wanted to meet Orcutt because of her interest in scientific matters—she happens to be the one in our family who reads books about brain research and puts together the stereo—but I suspected that her interest had something to do with rumors that a restaurant in Princeton, California, more or less on the way to Menlo Park, served fresh abalone.

Alice has a weakness for abalone, and, being a husband who does his best to anticipate even her unexpressed desires, I try to eat as much of it with her as possible. Abalone may be the one indestructible shellfish. Canned crabmeat tastes like Styrofoam. A bad version of she-crab soup in Charleston tastes like the sauce used on lobster Newburg by the third-fanciest French restaurant in Tulsa. The sort of shrimp hidden under a pound and a half of batter on what Midwestern menus call "French-fried butterfly shrimp" could as easily be turnips. Abalone seems to defy efforts to gussy it up. At Lazio's, a restaurant attached to a fish plant in Eureka, I once ordered something called Scalone—despite the fact that it sounded more like the water commissioner of Hoboken than something to eat—and what arrived, a sort of patty made out of abalone and scallops, was delicious.

Abalone is difficult to find in California these days. The shortage, according to one theory, may have something to do with efforts in recent years to preserve the sea otter, that cute little creature that tourists like to observe as it perches on rocks just off high-priced beachfronts and cleverly opens shellfish—shellfish that happen to be abalone. I have nothing against sea otters—we have what might be considered a shared interest or a community of taste—but I'm not certain that the lobby organized for their protection was aware of quite how much of what those adorable creatures were getting down. It's all a matter of priorities, I suppose, and mine have something to do with the fact that when someone mentions the delights of observing creatures use their manual dexterity to open shellfish, the creatures that leap to my mind are not sea otters off the beach in Monterey but oyster shuckers at the Acme in New Orleans.

Having filled ourselves with abalone, we found Dr. Orcutt, who turned out to be a man who spoke with the traditional detachment of a scientist unless he happened to be on the subject of eating blue crabs on the East Coast as a boy. Orcutt emphasized that he and his fellow researchers were still a long way from accumulating enough data to discover precisely what was causing the dearth of crabs in the waters outside San Francisco Bay. They may never know. Scientists are still not certain why the sardines that used to be so prevalent around the same area were some years ago replaced by anchovies; it may even be that the sardines existed in such profusion for what seemed like so many years merely because of some temporary imbalance in the ecological system, and that everything has now returned to normal. I have always thought of sardines as more normal than anchovies myself but, my understanding of such matters being so primitive that I spent an embarrassing number of years in the belief that marshmallows grew on bushes, I decided not to offer that opinion to Dr. Orcutt as something he might want to pass along to the sardines-and-anchovies crowd.

Orcutt's project was working on the theory that any one of several factors could have crippled the crab crop—some natural environmental variation, such as a change in water temperature, or man-made pollution in San Francisco Bay, or fishing pressure, or some combination of factors that reduced the crab stock below the level at which it could "snap back" from the low end of the cycle. Orcutt was certain of the answer to one question I had— why crabmeat that has been out of the shell for a while tends to taste like chopped Styrofoam. Exposure to the air, he said, oxidizes the crab's natural fats, and the fats are the source of the crab's flavor. The scientifically correct complaint to make when served tasteless crab in a restaurant is, I now know, "Waiter, this crab's natural fats must have been oxidizing since last Tuesday."

The fishermen who hang around Fisherman's Wharf were not as cautious as Orcutt about explaining why the crabs have disappeared. A fisherman asked about an unnatural absence of fish tends to speak with the assurance of an orthopedist who has been hired as an expert witness in a negligence case—and like the orthopedist, he is not troubled by hearing a colleague present conflicting testimony with equal authority. We found fishermen who believed that the crabs were destroyed because cities were dumping their garbage into the ocean, and we found fishermen who believed that the crabs were destroyed because some fools forced the cities to stop dumping garbage into the ocean, thus depriving the young crabs of food. There were a lot of fishermen who believed the problem was caused by the dumping of industrial wastes into San Francisco Bay. There were fishermen who believed that the crab drought, like a lot of other problems, can be traced to Russian trawlers. According to a fish processor I spoke with in Eureka, the Russians may have actually helped the crab supply there by taking a lot of hake, which feed on baby crabs, but that is not a theory I heard from fishermen. Before the United States declared a two-hundred-mile limit, American fishermen tended to resent the Russians not only for where they fished but for how they fished—from huge trawlers that are to the average American fishing boat what the largest supermarket in Orange County is to a mom-and-pop corner store. A group of American fishermen standing around a wharf are more likely to drop a kind word about gale-force winds than about the Russians.

•

Fisherman's Wharf puts less emphasis on the edible part of a shellfish than on the ashtrays or hula dolls that can be made out of its shell. After walking through the souvenir stands on the Wharf, an out-of-town visitor may find it rather astonishing to turn the corner and suddenly come upon fishing boats—real fishing boats, with names like *Skip-A-Lou* and *Baby Carl*. The effect is the same as traveling through the Pennsylvania Dutch country, amid manufactured hex signs and plastic horse-and-buggy reproductions and place mats with bad jokes written phonetically in a vaudeville Pennsylvania Dutch dialect, and coming across an Amishman riding down the road in a buggy that looks just like the miniature buggies in the gift shop. It is something of a shock to realize that the Pennsylvania Dutch actually exist, living there in the same area that sells pictures of them on ashtrays.

The fishing boats Alice and I saw at Fisherman's Wharf were not, of course, the source of the crabs we saw being cooked in the huge crab pots. The signs that said FRESH LOCAL CRAB were completely accurate only if Eureka is taken to be in the Greater San Francisco area. But the crabs were, in fact, the freshest that could be found in San Francisco; the trucks being sent every night from Eureka specifically serviced the crab stalls and the relatively few restaurants in town that are particular about freshness. The best way to eat Dungeness crabs in San Francisco is still to witness your fresh crab being dropped into boiling water by one of the Wharf's crab hawkers, dash a block or two down the Embarcadero to Boudine's Bakery three minutes before the crab is done, buy a loaf of sourdough bread just out of the oven, return on the dead run to the crab pot carrying a loaf of bread that is still hot, ask the hawker to crack the crab's shell ever so slightly, and adjourn to a bench overlooking the fishing boats.

Not many tourists do that; it's too much trouble, and it's too messy. Tolerance of messiness, of course, is based partly on familiarity with the mess; there are undoubtedly Midwestern tourists on Fisherman's Wharf who would think nothing of being up to their elbows in fried chicken or barbecued ribs but recoil at taking apart a Dungeness crab. The most popular item offered by the crab hawkers is not freshly boiled crab but something called a Walk Away Cocktail—crabmeat taken from the shell early in the morning, put into a small paper cup, and kept on ice while its natural fats, I now know, are oxidized like crazy. Alice tried a Walk Away Cocktail, and took on the expression she sometimes has when Abigail and Sarah ask for more ketchup to pour on their frozen fish sticks. A Walk Away Cocktail is also available with equally tasteless shrimp instead of crab, or a combination of shrimp and crab. Eating a combination shrimp-crab Walk Away Cocktail has all the excitement of eating bologna between two different brands of packaged white bread. It is not, however, messy.

If a research team systematically interviewed serious shellfish eaters about their most memorable shellfish experience, I suspect that the unifying theme of the testimony would be messiness. Ask anyone who truly loves shellfish about the best he has ever had, and the answer tends to be a story ending with the table being hosed down after the meal or mountains of shells being shoveled into trash bins. It is apparent to serious shellfish eaters that in the great evolutionary scheme of things crustaceans developed shells to protect them from knives and forks. Extracting fish from a shell tends to be time-consuming, but shellfish eaters are, as a group, patient. In fact, the most pedantic among them—those amateur professors of shelling who loiter around Chesapeake Bay—sometimes seem more interested in extracting crabmeat with finesse than in eating it.

American restaurants operate on the premise that most of their customers do not want to engage in that sort of dirty work just to get at food they are paying good money for. Tarantino's restaurant on Fisherman's Wharf has on its menu something called Lazy Man's Cioppino, described as "Famous local shellfish stew of the native fisherman. Prawns, clams, crabs, eastern oysters—with all the meat removed from the shell." I suspect that the popularity in America of frozen South African lobster tails can be accounted for by their being so easy to eat—the only other logical explanation being that Americans, for some reason, are attracted to the taste of unpainted papier-mâché if it is priced high enough.

To a restaurant proprietor, a customer who eats a simple dish with dispatch is a customer who is likely to turn the table over to another customer rather quickly. Even one of those East Side New York steak restaurants that bully the innocent into paying twenty-three dollars for a lobster would probably lose money on the most thorough lobster eater I know—a friend of ours in Nova Scotia named Russell Harnish—because of how long he would keep the table tied up while he was doing justice to the lobster. Russell is a methodical man. He takes a lobster apart the way a senior infantry sergeant disassembles an exceedingly complicated machine gun, and when he finishes his meal the lobster looks as though it might have been staked out on an anthill for a couple of weeks. I suppose that in the time it takes Russell Harnish to eat one lobster McDonald's sells twenty or thirty million hamburgers.

When we eat lobster with Russell Harnish, Alice spends a lot of time studying him, the way an apprentice silversmith might watch a master turn out a particularly difficult bowl. Alice is a practiced dismantler of lobsters herself, although the story making the rounds that she still has to show me how to break off the claws happens to be what the politicians call "untrue and completely out of context." It is generally true, though, that even after years of living in New York the two mysteries of the East that remain beyond the reach of an expatriate Midwesterner are the New York subway system and the proper eating of a lobster. Someone who comes to lobster eating or subway transportation late faces the sort of frustrations faced by someone who applies himself diligently to studying French with the realization that no matter how many hours he spends in the language lab there are thousands of words like "diaper pin" and "ball bearing" he will probably never know. We inlanders sometimes imagine we have conquered the subway, but our conquest, upon close examination by a native, usually consists of nothing more than some straight shots on the West Side IRT or some rather clumsy combination put together with the Forty-second Street shuttle. There are out-of-towners who have cornered the market in one thing or another in Wall Street and there are out-of-towners who command attention at Sardi's, but I have never met an out-of-towner who has broken the code of the BMT. We remain equally ignorant of the final mysteries of lobster dismemberment. But, the taste of a lobster not being a taste that has to be acquired, we wade right in, like cheerful hackers who have a fine time on the course while shooting a sixty-four for nine holes.

8

Dinner with Friends

WHEN WE'RE DRESSING to go to someone's house for dinner, Alice often tries to persuade me that there are ways of showing appreciation to the hostess other than having thirds. I suppose there are ways of displaying appreciation for an artist's painting other than writing out a check on the spot and snatching the painting from the wall, but is "My, how interesting" really what he wants to hear? There cannot be many cooks so confident in their skill that the possibility of their having, say, put too much salt in the soup does not occur to them when a dinner guest says, "Thanks, it was delicious but I couldn't eat another bite" or "I'm saving room for dessert."

"They know I can eat another bite, Alice," I try to explain, hoping that she has not noticed that I am having some mild difficulty getting my collar buttoned. "And how can I tell them I'm saving room for dessert when it is widely known that my policy with food is to eat it on a first-come-first-served basis?"

"It wouldn't hurt not to live up to your reputation one night," Alice says. "In fact, it wouldn't hurt to change your reputation."

"My mother told me always to be polite," I reply weakly.

When I'm on the road and someone asks me to dinner, I am sometimes able to phone Alice late in the evening to report that I have displayed the sort of restraint she so admires. There is some food that inspires abstemiousness even in me. Naturally, I try to avoid exposing myself to it. When someone I have met in another city suggests that I "come on out to the house" that evening, I believe I owe it to myself to try to figure out, as politely as possible, whether he is married to someone who is always pouring canned mushroom soup all over everything. A traveling man can't be too careful. I stall the invitation with some talk about whether my work will be finished by dinnertime, and then I try to feel around for what the percentages are of getting a better meal than I might find trying to sniff out a barbecue joint that uses real hickory wood or a Mexican restaurant that serves tripe. (I don't particularly like tripe, but, after many years of research, I have finally decided that its presence on the menu of a Mexican restaurant is a badge representing seriousness of intention.) Anybody who finds this approach to a dinner invitation callous or cynical or lacking in graciousness has not spent much time on the road.

"Where did you and your wife meet?" I might say to some politician in Toledo, supposedly making idle conversation but actually hoping against hope for the long shot that he took a war bride from an Italian village known throughout Europe for the perfection of its gnocchi. Or, speaking to a newspaperman in Cedar Rapids, I might say, "I guess the corn is pretty good out this way"—waiting to see if his response is an uninterested grunt or the information that he always waits until dinner is precisely three and a half minutes away before snapping a few cobs off the stalks in his back yard and passing them to his son, who is faster at short distances, to shuck as he proceeds at a dead run to the pot of boiling water waiting on the stove.

Now and then I am simply lucky. In Vermont once, having taken a wild guess that the couple in question might be the sort of people who would make the best use of what the land around them provided, I accepted a dinner invitation with a haste that Alice might have considered unseemly and was rewarded with a dinner that included a dish, made from apples and coarse maple syrup, that was probably the best dessert I have ever eaten. In El Paso, during a particularly bitter clothing workers' strike, I was asked by a priest known for his support of the strikers whether I might like to stay for a bowl of *chili verde*. The priest seemed to me to have demonstrated the sort of attention to detail often found in gifted cooks: when the company being struck ran a full-page newspaper advertisement that listed eight thousand "happy workers"—people who immediately became known as "happies"—the priest, with a patience that I have always associated with seminaries, counted the names and found 2,329. It also happens that I have never eaten a bowl of *chili verde* I didn't like. The *chili verde* was magnificent—the masterpiece, as I learned later, not of the priest but of a local woman who had a singularly delicious way of demonstrating her devotion to the parish.

The staggering apple-and-syrup dessert and the magnificent *chili verde* are memorable exceptions to a body of experience that runs more in the direction of canned mushroom soup. I may run across the Italian war bride in Toledo and then find out that nothing makes her feel more American than being able to serve frozen food right out of the package—an announcement she makes while I am shoving Sarah's favorite brand of fish sticks from one part of my plate to another. I fall for a young executive's eloquent declamation about the wonders of his wife's cooking, and discover, once it is much too late, that I am eating a dinner prepared by the St. Paul or Denver or Moline version of the newlywed gourmet-food mongers we used to refer to in New York as "the beef Stroganoff crowd."

"My, how interesting," I say to the hostess, while silently comforting myself with the reminder that I can at least look forward to beginning my telephone conversation with Alice that night by saying, "Alice, you would have really been proud of me this evening. A man with real willpower is a pleasure to behold."

•

One evening, after we returned home from a dinner during which I had managed to do the sort of eating that compliments the hostess on her cooking and takes care of any leftover glut at the same time, Alice tried the sympathetic approach. "I suppose one of the problems is that too many people we know are good cooks," she said.

"That is not my idea of a problem, Alice," I said. "In fact, compared to, say, the problem of spiraling worldwide inflation or the energy problem or the race problem in South Africa, it doesn't seem like a problem at all." Alice has not spent much time on the road herself.

In a way, of course, she was right. A lot of people we know in New York serve dinners that demand gestures of appreciation— sometimes two or three gestures, if there seems to be enough in the pot. Some of the people, I suppose, are reformed members of the beef Stroganoff crowd. Some of them went through a period of ingredient purity during which dinner conversations were so dominated by talk of how to prepare stone-ground flour or where to buy the true fig that I found myself imagining a cook pure enough to grind her own cleanser. Then, before all the talk of authenticity and purity could have any serious effect on my appetite, the period was passed, and so were the seconds.

One New York cook we know who never seemed to go through any of the unfortunate phases is a friend of ours named Colette Rossant, whose dinner invitations I have always treated the way a Savings and Loan lobbyist might treat a note asking him to a small poker game with the members of the Senate Banking Committee. Colette is French, and had had no trouble at all remaining so in the South Village, which everybody else thinks is an Italian neighborhood. The Italian *coteghino* sausage she buys from Mrs. Conevari on Sullivan Street is somehow transformed into extremely French *saucisson en croûte* by being carried a few hundred yards into her kitchen. She does her shopping daily, like any French housewife, and if she finds a loaf of bread not quite as fresh as she expects it to be, she does not hesitate to bring the matter up with the man who baked it. I have occasionally tried to envision what must happen among the shopkeepers of the South Village when Colette Rossant, the Scourge of Sullivan Street, starts out with her shopping bag over her arm. "She's coming! The lady's coming!" the butcher must shout, spotting her from the doorway as he sweeps out the store. The baker rushes over to snatch away the day-old bread he had slid onto the top of the bread pile for the unsuspecting. The fruit and vegetable men begin to police their orange displays and squeeze the wilted leaves off the outside of their lettuce. Unlike the Italian war bride in Toledo whose dinner table I dread, Colette defies Americanization. She is so far above frozen food that I have always suspected she may not keep ice cubes. The Rossants live within walking distance of our house, and Alice claims that when we are walking there for dinner she is often forced to grab me by the jacket two or three times to keep me from breaking into a steady, uncharacteristic trot.

Sullivan Street is the scene every June of the Feast of St. Anthony, an Italian street fair I happen to love. (I happen to love all Italian street fairs. In fact, I even love Armenian street fairs: the One World Festival held every fall by the St. Vartan Cathedral is one of my favorite annual events.) Lately the Italians who run St. Anthony's have been permitting some foreign-food booths to creep in. Unlike the Armenians, though—whose commitment to One World is so strong that Philippine bean-sprout fritters and even Tibetan dumplings are permitted right next to the stuffed grape leaves—the Italians keep the outlanders so far south of Houston Street, where almost all fairgoers start their eating, that few people could possibly make it to the Korean egg rolls or the Greek spinach pie without being so stuffed with sausage sandwiches and *calzone* and clams and pasta that they can only stare numbly at the *souvlaki* signs. One year, in the foreign ghetto, we noticed two teenage girls operating a booth whose sign said, of all things, CRÊPES SUZETTE.

"*Crêpes suzette!*" Alice said. "At St. Anthony's!"

The girls, of course, turned out to be Rossant daughters—like their mother, unreconstructed.

Once, a few days before we were due at the Rossants' for what Colette had promised to be a particularly worthwhile feast—the preparations for which, I assumed, had tradesmen as far uptown as Fourteenth Street quivering at their counters—I felt a cold coming on.

"A cold!" I said to Alice. "This is a disaster!"

"Are we comparing it now to spiraling worldwide inflation?"

"This is nothing to joke about, Alice," I said. "You know I always lose my sense of taste at some point during a cold."

As the evening approached, my taste buds seemed to wither away. While Alice was dressing for dinner, I was still desperately alternating wild gargling and nose-blowing in an effort to clear some taste. As soon as we walked in, I picked up a couple of pieces of celery from a bowl of *crudités* that Colette had put out with drinks. I could taste nothing. I staved off a serious depression by telling myself that celery doesn't have much taste anyway. Then I tried some *coteghino*. Nothing. A man who cannot taste Mrs. Canevari's *coteghino* cannot taste. I spent the rest of the evening trying to imagine, by texture and by the blissful looks on the faces of the other diners, what the food I was eating tasted like.

"What sin did I commit to deserve this?" I asked Alice when we got home.

"If I had to guess, I'd guess gluttony," Alice said.

An hour after we had gone to sleep, I woke up coughing. "Go take some cough medicine," Alice mumbled.

"I don't have any cough medicine."

"There's some of Abigail's in the medicine cabinet," Alice said. "Red. Be careful not to take the other red stuff—it's to make kids throw up if they eat something dangerous."

I stumbled off, and came back to bed. Ten minutes later, I sat straight up in bed, possessed by a wave of nausea.

"Oh, you haven't—" Alice said. But by the speed with which I was making for the bathroom, she knew I had.

Moments later I understood for the first time how those characters in Sholem Aleichem stories can find themselves talking personally to the Divinity. "There must have been some misunderstanding, Lord," I said, when I was able to talk. "I didn't even taste it in the first place."

9

British Boiled

"DON'T YOU MISS ENGLAND?" Alice, the family intellectual and crypto-travel-agent, asked me one winter. "If we flew from Halifax, we'd have all the money we saved by not flying all the way from New York, so we'd have money left over."

"I suppose we could use the surplus to endow a chair of economics somewhere," I said.

It was rather late in the year for Alice to be making summer travel plans. Usually she likes to have them in the ground by the autumnal equinox. I knew she was itching to go somewhere. A few years before, a bizarre plan we had concocted for a cut-rate trip to China had fallen through—it entailed joining an organization in Kansas City that I remember as the Cricket Camera Club—and not taking a trip to China is, according to Alice's Law of Compensatory Cashflow, the equivalent of a small killing in the New York State Lottery.

I don't mean that Alice is the only one in our family who likes to travel. I go along cheerfully, even though I spend so much of my time in hotels during the year on business that I can sometimes feel like Eloise all grown up. When I can't seem to find the key to my own house, it occasionally occurs to me that I may have absentmindedly dropped it into a mailbox, postage presumably guaranteed by Abigail and Sarah.

"England is not a bad idea," I said to Alice. "The potato *latkes* are dynamite."

"Is that what comes to your mind when you think about England?" Alice asked.

The potato *latkes* were definitely in my mind. I could see myself on Wentworth Street in the East End of London. It was Sunday morning. We had just come from picking our way through Cheshire Street, where an acquisitive tourist can obtain such national treasures as a pair of fatigues from the Suez campaign. I was standing at the counter of a store called M. Marks, ordering a hot, thick potato pancake that is served on a piece of waxed paper and is eaten while standing up—a method that gives the eater the additional pleasure of being able to jump up and down occasionally in delight.

"That's amazing," Alice said.

"You're right," I said. It was amazing. England's reputation for such food is so low that a foreign correspondent of our acquaintance who was posted to London some years later—a ferocious eater I'll call Charlie Plum—arranged to have shipped from the United States among his belongings not just four bottles of Arthur Bryant's barbecue sauce and several jars of crunchy peanut butter but also an entire case of kosher dills. Plum is an awesomely energetic ferreter-out of facts, but how would anybody know that right there among people who don't even know how to spell bagel—they spell it beigel, which, oddly enough, is the way they pronounce it—a wayfarer can purchase the single best stand-up potato *latke* in the English-speaking world.

"When most people think of England, they think of the Changing of the Guard or the British Museum or sheep grazing in the English countryside or men in bowler hats going to their clubs," Alice said.

"I can do without mutton, thanks, and club food stinks," I said. "Everybody knows that." There are a number of theories to account for the failure of English club food to taste like anything at all—nostalgia for public-school dining rooms and regimental mess halls, for instance—but I have always assumed that the phenomenon can be traced to a strong subconscious Anglo-Saxon belief that the tastiness of the food varies in inverse proportion to social position. The belief arrived on the East Coast of the United States from England intact with the early settlers; to this day, anyone obligated to attend a wedding at the most exclusive Long Island clubs has to make do with what tastes like Kraft Velveeta cheese sandwiches on Wonder bread (quartered and decrusted for a touch of class) and the sort of chicken à la king that brings groans from the regulars when it turns up at small-town Kiwanis luncheons.

I did have fond memories, though, that made me miss England as much as Alice did—memories that went beyond potato *latkes*, mostly in the direction of Chinese food. I know there is a widespread feeling that anyone with my priorities should look upon Great Britain more or less the way Charles de Gaulle used to—from a distance and down the nose. It is undoubtedly true that the English serve a number of dishes that can turn a serious eater pale—thrown into a mild state of shock by the thought that human beings have been existing on such substances for generations. (I have always been impressed, though, by how conscientious the English are about clearly labeling some of their most gruesome dishes, the way they might label dangerous medicine or a large hole in the pavement. It seems to me, for instance, that anyone who orders something called "meat and veggies" or "spotted dog" gets what he deserves. On the other hand, I must admit that in a North Carolina barbecue restaurant once, I myself ordered something called a "bag of skins," and was briefly irritated to discover that what came tasted very much like a carefully barbecued volleyball.) It does seem almost willful that at breakfast—the one meal at which an innocent traveler even in a provincial hotel has a good chance of tasting some good kippers and fresh eggs—the English refuse to serve toast until it has been hung out to dry, as if it were a pile of soggy linen.

It is also true that English food is no longer the only kind of food to be avoided in England. In recent years the place has become pockmarked with the kind of American hamburger joints that have cutesy names and less than adorable beef. The Continental cuisine palaces in England can be even more dangerous, since they tend to be as bloated with unjustified pretense as their American counterparts—those revolving domes on the top of Midwestern bank buildings that feature Sigma Chi sommeliers and three-paragraph descriptions of which canned vegetables are going to be poured over what type of frozen sole. The English style of Continental cuisine was planted, I've always thought, by some Anglophobic Frenchman who managed to persuade dozens of prospective restaurant proprietors and country-hotel keepers that the way to prepare sophisticated food was to stuff something with something—almost anything—else, and then to obscure the scene of the crime with a heavy, lava-like sauce. He demonstrated to all of them, for instance, how to stuff a chicken breast with a plum that is, in turn, stuffed with an almond. I wouldn't be surprised to hear that he is now experimenting with hypodermic needles to perfect a method of stuffing the almond with paté. Since the dishes that result from these acts of cumulative stuffing all taste and weigh more or less the same, Alice and I have always referred to them by a single generic name—Stuff-Stuff with Heavy.

Eating a meal in a Stuff-Stuff with Heavy joint in the company of English people who think of themselves as gourmets is like taking a final examination in a course you hadn't meant to sign up for in the first place. Is the wine appropriate? Are there enough forks? Are there enough waiters? Did the waiter flick the crumbs from the table on the proper side of the person who deposited them there?

Once, in a Stuff-Stuff with Heavy restaurant in Bath, I happened to notice a waiter passing with a platterful of potatoes that looked superior to the sort I was eating—my habit of keeping my eyes open for a chance to covet my neighbor's side dishes having remained unbroken even in the face of occasional warnings by Alice that a man who spends as much time as I do glancing around during a meal stands the risk of dropping most of it on his lap. Naturally, I asked the waiter for a bowl or two of what he was carrying, and, having been searching for a good opportunity to take advantage of a favorable rate of exchange on the pound, I offered to bear the cost personally.

"But these are Lyonnaise potatoes," he said. "They don't go with trout."

"Never?"

"Oh no, sir," he said.

"I think I'll have some anyway," I said. He looked uncertain as to whether he wanted to be in the role of accessory in the atrocity

I was about to commit. I began to feel rather uncertain myself. There was always the possibility that the waiter was a moonlighting biochemist who knew that trout and Lyonnaise potatoes produce a nearly always fatal chemical reaction if they meet in the upper colon.

Alice gave the waiter one of the smiles she reserves for assuring strangers that I am not lunatic in any dangerous way, and he gave me the potatoes—which, of course, turned out to be inferior to the ones I had been eating.

There would be no reason, though, for us to subject ourselves to any more Stuff-Stuff with Heavy joints. We could spend some time in Somerset, frying hog's pudding to a crisp and making fun of Jeffrey's eggs while gobbling up the soufflés Francie made out of them. I had no reason to be concerned about the possibility of our being dragged into any gentlemen's clubs in London. Alice and I have only one close friend who belongs to a London gentlemen's club, and we have what amounts to an understanding with him about it: we agree not to ridicule him for belonging to such an institution and he agrees not to take us there to dinner. We break our part of the agreement regularly, but he, being a gentleman, has been scrupulous about keeping his. I began to think not of what had to be avoided but of what could be savored. A satisfied look came across my face. "Yes, let's go to England this summer," I said.

"Are you really going to England just because you want a potato *latke*?" Alice asked.

"Of course not," I said, rather hurt. "You must think me a narrow fellow indeed. As it happens, I have just remembered the Great Dried Beef in the Sky we used to eat at the Chinese restaurant across from the Golders Green tube stop."

•

When I arrived in Golders Green one day in the middle sixties to meet an émigré politician for lunch, he said the neighborhood offered us a choice of eating at an English restaurant or a Chinese restaurant.

"May all the decisions you have to make in your political career be as simple as that one," I said.

I have been going to the Chinese restaurant across from the

Golders Green tube stop ever since. It has turned out, though, that the dishes I was so happy to find when I ate with the politician are available in a number of Peking-style restaurants in London, and that my favorite dish is no longer the dish we have always called the Great Dried Beef in the Sky (hidden behind some name like Beef with Chili Sauce on the menu) but fried seaweed, which tastes more like fried than seaweed and is worth a trip across the Atlantic on foot. England being the sort of place that encourages traditions, our family has developed a tradition of spending our first evening in London at the Chinese restaurant across from the Golders Green tube stop, even if Sarah has not even had enough time to acquire a beigel.

My strategy for eating in London was clear from the start: eat plenty of fried seaweed and dumplings and crispy duck and crab-with-ginger and dried beef and honey-apples at Chinese restaurants. Go regularly to first-rate Indian restaurants, which are almost as difficult to find in America as fried seaweed. Eat fish—whitebait or lemon sole or turbot served in some simple fish house, like the downstairs of Manzi's, instead of in one of those fish restaurants that seem to have contracted for a steady supply of Heavy from the Stuff-Stuff with Heavy joints. Find some decent pub food or consume two or three hundred pints of ale trying. Start each and every Sunday with a stand-up potato *latke* on Wentworth Street.

Even before we left for England, I recognized a couple of potential difficulties in the plan. The fish house would present no problem. London has fish restaurants that are very much like serious fish houses in America. Serious fish restaurants anywhere tend to be plain rooms staffed with the sort of waiters who nod silently as they take your order, and who probably seem so much alike because they come from the same village in Italy. (The exception is in San Francisco, where the city's two serious fish houses, Sam's Grill and Tadich Grill, are staffed with Dalmatians rather than Italians—the phenomenon I always assume San Francisco boosters have in mind when they say that their city is uniquely cosmopolitan.) But I have never had much luck turning up good pub food, despite such a strong inclination to give it the benefit of the doubt that I have occasionally found myself praising pub sausages for keeping their meat content low enough to guard against heartburn. There would also be a problem, I knew, with Alice's lack of enthusiasm for Indian food. On one trip to England, she had informed me—rather bluntly, I thought, after all these years—that she believed one Indian meal every week was quite enough for her.

"I don't suppose Ceylonese and Pakistani count as Indian," I said, hoping to salvage a little something.

"It all tastes the same," Alice said.

"Surely, the nations of the Third World, aspiring to their own distinct national identity—"

"Once a week," Alice said.

My plan for getting Alice in a receptive mood for Indian food included taking her for a couple of cream teas in the country and bringing her a box of chocolate truffles from a candy store in London called Prestat—Prestat truffles being what Alice is really thinking about when she pretends to be thinking about sheep grazing in the countryside and the Changing of the Guard. Alice's moderation evaporates upon exposure to chocolate. I have been with her when she insists that the Trattoria, an otherwise undistinguished Italian restaurant in the Pan Am building that has by far the best chocolate ice cream in New York, is "right on the way" from Chinatown to the Village. Her discussions on the variety of chocolate cake available in our neighborhood are so erudite that I would not be surprised to read someday that she was leading a symposium on that subject at the New School. The only commercial venture I ever heard her discuss with any enthusiasm at all was a store that she and another chocophiliac we know were going to start called the Chocolate Freak. When Alice's thoughts wander from chocolate in England, she does not begin thinking about the British Museum. She begins thinking about a bowl of fresh blackberries covered with Devonshire cream—or, really, a bowl of practically anything covered with Devonshire cream. I wouldn't be surprised to find her pouring Devonshire cream on eggplant or steak-and-kidney pie or *matzo brei*.

After Alice had absorbed a couple of dozen truffles and a gallon or two of Devonshire cream, I felt I might be able to take her to an Indian restaurant without having my *paratha* spoiled by thoughts that she was about to cause a nasty scene. On previous trips to

London, we had been taken to Indian dinners by a friend whose commitment to organizations working against the discrimination that exists toward immigrants from the Indian subcontinent and the Caribbean has been, I always assumed, a shrewd device for acquiring inside information on Indian restaurants. Our host at Alice's first post-truffle Indian meal was another friend with what I took to be a similarly selfish devotion to bettering race relations in Great Britain. Confident that he had at last found an Indian restaurant that would please Alice, he dismissed our previous guide as a specialist in the problems facing Jamaicans and Trinidadians—a man whose inside information did not extend past codfish and yams.

"Well, what did you think?" he asked Alice, after we had finally finished an elaborate five-course meal.

"The best Indian food I ever had," Alice said with a shudder.

•

"What do you suggest we eat in the place of Indian food?" I asked Alice the next day. I had just finished a very satisfying English breakfast of eggs and sausages and grilled tomatoes and kippers, but I had that anxious feeling I get sometimes in parts of the American South when, after finishing a fine Southern breakfast of eggs and grits and little country-sausage patties made into sandwiches with biscuits, I realize that the high point of the day may have passed before nine in the morning.

"Natural food in England is extraordinarily good," Alice said.

"You know health food disagrees with me," I said.

"Natural food is not the same as health food."

"It certainly isn't in my case," I said. "Unless long-term nausea is your idea of health." If one of her attacks of diet balancing had come over her, I told Alice, she could comfort herself with the reminder that the filling in one English sausage probably satisfies the minimum daily cereal requirement for six months.

I resolved to redouble my efforts to find decent pub food in London, or maybe a fish-and-chips café that actually fried the fish when it was ordered instead of in a mass fry-in with all the other fish at six in the morning. The closest fish-and-chips café of quality that I knew about was in Brighton. Several people had recommended as the best fish-and-chips restaurant in London a place that was noted for the length of its wine list—a place I naturally dismissed out of hand, the way I would dismiss a barbecue joint in Arkansas that also served lobster tails and chow mein. The pasties at the pubs I had been eating at in London tasted like meat and veggies cleverly repackaged in a crust hard enough to be of some use if the pub happened to be the sort of place where the patrons tend to start throwing things at each other late in the evening. Whenever hunger overcame me at a pub, I had taken to ordering a Ploughman's Lunch—basically cheese and a roll and chutney—on the theory that its ingredients at least remained immune from attack by the man in the kitchen. I found eating Ploughman's for that reason depressingly reminiscent of a defensive gin-rummy player I once knew whose strategy was based on ridding himself of all high cards as quickly as possible and was expressed in the motto "Lose less."

But was I ready for health food? Aside from the fact that it has always seemed bad for my health, what would people say? Most of my eating discussions are, after all, with the kind of people who could be categorized roughly as big hungry boys—people who offer to let me in on the supreme *tacito* joint in East Los Angeles if, in return, I promise to keep the information to myself and to search my mind for suggestions as to how someone with a strong pastrami habit can survive in Cheyenne, Wyoming. What would Fats Goldberg, the pizza baron, someone who believes that green vegetables should be consumed only by small furry animals, say if I answered his inevitable question about eating in England by telling him I hung around health-food shops, gulping down wheat berries and bean sprouts? Could I really discuss whole-grain bread with chili heads and knish freaks?

"Let's just stop in to see what they have," Alice said one day, as we passed a health-food store called Sesame, near Primrose Hill Park. "Maybe we can have a picnic in the park."

I hesitated. I was famished. Alice had suggested that if I didn't take a meal or two break from Chinese food I might start nodding off from monosodium glutamate. We were a long way from Brighton. I was a bit embarrassed about going back to the fish-and-chips place there anyway: on our previous visit I had, under some pressure from Alice, removed some of the batter from my fish, making me feel like a pudgy secretary who had saved a few calories by removing the top slice of bread from her chicken-salad sandwich at lunch. I glanced quickly up and down the street to make certain that Fats Goldberg was not lingering nearby. Then we went in.

I had to admit that the salad did not produce immediate queasiness. The quiche was a great improvement on those leaded Frisbees that have been delivered to us now and then in Stuff-Stuff with Heavy joints through the efforts of two strong men and a reinforced handcart. What seemed truly remarkable, though, was the pizza. Natural-food pizza! It was actually pizza ingredients—tomatoes instead of tomato sauce, for instance—spread on top of heavy, whole-grain bread and toasted under the grill, the way your mother used to toast the ham-and-cheese sandwich for you at lunch if you had behaved yourself all morning.

"You don't seem to be having any difficulty eating the pizza," Alice said.

"The dissolution of the British Empire is complete when what you buy in health-food stores tastes better than real food," I said.

"I think it's all marvelous," Alice said.

"Maybe we should head over to Golders Green," I said. "I feel okay so far, but it would ease my mind to be close at hand to an antidote. Just in case."

•

By the time we got back to England again, I had reason to be optimistic about what we would find there to eat. Charlie Plum, our foreign-correspondent friend, had been on the job in London for several months, and I assumed he had made a small hobby of checking out fish-and-chip joints. I had been informed by some other specialists in the field that a new fish-and-chips café on Lisson Grove was causing lines around the block. A flash memory of a Singapore noodle dish we had once eaten at Chuen Chung Ku, on Wardour Street, had inspired me to write Plum about investigating some of the Singapore restaurants that had opened in London. I phoned Plum as soon as we arrived. He said that I might like to have lunch at Sweetings, a plain fish house in the City, but his suggestions for the serious dinners we had planned were virtually all French restaurants.

I was astounded. "Could he have become a connoisseur of Stuff-Stuff with Heavy?" I asked Alice. "Who would have thought it of a man who travels with Arthur Bryant's barbecue sauce?"

What seemed to disturb Alice the most about my conversation with Plum was the news that in an effort to find the perfect dining spot he had eaten in sixty French restaurants in London within a few months. (When Plum's friends are asked to name his principal charms, they often mention relentlessness.) Alice feared that eating in that many London French restaurants in such a short time could lead to someone's entire system going into heavy-cream arrest.

The restaurant we decided on—a French seafood place in Chelsea called Le Suquet—did not appear to be in the Stuff-Stuff with Heavy tradition. The atmosphere was informal. The proprietors were obviously French people instead of one of those English couples who seem to use up a considerable part of their energies making certain they have the correct pronunciation of Bourguignon. Any suspicion I had that appearances might be deceiving—that a trout stuffed with a shrimp stuffed with an olive stuffed with a pimento was about to appear, submerged in white cream sauce à la Elmer's—was swept away by the appearance of a startling assortment of shellfish. There were mussels and clams and oysters and langoustines and crawfish—all of them giving every indication of recent experience in salt water.

"You must admit . . ." Alice said after a while, her voice emerging and then fading away from behind a teetering pile of empty shells.

"I suppose the debates all those years about whether or not to join the Common Market weren't meaningless after all," I said, as soon as I disentangled myself from a crab claw. "This is what they must have meant by 'entering Europe.' "

The meal at Le Suquet was very much in Alice's mind a couple of weeks later, when we returned to London from visiting the Jowells in Somerset and had only one meal left before returning home. Although we had made our usual trip to Golders Green—tradition must be observed—I still felt the need of more fried seaweed. I had not been able to find time for the fish-and-chips place that was said to be stopping traffic on Lisson Grove, and I still wanted to check out the Singapore places, which Plum had failed to investigate in his obsessive pursuit of the best French restaurant in London.

All of which does not explain how I found myself sitting across the table from Alice at a small French restaurant called Ma Cuisine—the other French restaurant Plum had enthusiastically recommended.

"You're doing this all for me," Alice said.

"It's nothing, really," I said, trying to remember precisely the expression Humphrey Bogart used when he arranged to have Ingrid Bergman fly off with Paul Henreid while he remained to face the Nazis with Claude Rains. "I'm sure I'll get some fish and chips someday. Probably."

The first course arrived. I had ordered red mullet soup. I tasted it. It was staggering. It was so good it immediately joined a sort of soup pantheon that sloshes around in the back of my mind— Gladee's chowder, for instance, and the gumbo we ate at the andouille gumbo cook-off sponsored by the Jaycees in Laplace, Louisiana, and some lentil soup Alice once made with a stock based on the carcass of a smoked turkey someone had sent us from Greenberg's in Tyler, Texas.

"This is really sweet of you," Alice said. "Considering how much you really like all of that disgusting fish and chips."

I shrugged modestly as I ate. It occurred to me that the line outside of the fish-and-chips place on Lisson Grove might not mean anything anyway, since English people like standing in line so much they often just queue up as a way to pass the time.

"It's very nice of you to come here just because I wanted to," Alice said.

"It's nothing," I said. "Really."

(1 0)

A Softball, a Lump

I ONCE BECAME ACQUAINTED with the plight of three young lawyers in Omaha who were painfully conscious of the city's limitation as a gastronomic capital—all of them having at one time or another tasted the delights of Kansas City.

"It's as if somebody prepared for the French foreign service in Paris or Lyons and then got assigned to Liverpool for the duration," I explained to Alice.

"Mmmm," Alice said. "Could you please pass the sour cream?"

Alice and I were having our discussion just after I had received a letter from one of the lawyers, a Creighton University law professor named Michael Fenner, informing me that he and his two colleagues at the bar had discovered the greatest steak house in the world—a place that served sirloin steaks he described as "the shape of a softball, only bigger."

"I better get on out there," I said to Alice. "Those young fellows are suffering, and somebody has to give them some encouragement."

"What makes you think they're suffering?" Alice asked. "He says right in the letter that they've discovered the best steak house in the world. It also says that he likes the food in Omaha, that Omaha has the best cheeseburger in the world, and that there are several other eating experiences in Omaha nobody should miss."

"Midwesterners are noted for making the best of any situation, Alice," I said. "I thought you knew that by now."

I understood how the attorneys in question were suffering. The one generalization that it may be safe to make about lawyers— except, of course, for the statistically incontrovertible one that this country has quite a few more of them than it has any need for— is that the profession includes a large number of serious eaters. Once, when some employees of a noted steak house in Washington were arrested on narcotics charges, the waiters involved found themselves with immediate legal aid from attorneys who had represented some of the most prominent Watergate figures, and the maître d' showed up in court with a partner in the firm headed by Edward Bennett Williams. One of the three Omaha lawyers, a hefty young man named Daniel Morisseau, who works for the Union Pacific Railroad, has about him such a palpable interest in food that, I later learned, a taxi driver who once took him and some other travelers from the Memphis airport to downtown hotels pointed out governmental and cultural sights to the passengers in general, then slowed down at a corner, looked straight at Morisseau, and indicated the entrance to the city's premier barbecue establishment.

In the rather informal survey I have taken over the years on intensity of interest in food by profession, lawyers rank only a few trades below concert pianists, who are as a group undoubtedly the most devout searchers-out of quality restaurants—a phenomenon I can account for only with the theory that concert pianists, who travel constantly, quickly come to realize that the alternative to finding a decent place to eat on their own is having dinner at the home of the chairman of the local Philharmonic's hospitality committee. Reporters rank pretty low in my survey, partly because of the curse they share with the Irish. I once ate regularly with the members of an American newsmagazine bureau in Paris who had the custom of eating lunch as a group every Saturday, and the restaurant they favored always turned out to have been chosen for the perfection of its dry martinis. Once they found a bartender who had mastered the art, they tended to follow him from restaurant to restaurant, the way a group of concert pianists would follow a gifted but temperamental sauce chef.

Once I had met the three lawyers in question, I realized I had been quite right about the extent of their misery in Omaha. None of the three had grown up there—they were raised and educated in various parts of Missouri and Kansas—so when they talked about restaurants with the sort of nostalgia that can sometimes make up for whatever the sauce lacked, they were talking about restaurants in some other city. The nostalgia did not seem to be associated with restaurants of their childhoods. Michael Fenner, who grew up in St. Joseph, Missouri, recalls having practically no interest in eating until he happened to go to law school in Kansas City—where he met Dan Morisseau, and where, judging from their reminiscences, the two of them must have had to pick out the words in their contract texts through the barbecue-sauce stains. Fenner also spent a few years in Washington, working for the Justice Department, and he shared quite a few meals there with John E. Smith, a lawyer from Atchison, Kansas, not far down the Missouri River from St. Joe, who was then working for Senator Dole and later became the house attorney of an Omaha trucking company. Fenner still likes to talk to Smith about eating in Washington—the Cuban food at the Omega and the Middle Eastern food at the Calvert Café and the chili at Hazel's Texas Chili Parlor. Fenner believes that Hazel's recipe was so secret that she carried it with her to the grave, although some other Washington eaters believe that it was handed down intact to a man with a tattoo, and still others believe that it was not the sort of recipe anyone would have to guard very closely. Fenner's favorite restaurant in the Washington area was the renowned Silver Spring fish house called the Crisfield Seafood Restaurant. He misses practically everything about Crisfield's.

"They know how to treat children," I heard him say once.

"They know how to treat oysters," said Morisseau, who did some eating in Washington himself.

The exchange came in the midst of one of the discussions the three lawyers have had about how the food in Omaha compares with the food in other cities they have lived in. They do all seem to like Omaha, and they have been adventurous about seeking out the food of ethnic groups that an Easterner might not expect to find in Nebraska—Mexicans, for instance, and Bohemians. But Morisseau, after some careful research, concluded that what passes for barbecue in Omaha is just beef covered with a mixture of ketchup, Tabasco sauce, and a concoction called liquid smoke. Fenner decided that Italian food in Omaha amounts to pouring red sauce over whatever happens to be on the plate—a Midwestern Italian variation of the way Alice uses Devonshire cream in England. A couple of years after Morisseau moved to Omaha, he made a trip to New York, and he had trouble shaking his astonishment at rediscovering that there are Italian restaurants without red sauce and Chinese restaurants without chow mein. For someone who has accommodated himself to the limited number of restaurants in a Midwestern city, the quantity as well as the quality of New York restaurants can be staggering. About the time Morisseau made his trip, someone published a book that dealt only with the Chinese restaurants of New York; it was two hundred and sixteen pages long, the authors having decided to limit themselves to eighty restaurants out of what the Chinatown Chamber of Commerce estimated to be about one thousand.

"We gave up a lot of food when we came here," one of the lawyers said during the discussion. "What we got was steak."

Omaha, of course, has a few dozen steak houses—typical Midwestern red-meat palaces except that, the proprietorship being almost universally Italian, the customary side dish is spaghetti rather than hash browns. But the steak house Fenner had mentioned, a place called Dreisbach's, is in Grand Island, Nebraska—a hundred and forty miles away.

Fenner and Smith and Morisseau had most recently eaten at Dreisbach's on the way to a law seminar in Kearney, Nebraska, but when I informed them that I was coming to Nebraska to cheer them up, they seemed untroubled about just driving out to Grand Island from Omaha for dinner. Morisseau—the only one of the three who might qualify in some circles as an Easterner, having been raised in Kirkwood, Missouri, near St. Louis—has a fondness for the West that encompasses pioneer history and Western railroads and driving across the flat reaches of Nebraska which have caused many other travelers to sum up the state as being "just too far across." Smith and Fenner once drove an hour and a half to Peru, Nebraska, to eat dinner in a restaurant called Peru Seasons. (They liked it, but the proprietors decided to move to Costa Rica.) The trip to Peru was an activity of an informal eating club that they and their wives and four other couples belong to. Every month or so the women of the club cook a special dinner out of a particular cookbook or from the cuisine of a particular country. Twice the club had lobsters flown in from Maine. The men handled one meal, in the summer, and, having traveled to Kansas City for the supplies, they held a sort of taste-off between the barbecue sauce provided by Arthur Bryant's and by Gates Barbecue, a worthy if less legendary competitor.

It is not the sort of club in which a lot of eating time is wasted on talk about the bouquet of the wine or the texture of the crêpes. When it's called anything, it's called the Omaha Gourmands. The most memorable remark made at any of its functions came when one member was finishing up some of the main course directly from the serving platter—an understandable way to pass the post-meal lull, as far as I'm concerned—and another member said, "Please don't eat the spoon." There was some talk of translating that into French and putting it on a club T-shirt. Morisseau is not a member of the club, but he may be even more interested in quantity than the Omaha Gourmands are, particularly when the quantity in question is of beef. Morisseau is what used to be called a "meat-and-potatoes man"—in his case, a lot of meat and plenty of potatoes. The steak rumor he is most interested in investigating is a tip that the Elks Club in Ogallala, Nebraska, serves a 28-ounce sirloin.

•

I had looked upon Fenner's letter not only as an opportunity to buck up the spirits of some exiles but also as an opportunity to try overcoming what I acknowledge is a strong prejudice against eating in steak houses. It is a prejudice I blame partly on living for too many years in the East, where the atmosphere in most steak houses is the strongest argument I know for vegetarianism. While the rest of the country is becoming littered with steak houses that have "themes" like Old Depot or Western Barn, the theme of New York steak houses remains The Big Shots Meet the Tough Guys. Doormen say "Okay, Mac" as they accept five dollars for parking a customer's Mercedes; waiters say "Yeah, lady" when a female patron asks if she may have the sixteen-dollar filet. The male customers tend to have the look of people who are proud of themselves for having just slipped the headwaiter about what they paid their secretaries that day and for figuring out some way to take it off their taxes. A lot of the female customers are prime specimens for a game Alice and I used to play to pass the time during intermissions at the Broadway theater—trying to guess how long some particularly glossy culture lover in the first eight rows spent dressing for the evening.

Aside from the fact that the atmosphere of most New York steak houses is a threat to anyone's digestion, I must admit that, unlike many of my countrymen, I do not feel the need of a pound or so of red meat every day or two to stave off the perils of anemia. My mother has often said that I am not a "real steak eater"—real steak eaters being, as I understand the term, people who hold up dessert for a long time while they gnaw on the bones.

I have long suspected, I must admit, that a blind taste test would be as embarrassing for the people who go on about the superiority of one steak restaurant or another as it would be for the people who take a blood oath of loyalty to a particular brand of Scotch—or as it already has been for a law professor who boasts about the unique splendor of his eggs. On the other hand, I do like steak. There used to be a steak restaurant on the outskirts of Kansas City I loved going to, but after I heard some rumors that it had switched from charcoal broiling to gas, I decided against returning—partly because R.C.'s fried-chicken restaurant interposed itself between the steak restaurant and town, and partly because I might find it embarrassing to finish off a twelve-ounce filet and still not know for certain whether the rumors were true.

•

Fenner's letter was, as Alice had said, enthusiastic about the eating opportunities in Omaha. He suggested that I come at least a day early to try some of the local specialties before we drove to Grand Island, although when I arrived he seemed to be strapped about where he and his wife and I should go for lunch. He had heard—incorrectly, as it later turned out—that the obvious place, a stockyards bar that served Mexican food and was called V.I.P. South, had closed. He settled on Joe Tess' Place, which specializes in scored carp. There is no mention of carp on the menu. Perhaps because the carp has had some difficulty overcoming a reputation as an ugly-looking beast that spends a lot of time nosing around in the mud, Joe Tess' menu has always identified the specialty merely as Famous Fish. Joe Tess charges sixty-five cents for a Famous Fish Sandwich, with an extra ten cents for specifying a rib or tail cut. The rib cut costs the same as the tail cut; it's the luxury of making the choice that costs a dime. Apparently, bitter words are spoken now and then at Joe Tess' Place when a diner who has paid a dime for specifying ribs finds that his dining partner got ribs just in the luck of the draw. There is some controversy about what the best part of a carp is, and there are a good many people who believe that there isn't any best part of a carp. Mike Fenner's wife, Anne, sounded like one of those. The most she could manage to say after trying her first plate of Famous Fish was "Well, that's got to be unique."

Her husband seemed discouraged. "You kind of hate being from a place that's famous for that," he said.

John Smith told us later that the secret is in the preparation. "In Atchison, you nail the carp to a board and lean it up against the fire until the board starts to get kind of black," he said. "Then you turn it over and nail it to the other side of the board and lean that next to the fire until that side of the board gets kind of black. Then you eat the board."

•

"Well, it's got to be kind of unique," I said, when Alice asked me on the telephone that night about our lunch.

"How about dinner?" she said. We had eaten dinner at a cheerful Bohemian bar whose proprietors had such a strong Midwestern feeling about not carrying the divisions of squabbling Europe to the New World that they furnished "extra gravy" designed, as far as I could tell, to apply equally to Polish sausages, German sauerbraten, and Hungarian goulash. I told Alice I thought the high point of the meal came when Morisseau responded to a choice of two vegetables by saying, "I'll take double dumplings—that other stuff grows under the ground."

"Is there a French restaurant there you could try?" Alice asked.

"A what!" Alice was perfectly aware of my having stated in public print that a good French restaurant would come to Omaha about the time decent barbecue hit the Paris suburbs. I was willing to admit that the French restaurants in London had been a pleasant surprise, but Great Britain happens to be a bona fide member of the European Economic Community. For years I have gone around the United States assuming that good food is available if the careful traveler sticks to regional specialties and the cooking of ethnic groups strong enough to have at least two aldermen.

"Don't forget about André's," Alice said. André's is a French bakery in Kansas City that I have never entered. For years I brushed off suggestions that I go there by saying that someone who had only a few days in town to get down what might be several months' supply of superior barbecue and fried chicken had no time for such frivolities as finding out what the western Missouri version of a brioche might taste like. Then, in 1976, Mimi Sheraton, the redoubtable food critic of *The New York Times*, wrote an article informing Republicans who were about to travel to Kansas City for their national convention that André's had croissants better than any she had ever been able to find in New York. Alice, it almost goes without saying, adores croissants.

"André's was a fluke, Alice," I said. "Like a magnificent potato *latke* in London. A Traveling Person has to play the percentages." According to the percentages, a fancy French restaurant in Omaha was likely to be long on menu descriptions and short on taste. On the other hand, Alice and I had missed a lot of croissants playing the percentages in Kansas City. Could I have been wrong all those years? How bad could, say, trout amandine in a Midwestern French restaurant be? I shuddered, having just remembered.

Omaha, of course, does have a fancy French restaurant. The next day, just out of curiosity, I asked Morisseau what it was like.

He dismissed it as not serving steak "except for the fancy kind."

"Good point," I said, regaining my confidence. I was ready to push on to Fenner's cheeseburger joint.

•

According to the plan the three lawyers had devised, we were stopping at Stella's Tavern, a hamburger place near the SAC air base, to stoke up for the drive to Grand Island. Morisseau arrived at Stella's with some random train talk he apparently considers appropriate to the beginning of any journey ("The Ford FAST's running on time. The ARRO's five minutes late. Trains are speeding the nation's vital resources to their destination so that American consumers can consume everything that can be scratched out of the ground") and some words for Smith's benefit on the trucking industry ("Will the slaughter on our highways never stop? Is there no end to the carnage wreaked by the Killer Trucks?"). Stella's served up, as Fenner had predicted, a quality cheeseburger. It was not Kansas City quality, perhaps, but certainly nothing that would force anybody back into nostalgia for a Cuban restaurant in Washington. The cheeseburgers were accompanied by red beer—beer that has been mixed, for reasons that defy the imagination, with tomato juice. Smith remarked that the red beer served some years before at Sellen's Pool Hall in Russell, Kansas, was better than Stella's, and I think he must have been right. Everyone was looking forward to the journey, although for long drives Morisseau prefers the stark plains of western Nebraska to the central part of the state, where he has been heard to complain, "There are trees blocking the view."

I asked about the steak served at Dreisbach's, thereby launching my companions into what I believe lawyers call a colloquy:

"It's like a softball—sort of round."

"No, more like a lump."

"I'd prefer to say 'round' rather than 'like a lump.' "

All the attorneys were willing to stipulate that the tenderness of Dreisbach's steak was beyond question. Fenner had written me that Dreisbach's furnished knives only on the chance that some diner might want to slice up the skin of his baked potato.

"My mother often says I'm not a real steak eater," I said as we waited for our steaks at Dreisbach's. No colloquy followed. My dinner companions exchanged what I interpreted to be wary glances. Dreisbach's was full, even though it was only about six. We had found ourselves arriving an hour and a half ahead of schedule, despite a stop at a café in Wahoo whose chocolate-chip cookies Smith admires and a tour of the Stuhr Museum of the Prairie Pioneer and a slowdown to practically a dead stop at every railway crossing so that Smith could demonstrate to Morisseau the difficulty any innocent citizen out for a drive has in crossing the Union Pacific tracks without breaking an axle. Dreisbach's had turned out to be a huge, windowless brick restaurant hidden in a string of franchise joints along a double lane just on the edge of Grand Island. A plaque in the lobby indicated an Award of Excellence for Bread and Rolls from the Wheat Division of the State Department of Agriculture. I was put off a bit by a subheading under "Soups" on the menu that said "Heinz Individual," but I was cheered by the sight of the other people in the dining room—mostly families, with a pleasant absence of either Big Shots or Tough Guys.

The steak did look like something between a softball and a lump. I rather enjoyed it, even though the waitress had acknowledged that it had been broiled with gas, not charcoal.

"Well," I said to the attorneys as I finished the last of it. "I've tasted worse steaks."

"That is not exactly the response we were looking for," Morisseau said.

"Your trouble is that Omaha is no Kansas City," I said.

"Omaha's not a lot of places," Fenner said, taking on a wistful, Crisfield's sort of expression.

"Well," Morisseau said, "at least you can come out here and eat steak without having someone shove cold spaghetti under your nose." Midwesterners are noted for making the best of any situation.

A couple of months after my trip I got a letter from some people who identified themselves as members of the Omaha Wine and

Food Society. They had heard about my visit. They said that had I merely visited the appropriate *haute cuisine* palaces my "tastebuds would have rather roamed among classic foods of excellence." That sounded enough like the sort of menu those *haute cuisine* palaces have to confirm my belief that I had been wise not to sample what I believe the international gourmets categorize as Cornhusker French.

I also received another letter from Mike Fenner. "Omaha has a Korean restaurant which we kept from you the first trip, and a place that serves excellent pan-fried chicken," he wrote. "There is also a wonderful place on the banks of an otherwise undeveloped stretch of the Missouri River. One can sit outside and eat catfish (much better than carp) or fried chicken (deep fat, I suppose) while watching the river roll by . . . There is plenty to come back for."

"They sound desperate," I said to Alice.

"I suppose you think the only honorable course is for you to go back and try to buck them up," Alice said.

I thought about my meals in Omaha for a while. "No," I finally said. "I think the biggest help I can be to those young fellows is to encourage them to get by on their own resources."

Goldberg as Artifact

I WAS NOT SURPRISED when I heard that the Smithsonian Institution had expressed an interest in the neon sign on Fats Goldberg's pizza parlor. I have always thought of Fats himself as an American artifact, although he is ordinarily regarded as a medical wonder rather than a piece of straight Americana. What has brought doctors around to the pizza parlor now and then to have a stare at Fats and poke him around a bit is not merely that he once lost some one hundred and sixty pounds—no trivial matter in itself, being a weight equivalent to all of Rocky Graziano in his prime—but that he has succeeded for nearly twenty years in not gaining them back. Apparently, keeping off a large weight loss is a phenomenon about as common in American medicine as an impoverished dermatologist. Because Fats is now exceptionally skinny, most people call him Larry instead of Fats. Nobody, as far as I know, has ever called him Mr. Goldberg. Alice and Abigail both call him Larry; Sarah, who likes to keep him distinguished in her mind from another friend of ours named Larry, has always referred to him as Larry Fats Goldberg the One Who Makes Pizza. I still call him Fats. Having known him in Kansas City long before he let his Graziano slip away from him, I have difficulty thinking of him as anything but a fatty. He has even more difficulty than I do. He is, he cheerfully admits, as obsessed with food now as he ever was. (Fats cheerfully admits everything, which is one reason nobody has ever thought of calling him Mr. Goldberg.) Convinced that remaining a stick figure is the only alternative to becoming a second mountain of flesh, Fats has sentenced himself to a permanent diet broken only by his semiannual eating binges in Kansas City and, during the rest of the year, a system of treats on Mondays and Thursdays which reminds many New Yorkers of alternate-side-of-the-street parking regulations. His semiannual eating binges are so gargantuan and so infectious that Alice makes a small hobby out of seeing to it that Fats and I are never in Kansas City at the same time.

After six or eight years in the business, Fats became rather restless with the life of a pizza baron. "You can't schlepp pizzas all your life," he often told me. He began phoning regularly for our reaction to the schemes he thought up for new lines of work. What Fats's schemes have always had in common is that they are invariably concerned with food and they are invariably among the worst ideas in the history of commerce. At some point, I reluctantly came to the conclusion that Fats may be like one of those novelists whom publishers speak of as having only one book in them. It occurred to me that, as far as moneymaking business schemes go, creating the brilliant bi-ethnic concept of Goldberg's Pizzeria might have just done Fats in.

Sometimes Fats seems to prefer discussing his schemes with Alice instead of me—perhaps because he is aware that people in Kansas City sometimes refer to her, in respectful tones, as a "gourmet cook." It is certainly not because she is more encouraging than I am about the commercial prospects of, say, an edible diet book or a pizza cone. In fact, I at least mentioned to Fats that a better name for Goldberg's Pizza Cone might be Goldberg's Pizza Cohen, before telling him that it was, by whatever name, one of the truly dreadful ideas of the decade. When Alice answers the telephone, says "Hi, Larry," and then says something like "That is just awful —one of your absolute worst," I know that the Larry she is talking to is Larry Fats Goldberg the One Who Makes Pizza. As far as I know, Abigail is the only person who has ever taken any of Goldberg's ideas seriously. When he began to talk a lot about an invention of his called a pizza pusher—a hard-plastic instrument that would allow someone to eat a piece of hot pizza without burning his fingers—she asked him about its progress every time she saw him. "I'd really like to try it," she always said. Abigail has actually eaten a trial version of a pizza cone—pizza dough rolled into the shape of a cone and then filled with what more pedestrian operators put on the top. "It's very good, Larry," she said. "It really is." Fats beamed.

I don't know how to account for Abigail's sympathy for the Goldberg schemes. It is true that when we go to Goldberg's Pizzeria on Sunday evenings Fats always lets Abigail make her own pizza; it is true that he regularly shows up at our house on Abigail's birthday carrying a heart-shaped pizza, with her initials done up in green pepper. But he has always performed those same services for Sarah, and the noise Sarah made when she saw the pizza cone defies any attempt at reproduction. My own response to ideas by Fats has been fairly consistent. When I hear about something like a scheme to produce an edible diet book, I usually say, "Fat Person, there are worse things than schlepping pizza."

Fats mentioned the Smithsonian accession during one of our Sunday evening visits to the pizzeria. Having had some time to reflect on it, he told us he was not at all surprised that a place like the Smithsonian Institution wanted his sign. "It was a nice piece of neon work," he said. As it happened, one of the regular customers at Goldberg's Pizzeria works for Chermayeff & Geismar Associates, the firm commissioned to design a five-year Bicentennial exhibit for the Smithsonian called "A Nation of Nations." When the customer suggested that Goldberg's sign might be suitable for a display that would amount to a selection of ethnic neon, Fats said, as he later remembered it, "You want me to take it down now or will you come back for it?" (A Smithsonian curator came back for it, Fats having in the meantime ordered a precise replica to take its place.) Fats's cooperation was based partly on an understandable pride ("There I'd be with Lucky Lindy and everybody") and partly on a quick calculation of how many pizza eaters might pass through the exhibit in five years.

It is natural for a restaurant proprietor to see publicity as a way of attracting customers, but Fats has probably been alone among his peers as seeing it also as a way of attracting a wife. Ever since his emaciation, in his mid-twenties, Fats has thought about finding an appropriate wife almost as much as he has thought about food, and he tends to regard publicity as a sort of singles ad. In the days when Alice thought Fats was serious about finding a wife, she used to spend some time trying to persuade him that his search should be less dependent on such devices as striking up conversations on Madison Avenue buses. Eventually, Alice decided that Fats did not genuinely want to get married, even if he found someone who, in addition to meeting all his other requirements, was willing to commit herself to a lifetime of semiannual eating binges in Kansas City. I still try to help by suggesting that some of his requirements are unreasonable—a requirement, for instance, that the prospect not be seeing a psychiatrist. I have tried to explain to Fats that among young women of certain backgrounds in New York seeing a psychiatrist is merely a ritual of the culture, like foot-binding once was among young women of certain backgrounds in China. Fats remains unconvinced. He thinks that anyone who sees a psychiatrist is "a little twitchy." Also, he says that when he thinks of his intended telling all to some psychiatrist, he himself feels "a little twitchy."

Fats has often been mentioned in the press—in articles about pizza or about men's fashions (his views on clothing are as deeply rooted in the fifties as his views on courtship and marriage; sartorially, he is best known for an addiction to saddle shoes) or about what celebrated New Yorkers like to do on Saturdays in the city ("Larry Goldberg, a bachelor who operates Goldberg's Pizzeria on 53rd Street and Second Avenue, said he spent his Saturdays at Bloomingdale's, where he rides the escalators and 'looks for girls' "). Somehow, though, Fats could never get over the fear that there were still a few people in New York who had never heard of Goldberg's Pizzeria. So in his travels around town he continued to spread the word by handing out small paper Goldberg's menus that list pizzas with names like "Moody Mushrooms" and "Bouncy Meatballs" and "SMOG" (sausage, mushrooms, onions, and green peppers)—the last a house specialty that Fats has described on the menu as "a gourmet tap dance." Extracting a menu from Fats has never required strenuous persuasion. "I don't press them into the hands of accident victims, or anything," Fats once told me. "But I did hand them out to the orchestra at Radio City Music Hall one night as they came out of the pit after the last show."

I thought I ought to go to the opening of "A Nation of Nations" with Fats; he was, after all, the only person I knew from whom the Smithsonian Institution had ever collected anything. Alice thought the trip was a good idea as long as Fats and I did not find it expedient to travel from New York to Washington by way of Kansas City. Fats has never been seriously tempted to break his regimen by the food of any other city. I have always found the food in Washington what might be expected of a city dominated by people who are willing to put up with the gray meat and spongy chicken of political dinners year after year merely for a seat in the Senate.

Fats was looking forward to the opening as his first trip to a museum in the role of a benefactor. He is not one of those New Yorkers who never seem to take advantage of the city's great museums. He long ago decided that museums are ideal places to strike up a conversation with someone who just might turn out to be the future Mrs. Fats Goldberg.

"On Sundays I schlepp through Central Park and stop for a rest on the steps of the Metropolitan," he once told us. "But I never go inside. The Metropolitan depresses me."

"You mean because of all those Egyptian tombs and everything?" I asked.

"No, it's mainly families," he said. "For girls the Whitney's the ticket. I usually work the Whitney on Sunday afternoons. I used to go in, but now I just work the lobby and save the buck and a half."

The subject of museums had come up suddenly, as I remember, during a conversation at our house about a business scheme Fats had concocted—a plan to offer a sort of food tour of New York that would take visitors from one ethnic delicacy to another for four or five hours.

"Fats," I said, "I hate to be the agent of your disillusionment once again, but I think you should know that many people do not customarily eat for four or five hours at a stretch. Many people eat breakfast and wait a few hours before eating lunch. Then they go about their business for a while, and then they eat dinner."

"Three meals a day!" said Alice, like some zealot who is always lying in wait for the opportunity to get a plug in for one wacky cause or the other.

Fats looked puzzled. When he is not on a diet—that is, when he is in Kansas City—he does not exactly divide his eating into meals, even if he does continue to use phrases like "Then on the way to lunch I stopped at Kresge's for a chili dog."

For several months he stopped talking about his ethnic-food tour and concentrated on the edible diet book, which many connoisseurs of Goldberg schemes believe to be his worst idea ever. "Don't you see it?" he would say. "The whole thing would be edible. Food coloring for ink. I haven't figured out what we could use for the paper, except maybe pressed lettuce, but we'll find something. Can't you just see Johnny Carson eating one on television! Each page would have menus for the three meals of the day, but one of the meals would be the page—so, for instance, you'd just eat that page for breakfast."

"If you ate the page for breakfast, Fats, how would you know what to eat for lunch and dinner?"

"It'd sell like crazy," Fats said, ignoring my quibble. "Bloomingdale's, Neiman Marcus, Marshall Field's. *Goldberg's Edible Diet Book*. I'd autograph them at the cookbook counter at Bloomie's. I hang around there a lot on Saturdays anyway. The cookbook counter is the best place in the store to meet girls."

•

On the flight to Washington for the opening of "A Nation of Nations," I asked Fats if I was about to witness the first visit he had ever made to a museum for any purpose other than to look for girls.

"Who said I won't be looking for girls tonight?" Fats answered. He is a man of strong habits. He acknowledged that he had a thick wad of paper menus in his suitcase. "If there's a flat place in front of the sign, I might just spread some out fan-style," he said. "It might be very artistic."

For the rest of the flight, Fats talked about some of his business

ideas—including a sort of singles restaurant that would feature Fats
as an auctioneer ("If only I could figure out what to auction, it
would be a natural"), and a Sunday morning catering service called
Brunch à la Goldberg, and a lecture tour as the Thin Evangelist.
The concept of the Thin Evangelist evolved, through a mutation
or two from an evangelical fat lady named Sister Sara Lee, who
was the main character in a skit performed by the monumentally
unsuccessful comedy team of Berkowitz and Goldberg—one of the
Fat Man's pre–pizza parlor schemes. It is central to the Thin Evangelist act that Fats begin each lecture by stepping out from behind
an air-filled plastic reproduction of himself as he looked when
he weighed three hundred and twenty pounds, and he told me he
had been concerned about the problem of the Goldberg balloon
springing leaks during all the traveling necessary for the lecture
circuit. Having heard some of the lines from the Sister Sara Lee
routine, I was prepared to tell Fats that his problems with the Thin
Evangelist act probably went beyond leakage, but he suddenly
seemed to lose interest in the lecture circuit in his enthusiasm to
explain the commercial possibilities of his plastic pizza pusher.
He seemed particularly proud that it had only one moving
part.

•

Fats had dressed carefully for the opening. He was wearing a faded
blue Western shirt with the collar spread back to display a V of
white T-shirt, peach-colored Levi's trousers, a Madras sports jacket,
and a pair of black-and-white Spalding saddle shoes with authentic
red rubber soles—a type of saddle shoe apparently as rare and difficult to replace as a 1947 DeSoto. Fats said he keeps the Spaldings
secreted in the back of his closet in their original box, to be taken
out only on special occasions. Having read in the press releases that
"A Nation of Nations" would include not only Thomas Jefferson's
desk and George Washington's mess kit but also an original ticket
booth from the 1923 Yankee Stadium and a selection of American
comic books, I felt obligated to warn Fats that an overzealous curator
might well snatch the saddle shoes from his feet and install them
in a display case between a pair of 1919 spats and a Dacron Nehru

jacket, circa 1968. "Keep both feet on the ground, Fat Person," I said.

We had dinner at a Georgetown fish house—a place that has on some occasions shown indications of being within fish-hauling distance of Chesapeake Bay and on another occasion raised the possibility in Alice's mind that the necks that had once been attached to the soft clam bellies served by Gage & Tollner were not being donated to the *Times* Hundred Neediest Cases after all. Fats ate very little—not because he was nervous about the opening but because it was neither Monday nor Thursday. At the Smithsonian he shifted from foot to foot while the opening ceremonies were going on. Then, the moment they had ended, he walked through the door of the main hall and strode purposefully toward the neon-sign display—not bothering to waste a glance at the Indian artifacts or the display of political buttons or the reconstruction of a 1940 Fort Belvoir enlisted men's barracks. Suddenly he was standing before an array of neon. A smile spread across his face. He looked prouder than I had seen him look since the time Abigail told him that his ethnic-food tour sounded like a lot of fun. The GOLDBERG'S PIZZERIA sign was in a central position, high above IRISH ROSE BAR-GRILL and WARSAW FOOT LONG. A discreetly designed caption said, "Goldberg's Pizzeria, 996 2nd Avenue. New York City. Designed by Fred Stenger. About 1971." Fats hesitated for a moment. Then he pulled some menus out of his Madras sports jacket and put them on a broad railing in front of the signs. A few minutes later, while Fats was at the other end of the display, grumbling about how much space had been given to huge McDonald's signs in foreign languages, an elegantly dressed man walked up to the railing, picked up some menus, and said to his companions, "I can't believe it—Larry Goldberg was already here." Spotting Fats, he said, "Don't you ever stop?" Then he started laughing.

"That was the guy from Chermayeff and Geismar," Fats said later. "He's a small anchovy."

"Is that like a Big Enchilada?" I asked.

"No, no," Fats said. "He has a small anchovy pizza when he comes in for lunch."

Fats seemed impressed by the exhibit ("Terrific, from start to finish") but disappointed by the crowd. He shook his head sadly as we left. "The Whitney's the ticket," he said.

•

"Did I ever tell you my idea for a fat belt?" Fats said as we sat on the plane back to New York.

"I'm sure you haven't," I said. "It sounds like the kind of thing I would have remembered. Maybe that was one you tried out on Alice."

"It would say 'You Are Fat' on the outside, and there would be a calorie counter on the inside," Fats said. "A little gimmick. You know—a little show business."

"I don't believe you should try that one out even on Abigail," I said. "I think that idea might be even worse than the edible diet book."

"I don't know why you say that," Fats said. "I've received nothing but huzzahs since I've discussed it with anybody. Peggy thought it was the best idea in the world."

"Peggy who?"

"Peggy Owens, my haircutter," Fats said. "She cuts my hair for three large SMOGs and three heart-shaped SMOGs."

"She sounds like an astute woman, Fats," I said. "But I'm not sure a talent for barter transfers well into modern merchandising. Also, I'm not sure why we're discussing such things when you should be telling me about your feelings on this historic occasion. Were you proud and humble last night?"

"I was proud and humble, and I thought it was a giggle," Fats said. "That a pizza schlepper would be there with all the biggies!"

•

Not long after the opening of "A Nation of Nations," Fats informed us that he had sold the pizza parlor—transforming himself into a pizza baron emeritus.

"I hope this wasn't based on any assumptions about hitting it rich with the pizza cone, Fat Person," I said. "I feel I should tell you that if Abigail said anything about having her finger on a lot of venture capital, she was talking through her hat."

"It's my greatest invention," he said. "We're just having a little trouble working out the right dough. My baker is getting a little twitchy."

Sarah and Abigail were also concerned about how Fats was going to support himself—and whether their Sunday kitchen privileges at Goldberg's Pizzeria were over. Fats assured us that he would still be at the pizza parlor in the role of consultant to the new owners. He said he even had a supply of free pizzas. The contract calls for Fats to receive one large SMOG a day—total of said SMOGs to be cumulative. We were there a few weeks later, and Fats presented Abigail with what he insisted on calling a "prototype" of the pizza pusher. Abigail lost a slice or two trying to eat with it, but that did not seem to affect her opinion of its usefulness. "It's a very good invention, Larry," she said. "Really."

(1 2)

Air Freight

WHEN ALICE AND I were walking through the American Pavilion at Expo '76 in Spokane, gazing at a pile of mangled appliances displayed as just one example of the crimes we had all been guilty of perpetrating against the environment, I thought I recognized a refrigerator that had been displayed spanking new in the Argentine Pavilion at the Brussels World's Fair in 1958. At that time, it was presumably being displayed to offer silent rebuttal to anyone who might have ever considered the notion that Argentina was incapable of cooling its own loin steaks. I don't feel responsible for solid-wasting refrigerators myself. Even if I did, I wouldn't be enthusiastic about paying admission to be reminded of it. I have disposed of no refrigerator since 1958. As it happens, though, almost superhuman restraint—the sort of restraint that many people, some of them in my own family, do not believe I possess—was required to avoid destroying the refrigerator we now own when the first and only breakdown in its history caused the spoiling of some crawfish *étouffée* I had just lugged all the way from Lafayette, Louisiana, under twenty pounds of dry ice. To this day, whenever I hear some environmentalist go on about modern man's tragic dependence on electricity, I think of my spoiled crawfish.

I don't mean to leave the impression that I always return from a trip with something for the freezer. The country ham I got in

Horse Cave from the Chaneys, for instance, was stored on top of my filing cabinet, Boots Chaney having assured me that it could be left out "for a year or two." The freezer, though, is often full. I have always operated on the assumption that being, say, within a couple of hours of Santa Fe and not dropping in to get some tamales from Mrs. Lina Rivera goes against the American belief in the value of enterprise shown and opportunities seized.

I came across Mrs. Rivera's tamales during a difficult period, when I was trying to gather some regional delicacies for a party that would demonstrate to some New Yorkers the sort of food they were being deprived of daily. There were enough complications to leave me with a permanent admiration for the patience of museum curators who put together shows by borrowing masterpieces from a variety of institutions and private collectors. First, I phoned the only man in southwestern Louisiana who had the facilities to airmail crawfish pies to New York, and he told me I had neglected to write him a thank-you note two years before, after he took me out in his boat on the Atchafalaya Basin. It took a day and a half to compose a letter of apology to him that Alice thought struck the right balance between abjectness and obsequiousness. Then Pat Uhlmann, a friend of ours from Kansas City, said that he would be willing to fly to New York on the day of the party with the necessary supply of Arthur Bryant's ribs, but only if we would refer to him in all correspondence as "Bearer of the Ribs, Keeper of the Sauce." Knowing Uhlmann to be a man of his word who merely happens to have some unusual ambitions—he once concocted a scheme, gracefully vetoed by his wife, to buy his birthplace and turn it into a national shrine—I finally agreed.

Then I discovered that the tamale supplier I had hoped to use for the party, a friend of ours who lives in Arroyo Seco, New Mexico, had turned her attention away from tamale making in the direction of goat raising. I was forced to telephone another friend in New Mexico, a psychiatrist in Albuquerque named Bob Bergman, who had no special credentials in the field of tamales. I did know Bergman to be an eater of considerable scope. He had just finished several years as chief of the mental health programs of the Indian Health Service—based in Window Rock, Arizona, on the Navajo

Reservation—and he seemed to have visited just about every restaurant in the country that is anywhere near any Indians. I suspect he has eaten at Dreisbach's more often than the lawyers from Omaha have. Being a pilot of some experience, he often made his rounds in a small private plane—a fact I have tried not to hold against him, even though the impression I always have while circling over LaGuardia in a commercial airliner that has been told to wait an hour for a runway is that dozens of private planes must be clogging the landing pattern, touching down with their loads of corporation executives and rock stars and political candidates and other people who would probably be doing everybody concerned a favor if they stayed home in the first place. Bergman just happened into Grand Island, Nebraska, one night when he had to make a stop between Aberdeen, South Dakota, and Plainview, Texas, and found the hospitality there extraordinary; it included literally being met by a red carpet, and being chauffeured to Dreisbach's and back by the motel manager. He then started stopping off whenever he was in the area. Sooner or later, he realized that other private pilots were doing the same thing. I told him that I thought all private pilots should fly to Grand Island, Nebraska, and stay there.

Bergman, acknowledging a lack of expertise in the field, agreed to search out a Spanish-speaking tamale specialist who would know for certain how to find the best green-corn tamales in New Mexico. A few days later he called to inform me that I might be looking for blue-corn tamales, since green and blue are the same word in Navajo. I began to worry that I had chosen the wrong tamale man.

"I didn't ask for a scholarly footnote," I told him. "I need tamales."

Bergman called the next week with a more encouraging report. A Spanish-speaking colleague named Gil Duran, who was from Santa Fe, had given him some serious assurances about the work of Lina Rivera. Duran had even volunteered to drive to Santa Fe with Bergman for the pickup. When I came through Albuquerque a couple of weeks later, Bergman handed over two sealed pasteboard boxes of tamales, packed in dry ice.

I tried to appear appreciative, but my concern about the tamales, which I had not tasted or even seen, must have been strong enough to communicate itself to a man in Bergman's line of work. "Don't worry—I'm sure they're great," he said. "Gil wanted to eat a couple of them on the way back from Santa Fe even though they were frozen solid." My trust proved well placed, of course. As it turned out, Lina Rivera is to tamales what Yonah Shimmel is to knishes.

•

The realization that my own trips need not be our only source of freezer treasures came to me one day when Fats Goldberg was about to fly off to Kansas City for one of his eating binges. He asked me if he could do anything for me while he was there—doubtless thinking that he was only making a polite gesture.

"Yes, Fat Person, as a matter of fact, there is," I said. "You can go to Arthur Bryant's barbecue restaurant and pick me up three pounds of spareribs, not forgetting a few handfuls of burnt edges, and then you can bring them back to New York and heat them up slowly in your pizza oven and watch me eat them—that's what you can do for me."

Since then Fats has a standing order from me. Once the ribs are safely in the freezer, I telephone the family that has been chosen to share the celebratory meal—the family having been chosen on the basis of strong Kansas City credentials or several years of extraordinary behavior. I have always assumed that my call touches off unrestrained joy throughout the fortunate household, although once, when the phone was answered by the strictly vegetarian roommate of a friend who had been selected, I was reduced to saying, "Just tell Henry the goods from Kansas City have arrived."

The arrangement has failed to work only once, when Fats returned from Kansas City bearing ribs but informing me that the burnt edges—the burnt edges of barbecued brisket which are presumably why both the Democrats and the Republicans held conventions in Kansas City within two years—had inadvertently been left in his mother's freezer.

"Are you telling me that your dear old mother in Kansas City stole my burnt edges?" I asked the Fat One.

"No, I just forgot them," Fats said.

"I certainly wouldn't have thought that of her," I said. "After all these years."

"She didn't do it," Fats said. "She doesn't even eat barbecue."

"I wouldn't have thought that of her, either," I said. "She always seemed very nice."

"Quit talking to Larry that way," Alice said. "They were just some burnt edges. It's not that important."

"I'm sorry, Fat Man," I said, trying to work up a smile for Fats and a glare for Alice. "I got excited."

Not that important! Why would Alice make a remark like that? Could it be, I began to wonder, that she had what one of Bob Bergman's colleagues might call a repressed hostility toward my attempts, as an old-fashioned American breadwinner, to assure my family a full larder against the possibility of drought or siege? Not long after the burnt-edges incident, Alice made still another suspicious remark. I was about to leave for LaGuardia Airport. Bergman happened to be on his way from Albuquerque to upstate New York, and had offered to hand over some tamales between planes.

"Must you really do this?" she asked me.

"I'd hate to think of poor old Bergman moping around LaGuardia all that time by himself, without even anybody to talk to," I said. "I think he may have as long as twenty-five minutes between planes."

"That's not why you're going," Alice said.

"He's also carrying chili verde," I admitted.

"I don't know why you've gotten yourself into this thing," Alice said.

It suddenly occurred to me that Alice may have overheard me say, "The goods from Kansas City have arrived," on the telephone and misunderstood the sort of substance I was dealing in. I tried to reassure her. "Don't worry," I said. "Green-corn tamales have been decriminalized."

•

Alice's real concern about the tamale drop was based, of course, on the suspicion that I would not start on the six-week raw-carrot torture she had devised for me if the freezer was filled with ribs, tamales, chili verde, Aunt Sadie's blintzes, and a number of other targets of opportunity. She has no strong moral feelings against tamales. On the other hand, the country ham I had acquired in Horse Cave through the good offices of the Chaneys had been drawing what I interpreted as disapproving glances from Alice for a few months whenever she happened to pass by my filing cabinet.

"If you're concerned about its appearance," I finally said, "I want you to know that Boots Chaney assures me the newspaper sticking to it is an authentic detail, like a piece of grit on a very expensive free-range egg." Kentucky is full of stories about sophisticates from the East ordering their first country ham, then throwing it away when it arrives because its appearance leads them to believe that a disaster has overtaken it in the mails. Although I tried to explain to Alice that the ham looked the way it was supposed to look, I also tried to face the fact that I was married to someone who had grown up in Westchester County, New York, blithely extracting the hearts from artichokes.

As it turned out, though, what Alice distrusted about the ham was the recipe Tom Chaney had typed for me. At first, I thought the stationery he used—with its legend about widows being tended and whiskey being hauled and lies being told—had given her the false impression that the Chaneys were not serious people when it came to ham. Alice was not bothered by the stationery. What bothered her was that Chaney's recipe, which called for baking the ham in a sort of crust that was then disposed of, said that only three hours and twenty minutes were required in the oven.

"According to what it says in James Beard, it should take about ten hours," Alice said.

"James Beard!" I said. "James Beard puts squid in his chili!"

James Beard, however worthy he may be in every other respect, does put squid in his chili. I am privy to this fact from having attended what must be described as an international chili confrontation in Manhattan at the home of a Hungarian gourmet. It is true that I find discussions about what properly belongs in chili to be on the same level of interest as detailed descriptions of new wonder diets or explanations of how to outperform the market, but I believe it would be fair to say that putting squid in chili is not what people in Kentucky would refer to as Down Home.

"I'm not going to have anything to do with fixing this ham,"

Alice said. At that moment, I remembered her commenting at the chili confrontation that she found the idea of squid in chili "very imaginative."

"I'll fix the ham," I said. I found an assistant, of course. In the kitchen I'm mainly an idea man, although I did have Abigail complimenting me on my Cheerios until she wised up at about the age of three. First, I phoned Tom Chaney, who sounded rather hurt when I asked him if the recipe could possibly be dangerous. "That has been the best country ham recipe in Kentucky since the mind of man runneth not to the contrary," he said. "If you're worried, you could use a meat thermometer, I suppose, although I would naturally never use no such a thing."

"Who shall we have over to eat the ham?" I asked Alice, after the meat-thermometer compromise seemed to give some assurance that guests would at least be safe.

"How about Bill and Genny?" Alice said.

It was not a suggestion that showed a lot of confidence in my ham. Genny Smith is a kindly person who would probably compliment the president of McDonald's on his Big Mac rather than hurt his feelings. Her husband, Bill, is widely known as the Man with the Naugahyde Palate. His standards of cuisine were set, rather rigidly, at the Bob's Big Boy outlet in Glendale, California, and he would not know a country ham from a parking meter.

My assistant and I began our task—scrubbing off several back issues of the Hart County *Herald*, and preparing the crust in precisely the manner directed by the Chaney family recipe. We put it in the oven and attached the meat thermometer. In exactly three hours and twenty minutes, the thermometer showed precisely the correct temperature for a ham that is ready to be eaten.

"Maybe the Beard recipe allowed for having the ham covered with truffles or *pâté de foie gras* or something," I told Alice.

My assistant removed the crust, and we served the ham. It was magnificent. Even Alice was dazzled.

"It's always nice to see you, Bill," I said to the man with the Naugahyde palate. "But I'm sort of sorry we didn't invite James Beard."

•

A few weeks later, I happened to be passing through Horse Cave, and I was able to report the triumph personally to Tom Chaney—repeating it a few hours later for Boots Chaney, and giving a shortened version to Aunt Daisie Carter.

"Tom says no hard feelings about the country ham," I told Alice on the telephone that night. "He's sending you a gift."

"How nice," she said. "What is it?"

"The local Cheddar," I said. "It's kind of a funny color, but Tom says you'll love it."

The Sound of Eating

AT LEAST I'LL KNOW what to say if a marriage counselor ever asks whether we have one subject that seems to provoke tension in our marriage again and again. "New Orleans," I will say. "Eating in New Orleans, counselor."

"Do you mean that the Chez Helène Incident was not an isolated incident?" the marriage counselor will say.

"Hardly," I will reply, as Alice sits without comment in the corner, stuffing herself with Prestat truffles covered with Devonshire cream.

"Would you like to talk about it?"

"Nothing would give me more pleasure," I will say. "Except perhaps eating in New Orleans, which nobody around here ever seems to let me do in peace." I will then present, in a calm and detached way, what the marriage counselor will come to know as the Jazz Festival Incident.

We had just decided to take in the New Orleans Jazz & Heritage Festival one spring when Alice said, "It would be a great time to visit some of those lovely plantation houses along the river."

I have nothing against plantation houses. I have gone without complaint once or twice to a plantation house outside New Orleans that has been made into a restaurant serving a passable copy of the baked oyster dish whose original inspired me to suggest that a statue be erected in Jackson Square of the inventor—Mrs. Lisa Mosca, of Mosca's roadhouse, in Waggaman, Louisiana. (My proposal calls for the statue to be carved out of fresh garlic.) I had to face the possibility, though, that Alice might be talking about visiting plantation houses that served no food whatsoever. Part of marriage, after all, is trying to protect one's husband or wife from potential weaknesses or excesses, and it occurred to me that Alice was in danger of developing an unhealthy interest in exteriors.

"How can you decide to go to a jazz festival in New Orleans, the birthplace of jazz, and theh talk about spending any of your time staring at a bunch of façades?" I asked Alice.

"Are you claiming that you're going there to listen to jazz?" she asked.

"Well," I said, confidently. I didn't think I should go any further than that. I do like jazz. I particularly like the sort of New Orleans street jazz heard at, say, a funeral held for a member of the Eagle Eye Benevolent Mutual Association or a Founder's Day Parade staged by the Jolly Bunch Social Aid & Pleasure Club—the sort of jazz nobody can hear without falling in behind the band and half-dancing down the street in a movement New Orleans people call "second-lining." I like the way jazz can be used in New Orleans to make what could be an ordinary event special. In fact, I once hired a jazz band to meet Alice as she arrived at the New Orleans airport from New York—a gesture, I might feel compelled to tell any marriage counselor, that was not made under the assumption that she would start talking about plantation houses or diet plans the moment she got off the plane. In fact, the jazz festival happened to be going on during the weekend I hired the band—although we were able to stop in only briefly, having a previously made engagement at the Crawfish Festival in Breaux Bridge. There was some difficulty finding a band that was free at the time Alice's airplane was scheduled to arrive, I remember, and a friend who was acting as what I suppose would be described as my band broker said, "How would you feel about having foreigners?"

"You mean from Houma or Morgan City or someplace like that?"

What my band broker meant, it turned out, was a band made

up of musicians from abroad who had come to New Orleans for the festival. There has always been a strong interest in New Orleans jazz in Europe and Japan; in the late fifties, when not many white people in New Orleans itself seemed very interested in New Orleans music, it used to be said that no jazz funeral was complete without a body, a band of music, and two Englishmen. The band that broke into "Hello, Dolly!" as Alice came down the ramp was led by a London antiques dealer who played trumpet as if he had grown up on Toulouse Street. I was not surprised. I have always believed that New Orleans jazz can be exported; it's the oyster loaves that won't travel.

Whatever my interest in jazz, though, it was true that my interest in attending the New Orleans Jazz & Heritage Festival had been aroused when a New Orleans friend of ours named Allan Jaffe told me what was available at the festival food booths. According to Jaffe, the eating side of the festival had developed over the years in a way that might make it possible for a jazz fan to eat jambalaya from Gonzales just a few steps from the booth where he had eaten andouille gumbo from Laplace on the way to eat boiled crawfish from Breaux Bridge.

My conversation with Jaffe had taken place over some baked oysters, cracked-crab salad, barbecued shrimp, spaghetti Bordelaise, and chicken Grande at Mosca's—Jaffe and his wife, Sandy, having whisked me to that Louisiana Italian shrine from the airport one evening after I had figured out that a traveler who truly wanted to get stuck between planes in New Orleans on the way from Mobile to New York could arrange it. Jaffe is thought of by most people in New Orleans as the manager of Preservation Hall, a jazz hall that was an important element of the New Orleans jazz revival in the early sixties, but he thinks of himself as a tuba player. He certainly has the sort of appetite that might be associated with a tuba player. Before Buster Holmes retired, Alice felt pretty much the same way about my going to Buster's restaurant on Burgundy Street with Jaffe as she did about my going to Kansas City with Fats Goldberg—although, as far as I can remember, none of the meals I ate at Buster's with Jaffe lasted more than four or five hours. "As much as I eat in New Orleans, though, I've only gained five pounds a year since I came here," Jaffe told me in the late sixties. "The only trouble is that I've been here nine years."

"Could it be that Allan Jaffe mentioned something about the food at the jazz festival that night you stopped to eat at Mosca's on the way back from Mobile?" Alice asked.

That is what I mean by suspicious questions. I can't imagine what led Alice to believe that Jaffe and I talked about the jazz festival at that dinner; as I remember, I reported to her at the time that our conversation had consisted mainly of speculation on whether or not Mrs. Mosca maintained her own garlic ranch hidden away somewhere in St. Bernard Parish. (Alice had raised the subject of garlic herself the morning after I arrived home from my Mosca's layover; she had not heard me when I crept quietly into the bedroom at two or three in the morning, she said, but while stirring in her sleep sometime before dawn, she had gathered from the presence of a strange odor that a wild beast had somehow found its way into the room.)

Confronted with the truth about my conversation with Jaffe, I told Alice that eating all sorts of Louisiana specialties at the festival instead of having to drive all over the state to find them should appeal to any citizen eager to do his or her part in conserving our country's limited supply of fossil fuel.

"To you a jazz festival is just eating with background music," Alice said.

"Jazz and *heritage* festival," I reminded her. "It's called the New Orleans Jazz & Heritage Festival. And what do you think the heritage of New Orleans is—macramé? In New Orleans, heritage means eating."

•

"With so much going on at the Fair Grounds, one has to be fairly well prepared ahead of time to catch as many good acts as possible on a given day," I read in *The Courier*, a New Orleans weekly, after we got into our hotel room. "This year there are five stages, three smaller gazebos (labeled A–C), a jazz tent, and a gospel tent." I could see the problem. In the eight years since we had stopped briefly at the jazz festival on our way to Breaux Bridge to eat crawfish (or, really, on our way to Opelousas to eat roast duck and dirty rice on our way to Breaux Bridge to eat crawfish), the festival had grown from a two-day event held at a local square to a huge undertaking that covered the Fair Grounds racetrack with people for two three-day weekends in a row. Since we had come for the second weekend, we had the opportunity to prepare ourselves by telephoning a New Orleans friend named Gail Lewis for whatever tips she could offer from having attended the first round. "The crawfish is expensive but good," Gail told me. "There's okay red beans and rice. Stay away from the oyster pie. Also skip the fettuccine unless you're nostalgic for your mother's macaroni-and-cheese."

"Gail says the red beans and rice are okay," I told Alice. "She didn't try the oyster loaves, so we might have to stop at the Acme to have two or three before we go out, just in case. The ladies from the Second Mount Triumph Missionary Baptist Church have a booth again selling the fried chicken that apparently caused Jaffe to seek salvation last year. I think everything's going to be all right."

Alice was on the other side of the room, looking at an old-fashioned map that decorated the wall. I went over to read the map's inscription. It said, *Plantations on the Mississippi River from Natchez to New Orleans, 1858.*

"Don't pay any attention to that map, Alice," I said. "It's nothing but a reproduction."

•

During another planning session that evening—a planning session held at Mosca's with fourteen of our closest advisers in attendance—I realized that the jazz festival had intensified a problem we always have in New Orleans: we never seem to have time for enough meals. There are simply too many restaurants in town that have been mentioned in sentences that begin, "We can't leave without going to . . ." The problem is serious under the best of circumstances—partly, of course, because of Alice's strange fixation on having only three meals a day—and the necessity of eating for a couple of hours each day at the jazz festival would make it even more acute.

"Anthropologists have found that in many societies four or five meals a day are the norm," I told Alice halfway through dinner, just after someone at the table had mentioned a smashing soul-food rival to Chez Helène that had been unearthed in Gretna since our previous visit.

"Don't feel you have to keep up with Jaffe tonight," Alice said, ignoring what I thought had been a rather interesting anthropological fact for a layman to have invented. "Remember, he's a tuba player."

The meal was magnificent. After we were through, Jaffe, who had done the ordering, confided to me his suspicion that we had just ordered precisely the same meal for sixteen that we had ordered for three the night he and Sandy had rescued me from the airport.

"There must be some mistake," I said.

"Maybe," Jaffe said. "But tonight I'm not too full."

•

At some point in its development, the New Orleans Jazz & Heritage Festival turned into the sort of pleasantly unstructured, laissez-faire celebration that Mardi Gras used to be before it absorbed successive body blows from the youth cultures associated with Fort Lauderdale and Woodstock. Some people stand in front of a stage all day, clapping to bluegrass or amen-ing to gospel. Some people stake out a small section of Fair Grounds grass and hold an eight- or nine-hour family picnic, probably listening to nothing much beyond the sound of their own chewing unless one of the marching brass bands happens to wander within earshot. Some people stroll from traditional jazz to Cajun to contemporary jazz, stopping between tents and stages now and then to watch a brass band or some of the brightly dressed high-steppers the jazz festival calls Sceneboosters. Cajun happens to be a type of music I find particularly appealing —partly, I must admit, because for me it carries memories of crawfish, the first good Cajun band I ever heard having been Celbert Cormier and His Musical Kings at the Breaux Bridge Crawfish Festival.

"It's hard to know where to begin," Alice said, when the music started.

"I know what you mean," I said. "There are thirty-two different food booths."

By that time I had already paid my respects to the ladies of the

Second Mount Triumph Missionary Baptist Church, whose potato salad turned out to be even better than their chicken, and, not wanting to provoke any schisms among the Baptists, I had also sampled the barbecued chicken being sold by the ladies of the Second True Love Baptist Church. I also felt I should try both versions of jambalaya being offered, and both versions of red beans and rice. Fair is fair.

Three hours after we had arrived at the Fair Grounds I was settled under a tree, almost too full to finish my second hot-sausage po' boy.

"I think you've eaten just about everything that's for sale here," Alice said.

"Not quite," I said. "I refused to eat the avocado-cheese-and-sprout sandwich as a matter of principle. If health food is part of the heritage around here, so is the polka."

"I'm beginning to think we're not going to make it out to the plantation houses this trip," Alice said.

"Probably not," I said. "That would mean we wouldn't have time to go to the lakefront for boiled crabs. Of course, if we treated that lakefront crab eating as a snack rather than as a meal, sort of like tea—"

"I suppose we can at least take a drive to the Garden District," Alice said, paying no attention to what I thought was an extremely sensible solution to one of our scheduling problems.

"Good idea," I said. "There's a place in the Irish Channel whose po' boys I want to try—just a taste, not for dinner or anything—and we could cut through the Garden District on the way."

"Do you want to hear some more music first?" Alice asked.

"Let's go to the gospel tent for a while," I said, rising with some difficulty. "I want to pray for a good harvest."

Weekends for Two

IN MY VERSION OF a melancholy walk on the waterfront, I find
myself walking through a cold Atlantic mist along the docks of some
East Coast city, wearing a trenchcoat with a turned-up collar, making the best approximation of footsteps echoing on the cobblestones
that can be expected from a man wearing crepe-soled shoes, and
ducking into a passage that turns out to be the entrance to a gourmet
kitchen-supply shop called something like the Wondrous Whisk—
where I soberly inspect imported French cherry pitters and antique
butter molds and Swedish meat slicers. The melancholy is produced
by wondering why someone who cannot cook spends so much of
his time in gourmet kitchen-supply shops. (Was the Cuisinart food
processor I bought Alice for Christmas really for me? Could that
also have been true of the slicer I bought my mother in 1949 after
I saw a man at the Missouri State Fair use one to cut a tomato into
slices as thin as playing cards and then spread them into a fan shape
on the cutting board, like Doc Holliday showing his aces?) There
are some people, of course, who find melancholy aspects in the
prospect that, at the present rate of brick-exposing and paint-
stripping and beam-uncovering, all old warehouses in all port cities
will someday be thoroughly renovated as shopping areas that feature
gourmet kitchen-supply shops and purveyors of hardwood toys and
restaurants with names like the Purple Endive.

When old warehouses and abandoned factories all over the country started being scrubbed up into boutiques, we Traveling People accepted them more or less the way we had accepted the advent of Holiday Inns—at first marveling at their presence, and then grumbling that they all looked alike. The brick exposed in Ghiradelli Square in San Francisco tended to look like the brick exposed in Pioneer Square in Seattle, which had some similarity to the brick exposed in Old Town, Chicago, or Underground Atlanta or Old Sacramento or the River Quay in Kansas City or Larimer Square in Denver or Gas Light Square in St. Louis or the Old Market in Omaha. I still walk through them regularly—the chic ones and the tacky ones, the ones whose buildings do evoke the history of a city and the ones whose buildings seem a comment only on the history of American brick. I find myself with the sort of conflicting impressions that might be expected of someone who has an aversion to names like the Wondrous Whisk and a weakness for the gadgets that stores with names like the Wondrous Whisk have in them.

Sometimes, on my walks, I speculate that this postindustrial society may have in ten or twelve years produced more handmade pottery than was produced by all of the primitive clay-fashioning societies in the history of the world. Sometimes I am grateful that in an era of suburban chain bookstores run like suburban chain shoe stores it seems natural for a place like Portland's restored waterfront to have a children's bookstore whose proprietors have actually read the books they sell. Sometimes I am fearful that my commitment to civil liberties will someday collapse in the face of a proposal that all producers of macramé be jailed without trial. I have already convinced myself that there are no First Amendment problems about a law that would require shopkeepers to refrain from describing animals or vegetables as being colors the animals or vegetables in question do not happen to come in. If someone wanted to name a bar after an elephant, he would simply have to call it the Gray Elephant or the Dun-Colored Elephant. The Blue Strawberry would be out, which is a pity, since Alice and I once had a spectacular meal in a restaurant by that name on the restored waterfront of Portsmouth, New Hampshire.

"Maybe you could make an exception in this one case," Alice said, after finishing a dessert of huge strawberries served with brown sugar for dipping. Alice is always at her most tolerant after dessert.

"A rule's a rule," I said.

I was on a tour of restored shopping areas along the Atlantic Coast, and Alice had joined me in Boston for the weekend—partly because she wanted to see the Quincy Market restoration on the Boston waterfront, but mostly, I had grown to suspect, because she wanted to go to Steve's, an ice-cream parlor in Somerville known not only for its homemade ice cream but also for its policy of "mixing in" ingredients that range from fresh blueberries to chopped-up Heath bars.

"Is Steve's Ice Cream what comes into your mind when you think of Boston?" I asked Alice. "Most people think of the Boston Common or Old North Church—or maybe Locke-Ober's, which at least has some characteristics of the traditional fish house."

Alice considers ice cream at Steve's to be an appropriate end to any meal eaten in the Boston area—an area that, in her definition, easily encompasses Portsmouth, New Hampshire. She does not except meals that seem to have ended once already with strawberries dipped in brown sugar. Even with the end of the meal decided, though, we ran into difficulty one day around the restored waterfront of Boston figuring out what to do about the beginning and the middle. The restaurants in such neighborhoods always make me wonder how the word gets around. How, for instance, do all local television newscasters, without having an opportunity to see each other on the air, manage to know when to lower their sideburns three-quarters of an inch or narrow their collars an inch and a half so that they can look precisely alike? How do the proprietors of exposed-brick/hanging-plant/butcher-block-table restaurants in New England know what is being served in exposed-brick/hanging-plant/butcher-block-table restaurants in Seattle? They don't seem to be the type who attend industry conventions. Did the spread of spinach-mushroom-and-bacon salad just happen, or was it engineered by some brilliant agent of the spinach interests trying to pull another Popeye? Who spread the word on putting a celery stalk in a Bloody Mary? Was it the word spreader who told everyone about serving

Bloody Marys in goblets? What's his angle? How does everybody know what sort of cheese to have melted on the special bacon-cheeseburger? And which enemy of the language figured out the names? Walking through Quincy Market, we first passed a restaurant called the Magic Pan. Then—after passing a fruit-and-vegetable stand identified by a piece of black-and-white graphic art that appeared to my untutored eye to be a sixteenth-century radish—we came upon a restaurant called the Proud Popover. Then we left Quincy Market and went to Locke-Ober's for lunch. I felt the need to eat at a restaurant named after something that had no astonishing properties whatsoever.

•

It is customary, of course, for the wives of traveling men to join them for the weekend now and then in pleasant cities like Boston, but ordinarily Alice and I are not among the New Yorkers who are eager to "get away for the weekend." Why would anyone want to get away from a city that has a thousand Chinese restaurants? When we return from Nova Scotia in September, the first conversation I fall into about local restaurants often leads me to believe that, far from wanting to spend much time away from the city, I may not even want to leave the neighborhood. The conversation usually takes place in a nearby corner grocery store known locally as Ken & Eve's—a place so friendly that Abigail and Sarah and I would probably use it as our after-school hangout even if it did not have the attraction of old-fashioned gum-ball machines and did not happen to be the exclusive outlet (on a consignment basis) for Keen's Specials, the chocolate-chip cookie to which all other chocolate-chip cookies cannot be compared.

By the time I have my restaurant conversation at Ken & Eve's, I have usually made a quick tour of the neighborhood, just to make certain that everything is as I left it the previous spring. Once, riding my bike down Carmine Street on a crisp fall day, I noticed a sign saying C. P. SALUMERIA ITALIANA over what was supposed to be Frank's Pork Store. I screeched to a halt. Frank's Pork Store had offered one of the true delicacies of the neighborhood—a sandwich of what was called simply "hot cooked salami," made fresh every morning and served warm, with some minced green peppers on top. The sandwich was supposedly "takeout," but I never made it out of the store with one intact. The three men who operated Frank's were always indulgent about someone's wanting to wolf down a takeout sandwich while standing at the counter rather than taking any chances about the salami cooling off. It was always the sort of place where a few bottles of liquor and some paper cups were left on a counter during the Christmas season so that the customers would not be put in the position of offering each other holiday greetings empty-handed.

I parked my bike and raced into the store, shooting a quick glance on the way toward Bleecker Street to make certain that the luncheonette with the remarkable minestrone was still there. At that moment nothing seemed safe. The previous spring, after all, the bakery across Carmine Street that had been, as far as I know, the single source for a type of Italian ring bread made with oregano and lard and cheese and salami had gone out of business—with hardly a murmur from those people in the Village who are always going on about the need to preserve endangered species from extinction.

I burst into the pork store to find behind the counter the same three men who had always been behind the counter. Two of them, it was explained to me, had bought the store from the third— Frank—six years before, and they had finally got around to changing the sign.

"All is not lost!" I said, more dramatically than I had meant to. They looked at me oddly, and to cover my embarrassment, I ordered a hot cooked salami sandwich—extra meat, please, and some green peppers on top.

I then went to Ken & Eve's for the first neighborhood-restaurant conversation of the fall. Like most conversations at Ken & Eve's, it included everybody who happened to be in the store:

"What do you hear about the new Japanese place on Charles?"

"Dynamite! Great sushi. The best soft-shell crabs we've ever eaten."

"You talking about that great new fish place on Hudson?"

"What great new fish place on Hudson?"

"The Danish takeout place with the gravlax and the herring?"

"No, that's on Bleecker."

"On Greenwich?"

"At that new place on Greenwich last night, Eve had a chocolate-mousse crêpe for dessert. Fantastic!"

"Sounds disgusting."

"Chocolate-mousse crêpe! I better get home and tell Alice."

·

Alice and I, of course, are not completely at a loss for words when we stumble into one of those conversations about the value of married couples picking a favorite weekend spot to dash off to now and then without the children—conversations that have always reminded me of talk-show appearances by the sort of pop psychologist who wears a turtleneck sweater and calls the host by his first name. "Reading," I say when it came my turn to mention our special getaway place.

"Reading, Pennsylvania!" someone always says. Explaining our fondness for Reading is particularly difficult if the group includes one of those people whose tastes run strongly to exquisitely restored country inns with authentic eighteenth-century details and noisy nineteenth-century plumbing.

"You must be joking," the doctrinaire aesthete says. "Isn't Reading just a grimy factory town?"

"Not particularly grimy, as far as I know."

"Is there some sort of country inn near there?"

"There's a motor inn between a cornfield and a shopping center in the suburbs. On the weekends, it has what amounts to a private glassed-in swimming pool. The Sunday *Times* can be reserved at the desk."

"Is there something historic about the buildings? Old row houses or something?"

"Well, there are row houses, but I would say they qualify as historic only in that they give some indication that Reading was once the territory of the single most talented aluminum-awning salesman in the United States."

Alice and I are not actually experts on the architecture of Reading, since we visited the town for some years before we ever saw it in the daytime. We tended to spend most of Saturday in Lancaster County—where Alice likes the quilts and I like the sausages—and head straight for our suburban motel in the evening. On Sunday morning the route we customarily took to the Dutchman's Diner, near Adamstown, happened to bypass the city. At the Dutchman's, the breakfast specials include such local delicacies as country scrapple—cooked crisp, at Alice's instruction, with a poached egg on top—and creamed chipped beef on home fries. The Dutchman's has the added attraction of a twenty-cent surcharge on any breakfast that is ordered after eleven-thirty in the morning —meaning that someone who feels guilty about not getting around to breakfast until the morning church crowd is drifting in for Sunday midday dinner is given the opportunity to pay the wages of sin, but at well below union scale. The only time we spent in Reading itself was on Saturday night, when we had dinner at Joe's—making our way there by a route that permitted me to be sure that one of my favorite American restaurant signs (HOF BRAU CAFE—ITALIAN CUISINE, SEAFOOD) was still in place. Joe's, which specializes in wild mushrooms, does its very best to be a pretentious restaurant —a headwaiter in formal dress, a fancy menu, a room for diners to inspect bottles of the wines available—but the pretension melts away with the first taste of the mushroom soup. I have occasionally mentioned to Alice the possibility of trying a Mao-like running meal in Reading sometime—eating the mushroom soup at Joe's and then dashing across the street to try some of the specialties at Stanley's, which has been identified as "one of the most famous watering holes in Reading" by the authoritative *A Beer Drinker's Guide to the Bars of Reading*, by Suds Kroge and Dregs Donnigan ("Dedicated to our wives"). Alice has always seemed unenthusiastic about leaving for Stanley's after the soup, and, aware that these weekends are supposed to be special, I haven't made an issue of it.

On Sundays, after our stop at the Dutchman's Diner, we wander through one of the nearby antiques markets—Renninger's or Shupps Grove. Shopping is so much a part of any American vacation, of course, that a visitor to Atlantic City strolling along the boardwalk in his swimming suit on an August afternoon is offered several opportunities to buy a fur coat. Our first glimpse of Reading by daylight, in fact, came because we wanted to observe the phenomenon of thousands of people being bused in from all over the East Coast to entertain themselves with a day of pure shopping—Reading having rather suddenly become the Factory Outlet Capital of the World. "We're really here to observe," I had to remind Alice as she started to work her way methodically down a rack of little girls' dresses that had tiny alligators on them. "It's the phenomenon I thought you might be interested in."

I don't know whether there is any validity to the theory that acquisitiveness in America is, like crippling debt, a natural concomitant of family life and a permanent address, but it is true that I didn't buy much before I knew Alice. I worked for a while in Europe when I was young and single, and when I returned I ran into trouble at customs because I had nothing to declare. All around me my fellow citizens were flashing French perfume and Swiss watches and English china. When the customs man asked what I had bought during a year out of the country and I told him I couldn't think of anything, he acted as if he might place me under arrest for Aggravated Prevarication. "Nothing?" he said incredulously. I tried to conjure up a picture of myself in some shop buying the specialty of the region, but no shop appeared. Instead, I kept seeing my draft-board physical examination, during which an Army sergeant, holding a form on a clipboard in front of him, had demanded three identifying marks or scars from a frightened and patently unblemished young farm boy who was standing next to me. ("I'm awful sorry, sir," the farm boy said, feeling desperately around his palpably smooth chin and searching for evidence of so much as a freckle on his chalk-white shoulder. "Three marks or scars," the sergeant kept saying.) Finally, I told the customs man I had bought a pair of pants, and he signed my declaration.

I have thought of that scene as I place something like a Victorian hatbox full of Javanese puppets on the counter in front of the customs man and explain that some posters for Abigail's room have been sent ahead—although the dolls both girls are carrying were in fact purchased in England, notwithstanding their similarity to the dolls I bought them in eastern Kentucky to go with the ones I tracked down, in an investigative tour de force, at a small shop in Charleston, South Carolina. The customs man nods, knowing before he asks me that I will be just under the exemption limit. I have been spotted as the type who would have phoned the consulate to make certain that a four-year-old girl is entitled to a hundred-dollar exemption despite her inability to sign her name to a traveler's check. He waves me on—a wise bartender waving good night to a heavy-drinking regular who always manages to stop just before he becomes sick or dangerous. The real answer to the customs man's inquiry about what I have to declare is "A greedy nature, sir."

Still, we rarely buy anything on those Sunday mornings at Renninger's—partly because the prices reflect the fact that there is hardly anything left on the entire continent that is not valued as a part of somebody's collection of something or other. The grotesque lamp base that discourages speculation on what the shade must have looked like turns out to be a find for the collector of "early electrical." Even if we don't buy any of what the voice over the loudspeaker calls "antiques, collectibles and investment items," though, we never leave disappointed. I can always find the funnel-cake stand. Funnel cake is a plateful of twisted dough that has been cooked in oil, covered with powdered sugar, and served piping hot—a regional specialty that some connoisseurs believe to be of about equal harm to the fingers, the clothing, and the stomach lining. Alice, muttering about the grease content as she nibbles on the edges of my funnel cake, always moves in the direction of Pauline Thompson's lunch counter—the only place in the state, as far as I know, that serves coal-black chocolate cake. Mrs. Thompson's cake is the sort of black that in some light looks almost blue. Its origin was apparently in the misdelivery of some dark chocolate to a restaurant Mrs. Thompson once ran—an accident she had the wit to exploit, like an alert chemist who notices that the medicinal substance he has accidentally spilled seems to have a remarkable cleansing effect on the suede of his shoes.

For Alice, dark chocolate is a specialty within a specialty—reminiscent of a collector I once came across at Renninger's who liked all ice-cream scoops but concentrated most of his energies on acquiring the ice-cream scoops that had been manufactured by one particular company. I have heard Alice dismiss elegant and outrageously expensive goodies as "mostly milk chocolate" in a tone of voice rather like the one Francie Jowell uses to say "foreign vegetables."

Alice's feeling of tolerance and well-being after dessert at the Blue Strawberry in Portsmouth is nothing compared to the expansive mood she is in after a piece of Mrs. Thompson's coal-black cake. She seems so agreeable to any adventure, in fact, that I often find myself ending the weekend with a note of regret—regretting the fact that there are no Indian restaurants within miles of Adamstown, Pennsylvania.

•

When Alice discovered that the Bonaventure Hotel in Montreal had special weekend rates, I pointed out that the Bonaventure was bound to lack scrapple, not to speak of the Sunday *Times*. The Bonaventure is run by Western International, one of the more tasteful creators of the new boffo-architecture hotels that permit those traveling salesmen who used to spend evenings on the road sitting numbly in an Esther Williams movie to pass their time staring at the lobby—watching other traveling salesmen ride up and down in glass elevators, or making bets on whether anyone will take a dive from the sixteenth floor of the atrium lobby, or gazing into a half-acre lake that reminds them of the plumbing emergencies their wives are likely to report as soon as they call home.

"The Bonaventure is a lovely hotel," Alice said.

"Western International is weak on costumes," I said. The first time I walked into the Bonaventure lobby I was astonished to find that the bellhops were all Chinese dressed in coolie costumes. I had assumed that there must have been some Chinese phase of Montreal history I didn't know about, but when I went to the Crown Center in Kansas City—a hotel that has, with a rather individualistic vision of environmental protection, preserved part of the hillside it was built on within the lobby—I found the doorman to be an exceedingly tall black man dressed as a Russian folk dancer. The doorman at the Century Plaza, a Western International Hotel in Los Angeles, is dressed as an English Beefeater. I wouldn't be surprised to check in at a Western International Hotel in Nebraska and find that the room clerk is a Puerto Rican dressed as a Southern planter or an Apache done up as a French merchant seaman.

"It has a nicer swimming pool than the one in Reading," Alice said. It is true that the Bonaventure has, in one of its interior courtyards, an outdoor swimming pool that is open year round, but I doubted whether Alice and I would venture into it in January. Steam rises from it in the winter, so that someone observing the action from the lobby is unable to ascertain whether people swimming in ten below zero air are wearing expressions of serenity or intense pain. The temperature of the Reading pool was always approximately that of Lake Lotawana in August.

"Was it the salmon or the Arctic char that was so marvelous at Chez Pauzé the last time we were there?" Alice asked. "It's been so long I've forgotten."

"It has been a long time," I said, reaching for the telephone to call Air Canada.

Once we were in Montreal, of course, I had little time to inspect the Bonaventure's design elements; I was buried in food guides, cramming away like a law school graduate about to take his last shot at the bar exam. I was looking forward to French food, but it had become obvious from all the data that the local cuisine of Quebec was not French but French-Canadian. Eating French food in Montreal is obviously not the equivalent of eating French food in Omaha, but it could be considered parallel to eating Spanish food in El Paso.

"We really ought to have a French-Canadian meal before we leave," I said to Alice.

Alice started thumbing through the food guides. "Well, here's a place that seems to specialize in baked beans in maple syrup," she said. "That must be quite authentic; I can't think of any other reason for serving it."

"There must be other places."

"Yes, here's one that specializes in pig's knuckle stew," she said. "Or maybe you'd like to try one of your Mao meals—pig's knuckle stew here, baked beans in syrup there, then another spot for French-Canadian ham hocks."

"It's always a shame to miss the local specialties," I said, although I was beginning to experience some of the appetite loss I suffered in Martinique when I read Dr. Nègre's description of "a bat worthy of the plate."

"How about that Italian restaurant that was supposed to be so good?" Alice said.

"How can we eat Italian food in a city famed for its own version of French cuisine?" I asked.

"What is New Orleans famous for?"

"Its own version of French cuisine."

"What's your favorite restaurant in New Orleans?"

I paused for reflection, and a school of Mrs. Mosca's barbecued shrimp swam into my mind. (That often happens when I pause for reflection.) "Let's try the Italian place," I said.

We took a taxi to Rue Notre Dame Ouest, a drab street next to the railroad yards, and went into a restaurant called Da Giuseppe. Fifteen minutes later we were eating something called Fettuccine Danielle—fettuccine with cream and mushrooms and sausages put together in a way that rendered me practically speechless. Marriage, as I have often remarked, is not merely sharing one's fettuccine but sharing the burden of finding the fettuccine restaurant in the first place. "Alice," I said, as I rolled some fettuccine around my fork as quickly as I could roll, "I'm certainly glad you decided to come along."

(15)

Alice's Treat

WHEN I LEARNED that space limitations would make it impossible for Alice to come with me to a special dinner that was to be prepared in New York by Paul Bocuse, the renowned Lyonnais chef, I secretly resolved to take her to the annual wild-game supper of the United Church of Christ, in Bradford, Vermont. I try to do right by her. Since Alice had spoken for years of wanting to eat a meal prepared by Bocuse, I was determined to make up for the Bocuse bash with a special event she would find particularly appealing—a determination that was not weakened even when she rather overdid her bewilderment at how I happened to have been invited by the publishers of Bocuse's new cookbook to a dinner held for grown-up food writers. I knew that Alice enjoys church suppers as much as I do. I also knew that she enjoys dishes like prime ribs of beef and steak more than I do—I have always had trouble disassociating such food from testimonial dinners—and I figured that anyone who liked beef was bound to be delighted by buffalo or bear.

When I casually mentioned that the date of the Bradford wild-game supper, an annual event of national renown, was approaching, Alice said, "It's occurred to me lately that it's the idea of church suppers I like more than the food."

"This one is different," I assured her. "Some years they have moose." Then I broke the news: through some strenuous efforts, I had managed to obtain two tickets to the wild-game supper for us. "You can eat French food anytime," I told her. "This is something special."

Alice did not look instantly ecstatic. "Let me get this straight," she said. "Because I won't get to go to a dinner cooked by Paul Bocuse, I get to eat moose in Bradford, Vermont?"

"They don't have moose every year," I said. "I don't want to oversell this."

•

The Bocuse dinner was held at Lutèce, a distinguished East Side French restaurant that has a custom of leaving prices off all menus except the one given to the host of each party—presumably on the theory that guests should not have to run the risk of having their digestion impaired by the price of the quenelles. We have been taken to dinner there a couple of times by Pat Uhlmann, Bearer of the Ribs, Keeper of the Sauce. As the host of a dinner at Lutèce, Pat has the custom of announcing the price of any dish his guests mention. If Alice says, "I'm thinking about having the *saumon farci en croûte* to start," he'll say something like "A steal at eight dollars and fifty cents." He says it's only fair to give his guests some idea of how warmly they should thank him.

For the Bocuse dinner, I was fortunate enough to be seated next to our friend Colette Rossant, the cook of my dreams, who had translated Bocuse's cookbook from the French. Colette told me that she had taken Bocuse shopping for ingredients in the Village —introducing him to some of the tradesmen she terrorizes daily. They stopped for breakfast at the soda fountain of Bigelow's Pharmacy, a late-morning Village hangout that happens to be only a few hundred feet from Balducci's, the legendary produce store. Bocuse ordered fried eggs, Colette said, and when the counterman asked if he wanted them sunny side up or over, he replied, "As the chef desires."

I was naturally pleased to have Colette at my ear to explain what was going down. It gave me the sort of security I have always felt when Alice is in the seat next to me at a foreign film to let me in on the meaning of the symbolism. (We long ago decided that any foreign film I understood outright can be fairly criticized for heavy-handedness.) Just how fortunate I was to have a specialist nearby was brought home to me after the first course—two pieces of terrine—when Colette said, "I preferred the woodcock to the hare," and somebody down the table said, "Oh my God! You mean they were different?"

Bocuse, wearing an immaculate chef's outfit, was slicing the terrine himself. Although the rest of the meal had been prepared by Bocuse and his assistants in Lutèce's kitchen, he had brought the terrine from France; his method of clearing customs without causing a lot of tiny rules to be quoted had apparently been to choose a customs inspector who looked stout enough to put the matter into perspective. Bocuse, I was pleased to see, had the build of an understanding customs inspector himself, and seemed to have no sympathy for the low-calorie French cooking that has lately become fashionable. "Without butter, without eggs," he said to his guests, "there is no reason to come to France." I was happy to have some confirmation of my assumption that no sane person would enter one of those French retreats that specialize in three-star diet food without having taken the precaution of strapping a flask of heavy cream to his ankle.

When the fish course was served, Colette told me that *loup en croûte*—or sea bass *en croûte* in our case, since the *loup* does not swim this far from France—was a very old French dish. It occurred to me that I might be able to tell Alice that the fish was nothing particularly novel or unusual. I even thought of asking Colette whether the word "common" could fairly be applied to the dish— until I tasted it. "A very old French dish," Colette repeated. "But this happens to be the best I ever tasted."

Through the rest of the dinner, I found myself trying to concoct uninteresting ways of describing what we were eating to Alice. I could describe the main course as "sort of plain veal," I thought, but could I get away with saying that the macaroni au gratin that accompanied it was done on the same principle as a Kraft dinner? How was I to describe the *oeufs à la neige* that were served between the *fromage de France* ("just some cheese") and *gaufres de grand-mère Bocuse* ("a piece of cake")?

"What was it like?" Alice said sleepily when I finally walked into our bedroom at around twelve-thirty.

"I brought you some chocolate candy," I said. "He gave it out at the end of the meal. I also brought you some cake. Chocolate cake. *Gaufres de grand-mère Bocuse*, actually."

"Was the dinner any good?"

"Also some cookies. I knew you'd love the cake. I just had a bite or two myself, then I said to the waiter, '*Avez-vous* aluminum foil?' "

"Was the meal any good?"

"Not bad, really. Not too bad."

"What'd you have?"

"Oh, some fish, and meat, and some hard egg-white stuff. You know—that sort of thing."

"Hard egg-white stuff?"

"Did I tell you I brought you some candy? Also some matchbooks."

•

"They're going to have hare at the United Church of Christ, just like at Lutèce," I told Alice when I phoned her from Bradford the day before she flew up for the dinner. I had gone to Vermont in advance to watch some of the preparations. "It's rabbit pie instead of *terrine de lièvre*, but a bunny's a bunny, right?" I was trying to reassure Alice. Somehow, she had got it into her mind that one of the meats to be served at Bradford was polecat—a misapprehension that I feared was preventing her from viewing the wild-game supper as a class event. "There's no moose this year, but they have moufflon ram instead," I went on. "Not just moufflon ram roast but also moufflon ram loaf. And where else could you get buffalo burgers or bear chops? And no polecat, Alice. I want you to know that nobody around here is even absolutely sure what a polecat is. This is going to be a special event."

"I'm sure it'll be lovely," Alice said, in the voice she sometimes uses to comment on my fourth helping of ribs.

I tried to explain to Alice that the United Church of Christ wild-game supper was the Super Bowl of church suppers—out of the class of the kind of church supper she had occasionally referred to as the

Annual Starch Festival. Even when it began, in the fall of 1956, it was staged for outside wild-game connoisseurs rather than the local folks—apparently on the sound theory that if a lot of city-bred hunters from Massachusetts were going to swarm into the area every autumn and mow down farm animals while trying to shoot deer, they might as well have a few dollars taken off of them for a good cause before they went home. I told Alice that twelve hundred people were going to be served at the church supper—moving through a buffet line from three in the afternoon until ten at night—and that we were fortunate to be among them, since almost that many had to be turned away. Eris Eastman, the supper's co-chairman, had told me that three young men drove to Bradford all the way from Long Island on the day tickets went on sale at the church, a month before the dinner, simply because they were not willing to trust their luck to the mails. I saw no reason to add Mrs. Eastman's comment that the young men must have been out of their minds.

I also saw no reason to talk to Alice much about the presence on the menu of beaver. Too close to polecat. Marcia Tomlinson —who, along with her husband, Gary, is in charge of cooking for the wild-game supper—told me that there were actually people who came to Bradford every year specifically to eat beaver. "They pass up the pheasant and rice," she said. "They consider that 'restaurant food.' " Apparently, though, a lot of people who are willing to eat most wild game draw the line at beaver—including Mrs. Eastman. ("I'm not sure but what I'm prejudiced," she told me.) There happens to be a theory in Bradford that the game supper was inspired partly by a beaver supper a local man named Richard Shearer used to throw for his pals every year at the Legion hall, but I thought Alice would be more interested in hearing how the supper was founded by Cliff and Helen McLam after they moved to Bradford from East Corinth, where they had run a very successful chicken-pie supper for the Congregational church. "East Corinth is still renowned for its chicken pie," I told Alice on the phone. Alice didn't say anything.

•

Just before Alice arrived, I bought her a copy of the recipe book the game-supper people had just published. At first glance it seemed rather specialized—the pheasant-and-rice recipe, for instance, yields six hundred portions—but I figured that Alice could make a nice game dinner for two someday merely by dividing all the measurements by three hundred. As far as I could tell from watching the preparation, the Bradford secret for cooking wild game was to subject it to so much soaking in vinegar and water and so much cooking that a diner might have as much difficulty in distinguishing between wild and domestic as some of the visiting hunters always do (in the three days before the game supper, the farm animals that had been felled by gunshots in the area included two horses and a tethered sheep). Aware of the problem of distinguishing between, say, bear sausage and wild boar sausage—particularly when they are crammed on a plate that also contains buffalo, coon, rabbit, moufflon ram, venison, pheasant, and, in some cases, beaver—the church women who pile meat on the plates at the serving line implant in each portion a color-keyed toothpick.

"Aqua is bear," I said to Alice as we finally sat down to eat. Our plates were piled high with meat—about a pound of meat on each plate, according to Gary Tomlinson's estimate. There were bowls of mashed potatoes and gravy and squash and shredded cabbage on the table. Alice pushed around among the toothpicks for a while. She seemed to be taking very small bites.

"I'm told the venison chops should be eaten as soon as possible," I said. "If they've been off the stove too long, the grease congeals."

"Ummm," Alice said. "What'd you say the course after the *loup en croûte* was at Lutèce?" *Quasi de veau bourgeoise* was what she had in mind.

"It was what the French call middle-class veal," I said.

Somewhere down the table somebody said, "I've lost my rabbit livers." It was not easy to keep the various meats separated on the plate, and the toothpicks were not as much help as they might have been if the colors had been more distinctive. I was having some difficulty figuring out where aqua ended and green began. I had already complimented the beaver ("It seems harmless enough") before I realized that what I was eating was marked not with pink but with orange—buffalo. I thought it only fair to remind Alice that at least one of the grown-up food writers at the Bocuse dinner had been unable to distinguish between woodcock and hare.

Alice did not seem to be eating much at all. "The wild boar sausage tastes pretty much like sausage," I said in encouragement.

Alice stared at her plate. Finally, she said, "Could you please pass the squash?"

Fifteen or twenty minutes later, when someone came to clear away our dishes, Alice said, "I notice that you uncharacteristically failed to clean your plate." It was true that I had eight or ten ounces of meat left, although I had probably eaten another four or five ounces in sausages during the day as I watched the preparations. When I had finally figured out which toothpick was pink, I realized that I had spoken too soon about the harmlessness of the beaver. My venison chop had shown some evidence of being fairly long off the stove.

"Well, as you know, I'm not really much of a meat eater," I said.

"While I, on the other hand, have always had this thing about coon pie," Alice said. I gathered from her tone that the Bradford United Church of Christ wild-game supper, an event that seemed to please many diners to the point of seconds and thirds, might have been a disappointment for her.

"I'll make it up to you, Alice," I said. "The Methodist church in West Fairlee is having a chicken-pie dinner tomorrow and I'm pretty sure I can get hold of two tickets."

•

This is certainly not the West Fairlee Methodist Church, I thought to myself, several months later, as Alice and I sat down for dinner at Paul Bocuse's restaurant in Lyons. How someone with nothing more than a simple chicken-pie sort of gesture on his mind happened to end up in France is, oddly enough, rather easy to explain: Alice had just turned forty. (I make that revelation in direct retaliation for her observation some years ago that I had just passed the age limit for joining the Transit Authority Police.) I should make it clear that I did not present Alice with a trip to France as a fortieth-birthday gift. I was simply trying to find a restaurant adequate to the occasion.

Alice is serious about celebrations. Finding a restaurant for even an off-year birthday dinner has always been a problem. She has been consistently unenthusiastic about holding her birthday dinner in Chinatown; she says the restaurants we frequent there are lacking in celebratory atmosphere. I once offered to hold the dinner during Chinese New Year—a period of enormous celebration throughout Chinatown every February—but she declined on the rather prosaic ground that her birthday happens to be in May. For a few years, Alice seemed pleased with the custom of a long birthday lunch at La Petite Ferme, a tiny restaurant in our neighborhood. Then La Petite Ferme moved uptown, and Alice's response to the notion of trudging up there on a balmy May afternoon was to quote a phrase usually attributed to a traveler in France named Esther Kopkind—*quel schlepp*. Our attempt to have a birthday dinner in some other New York French restaurant expensive enough to mark the occasion ended rather badly at the Box Tree—a small East Side place whose seating arrangements seemed to have been designed by the man who did the IRT uptown local. When our check arrived inside an early-nineteenth-century book whose pages had been hollowed out to form a little box for that purpose, Alice remarked that some rule ought to prevent restaurant pretension from extending to the destruction of books.

A man who was sitting at the next table—and was therefore just short of toppling into the birthday girl's lap—said, "Are you a librarian?" The waiter informed us, with some disdain, that delivering the check in a hollowed-out book was an authentic custom of seventeenth-century France or sixteenth-century England or some other high-priced civilization—failing to add that their customs also included the flogging of debtors and the medicinal application of leeches.

Knowing that something special would have to be done for Alice's fortieth birthday, I offered to take her to Arthur Bryant's, in Kansas City. She declined, even though I informed her of rumors that Mr. Bryant had recently painted a wall and had acquired a new Royal Crown Cola machine that some customers found quite attractive.

"Well, I guess we better go to Bocuse's place in Lyons then," I said.

Alice looked suspicious. "Are you just feeling guilty about the Bocuse dinner at Lutèce and all that burnt polecat?" she said.

"You know I've never had any guilt of transatlantic magnitude," I said. "I just want to avoid one of those East Side joints."

"You're offering to take me to Paul Bocuse in Lyons because I don't want to have my fortieth-birthday dinner at Arthur Bryant's or Phoenix Garden?"

"Well, that was very good chipped beef on toast you made me on my fortieth, Alice," I said. "And I'm sure if you had known at the time that the chipped beef on English muffin at the coffee shop in the Stanford Court Hotel was even better, you would have arranged for me to be in San Francisco to eat it."

"And you're asking me to go to France just because you think it might be the perfect place for my birthday meal?" Alice asked, still sounding unconvinced.

"Well, to tell you the truth, Alice," I said, "I think I'd like another crack at that *loup en croûte*."

"I accept," Alice said.

•

"This is only the best thing I've ever eaten," Alice said. She had just swallowed her first bite of Bocuse's *foie gras*. I was relieved. The previous evening we had warmed up by having dinner with a friend at another three-star restaurant called Alain Chapel, and I was afraid Alice might have been put off her feed for the entire week by a maître d' so supercilious that he managed to remind everyone at the table of a different despised grade-school teacher.

Alice's appetite seemed fine. She tracked down every morsel of *foie gras* on her plate, and she seemed to be enjoying the *loup en croûte* even before I reminded her that Colette had praised it as the daddy of all *loups en croûte*. She finished her *volaille de Bresse en chemise*, and her eighty or ninety varieties of *chèvre*, and her *gaufres de grand-mère Bocuse*. At Paul Bocuse, Alice is a Clean-Plate Ranger.

"Did it seem okay?" I asked.

"Well, I have to say this," Alice said. "I didn't need different-colored toothpicks to tell the *foie gras* from the *loup en croûte*."

I had tried to be attentive to the meal myself after realizing that the truffle soup I ate as a first course could be honorably compared with the andouille gumbo turned out by the Jaycees of Laplace, Louisiana. In fact, my soup pantheon had to be expanded by several gallons in France. A couple of days after the Bocuse dinner, at a sleek hotel in St.-Jean-Cap-Ferrat, I had a fish soup— *soupe de poissons de roche, rouille et croûtons dorés*, to be exact— that was so good I was almost able to forget how much it cost. On our last day in France we realized we might be able to sample a soup that was said to be even more spectacular—a sort of Provençal version of bouillabaisse called *bourride*, which is one of the specialties of a place on the Nice docks called L'Âne Rouge. With careful planning, we figured, we could take a quick tour of the renowned Maeght Foundation museum in St.-Paul-de-Vence, then nip down to L'Âne Rouge more or less on the way to the Nice airport.

The careful planning did not, as it happened, take into account the time required to decide whether the Provençal dolls for Abigail and Sarah ought to be knitting or weaving or carrying a basket of clams or plucking a chicken. By the middle of the morning it was clear that touring the museum would leave us no time for *bourride*.

"It's supposed to be a marvelous museum," Alice said.

"I'm sure it is," I said. "Why else would we have seen six busloads of tourists go in there?"

"There are a lot of Giacomettis," Alice said. She paused. "On the other hand," she went on, "there are a lot of Giacomettis in New York."

"Plenty of Giacomettis," I said.

Alice didn't say anything for a while. She had a thoughtful look on her face. I hoped the thoughts were about the mountain of shellfish she had downed at Le Suquet in London, mixed with thoughts about the sort of seafood a restaurant on the Nice docks might consider worthy of its table. "Let's go to Nice," Alice said.

Did she realize what she was saying? "Well, okay," I said. "If that's what you want, Alice, let's eat."

THIRD

HELPINGS

(1 9 8 3)

(1)

Spaghetti

Carbonara Day

I HAVE BEEN CAMPAIGNING to have the national Thanksgiving dish changed from turkey to spaghetti carbonara. In a complicated way, it all has to do with my wife, Alice. There came a time when Alice began to refer to a certain sort of people I have corresponded with over the years—the sort of people who are particularly intense about, say, seeking out the best burrito in East Los Angeles—as "food crazies." She spoke of them as bad company. She even spoke, I regret to say, as if I might be in danger of becoming a food crazy myself. I knew I had to do something. What I decided to do was launch a campaign to have the national Thanksgiving dish changed from turkey to spaghetti carbonara.

At one time, Alice had displayed a certain sympathy for my approach to eating. Maybe "understanding" would be a better word. When I began traveling around the country in the line of duty some years ago, she understood that if I didn't devote a certain amount of my time to searching out something decent to eat I would find myself having dinner in those motel restaurants that all buy ingredients from the same Styrofoam outlet or in that universal Chamber of Commerce favorite that I began referring to as La Maison de la Casa House, Continental Cuisine. That is not a fate to wish on a husband simply because he may have an irritating habit or two— insignificant ones, really, like a tendency to eat from the serving bowl late in the meal.

When did it all begin to change? The signs, I now realize, were there almost from the start. Why, I should have asked myself, do dinner-table conversations at our house so often turn to the perils of gluttony? Why had Alice continued to preach the benefits of limiting our family to three meals a day even after I presented incontrovertible scientific evidence that entire herds of cattle owe their health to steady grazing? Why, in planning a trip to Sicily, would Alice seem so insistent on staying in towns that have world-renowned ruins, whether those towns are known for their *pasta con sarde* or not? Looking back, I realize that I shouldn't have been so surprised on that dark and rainy night—we had just arrived in a strange town after a long trip, and I was inspecting the Yellow Pages in the hope of happening upon some clue as to where a legitimate purveyor of barbecue might be found—when Alice uttered those dreaded words: "Why don't we just eat in the hotel?"

Naturally, I tried to put everything in context. Around that time, I happened to read in the *Dallas Morning News* that a French-man who goes by the name of Monsieur Mangetout had been hired to entertain at a Dallas waterbed show and had done so by eating several cocktail glasses, a few dozen razor blades, and about a third of a queen-size waterbed, including the pine footboard with brass brackets.

"Now that is excessive," I said to Alice. "The article says that he once consumed fifteen pounds of bicycle in twelve days, and he's negotiating with Japan to eat a helicopter."

The point I was trying to make to Alice—who, I must say, was not really keeping up her end of the conversation—was that compared to somebody like M. Mangetout (who, I hasten to admit, is obviously on one extreme), I am someone of moderate appetite. When M. Mangetout talks about eating junk, after all, he is not talking about those packages of roasted sweet-corn kernels from Cedar Rapids that I love. He is talking about eating junk. Just as an example, I have never eaten so much as a pound of bicycle. Although Alice may criticize me for always showing my appreciation of the hostess's cooking by having a second helping—to be perfectly honest, what she criticizes me for is showing my appreciation of the hostess's cooking by having a third helping—I can see myself acting with considerable restraint at a dinner party at which the main course is, say, queen-size waterbed ("No, thank you. It was delicious, but I couldn't eat another bite"), even though I might risk spending a sleepless night from worry over the hostess's feelings or from the effects of the first helping.

The comparison I drew between me and M. Mangetout did not impress Alice. I began to see that the problem was not context but point of view. Seen from the right point of view, for instance, someone who seems intent on obtaining a fair sampling of foodstuffs wherever he happens to be is engaged in serious research—not research done for the purpose of, say, probing for soft spots in the New England fast-food taco market, but the sort of pure research that in more cultivated times was often done by educated gentlemen interested in knowledge for its own sake—and the appropriate way to comment on such research would not be with phrases like "You're making an absolute hog of yourself."

What better way to demonstrate one's seriousness than to start a campaign to change the national Thanksgiving dish from turkey to spaghetti carbonara? Alice would see some serious historical research going on, right under her own roof. Our daughters might be convinced that my interest in food is far too complicated to be summed up with the phrase "Daddy likes to pig out." They are always being told that an informed citizenry is the cornerstone of democracy, after all, so they could appreciate the value of informing the citizenry that the appropriate Thanksgiving dish is spaghetti carbonara. The adventure inherent in such a campaign might even stir their souls sufficiently to free them from what I regard as a crippling dependence on canned tuna fish.

It does not require much historical research to uncover the fact that nobody knows if the Pilgrims really ate turkey at the first Thanksgiving dinner. The only thing we know for sure about what the Pilgrims ate is that it couldn't have tasted very good. Even today, well-brought-up English girls are taught by their mothers to boil all veggies for at least a month and a half, just in case one of the dinner guests turns up without his teeth. Alice and I did have a fine meal of allegedly English food in New York once, at the home of a friend named Jane Garmey—it included dishes with those quaint names the English give food in lieu of seasoning, like Aunt Becky's Kneecap—but I suspected that Jane had simply given real food English names, the way someone might fit out a Romanian with a regimental blazer and call him Nigel. I liked the meal well enough to refrain from making any of the remarks about English cooking that I often find myself making when in the presence of our cousins across the sea ("It's certainly unfair to say that the English lack both a cuisine and a sense of humor: their cooking is a joke in itself"), but I can't get over the suspicion that hidden away somewhere in the Garmey household is a French cookbook that has a recipe for something called *La Rotule de Tante Becky*.

It would also not require much digging to discover that Christopher Columbus, the man who may have brought linguine with clam sauce to this continent, was from Genoa, and obviously would have sooner acknowledged that the world was shaped like an isosceles triangle than to have eaten the sort of things that English Puritans ate. Righting an ancient wrong against Columbus, a great man who certainly did not come all this way only to have a city in Ohio named after him, would be a serious historical contribution. Also, I happen to love spaghetti carbonara.

•

I realize that these days someone attempting to impress his own wife and children with his seriousness might be considered about as quaint as Aunt Becky's kneecap. Where we live, in New York City, just having a wife and children is considered a bit quaint. I sometimes think that someday we might be put on the Grayline Tour of Greenwich Village as a nuclear family. As I imagine it, the tour bus pulls up to the curb in front of our house, after the usual stops have been made at Washington Square Arch and Aaron Burr's stable and Edna St. Vincent Millay's brownstone and Stephen Crane's rent-controlled floor-through. As the tourists file out, a fat lady in the back of the bus says, "How about the hippies? I want to see the hippies." Instead, they see us—an American family. Mommy and Daddy and their two children are having dinner. Mommy asks Abigail what she did in school all day, and Abigail describes a math problem that Daddy doesn't understand. Mommy is helping Sarah cut her meat. Mommy is telling Abigail to sit up straight. Daddy is telling Sarah that if she doesn't stop playing with her meat he will arrange to have her sent to a foster home. Mommy is discussing the perils of gluttony. Daddy is being manipulated by Abigail and Sarah, who want a cat. Mommy says Daddy hates cats. Daddy says it's not that he hates cats—Daddy doesn't want to teach Abigail and Sarah prejudice—but simply that he has never met a cat he liked. Mommy is helping Daddy cut his meat. After a while, the tourists seem to grow restless. The sight did seem unique at first, but it has begun to remind them of reruns of the old *Ozzie and Harriet* show. The tour guide, discerning their mood, leads them out the door. The fat lady says, "Now can we see the hippies?"

The tourists might assume that such a family celebrates Thanksgiving every year with a traditional meal at that same dinner table. Not so. When it comes to national holidays, there is a quiet war for hearts and minds going on in our family—it is fought over Halloween and Christmas—and Thanksgiving has tended to get overlooked as territory that is not hotly contested by either side. Halloween is my holiday. For days before Halloween, people who telephone me have to be told by Alice, "He's in the basement making sure that the witch piñata is still in good enough shape to hang out the window" or "He's upstairs trying to decide whether the ax murderer's mask goes better with his Panama or his Stewart Granger bush hat." I'm always in town for Halloween. Even if I didn't happen to enjoy walking in the Village Halloween parade in my ax murderer's mask, I would feel it my duty to be there because of the long-established role of a father in passing on important cultural traditions to the next generation. Alice's attitude toward Halloween, I regret to say, borders on the blasé. By the time Halloween comes, Alice is already thinking about Christmas, a holiday whose modern celebration always makes me wonder whether December might be a nice month to spend in Saudi Arabia. As a result, we engage in one of those quiet struggles common to marriages of mixed cultural emphasis. If I were not in town to press my case on Halloween, I sometimes think, my girls might find themselves spending October 31 trimming a Christmas tree—pausing now and then to hand out tiny "Joyeux Noël" wreaths to the visiting trick-or-treaters.

Being a kind of demilitarized zone, Thanksgiving has often been celebrated away from home. It was at other people's Thanksgiving tables that I first began to articulate my spaghetti carbonara campaign—although, since we were usually served turkey, I naturally did not mention that the campaign had been inspired partly by my belief that turkey is basically something college dormitories use to punish students for hanging around on Sunday. I did bring up some aesthetic advantages of replacing turkey with spaghetti carbonara—the fact, for instance, that the President would not be photographed every year receiving a large platter of spaghetti carbonara from the Eastern Association of Spaghetti Carbonara Growers. (As King Victor Emmanuel may have said to his Chancellor of the Exchequer, spaghetti doesn't grow on trees.) I spoke of my interest in seeing what those masters of the floatmaker's art at Macy's might come up with as a 300-square-foot depiction of a plate of spaghetti carbonara. I reminded everyone how refreshing it would be to hear sports announcers call some annual tussle the Spaghetti Carbonara Day Classic.

I even had a ready answer to the occasional turkey fancier at those meals who would insist that spaghetti carbonara was almost certainly not what our forebears ate at the first Thanksgiving dinner. As it happens, one of the things I give thanks for every year is that those people in the Plymouth Colony were not my forebears. Who wants forebears who put people in the stocks for playing the harpsichord on the Sabbath or having an innocent little game of pinch and giggle? In fact, ever since it became fashionable to dwell on the atrocities committed throughout American history—ever since, that is, we entered what the intellectuals call the Era of Year-Round Yom Kippur—I have been more and more grateful that none of my forebears got near this place before 1906. When it comes to slavery and massacring Indians and the slaughter of the American buffalo and even the assorted scandals of the Spanish-American War, my family's hands are clean. It used to be that an American who wanted to put on airs made claims about how long his family has been here. Now the only people left for our family to envy are the immigrants who arrived in the last decade or so. They don't even have to feel guilty about the Vietnam War.

Finally, there came a year when nobody invited us to Thanksgiving dinner. Alice's theory was that the word had got around town that I always made a pest out of myself berating the hostess for serving turkey instead of spaghetti carbonara—although I pointed out that even if a hostess had taken some offense at the mention of my campaign, she must have forgotten all about it in the glow of hearing me ask for thirds on stuffing. Abigail and Sarah, I'm happy to say, did not believe that our lack of invitations had anything at all to do with my insistence on bringing the spaghetti carbonara issue to the attention of the American people at any appropriate opportunity. They seemed to believe that it might have had something to do with my tendency to spill cranberry sauce on my tie.

●

However it came about, I was delighted at the opportunity we had been given to practice what I had been preaching—to sit down to a Thanksgiving dinner of spaghetti carbonara. In the long run, I saw it as an opportunity to inspire our daughters to seek the truth and test frontiers and engage in pure research and never settle for eating in the hotel. In the short run, I saw it as an opportunity to persuade Sarah to taste spaghetti carbonara. Sarah does not taste casually. Abigail has expanded her repertoire to the point of joining us in the ritual lobster supper we always have in Maine on the way to Nova Scotia, where we live in the summer, but Sarah celebrates that occasion each year with a tuna-fish sandwich. ("The tuna fish here is excellent," she always says.) If Sarah is finally persuaded to try something new, she usually cuts off the sort of portion I have come to think of as a microbite, chews on it tentatively, swallows it, and says, "It's okay but I'm not crazy about it."

Confident that our family was about to break new ground, I began preparations for Thanksgiving. I did some research on what ingredients would be needed for the main course. I prepared for any questions the girls might have about our forebears:

"Was Uncle Benny responsible for the First World War just because he was already in St. Joe then?" Abigail might ask.

"Not directly," I would say. "He didn't have his citizenship."

"Is it really true that your grandparents got mixed up about

American holidays when they first got to Kansas City, and used to
have a big turkey dinner on the Fourth of July and shoot fireworks
off in Swope Park on Thanksgiving?" Sarah might ask.

"At least they had nothing to do with snookering the Indians
out of Massachusetts," I would be able to say. "Be thankful for
that."

Naturally, the entire family went over to Raffetto's pasta store
on Houston Street to see the spaghetti cut. I got the cheese at Joe's
Dairy, on Sullivan, a place that would have made Columbus feel
right at home—there are plenty of Genoese on Sullivan; no
Pilgrims—and then headed for the pork store on Carmine Street
for the bacon and ham. Alice made the spaghetti carbonara. It was
perfection. I love spaghetti carbonara. Sarah, a devotee of spaghetti
with tomato sauce, said, "I'm not crazy about it," but she said it
in a nice, celebratory kind of way. After a few forkfuls, we paused
to give thanks that we weren't eating turkey. Then I began to tell
the children the story of the first Thanksgiving:

In England, a long time ago, there were people called Pilgrims
who were very strict about making sure everyone observed the Sabbath and cooked food without any flavor and that sort of thing, and
they decided to go to America, where they could enjoy Freedom
to Nag. The other people in England said, "Glad to see the back
of them." In America, the Pilgrims tried farming, but they couldn't
get much done because they were always putting their best farmers
in the stocks for crimes like Suspicion of Cheerfulness. The Indians
took pity on the Pilgrims and helped them with their farming, even
though the Indians thought the Pilgrims were about as much fun
as teenage circumcision. The Pilgrims were so grateful that at the
end of their first year in America they invited the Indians over for
a Thanksgiving meal. The Indians, having had some experience
with Pilgrim cuisine during the year, took the precaution of taking
along one dish of their own. They brought a dish that their ancestors
had learned many generations before from none other than Christopher Columbus, who was known to the Indians as "the big Italian
fellow." The dish was spaghetti carbonara—made with pancetta
bacon and fontina and the best imported prosciutto. The Pilgrims
hated it. They said it was "heretically tasty" and "the work of the

devil" and "the sort of thing foreigners eat." The Indians were so disgusted that on the way back to their village after dinner one of them made a remark about the Pilgrims that was repeated down through the years and unfortunately caused confusion among historians about the first Thanksgiving meal. He said, "What a bunch of turkeys!"

As is traditional toward the end of a Thanksgiving family meal, I was content. I considered the campaign a success even if no other family converted. Everything seemed possible. I could see the possibility of doing pure research (not "pigging out") around the country in the company of like-minded researchers (not "food crazies"). I could see the possibility of inspiring Sarah to try dishes far more exotic than spaghetti carbonara. I could see the possibility of Alice's thinking that someone given to serious inquiry might have a third helping out of an honest curiosity about whether it could taste even better than the second. I had a third helping of spaghetti carbonara.

2

An Attempt to Compile

a Short History of the

Buffalo Chicken Wing

I DID NOT TRULY APPRECIATE the difficulties historians must face regularly in the course of their research until I began trying to compile a short history of the Buffalo chicken wing. Since Buffalo chicken wings were invented in the recent past, I had figured that I would have an easy task compared to, say, medievalists whose specialty requires them to poke around in thirteenth-century Spain and is not even edible. Alice, I must say, was unenthusiastic about the project from the start. It may be that she thought my interest in pure research could lead me into searching out the origins of just about any local specialty I might contemplate eating too much of—how the cheese-steak got to Philadelphia, for instance, or why Tucson is the center of interest in a Mexican dish called *chimichanga*, or how people in Saginaw came to begin eating chopped-peanuts-and-mayonnaise sandwiches, or why a restaurant I once visited in the market area of Pittsburgh serves sandwiches and French fries with the French fries inside the sandwiches. I assured her that I had no intention of extending my inquiries as far as chopped peanuts or interior French fries, although I couldn't fail to point out that she had, in a manner of speaking, expressed some curiosity about the Pittsburgh sandwich herself ("Why in the world would anybody *do* such a thing?").

I saw the history of the Buffalo chicken wing as a straightforward exercise, unencumbered by the scrambled folk myth that by now must be part of the trimmings of something like the Philadelphia cheese-steak. There happens to be extant documentation identifying the inventor of Buffalo chicken wings as the late Frank Bellissimo, who was the founder of the Anchor Bar, on Main Street—the form of the documentation being an official proclamation from the City of Buffalo declaring July 29, 1977, Chicken Wing Day. ("WHEREAS, the success of Mr. Bellissimo's tasty experiment in 1964 has grown to the point where thousands of pounds of chicken wings are consumed by Buffalonians in restaurants and taverns throughout our city each week . . .") I would not even have to rummage through some dusty archive for the document; the Anchor Bar has a copy of it laminated on the back of the dinner menu.

I had the further advantage of having access to what people in the history game call "contemporary observers"—a crowd of serious chicken-wing eaters right on the scene. A college friend of mine, Leonard Katz, happens to be a Buffalonian—a native Buffalonian, in fact, who became a dean at the medical school of the State University of New York at Buffalo. I have also known his wife, Judy, since long before the invention of the chicken wing. She is not a native Buffalonian, but she carries the special credentials that go with having been raised in New Haven, a city that claims to have been the scene of the invention of two other American specialties—the hamburger and the American pizza. Although Leonard Katz normally limits his chicken-wing consumption to downing a few as hors d'oeuvres—a policy, he assured me, that has no connection at all with the fact that his medical specialty is the gastrointestinal tract—the rest of the family think nothing of making an entire meal out of them. Not long before I arrived in Buffalo for my fieldwork, Linda Katz had returned from her freshman year at Washington University, in St. Louis—a city where, for reasons I do not intend to pursue, the local specialty is toasted ravioli—and headed straight for her favorite chicken-wing outlet to repair a four-month deprivation. A friend of Linda's who returned from the University of Michigan at about the same time had eaten chicken wings for dinner four nights in a row before she felt fit to carry on. Judy Katz told me that she herself eats chicken wings not only for dinner but, every now and then, for breakfast—a pattern of behavior that I think qualifies her as being somewhere between a contemporary observer and a fanatic.

On my first evening in Buffalo, the Katz family and some other contemporary observers of their acquaintance took me on a tour of what they considered a few appropriate chicken-wing sources—out of what is said to be several hundred places in the area where Buffalonians can order what they usually refer to simply as "wings"—so that I could make some preliminary research notes for later analysis. The tour naturally included the Anchor Bar, where celebrated visitors to Buffalo—say, a daughter of the Vice President—are now taken as a matter of course, the way they are driven out to see Niagara Falls. It also included a noted chicken-wing center called Duffs and a couple of places that serve beef-on-weck—a beef sandwich on a salty roll—which happens to be the local specialty that was replaced in the hearts of true Buffalonians by chicken wings. In Buffalo, chicken wings are always offered "mild" or "medium" or "hot," depending on how large a dose of hot sauce they have been subjected to during preparation, and they are always accompanied by celery and blue-cheese dressing. I sampled mild. I sampled medium. I sampled hot. It turned out that there is no sort of chicken wing I don't like. As is traditional, I washed down the wings with a number of bottles of Genesee or Molson—particularly when I was sampling the hot. I ate celery between chicken wings. I dipped the celery into the blue-cheese dressing. I dipped chicken wings into the blue-cheese dressing. (I learned later that nobody in Buffalo has figured out for sure what to do with the blue-cheese dressing.) I tried a beef-on-weck, just for old times' sake. I found that I needed another order of hot, plus another bottle of Molson. After four hours, the tour finally ended with Judy Katz apologizing for the fact that we were too late for her favorite chicken-wing place, a pizza parlor called Santora's, which closes at 1:00 a.m.

The next morning I got out my preliminary research notes for analysis. They amounted to three sentences I was unable to make out, plus what appeared to be a chicken-wing stain. I showed the stain to Judy Katz. "Medium?" I asked.

"Medium or hot," she said.

•

Fortunately, the actual moment that Buffalo chicken wings were invented has been described many times by Frank Bellissimo and his son, Dom, with the sort of rich detail that any historian would value; unfortunately, they used different details. According to the account Frank Bellissimo often gave over the years, the invention of the Buffalo chicken wing came about because of a mistake—the delivery of some chicken wings instead of the backs and necks that were ordinarily used in making spaghetti sauce. Frank Bellissimo thought it was a shame to use the wings for sauce. "They were looking at you, like saying, 'I don't belong in the sauce,' " he often recalled. He implored his wife, who was doing the cooking, to figure out some more dignified end for the wings. Teressa Bellissimo, presumably moved by her husband's plea, decided to make the wings into some hors d'oeuvres for the bar—and the Buffalo chicken wing was born.

Dom Bellissimo is a short, effusive man who now acts as the bustling host of the Anchor Bar; his friends sometimes call him Rooster. He told me a story that did not include a mistaken delivery or, for that matter, Frank Bellissimo. According to Dom, it was late on a Friday night in 1964, a time when Roman Catholics still confined themselves to fish and vegetables on Friday. He was tending the bar. Some regulars had been spending a lot of money, and Dom asked his mother to make something special to pass around gratis at the stroke of midnight. Teressa Bellissimo picked up some chicken wings—parts of a chicken that most people do not consider even good enough to give away to barflies—and the Buffalo chicken wing was born.

According to both accounts, Teressa Bellissimo cut off and discarded the small appendage on a chicken wing that looks as if it might have been a mistake in the first place, chopped the remainder of each wing in half, and served two straight sections that the regulars at the bar could eat with their fingers. (The two straight pieces, one

CALVIN TRILLIN (272

of which looks like a miniature drumstick and is known locally as
a drumette, became one of the major characteristics of the dish; in
Buffalo, a plate of wings does not look like a plate of wings but
like an order of fried chicken that has, for some reason, been reduced drastically in scale.) She deep-fried them (or maybe "bake-
barbecued" them), applied some hot sauce, and served them on a
plate that included some celery from the Anchor Bar's regular an-
tipasto and some of the blue-cheese dressing normally used as the
house dressing for salads. If the regulars were puzzled about what
to do with the blue-cheese dressing, they were presumably too grateful to say so.

The accounts of Dom and Frank also agree that the wings were
an immediate success—famous throughout Buffalo within weeks.
In the clipping libraries of the Buffalo newspapers, I could find only
one article that dealt with the Bellissimo family and their restaurant
in that period—a long piece on Frank and Teressa in the *Courier-
Express* in 1969, five years after the invention of the chicken wing.
It talks a lot about the musicians who appeared at the Bellissimos'
restaurant over the years and about the entertainers who used to
drop in after road shows. It mentions the custom Teressa and Frank
had in times gone by of offering a few songs themselves late on a
Saturday night—Teressa emerging from behind the pasta pots in
the kitchen to belt out "Oh Marie" or "Tell Me That You Love
Me." It does not mention chicken wings.

Maybe Dom and Frank Bellissimo got fuzzy on dates after
some time passed. By chance, my most trusted contemporary observers, the Katzes, were living out of the city during the crucial
period; Linda Katz looked surprised to hear that there had ever been
a time when people did not eat chicken wings. The exact date of
the discovery seemed a small matter, though, compared to the
central historical fact that, whatever the circumstances, the first
plate of Buffalo chicken wings emerged from the kitchen of the
Anchor Bar. It seemed to me that if a pack of revisionist historians
descended on Buffalo, itching to get their hands on some piece of
conventional wisdom to refute, they would have no serious quarrel
with the basic story of how the Buffalo chicken wing was invented—although the feminists among them might point out that

the City of Buffalo's proclamation would have been more accurate if it had named as the inventor Teressa Bellissimo. The inventor of the airplane, after all, was not the person who told Wilbur and Orville Wright that it might be nice to have a machine that could fly.

•

"A blue-collar dish for a blue-collar town," one of the Buffalonians who joined the Katz family and me on our chicken-wing tour said, reminding me that an historian is obligated to put events in the context of their setting, even if his mouth happens to be full at the time. Buffalo does have the reputation of being a blue-collar town—a blue-collar town that during the winter is permanently white with snow. Buffalonians who do much traveling have resigned themselves to the fact that the standard response to hearing that someone comes from Buffalo is a Polish joke or some line like "Has the snow melted yet?" Buffalo has always had a civic morale problem; one of the T-shirts for sale in town reads *Buffalo: City of No Illusions.* Now that it is common to be served a dish called "Buffalo chicken wings" in places like Boston or Atlanta, is the problem being exacerbated by Buffalo's identification with a local specialty made from what is considered to be one of the chicken's less majestic parts? Frank Bellissimo seemed to argue against that interpretation. "Anybody can sell steak," he once said. "But if you sell odds and ends of one thing or another, then you're doing something." The celebrated visitors who troop through the Anchor Bar are, after all, almost always favorably impressed by Buffalo chicken wings. Craig Claiborne, the renowned food writer for *The New York Times,* proclaimed them "excellent" in one of his columns—although he may have undercut the compliment a bit by saying in the same paragraph that he had remained in Buffalo for only three hours.

A Buffalo stockbroker named Robert M. Budin once wrote a piece for the *Courier-Express* Sunday magazine suggesting, in a lighthearted way, that the city adopt the chicken wing as its symbol. Budin's piece begins with two Buffalonians discussing what had happened when one of them was at a party in Memphis and was asked by a local where he was from. Deciding to "take him face on," the visiting Buffalonian had said, "I'm from Buffalo." Instead of asking if the snow had melted yet, the local had said, "Where those dynamite chicken wings come from?"

"You mean positive recognition?" the friend who is hearing the story asks. It becomes obvious to the two of them that Buffalonians should "mount a campaign to associate Buffalo with chicken wings and rid ourselves of the negatives of snow and cold and the misunderstood beef-on-weck." Budin suggested that the basketball team be called the Buffalo Wings, that the mayor begin wearing a button that says *Do Your Thing with Wings*, and that a huge statue of a chicken wing (medium hot) be placed in the convention center.

When I telephoned Budin to inquire about the response to his suggestion, he said it had not been overwhelming. He told me, in fact, that he had embarked on a new campaign to improve Buffalo's reputation. Budin said that a lot of people believed that the city's image suffered from its name. I remembered that his Sunday-magazine piece had ended, "Buffalo, thy name is chicken wing." Surely he was not suggesting that the name of the city be changed to Chicken Wing, New York. No. What should be changed, he told me, was not the name but its pronunciation. He had taken to pronouncing the first syllable as if it were spelled "boo"—so that Buffalo rhymes with Rue de Veau. "It has a quality to it that lifts it above the prosaic 'Buffalo,' " he said.

Maybe. But I suspect that it's only a matter of time before Budin tells some corporate executive in Memphis or Cincinnati that he is calling from Boofalo and the executive says, "Has the snoo melted yet?"

●

On my last evening in Buffalo—just before the Katzes and I drove out on Niagara Falls Boulevard to try the wings at a place called Fat Man's Got 'Em, and just before I got final instructions from Judy Katz about the cardboard bucket of wings I was planning to take back to New York from Santora's the next day, in the way that a medievalist might haul home a small thirteenth-century tapestry ("Get the big bucket. Whatever's left over will be fine the next morning")—I met a man named John Young, who told me, "I am actually the creator of the wing." Young, who is black, reminded me that black people have always eaten chicken wings. What he invented, he said, was the sauce that created Buffalo chicken wings—a special concoction he calls mambo sauce. He said that chicken wings in mambo sauce became his specialty in the middle sixties, and that he even registered the name of his restaurant, John Young's Wings 'n Things, at the county courthouse before moving to Illinois in 1970.

"If the Anchor Bar was selling Chicago wings, nobody in Buffalo knew it then," Young said. "After I left here, everybody started chicken wings."

Young, who had returned to Buffalo a few months before our talk, told me that those who had copied the dish must be saying, "Oh, man! The original King of the Wings is back. He's fixin' to do a job on you." In fact, Young said, he was pleased to see so many people in Buffalo make money off his invention—a magnanimous sentiment that I had also heard expressed by the Bellissimos.

The wings Young invented were not chopped in half—a process he includes in the category of "tampering with them." They were served breaded, covered in mambo sauce. It is true, a local poultry distributor told me, that John Young as well as Frank Bellissimo started buying a lot of chicken wings in the middle sixties, but there was no reason for the distributor to have kept the sales receipts that might indicate who was first. First with what? I thought, as I sampled an order of medium and an order of hot at Santora's while picking up my bucket-to-go. Was the Buffalo chicken wing invented when Teressa Bellissimo thought of splitting it in half and deep-frying it and serving it with celery and blue-cheese dressing? Was it invented when John Young started using mambo sauce and thought of elevating wings into a specialty? How about the black people who have always eaten chicken wings? The way John Young talked, black people may have been eating chicken wings in thirteenth-century Spain. How is it that historians can fix the date of the Battle of Agincourt with such precision? How can they be so certain of its outcome?

3

Divining the

Mysteries of the East

PEOPLE WHO ARE always saying that scholarship is of no use in the practical business of everyday life apparently do not know about James D. McCawley, professor of linguistics at the University of Chicago, who is able to read the signs on the walls of Chinese restaurants. Unlike some of the rest of us, McCawley can enter a Chinese restaurant secure in the knowledge that his digestion will not be impaired by the frustration of watching Chinese customers enjoy some succulent marvel whose name the management has not bothered to translate into English. Unlike some of the rest of us, McCawley does not have to subject himself to puzzled stares from Chinese families while hovering close to their plates in an effort to divine by shape and smell what sort of braised fish dish seems to be making them so happy. Unlike, say, Bill Helfrich, a man I know who moved to Bar Harbor from New York—presumably driven from the city by the agonies of monolingual eating in Chinatown—McCawley has never been reduced to carrying in his wallet a note that says in Mandarin, "Please bring me some of what that man at the next table is having." McCawley can read the specials listed on the wall. Nobody can hide any crisp-skin deep-fried squab from McCawley. McCawley does not find himself inquiring in painfully enunciated English about a mysterious listing only to be dismissed by the waiter with a curt "You no like." McCawley does not have to make do with translations on the menu like "Shredded Three Kinds." McCawley does not spend half the meal staring at his neighbor's bean curd with the particularly ugly combination of greed and envy so familiar to—well, to some of the rest of us.

I realize that those who scoff at knowledge for its own sake would argue that McCawley could have learned to read Chinese without subjecting himself to three years of graduate work at M.I.T. in subjects like phonology and lexicography and semantics and syntax. He could have simply stuffed down a short course in Chinese characters at Berlitz, the scoffers would say, like some sales representative about to embark for Peking with the goal of putting a can of Reddi-Wip in every Chinese home. There is a significant difference. The true scholar shares the fruit of his research through teaching and publication. Although students who arrive at the University of Chicago to study linguistics may expect to receive as orientation material nothing more than the customary map of the campus and a list of the departmental regulations governing the use of reserved books at the main library, what they get includes a packet of half a dozen menus from Chicago Chinese restaurants "collected and translated by James D. McCawley."

The menu translations do not even constitute McCawley's most ambitious work in the field. Among his writings—most of which have titles like "The Role of Notation in Generative Phonology" or "Morphological Indeterminacy in Underlying Syntactic Structure" or "Lexicographic Notes on English Quantifiers"—is a document called "The Eaters' Guide to Chinese Characters." A 53-page typescript accompanied by a 140-page glossary, the "Eaters' Guide" uses a system of character classification adapted from the Japanese in an attempt to free the non-Chinese-speaking eater forever from the wretched restrictions of the English menu. "One of my linguist friends suggested that it might be a service to mankind," McCawley has said of the guide. "And to him in particular." McCawley has even offered to teach a course in Chinese-menu reading as part of the university's extension program, but it has apparently been delayed by some difficulties in arriving at a suitable title. According to McCawley, officials of the extension program thought that Menu Chinese was not a course title appropriate to an institution with the august academic reputation of the University of Chicago, and were not impressed when he, attempting to take their concerns into consideration, offered as an alternative title Aristotle, Freud, and the Chinese Menu.

It seems to me that McCawley's scholarly achievements in the field of Chinese menus are all the more impressive in view of the fact that he doesn't happen to speak Chinese. His doctoral thesis required him to learn Japanese, and many Japanese characters are close to Chinese characters—or were before some postwar modifications in Chinese writing that, fortunately for McCawley, a lot of owners of American Chinese restaurants were not in China to find out about. Starting in the early seventies, McCawley simply built on his knowledge of Japanese characters, with the help of a lot of research into Chinese cookbooks and some extensive fieldwork in Chinese restaurants—during which, for all we know, someone who did not fully understand McCawley's goals and methods might have been saying, "You're making an absolute pig of yourself."

I suppose some people might consider "The Eaters' Guide to Chinese Characters" the product of a hobby, albeit a hobby that happens to result in a service to mankind, but I'm happy to say that McCawley doesn't see it that way. He does not draw severe distinctions between his outside interests—principally food and music—and the field in which he makes his living. A lot of his colleagues seem to feel the same way—linguistics being, for one reason or another, a field that attracts a lot of musicians who like to eat. A graduate student of linguistics whom I met with McCawley—we were all eating in a Korean restaurant—told me that when she was studying at the University of Michigan the newsletter of the Linguistics Department seemed to consist mainly of recipes. At the annual party McCawley throws for St. Cecilia's Day, honoring the patron saint of musicians, he is ordinarily able to put together a small orchestra of linguists. (The other annual party he gives is on October 9, in celebration of the only national holiday anywhere having to do with linguistics—the commemoration in Korea of the day in 1446 when *han'gul*, the Korean alphabet, was officially adopted.) When McCawley's students and colleagues published a sort of antic Festschrift in his honor in 1971—it was called "Studies Out in Left Field: Defamatory Essays Presented to James D. McCawley on the Occasion of his 33rd or 34th Birthday," and it included a large section called "Pornolinguistics and Scatolinguistics"—the title on the cover was superimposed on the menu of a Chinese restaurant. In the same spirit as the Festschrift, McCawley once presented to the University of Chicago Hillel Foundation's annual Latke-Homantash Symposium a paper on "Some Hitherto Unrecognized Implications of the Chinese Terms for Latkes and Homentashen"—although after several readings I'm not certain I understand precisely what those implications are.

I suspect that part of what has led McCawley's students and colleagues to admire him enough to do a Festschrift in his honor is his ability to discover a scholarly meeting, a concert, and an interesting restaurant in the same city at the same time. Discussing the Philosophy of Science Association meeting in Toronto, he may digress on the advantages of having a Toronto colleague whose research in Chinese syntax has enabled him to know that the proprietors of what seems to be a Szechuan restaurant on Spadina Avenue are actually natives of Jiangxi Province who can, upon request, turn out a proper Jiangxi banquet. Right in his own department, of course, McCawley has access to colleagues who, for example, may have done enough fieldwork in the dialects of southeastern Europe to become expert in Greek cuisine, and he has no rigid notions of interdepartmental rivalry that might prevent him from dipping into the Department of Far Eastern Languages and Civilizations if the need should arise. Not all members of the Linguistics Department, after all, have a particular interest in foreign languages or foreign cultures or even foreign food; even those who do may have acquired expertise from their fieldwork that is not obviously transferable to the gastronomic challenges of Chicago. For instance, one of McCawley's colleagues, Jerrold Sadock, has done a lot of work on Greenlandic Eskimo, and there are as yet no Greenlandic Eskimo restaurants in Chicago. It is not a cuisine whose absence distresses McCawley, since the recipe Sadock remembers best begins, "Kill and gut one seal, stuff the body cavity with auks, sew up, bury in sand, dig up in six months."

•

A scholar who makes no priggish distinction between knowledge of phonology and knowledge of *latkes* is obviously my sort of scholar. From the first time I heard about McCawley, I figured I could learn a lot from him. Although the course he teaches in the Linguistics Department at the University of Chicago, Justification of Linguistic Units, sounds worthwhile, the course I was hoping to get a head start on was Aristotle, Freud, and the Chinese Menu. I have been frustrated for years by the Chinese wall signs in Chinatown. I have publicly admitted that when Alice taught a class at City College which included some Chinese students not long in this country I suggested wall-sign translation as an exercise that might be just the thing for polishing their idiomatic English. I have also revealed in public print that I often have fantasies of having been selected by the State Department to take Mao Tse-tung on eating tours of New York that include Chinatown—and that Mao always brings along his interpreter. On trips to Chinatown with my family, I was becoming increasingly sensitive about the fact that whenever I leaped from my chair to follow some waiter who passed by carrying an obviously fantastic bean-curd dish resembling nothing described on the English menu my daughters tended to say "Daddy—please" in the same way Sarah says "Daddy—please" to indicate that she finds it embarrassing to walk to the grocery store with someone who happens to be singing "The Streets of Laredo." I needed help.

The first time I caught up with McCawley was when he was on a visit to New York. As I understood the purpose of the visit, he had agreed to deliver a lecture called "The Nonexistence of Syntactic Categories" at Columbia University and at the Bell Laboratories, he was desperately interested in attending two Janáček operas that the City Opera was going to produce on successive evenings, and he wanted to sample the goat curry at a Trinidadian restaurant on Nostrand Avenue in Brooklyn. I had arranged to fly back to Chicago with him, for a sort of short-course in his methodology, and I suggested that we meet the day before our flight for a tea lunch at a place in Chinatown called H.S.F.—giving him a chance to pick up some Chinese ingredients at the Kam Man supermarket on Canal Street and giving me a chance to get some translation done closer to home than Chicago.

My translation needs at H.S.F. did not have to do with menus. Tea-lunch—or *dim sum*—restaurants are about the only places in Chinatown that do not drive me mad with linguistic frustration, since the food-service system common to all of them might almost have been designed to soothe the fears of monolingual gluttons. Waiters pass up and down the aisles with carts or trays holding small plates of dumplings or shrimp balls or noodles or some other *dim sum* specialty, the customer takes a plate of whatever appeals to him, and a waiter slightly senior to the passers arrives at the table at the end of the meal to tally up the bill by counting the number of plates on the table—a system that somehow does not tempt too many customers to gain the double benefit of more china and a smaller bill by slipping some of the plates into their pockets. Although I have never met a *dim sum* passer who spoke English well enough to explain what was inside the dumplings he was passing, my method of eating a tea lunch requires no Chinese: I simply take some of absolutely everything offered.

My purpose in luring McCawley to H.S.F. was based on a suspicion that a Chinese wall sign I had noticed there was in fact not a list of special dishes but an explanation of some changes in the restaurant which had struck some of its customers as distinctly un-Chinatown. H.S.F. used to be called Hee Seung Fung. Not long after it started going by its initials, it was redecorated in a rather sleek style that was conspicuously lacking in both dragons and pagodas. It opened a branch uptown. For a time, it made some of its *dim sum* available in frozen form at Bloomingdale's. I figured that the wall sign said something reassuring to Chinese-speaking customers—"Don't be put off by the trendy flash done for the benefit of the wide eyes, because we're still just folks," or words to that effect.

McCawley turned out to be a man with a heavy mustache, full sideburns, and shoulder-length dark hair. He looked like a sixties radical gone not quite respectable. He had lived in Glasgow until he was six and in Chicago after that—giving him a way of speaking so much his own that it is probably of no interest to those of his sociolinguistic colleagues who study accents and dialects. I explained the task at hand as we entered H.S.F.

"Two?" the waiter who approached us said.

McCawley stopped in his tracks and stared at the wall sign. "The first column says black-bean steam fish something or other," he said. "Whatever that last character is."

"Are you sure it doesn't say anything about Bloomingdale's?" I asked.

McCawley, without saying whether or not he knew the Chinese character for Bloomingdale's, assured me that the wall sign simply listed some of the specialties that could be ordered at dinner. He tried the first column again. Turning to the waiter who had greeted us, he said, "What the bloody hell is that last character?"

The waiter looked blank for a moment. Then he said again, "Two?"

•

Until I spent a couple of days in the company of James McCawley, I had not thought of Chicago as an Oriental city. Among wandering eaters, it is probably best known for the pirouettes its restaurants manage in what other cities think of as the straightforward business of turning out pizzas. It seems to me that over the years a lot of the conversations I have had in Chicago have concerned authentic Chicago pizza or deep-dish pizza or double-crusted pizza or a pizzalike object known as a *panzerotti*. The fame of Chicago pizza now extends well beyond the city limits. There are places in London jammed with Englishmen eating Chicago pizza in an atmosphere distinguished by Cubs pennants and framed front pages of the *Chicago Daily News* and election posters urging yet another term for Richard Daley. The sort of pizza our friend Fats Goldberg, the thin New York pizza baron, began serving in Manhattan in the sixties was the Chicago version of the beast. Fats claims that he developed his own recipe for Chicago pizza, but he acknowledges that, like most disciples who have carried the Chicago version to the outside world, he took a crack or two at stealing the recipe developed by a pioneering Chicago parlor called Pizzeria Uno. According to Fats, the plan was for him to stand in the alley next to Uno's kitchen pretending to spoon with a volunteer sweetie while glancing regularly through the window to absorb the secrets of the craft. What the Fat Man had neglected to consider in planning his operation was the cold wind coming off Lake Michigan in February; the volunteer didn't mind a little necking, but she had not signed up for frostbite. The ersatz lovebirds abandoned their post before the pepperoni went on.

McCawley doesn't talk much about pizza or any other foodstuff with origins in Europe. He alone seems to treat Chicago as a sort of prairie Hong Kong. His "Notes on Access to Interesting Food in Chicago," prepared for the students and faculty of the Linguistics Department, lists as its ethnic categories Chinese, Japanese, Korean, Thai, Indian, and Other. He was able to pick his way through an Indian menu pretty well even before he started studying Hindi in preparation for a trip to India he was planning to take a few months after my visit. Although he celebrates Korean *han'gul* more confidently than he reads it, a steady supply of *han'gul* readers seems assured by the fact that Koreans are particularly drawn to graduate studies in linguistics—a natural result, perhaps, of being let out of school year after year in honor of an alphabet. In addition to a fair-sized Chinatown, Chicago has any number of Korean restaurants and several Thai restaurants and a clutch of Indian restaurants, including one valued so highly by the linguistics crowd that it has catered the annual meeting of the Chicago Linguistics Society. With McCawley in Chicago, I ate *Mutter Panir* at the Moti Mahal Restaurant, and *Yook Hoi* at a Korean restaurant called Cho Sun Ok, and *Panang Nue* at Friend, a Thai restaurant—all the while confident that I was eating what I was intended to eat rather than some chop-suey equivalent put on the English menu to pacify the passing meter reader or paper-supply salesman who happened to drop by because he suddenly got hungry while on his rounds. McCawley would simply find a scrap of paper (usually a deposit slip from his checkbook), write our order in the appropriate alphabet, and hand it to the waiter along with an English "Thank you."

Our Chinese meal was at a place called Chinese Deli. Its non-English-speaking customers presumably call it something else. When we discussed names given to Chinese restaurants—I admitted to a weakness for the name of a Los Angeles place called Yangzee Doodle—McCawley said that in Australia he once came upon a restaurant that was called Epping Chinese Restaurant in English and was identified by its Chinese characters as a restaurant called Occidental Food. A wall sign in the Chinese Deli listed all sorts of dishes that were not on the English menu. Among the delicacies available to readers of Chinese characters, McCawley announced, were chicken feet with black beans, and salted mustard greens with goose intestines. I like to think that I'm as fond of chicken feet as the next fellow, but goose intestines are the sort of thing that makes me suspect that those Chinese waiters were correct a number of times when they said, "You no like." I put aside my doubts. The store of mankind's knowledge was not expanded by scholars who failed to seek because of fear of what they might find. "These goose intestines are not bad," I said to McCawley when our meal had been delivered. The sincerity of the compliment was not really undercut, it seems to me, by the possibility that I was eating the Chicago version of chicken feet.

McCawley had been kind enough to give me a copy of "The Eaters' Guide to Chinese Characters," and I intended to apply myself to learning how to use it. "Will I really be able to read the wall signs in Chinatown?" I asked.

"If they're printed," McCawley said. "Script is a little more difficult." The growing use of modern Chinese modifications adds another difficulty, he explained, not to speak of the euphemisms that Chinese often use in describing food. For instance, before we left H.S.F., McCawley had told me that the final character in the sign he found troublesome was "cloud," which might have been a euphemism for fish stomach or might not have been. Later, he decided it was a nonstandard character for wonton.

On the way back to New York, I studied the guide. It looked as if it required about the application necessary to get through a graduate course in phonology at M.I.T. Also, if even McCawley sometimes had difficulty telling characters apart, it was obvious that a novice might often order what appeared to be wonton only to be brought fish stomach—fish stomach he would have to eat unless he wanted to risk having the waiter come over to say, "I told you you no like." Linguistic research began to seem even more complicated than history. I decided I would ask McCawley to do one more translation for me, from English to Chinese—a note that said, "Please bring me some of what that man at the next table is having."

(4)

Confessions of a

Stand-up Sausage Eater

I SUPPOSE I WOULD HAVE given up the Feast of San Gennaro years ago if I'd had any choice. San Gennaro has always been the largest Italian festival in the city, and for a long time now Mulberry Street during the Feast has been crowded enough to give the impression that, for reasons lost to history, Manhattan folk customs include an annual outdoor enactment of precisely the conditions present in the IRT uptown express during rush hour. In September, the weather in New York can be authentically Neapolitan—particularly on a street that is jammed with people and sealed on both sides with a line of stands where vendors are boiling oil for *zeppole* or barbecuing *braciole* over charcoal. Occasionally I have become irritated with the Feast even on evenings when I have no intention of attending it, since I have become one of those Manhattan residents who get testy when some event brings even more traffic than usual into the city from the suburbs. Those of us who migrated to New York from the middle of the country may be even less tolerant of incursions by out-of-towners than the natives are. I suppose I might as well admit that, in some particularly frustrating gridlock on some particularly steamy fall day, I may have shouted, "Go back where you came from, you rubes!" in the direction of a lot of former New Yorkers who now live a mile or two into New Jersey—an outburst that would have been even ruder if the objects of my irritation had not been safely encased in soundproof air-conditioned cars.

The traffic congestion caused by San Gennaro is particularly irritating to me because Mulberry Street lies between our house and Chinatown, and the Feast happens to fall at the time of year when I return to the city from a summer in Nova Scotia suffering the anguish of extended Chinese-food deprivation. For Occidentals, we eat very well in Nova Scotia. Around the middle of August, though, even as I'm plowing through a feast that may include mushroom soup made from wild mushrooms we have gathered in the woods and halibut just off the boat and sugar-snap peas so sweet that even Sarah (whose last recorded expression of enthusiasm for eating anything green came at a street fair that was selling green cotton candy) has been witnessed eating them straight off the vine and freshly baked bread and blueberry pie made from wild blueberries, I become acutely aware of how many miles, nautical and overland, stand between me and Mott Street.

Practically feverish with visions of crabs sloshing around in black-bean sauce, I detour around the Feast in a journey that seems to get longer every year, as the lights of San Gennaro push farther and farther uptown from the heart of Little Italy toward Houston Street, on the edge of the Lower East Side. It would not surprise me, I think, if one of these years commuters from Westchester County pouring out of Grand Central Station some hot September morning walked smack into a line of *calzone* and sausage stands that had crept up in an unbroken line fifty blocks from Grand Street. The vendors, dishing out food as fast as they can, will still have time to complain to the account executives and bank managers they're serving about having been assigned a spot too far from the busiest blocks of the Feast.

I love the elements of San Gennaro that still exist from its origin as a neighborhood festival transplanted practically intact from Naples by Little Italy immigrants—the statue of the saint with dollar bills pinned beneath it, for instance, and the brass band that seems to consist of a half-dozen aging Italians and one young Chinese trumpet player—but the Feast has felt considerably less like a neighborhood celebration in recent years, partly because its size has inevitably brought along some atmosphere of mass production, partly because of the inclusion of such non-Neapolitan specialties as piña coladas and eggrolls and computer portraits, and partly because of the self-consciousness represented by *Kiss Me—I'm Italian* buttons. Also, I find that I can usually catch the brass band during the year around the Chinatown part of Mulberry, below Canal Street; it often works Chinese funerals. The gambling at the Feast does not attract me, and the stuffed animals that are awarded for making a basket or knocking down milk bottles hold no appeal for someone whose family policy on stuffed animals is moving slowly, in the face of some resistance, toward what the Metropolitan Museum of Art used to call deaccessioning.

Still, there I am at San Gennaro every year—admitting to myself that I rather enjoy pushing my way down Mulberry at a time when Neapolitan music is coming over the loudspeakers and operators of games of chance are making their pitches and food smells from a dozen different booths are competing in the middle of the street. My presence is easily explained: I can't stay away from the sausage sandwiches.

As it happens, we live right around the corner from the South Village, an Italian neighborhood where the sort of sausage sandwiches served at Italian feasts—hot or sweet sausage jammed into a roll with a combination of fried pepper and onions as dressing—can be bought any day of the year in comfortable surroundings, which may even include a stool at the counter. I never buy one. Gradually, it has become clear to me that uncontrolled, year-round eating of sausage sandwiches is not an acceptable option for me. It was instinct more than conscious decision—the sort of instinct that some animals must use to know how many of certain berries to eat in the woods. Alice, who at our house acts as enforcer for the nutrition mob, does not have to speak on the subject of how much devastation a steady diet of Italian sausage could wreak on the human body. The limits are set. I have a sausage sandwich whenever I go to San Gennaro. I have a sausage sandwich at the Feast of St. Anthony, on Sullivan Street, in the spring. If I'm lucky, I might stumble across one of the smaller Italian feasts in Little Italy—I always come back from Chinatown by a circuitous route through there, just on the off-chance—or find a sausage stand that has attached itself to some Village block party. Otherwise, I do without. When I go back for visits to Kansas City, my hometown, and I'm asked by my old high-school friends how I possibly survive in New York, I tell them that the way I survive is simple: I only eat sausage sandwiches standing up.

I am not the only seasonal eater in New York. There is a time in the fall when a lot of people who have spent August in some rural setting—talking a lot of brave talk about how there is nothing better than a simple piece of broiled fish and some absolutely fresh vegetables—come back to the city and head straight for the sort of food that seems to exist only in close proximity to cement. One September I noticed one of them while I was waiting in line at Joe's Dairy on Sullivan Street—right across the street from St. Anthony's, the church that sponsors my spring sausage eating. As it happened, my own mission was seasonal—although one sort of business or another takes me to Joe's all year round. In the early fall, when farmers are still bringing their produce into Manhattan for Saturday-morning markets, it is possible to make a stop at the farmer's market in the West Village, pick up some basil and some tomatoes that actually taste like tomatoes rather than Christmas decorations, stop in at Joe's for mozzarella so fresh that it is still oozing milk, and put the tomatoes and mozzarella and basil and some olive oil together to create something that tastes almost too good to be described as salad. The man in front of me at Joe's Dairy was looking around the shelves as if he were a Russian defector getting his first look at Bloomingdale's. He asked for Parmesan cheese. He asked for Romano. He bought some mozzarella. "Jesus Christ! I just had a roast-pork sandwich at Frank's!" he suddenly said. "Boy, am I glad to be back in the city!" Everybody in the store nodded in sympathy.

•

When I walk down Mulberry Street, just below Canal, during the Feast of San Gennaro, I am strongly affected by what I suppose could be called border tensions: I feel the competing pulls of sausage sandwiches and flounder Fukienese-style. The street just east of Mulberry is Mott, the main drag of Chinatown. There was a time not many years ago when Mott and a few side streets seemed to constitute a small Chinese outpost in the middle of a large Italian neighborhood; those were the days when a Chinese candidate for the New York State Assembly endeared himself to me by telling a reporter from the *Times* that he was running against the Italian incumbent—Louis DeSalvio, the permanent grand marshal of the Feast of San Gennaro—even though he realized that he didn't have a "Chinaman's chance." Over the past ten or fifteen years, though, a surge of Chinese immigration has revitalized Chinatown and pushed out its boundaries—past the Bowery and then East Broadway in one direction, across Mulberry Street in the other. On Mulberry Street below Canal, the *calzone* stands and beer carts of San Gennaro stand in front of Chinese butcher shops and Chinese importing companies and Chinese produce stores. "They left us three blocks," an official of San Gennaro told me while discussing the Chinese expansion. The blocks between Canal and Broome are still dominated by the robust Italian restaurants that represent the tomato-sauce side against the forces of Northern Italian cream sauce in what has been called the War of the Red and the White. Even on those blocks of Mulberry, though, some of the windows of second-floor offices have sprouted Chinese writing. There are a lot of Italians left in the tenements of Mulberry Street, but a lot of Italians have moved away—returning only temporarily to shop on Grand Street or sit in one of the coffeehouses or eat sausage sandwiches at the Feast of San Gennaro. The Feast is still run by the grandson of the man who founded the Society of San Gennaro, Napoli e Dintorni, in 1926, but he lives on Staten Island.

Foreign food—non-Italian food, that is—began to creep into San Gennaro and some of the other Italian feasts several years ago, but not from Chinatown. There were some Korean booths and an occasional taco stand and some stands at which Filipinos sold barbecued meat on a stick and fried rice and lo mein and egg rolls and an unusual fritter that was made with vegetables and fried in oil. When I first came across the foreign booths, I decided that the purist belief in restricting Italian festivals to Italian food was narrow-minded and artificial—a decision that was based, I admit, on a certain fondness for the vegetable fritters. These days, any street event in New York—a merchants' fair on Third Avenue, a block party on the West Side—is certain to have at least one Filipino food stand, and a feast the size of San Gennaro will have half a dozen. At the annual One World Festival sponsored by the Armenian diocese—a festival that has always been so aggressively ecumenical that I wouldn't be surprised to discover someday that a few spots had been assigned to food stands run by Turks—the stands selling Armenian *lahmajun* and *boereg* and *yalanchi* and *lule kebab* seem almost outnumbered by stands selling what are sometimes called "Filipino and Polynesian specialties." The man in charge of assigning spots for San Gennaro once told me that if no attempt were made to maintain a balance—and a Feast that is not overwhelmingly Italian would obviously be unbalanced—Mulberry Street would have ten Filipino stands on every block. I have asked Filipino vendors how they accounted for so many of their countrymen being in the street-fair game, but their explanations have never gone much beyond the theory that some people made money at some street fairs in brownstone neighborhoods and other people decided to get in on a good thing. It may remain one of those New York ethnic mysteries that outlanders were not meant to understand. Why are so many fruit-and-vegetable stores that were once run by Italians and so many fruit-and-vegetable stores that previously didn't exist run by Koreans? Why have I never seen a black sanitation man? Why are conversations among vendors of hot dogs at the Central Park Zoo conducted in Greek?

Selecting my sausage sandwich at San Gennaro requires a certain amount of concentration. At San Gennaro, after all, there are always at least thirty stands selling sausage sandwiches. I don't mean that I do nothing else at the Feast. In the spirit of fostering intergroup harmony, I sometimes have a vegetable fritter. I often have a few *zeppole*—holeless doughnuts that are available almost exclusively at Italian feasts. I have a couple of beers, muttering about the price, or some wine with fruit. Mainly, though, I inspect sausage stands —walking slowly the length of the Feast and maybe back again before I make my choice. About halfway through my inspection, I can expect to be told by another member of the party—Abigail and Sarah are ordinarily the other members of the party—that all sausage stands look alike, or maybe even that all sausage sandwiches taste alike. I tell them that they certainly weren't raised to believe that all sausage sandwiches taste alike. I tell them that their expertise in this matter is seriously limited by the refusal of either of them to taste an Italian-sausage sandwich. I remind them that a researcher who is satisfied with a less than adequate sampling risks flawed results. I keep looking.

The stands always look familiar to me. A lot of the food vendors at Italian feasts in Manhattan make a business of going from feast to feast around the New York area from spring to fall. In Little Italy, it is assumed that the food-stand operators spend the rest of the year in Florida, living like kings off the sort of profits that must be accumulated by anyone who sells a tiny plate of ziti with tomato sauce for three dollars cash and doesn't have to furnish so much as a chair or a countertop. Among New Yorkers, it is practically an article of faith that anyone who runs what seems to be a small seasonal business—the ice-cream man in the park, for instance— can be found on any cold day in February casually blowing hundreds of dollars at some Florida dog track. Although I recognize the stands, I can never seem to keep in my mind which one has served me the best sausage sandwich. The last time I went to San Gennaro, the final inspection was carried out on a rainy weekday evening in the company of both Abigail and Sarah. I was convinced that the stand I had patronized at St. Anthony's the previous spring—ac-quiring a sandwich the memory of which I carried with me through the summer—was called by someone's first name. All the sausage stands at San Gennaro seemed to be called by someone's first name. Had it been Dominic's? The Original Jack's? Rocky & Philly's? Tony's? Angelo's? Smokin' Joe's? Staten Island Frank's? Gizzo's? Lucy's?

There was nothing to do but inspect each stand—Abigail and Sarah tagging along behind me, already full of pasta. I looked for a stand that was frying the sausages on a griddle rather than grilling them over charcoal—and displaying peppers and onions that had been sliced and cooked precisely to my requirements. It was amazing

how many sausage stands qualified. My daughters began to remind
me that it was a school night. I told them that I would write them
notes if they overslept the next morning ("Abigail had to be up late
to take advantage of an unusual opportunity to observe the process
of pure research"). Under some pressure, I stopped in front of Staten
Island Frank's—or maybe it was the Original Jack's; even now the
names run together—and said, "This is it." When I started to eat,
I was convinced that I had chosen brilliantly—until we passed a
stand that I hadn't noticed before. It was serving sausages, with
correctly fried peppers and onions, on marvelous-looking rolls that
had sesame seeds on top of them.

"Sesame-seed rolls!" I said. "Nobody told me about sesame-
seed rolls!"

"Take it easy," Abigail said, giving me a reassuring pat on the
arm. "You can have one on a sesame-seed roll next year."

"Not next year," I reminded her as we headed home. "At St.
Anthony's in June."

5

An Attempt to

Compile the Definitive History

of Didee's Restaurant

MY FIELDWORK IN BUFFALO was not actually my first fling at historical research. I once went to Louisiana determined to write the definitive history of Didee's restaurant, or to eat an awful lot of baked duck and dirty rice trying. I'm quick to take up scholarly challenges in southern Louisiana. Once, I went to Mamou, Louisiana, to observe the Cajun Mardi Gras celebration because I had heard that the traditional ride of Cajun horsemen around the countryside in search of chickens for the Mardi Gras chicken gumbo often comes to a halt so that the celebrants can drink beer and eat boudin. The Cajun Mardi Gras happens to be a particularly jovial event, but I have to say that I would observe the annual conference of the society of water-treatment-plant engineers if I had reason to believe that it was interrupted every so often so that the participants could drink beer and eat boudin. At the Mamou Mardi Gras, I ate a lot of boudin while I was standing in fields chosen as rest stops —squeezing the mixture of pork and seasoning and rice out of the sausage casing with one hand and holding the wash-down can of beer in the other. It wasn't far from my normal style of boudin eating; I normally down boudin while standing in the parking lot of some Cajun grocery store that has managed to snatch me off the road by displaying in its window a hand-lettered sign that says HOT BOUDIN TODAY. The Mamou boudin seemed particularly good, although I may have simply been in a particularly good mood because of the knowledge that even after all the boudin was gone we still had the chicken gumbo to look forward to. As I ate boudin in Mamou, it occurred to me that if sausage fanciers ever have our own annual conference I might find myself responding to a panel of experts who had concluded that there is little in common between boudin and East Coast Italian sausage by rising to remind the panel that both are normally eaten standing up.

Trying to compile the definitive history of Didee's restaurant wasn't easy. In fact, I might have given up the history game right there if it hadn't been for the baked duck and dirty rice. The event that had attracted my attention obviously qualified as what historians are always calling the End of an Era—the perfect moment to slip in with a definitive history. The proprietor of a tiny, family-run restaurant in a nearly abandoned section of Baton Rouge's black commercial district—Didee's, a name that had represented stupefying baked duck in Louisiana for this entire century—had sold name, duck recipe, and franchise rights to a go-go New York mini-conglomerate that talked about making him "the Colonel Sanders of the duck business." All that may strike professional historians as a simple enough tale of American commerce, but once I had arrived at Didee's and begun my research—interviewing the proprietor, Herman Perrodin, while downing a bowl of his seafood gumbo and feeling grateful for my working conditions—I realized that no tale involving Herman Perrodin was likely to be a simple tale. There was no doubt that his grandfather, Charles Adrian Lastrapes, founded the original Didee's in Opelousas, Louisiana, around the turn of the century—Perrodin's mother, Clara Lastrapes Perrodin, and her husband opened a separate Didee's in Baton Rouge in 1952—but Herman Perrodin did not fit snugly into the role of an unspoiled folk chef nurturing an old family recipe. A tall man in his fifties with a sort of lubricated manner of talking, Perrodin occasionally described himself as a "poor little old dumb boy born in a sweet-potato patch in Opelousas, Louisiana," but he also described himself as being a better chef than Paul Bocuse. "*La nouvelle cuisine!*" he said to me, drawing out the last word in astonishment at the sort of thing dumb folks will believe. "Don't tell *me* about

la nouvelle cuisine! I've been doing *la nouvelle cuisine* all my god-
damn life!"

The early history of Didee's restaurant, Perrodin assured me,
was not all that complicated. Charles Adrian Lastrapes started serving baked duck and baked chicken and Creole gumbo and oyster
loaves while running what newspaper features about Didee's usually
refer to as a coffee shop and what Perrodin figured for a gambling
den or a bootlegging operation. Lastrapes was always known as
Didee, pronounced to rhyme with high tea—a meal, I hardly need
add, that anyone fortunate enough to eat the daily fare of Opelousas
would undoubtedly regard as some form of corporal punishment.
Opelousas is about sixty miles west of Baton Rouge, in the section
of Louisiana long dominated by the French—an area where a noted
gumbo is discussed with the seriousness it deserves, and where a lot
of black and white people seem to have the same last names as well
as approximately the same complexions, and where attitudes toward
the more enjoyable of the Seven Deadly Sins are the sort of stuff
sermons are made of in Shreveport. Didee's was always a restaurant
for white people, although the Lastrapes were what are sometimes
called "people of color," or Creoles. There are those in Louisiana
who object to the word "Creole" being used to designate people of
mixed race rather than the white descendants of the colonial French,
and there are those in Louisiana who believe that people who serve
the sort of baked duck that Didee Lastrapes and his second wife,
Miz Anna, put out for so many years in a little restaurant just off
the courthouse square in Opelousas can call themselves anything
they please.

"This is edible gumbo," I said, while Perrodin paused between
stories of a childhood in Didee's kitchen and stories of his wanderings
around the country after he left Opelousas as a teenager ("I'm the
traveling, adventurous, aggressive black sheep of the family"). He
agreed that the gumbo was at least superb. In southern Louisiana,
it is customary for a serious cook to assume the preeminence of his
version of anything. Perrodin's son, Charles, who struck me as
relatively reserved, said to me later that day, "You ever taste our
shrimp *étouffée*? You taste our *étouffée*, you'll throw rocks at other
people's *étouffée*."

Didee Lastrapes died in the mid-forties, Perrodin said, but the Opelousas restaurant remained open under Miz Anna's stewardship until her death in 1970.

"Then Dee Dee's opened where Didee's had been," I said, introducing a complication I already knew about and opening what I believe the methodology specialists at the American Historical Association conferences refer to among themselves as a real bucket of worms.

Perrodin dismissed Dee Dee's with a wave of his hand.

What happened, I knew, was that Thomas and Tony Blouin, who had worked for Miz Anna for years, reopened the restaurant, choosing the name Dee Dee's for reasons Thomas Blouin once summarized pithily for a visiting reporter: "So people would know it's the same but different." I once ate at Dee Dee's. In 1972 Alice and I stopped in Opelousas on our way—well, more or less on our way—to the Breaux Bridge Crawfish Festival. I remember Alice speculating on the ingredients in the dirty rice, in the tone of voice a bomb-squad man might use to discuss how the terrorists rigged up something small enough to fit into a satchel but powerful enough to destroy a wing of the post office. As I remember, we had a fine meal, although I may have simply been in a particularly good mood because of the knowledge that even after the duck was gone we had the crawfish to look forward to.

"Did you think the food was any good at Dee Dee's?" I asked Perrodin.

He waved his hand again. "A lot of people can do things and a lot of people have to be directed," he said. "It went kerplop, and now they're cooking on the offshore oil rigs or something."

For most of the history we had been discussing, Perrodin was not what the historians call a primary source. The wanderings he had begun as a teenager kept him out of Louisiana until he went to Baton Rouge for a few years in the late fifties to help out his father, Arlington Perrodin, as a sort of catering manager. Perrodin told me that the jobs he had held around the country as a waiter or bartender or cook or manager would take four years to list. He could present a ten-minute declamation on what he learned along the way about which tastes are received where in what he called the "sculpture of the mouth" or on what he learned about herbs alone ("I'm like a perfumer. I mean it. I'm telling you. I studied the herbs for five years. I could tell you more about herbs than the man who wrote the book"). He could also present a declamation on the high life, and on the personal lesson he learned when he was sent to prison in Texas in 1970 as a heroin user. Perrodin talked about his drug habit the way he talked about his gumbo. One minute, while mentioning the last spice in a recipe that gives it "that zing—*respect*, I call it," he would slam his hand on the table and say, "*Voilà*! Now I got your whole mouth lit up!" A few minutes later, he would fling both hands toward the ceiling and say, "A quarter of a million dollars flowed through these arms!"

When Arlington Perrodin died in 1976, a few years after Herman had come home for good, Didee's was not far from kerplop itself. It had been mentioned in national magazines; movie stars had written raves in its guestbook; the Confrérie de la Chaîne des Rôtisseurs (le Chapitre de Nouvelle-Orleans) had included on one of its formal menus *Canard à la Didee, Rize au Fave, Les "Mustard Greens*." But not many Baton Rouge people came to eat. The neighborhood was evaporating around Didee's, and Herman Perrodin could not seem to raise the capital to move or even to advertise. "You can't do anything without money," Perrodin said. "Cash money. No checks."

In 1974, a review by Richard Collin in the *New Orleans States-Item* suggesting that Didee's would flourish if it moved to New Orleans had resulted in a number of proposals, but every one of them had fallen through. During the last year of Arlington Perrodin's life, Herman took a fling at a scheme by some young Baton Rouge entrepreneurs to feature Didee's cooking in Aspen—a flop from which he acquired nothing but an interest in skiing to add to his taste for the high life. There were other offers, but Perrodin dismissed them as schemes in which he might do a lot of work without seeing any money. "I'm not waitin' for no net," he explained to me. "You can have all the net you want. Give me the gross."

After three-quarters of a century of his family's building the reputation of Didee's, the way Perrodin analyzed it, he had found himself in the position of an unappreciated and—even worse—

undercompensated genius. There was Paul Bocuse, according to Perrodin's calculations, making fifteen thousand dollars for catering a meal, and there was Herman Perrodin doing all of his own cooking and ordering and bill paying and, sometimes, sweeping up—and still never taking in more than a few hundred dollars on a good day. "I got obligations and I got a life-style," Perrodin told me. "I'm not satisfied with the way I'm living. I'm not satisfied with the home I live in. I'm not satisfied with the car I drive."

Enter Omni Capital Worldwide, Ltd., go-go miniconglomerate whose name might be taken as another way of saying, "All Money Everywhere."

•

I had lunch at Didee's with Herb Turner, who had moved to Baton Rouge from Fort Lauderdale a couple of years before to run Omni Capital's operations in Louisiana. Turner struck me as very go-go himself. He said he had been so busy that he hadn't had time to get rid of his second Cadillac before buying his third. The previous few days had been particularly hectic, he said, because he had a guest in town—a very close personal friend who happened to be Frank Sinatra's bodyguard.

I knew I was digressing from the history of Didee's, but I couldn't resist the obvious question: "Who's watching Frank?"

"Frank's okay," Turner said, digressing himself into show business for some encouraging stories about Eddie Fisher's comeback. As it happens, Fisher once ate at Didee's, and left a rude remark about Elizabeth Taylor in the guestbook. Arlington Perrodin covered that page with clear plastic for protection.

Omni Capital, Turner told me, had been founded in New York as a tax-shelter consulting business by one investment banker who was also a CPA, and another who was also a Hollywood booking agent. In describing its history, he and another Omni executive who had joined us for lunch used the word "roll" a lot. They talked about rolling out of tax shelters into film distribution, and rolling out of timberland into housing developments. It seemed natural enough to roll out of housing developments into baked duck and dirty rice. In fact, on those rare evenings when I find myself in a place where the only alternative to sitting like a condemned man in the motel dining room is starvation, rolling into baked duck and dirty rice is something I've thought about a lot myself.

What Omni was planning, Turner said, was to build a prototype Didee's near the Baton Rouge Country Club—a Garden Room that could be adapted for private parties, an Acadian Room with beams of distressed wood, a good bar. If the prototype succeeded, Didee's Famous Restaurant, Inc., the corporation formed for the occasion, would start franchising. Turner said Omni planned to send out Didee credit cards, carrying preferential reservation privileges, to five thousand business contacts in the state. "That'll take care of that," he said. "I can't imagine the general public getting a shot at that restaurant."

"The duck is delicious," I said to Perrodin. I happen to like duck. I don't think I like it as well as Alice does. When it comes to partiality to ducks, Alice is outdone by nobody except, perhaps, other ducks. In the jockeying that goes on during the decision-making concerning what dishes are to be ordered in a Chinese restaurant, Alice always says something that has to do with duck. "You know, this place seems like the kind of place that would have great duck," she'll say, apparently having figured that out from the shade of Formica on the tabletops. I don't mean to complain: our friend William Edgett Smith, the man with the Naugahyde palate, always says something like "You know, this place seems like the kind of place that would have great egg foo yung." I do like duck. I particularly liked Herman Perrodin's duck. It was by far the best thing on the plate—moist on the inside and crisp on the outside, with no fat in sight. I suppose I might have found the duck particularly satisfying because I realized that, as a member of the general public, I might be having my last shot at it.

•

As soon as I arrived in Opelousas, I was assured that the New York miniconglomerate had signed the wrong man. "They didn't do enough research before they closed the deal," one of the breakfast regulars at the Palace Café, on the courthouse square, explained to me. In Opelousas, the Perrodins' Baton Rouge version of Didee's was barely acknowledged ("I think they started some kind of catering service over in Baton Rouge"). From the way Baton Rouge was discussed at the Palace, I got the idea that anybody in Opelousas who has business in the capital waits until he gets back home to eat. Baton Rouge was described as a place where the state government and the petrochemical industry have drawn so many people from places like north Louisiana or even Mississippi that there might not be a tableful of eaters in the entire city who know the difference between splendidly prepared duck and the kind of fowl that might be considered edible by Baptists. Herman Perrodin could hardly have learned the secrets of baked-duck cooking from Didee as a boy, I was told by a man who had delivered milk to the restaurant for many years, since Didee was accustomed to sitting out on the sidewalk whittling while his wife did the cooking. The dairyman said Herman would not have been around the restaurant much anyway; even as a boy, he was apparently what people in Opelousas call "kinda sporty."

As if that were not complication enough, a lawyer in Opelousas who once had some business with Thomas Blouin, the proprietor of Dee Dee's while it lasted, informed me that Blouin had recently come off the oil rigs to take a job cooking at a restaurant between Opelousas and Lafayette, where he was prepared to cook the true Opelousas stupefying baked-duck dinner for me and most of the law firm of Sandoz, Sandoz & Schiff. At the restaurant, a place called Carroll's, near Evangeline Downs racetrack, I was pleased to find that Sandoz, Sandoz & Schiff lawyers are the sort of lawyers who find it easier to get down to cases if they have a pile of boiled crawfish to work on while they talk. What they talked about mainly was food. "Her oyster loaf was a knockout," one of the lawyers said, recalling how Miz Anna would scoop the middle out of a perfect French loaf and replace it with succulent fried oysters. That reminded another member of the firm about stopping in after work with a large pot he kept in his car and having Miz Anna fill it with seafood gumbo before he went home. As they talked, the lawyers deftly peeled crawfish and popped them into their mouths. It occurred to me that if a society of sausage fanciers was ever founded, the firm of Sandoz, Sandoz & Schiff might be a good bet for general counsel. "If it please the court," the firm's litigation partner would say in our defense, "I would ask that the term 'food crazy' used by this witness be stricken from the record." Conferences would be held in grocery-store parking lots, where the officers of the association and their attorneys could lean up against a Pontiac and chomp away at boudin. The bylaws drawn up by Sandoz, Sandoz & Schiff would make it clear that all association business would be suspended on those days when, as is sometimes said in southern Louisiana, "the crawfish are walking right across the highway."

About the time we had knocked off our first conversational bowl of crawfish, Thomas Blouin came out from the kitchen to sit down with us for a while before putting the finishing touches on the meal. He turned out to be a rather modest man, as southern Louisiana cooks go, although he did admit later in the evening that he could prepare wild duck, a notoriously difficult fowl to cook, so well that it tasted like lemon pie. As Blouin told me about his training under Miz Anna, first as a waiter and then as a cook, the lawyers said, "See!" and "Listen to that!" and "He knows his onions!" When I asked who had the real Didee recipe for duck, Blouin said, "You're fixin' to eat the recipe." The duck was delicious, if not quite as crisp as Herman Perrodin's. The dirty rice—a sort of rice dressing made with chicken liver and chicken gizzard and onion and bell pepper and celery and garlic and spices and oil—was staggering, although I speak as someone who had to go to a franchise fried-chicken place to find a dirty rice he didn't like. When I accepted Blouin's kind offer of another bowl of rice, there were cheers at the table, and a couple of lawyers clapped Blouin on the back. "They signed the wrong man," one of them said. "What'd I tell you." I couldn't help but wonder whether Henry Steele Commager had ever found himself in a similar situation.

•

"Why, I bet he learned more about cooking on the oil rigs than he knew when Miz Anna died," Perrodin said when I reported the Opelousas theory about who knew how to cook Didee's duck. I had arrived back in Baton Rouge in time for a late lunch. Perrodin tossed off a few more disparaging remarks about Blouin, and then sat down to tell me how *maquechou*, a sort of stewed-corn dish the Omni executives and I had been served at Didee's with lunch, was prepared by a cook who really knew how to get your whole mouth lit up.

"But will they be able to do that sort of thing at a Didee's franchise in Alexandria or Shreveport?" I asked after Perrodin had finished a five-minute speech that included pulling his tongue out now and then to show me which part of the mouth was affected by which flavor. "Aren't you afraid they'll take shortcuts with preparation and ingredients?"

Perrodin leaned way back in his chair and stared at me, as if to make certain I had not disappeared from dumbness. "That was *canned* corn you had in the *maquechou*," he said. "What I was just explaining to you was the authentic way to do it. Who the hell's got time to do that?"

Thinking back on the meal, I remembered that when one of the Omni executives mentioned his company's roll into real estate, it had occurred to me that Perrodin's dinner rolls had the look of packaged hamburger buns about them. "But how about the duck?" I asked. "Doesn't that take a lot of care and experience—all that time in your grandfather's kitchen learning the secrets?"

"There are no secrets," he said. "Any idiot could do it. Why, I could stay home and tell you how to do it over the phone, and I bet *dollars* it would come out the same."

He took a fork and poked around at the duck I was eating. "Shortcuts!" he said. "This duck was cooked last night. I reconstituted it by putting it back in natural sauce just to get it warmed through. When somebody orders it, I take it out of its natural gravy and put it under the salamander and let this overhead-broiler heat come down on it, and it brings it back just like I took it out of the oven."

As Perrodin expanded on the subject, shortcuts began to sound as dramatic as spectacular gumbo or a serious heroin habit. "Why, I can take almost any kind of canned vegetable and I'll defy you to tell me if it's fresh," he said. "Shortcuts! I'm the *master* of the shortcut. I mean to tell you."

6

Ordering in Japanese

ALL IN ALL, I spend a lot of time—time other people might spend worrying about their tax situation or the Bomb—worrying about the possibility that I might go right through a meal somewhere and still miss the good stuff. That's what worried me about going to Tokyo. How was somebody who couldn't seem to master a few wall signs in an American Chinatown going to figure out what the special of the day was in Tokyo? Talk about the Mysteries of the East! Even in European countries that are thoughtful enough to conduct their business in the Roman alphabet, I often get edgy during meals because of a suspicion that the regulars are enjoying some local specialty that the management has hidden from travelers by listing it on the menu in a foreign language. Once, while Alice and I were eating lunch in a Sicilian city called Piazza Armerina, I became nearly frantic at not being able to figure out what was meant by the special of the day listed as *bocca di lupo*—a dish my high-school Latin led me to believe was called Mouth of the Wolf. Before placing an order, I thought it prudent to confirm my assumption that the phrase was not meant literally, but no such dish was listed in the dictionary of menu terms that I keep with me at all times in a foreign country—the way some travelers always carry their passport and a carefully hidden American fifty-dollar bill. The waiter spoke no English, and he just looked puzzled when I, having quickly exhausted my Italian, cleared my throat and did what seemed to me a passable wolf imitation. We never did order the special of the day, and I have assumed ever since that it is only a matter of time before we run into some old Sicilian hand who says, "I hope you got to Piazza Armerina for some of that marvelous *bocca di lupo.*"

I was thinking of *bocca di lupo* as Alice and I flew over the Pacific on the way to our first stay in Tokyo. I like the Japanese food served in New York, even though I have sometimes heard Alice discuss the purity of Japanese ingredients—the sort of talk that can ordinarily put me off my feed. What was to be found in Tokyo would presumably be even better, but how were we meant to find it? "How am I going to get along in a place as foreign as Japan when even an Italian menu can cause me to bay in a public place?" I asked Alice.

"Where's your spirit of adventure?" Alice said. She reminded me what I had said about pushing out frontiers in the interest of pure research—and conveniently forgot that she had not been eager to take a flier on *bocca di lupo* herself.

I settled down to my airplane reading—a book that displayed colored pictures of Japanese dishes and explained what they were. "The word for noodles is *udon,*" I announced right away. I always take the precaution of learning the word for noodles before entering any country, just in case. "Unless you want the polite form," I went on, "which is *o-udon.* That's what I mean about mystery: why would anyone want to be anything but polite about noodles?"

My precaution turned out to be well taken. "*O-udon!*" I was able to shout, politely, during a stroll on our very first morning in Tokyo, as I stopped Alice in her tracks and pointed to a store window beyond which someone was rolling out noodle dough. By then, I was already feeling much less concerned about the possibility that the language barrier could lead to my starvation. Having arrived in Tokyo the previous evening tired from the flight, we had gone no farther for dinner than the hotel's sushi restaurant—where it became apparent that someone sitting at a sushi bar, rather than at a table, can get his fill simply by pointing at the fish on display. Sitting at the bar is the best place to eat sushi anyway, since a good sushi chef puts on a good show—responding to any order with an almost military "*Hai!*," a couple of taps with his knife to get the rhythm, some quick strokes at the raw fish, an abrupt jab to plant the fish in a ball of rice, and a flick of the wrist as he places the finished product on the bar in front of you. According to a pocket-size sushi-identification chart we picked up on the way in, we managed, without saying a word, to eat tuna, belly of tuna (I thought I might like a country that troubles to distinguish among cuts of tuna), abalone, salmon roe, sea urchin, "interior of arch shell," and, finally, some mysterious but fantastic mixture of fish and herbs that we ordered by displaying enthusiasm as it was being prepared for someone else.

"*Aji no tataki,*" I had said the next morning, after a long session with my food-picture book.

"Does that mean 'I ate too much' in Japanese?" Alice asked.

"It's what we had last night at the end of the meal," I said. I read from the text: " 'Small pieces of pompano chopped and mixed with onions, ginger, and sometimes leeks.' " My confidence was growing, and it wasn't depleted by noticing that other sources identified *aji* as horse mackerel or a type of herring. I felt that I had broken the code.

By the time we stood in front of the store window admiring the technique of the noodle maker, it had also become apparent that we had another great demystification device at our disposal—the Japanese custom of restaurants displaying in their windows full-size, absolutely realistic models of whatever dishes they're offering. We had spent the morning wandering around Asakasa, a neighborhood of small shops and a serious temple and a pleasant little amusement park where I had lost badly in hand wrestling to a mechanical sumo wrestler, and a lot of what we had paused to admire had been models of sushi and sashimi and tempura and noodles and lightly fried fish—my idea of window shopping. When we reached the noodle shop, I realized that I was famished. One of the models it displayed looked particularly tempting—a large bowlful of soup with thick white noodles and two huge mushrooms and a bean-curd cake. We marched into the restaurant—a small, immaculate place—and I beckoned the proprietor to come with me. He was polite but hesitant. Did he think that I may have once suffered some slight at his hands which he had long ago forgotten and was now, as they say in the saloons, inviting him to step outside? Had some recent article comparing Japanese and American crime statistics put him on his guard to the point where he suspected that going outside with me might give Alice a shot at the cash register? Could he possibly have mistaken me for some sort of exchange-program public-health inspector who might object to noodles being made in the window? I could reassure him on that point by informing him that, quite the contrary, I had once offered to establish a defense fund for a barbecue man on the west coast of Florida who had allegedly assaulted a public-health inspector for suggesting that he clean his grill more than once a year—except that I don't know how to reassure in Japanese.

Whatever misgivings the noodle-shop proprietor had, though, were overcome by his courtesy. He stepped outside. We studied the window together. As I tried to indicate what I wanted, I realized that my menu dictionary was remiss in offering me translations only for words like "grilled" and "well done." What I needed to know how to say in Japanese was "No, not that one—the one just behind it, near the corner." In a moment, though, he gave a quick nod, we went back inside, and a waitress brought to the table a precise replica of the replica. It was delicious. It cost the equivalent of two dollars.

"No wonder the crime rate is so low in Japan," I said to Alice. "Everybody must be very, very happy."

•

"*Tako yaki*," I said to Alice, as we stood in front of a street vendor and watched him pour batter into the rows of half-circle indentations of an iron griddle—like one of those college kids at Williamsburg demonstrating how musket balls were made. "It's listed right here in the book under Street and Festival Foods." What we were attending was not a festival but an astonishing ritual that happens with enough regularity to draw a few dozen street vendors. Every Sunday afternoon, a boulevard near the Olympic stadium becomes filled with thousands of Japanese teenagers who arrive in groups of a dozen or so, the members of each group dressed identically in costumes of the fifties. Each group gathers in a circle around a huge tape recorder that is playing songs like "Rock Around the Clock" and "Let's Go to the Hop," dances a carefully choreographed version of the twist in unison, and somehow seems very Japanese doing it. Naturally, I tried a *tako yaki*, but then I discovered a problem with eating completely foreign foods which I hadn't anticipated: was it possible that I didn't like *tako yaki* or had I stumbled across the one *tako yaki* stand that knowing *tako yaki* eaters always avoid? I had to have several versions of *tako yaki* to settle that question—as it turns out, I don't like *tako yaki*—but then I fell into the same trap with four or five other street foods. By the time I could announce with certainty that I liked the fried buckwheat noodles being sold at half a dozen stands, I felt I had rocked several times around the clock. "There's no substitute for an adequate sample," I said to Alice.

My confidence continued to grow. At a sushi bar near the central fish market, I realized that I did not have to remain silent when I pointed at a delectable-looking piece of tuna. I could point and say anything I wanted to—"Tippecanoe and Tyler too" or, "*Où se trouve la plage?*" The results were the same. "*Hai!*" the sushi chef would bark, and tap his knife a couple of times on the cutting board in anticipation. All sorts of Japanese restaurants tend to display their food, so we found that at, say, a *yakitori* restaurant—a restaurant that specializes in grilling various parts of a chicken and various vegetables over charcoal—we could get whatever we wanted grilled by simply pointing to it and saying "*Semper fidelis*" or "You wanna buy a duck?"

Also, we discovered the food halls of the department stores. All the large department stores devote their bottom floor or two to food—not just packaged food but fish and produce and salads and pastry and just about anything else anybody could think of to eat. Not only that—they give samples. "I can't believe it," I said to Alice as we walked through the ground floor of a department store on the Ginza, politely trying out the shrimps and the dumplings and the salmon and the rice cakes. "It's a Japanese bar mitzvah. A person could have lunch here."

"I think you just did," Alice said.

I would maintain that I had not actually eaten lunch—I offer as proof the fact that just a few minutes later I ate lunch at a little *yakitori* place called Torigin, around the corner—but Alice may have been right in remarking that I had attracted the attention of some salesclerks. If I lived in Tokyo, I suppose that could get to be a problem: I can imagine the clerks whispering to each other as I walked off the escalator around the middle of some pleasant weekday, "He's here—the foreign one who eats." They would snatch their toothpicks off the sample tables. An assistant manager would approach me, smiling broadly, and lead me firmly toward the elevator, with a grip like a mechanical sumo wrestler. Smiling, he would say, "How nice to see you again. Perhaps you would like to visit our fine selection of notions and gifts on the fifth floor."

•

Of course, some mysteries remained unsolved. On a trip to Kyoto, we went directly from a traditional breakfast at a Japanese inn to the garden of the Ryonaji Temple, a garden whose simple perfection inspires people to contemplate all sorts of profundities as they gaze upon it, and all I could think of as we stood there was "What could that orange thing next to the fish possibly have been?" Of course, errors were made. Occasionally we would point to something being greatly enjoyed by some diners a few tables away only to find when it arrived that it fell in that category of small sea creatures and odd weeds that a longtime Tokyo resident named Ellen Reingold has summed up evocatively as "low-tide stuff."

Usually, though, a mistake did not mean disaster. On the morning I visited the central fish market, for instance, I made a mistake while ordering my third breakfast. My first two breakfasts had gone off without a hitch. I had started eating at about seven-thirty, with some very good noodles in broth. By then, I had spent a couple of hours wandering around the market, a place I found almost as astounding as the boulevard of dancing teenagers. In what seemed to be acres of market shed, thousands of fish were arranged with military precision for inspection by the people who would bid for them. Most of the fish were displayed in neat stacks of white Styrofoam boxes—so that, depending on size, a box might contain one mackerel or twenty-four perfectly aligned smelts. The huge tuna were lined up outside in precise rows, with a steak-size flap pulled back on each fish for inspection of the meat. The place was so clean and the fish so fresh that I suppose it might have struck some people as a confirmation of the purity of Japanese ingredients, but it just made me hungry.

After my noodle breakfast and a sushi breakfast, I pressed my face against the window of a tiny lunch counter where the short-order man started what seemed to be an onion stew in a frying pan, dropped what I took to be a breaded halibut steak into a deep-fat fryer, switched the steak to the frying pan after a while, broke an egg on top, and then put a cover on the frying pan to let the whole concoction cook together. It looked so good that I went in pointing. The halibut steak turned out to taste a lot like a pork cutlet. *Tongetsu!* After some consultation with my portable research library, I finally realized I was eating a version of *tongetsu*—a pork dish popular in inexpensive Japanese restaurants. "And excellent *tongetsu* at that," I said, drawing some of the same sort of looks that I had provoked in Sicily with my wolf imitation. "My compliments to the chef."

The most serious problem was in restaurants that were too sophisticated to have food models in the window but too Japanese to have a menu in English. One evening we wandered into a restaurant whose specialty seemed to be a fish stew that was cooked at the table—a sort of marine *sukiyaki*. Nobody spoke English. We went with the specialty—although I could see from observing some other diners that it was going to involve having someone hover around the table, picking bits out of the bubbling pot and encouraging us to eat. We had just had two straight meals like that—a constantly attended dinner at a Japanese inn followed by lunch at a fine *sukiyaki* place near the restaurant-supply area, where we had gone to buy some sushi models—and I was beginning to feel like a college freshman who arrives home late one night for his first Christmas vacation and is not allowed to go to sleep until he sits at the kitchen table eating some of his mother's specialties under the watchful eye of his mother ("You don't want any Swedish meatballs? You've always loved my Swedish meatballs. Here, have some Swedish meatballs"). Some of the fish in the pot looked very mysterious.

Alice picked up a roundish lump with a black appendage on it, and peered at it suspiciously.

"A pure ingredient," I said helpfully.

She tried the black appendage.

"Shrewd of you to bite off the toe before you start on the body," I said.

Alice picked carefully at the remainder of the beast. "It's not bad," she said, "although I wish I knew what it was."

"Well, this is strictly a fish restaurant," I said. "Otherwise, I might conclude that we'd found, at long last, Mouth of the Wolf."

7

A Real Nice Clambake

I THINK IT'S ONLY PRUDENT to be wary about accepting an invitation to attend a clambake at a gentlemen's club. I always thought of a clambake as a long picnic whose atmosphere is somewhere between informal and roistering—the sort of event that ends up late in the evening with bad sunburns and worse singing and a demand by the big fellow who has had too much beer that everyone help him display his strength by forming a pyramid on his stomach. Wouldn't a gentlemen's club version of that event result in a lot of sand getting down into the leather armchairs? My suspicion that a gentlemen's club might be an unusually formal setting for a clambake was confirmed by the person who had in fact phoned to invite me to a clambake at the Squantum club, in Providence—a newspaper reporter named Donald Breed. Breed hadn't been a member of the Squantum long, and he confessed that when he showed up for his first clambake wearing a sport coat but no tie he was drawn aside by the steward, who reminded him, in a kindly sort of way, that he was not properly dressed for the occasion. I had to confess that I was wary about accepting an invitation to eat anything at a gentlemen's club. Although I naturally deplore those researchers who make unseemly efforts to elbow ahead of their colleagues in publishing particularly flashy findings, it happens to be a matter of record that I was first in print with the discovery that the tastelessness of the food offered in American clubs varies in direct proportion to the exclusiveness of the club. After many years of trying to ascertain the cause of this phenomenon, I even came up with a rather persuasive theory: the food in such places is so tasteless because the members associate spices and garlic and *schmaltz* with just the sort of people they're trying to keep out.

When I spoke to Breed on the telephone, I got the impression that the Squantum club is, as men's clubs go, fairly flexible about bloodlines—although not to the point of retaining a chef who goes heavy on the oregano. Breed told me that the Squantum had actually been founded in the mid-nineteenth century by people who were drawn together by a strong interest in eating seafood—it is built on a point that juts into Narragansett Bay—and that it had never strayed from the values of its founders to the extent of installing anything like a golf course or a sauna bath. Breed said that the Squantum bake could provide a sort of warm-up for the first public bake of the season at Francis Farm a few days later—Francis Farm, in Rehoboth, Massachusetts, not far from Providence, being a place that stages clambakes of the sort that last all day and include horseshoe pitching and may even feature, now and then, a big fellow who wants everyone to form a pyramid on his stomach. I told Breed that I would be pleased to join him at the Squantum, and he asked me—in the discreet way people ask, now that we have passed through an era in which anybody might show up anywhere wearing anything—if I happened to own a necktie.

•

Like a lot of serious shellfish eaters I have encountered over the years, Breed had a landlocked childhood—in northwestern Illinois, near the Wisconsin state line. He was fortunate enough to come to roost in a section of the Northeast where the custom of clambakes remains strong. People all over New England, of course, have always baked clams on the beach—built a fire of hardwood over stones that will retain the heat, then piled on four or five inches of rockweed that pops and sizzles as it steams—but the custom seems particularly institutionalized around Providence. Elderly people in the area speak of going by horse and buggy earlier in the century to annual clambakes that are still being held—the Hornbine Church Bake, for instance, or the Moosup Valley Grange Bake. There are said to be old-timers around Providence who can tell from the taste of a clam not just where it came from but whether it was baked over oak or cherry.

Around Narragansett Bay, in fact, the tradition of clambakes seems to have outlasted the clams. Although there are still enough quahogs in the bay for chowder, the clams that are actually baked on a clambake tend to be soft-shell clams trucked in from Maine. The Narragansett clam supply has been cut by pollution, of course, but some studies done at the University of Rhode Island indicate that an equally serious threat to the supply of clams and flounder and cod and tuna and the other seafoods traditionally eaten in this country is the rigidity of American notions about which fish is and which fish is not fit to eat. A project at U.R.I. has done what it could do for the popularity of such "underutilized species" as the ocean pout, a fish that looks almost as bad as it sounds, and the dogfish, which the Rhode Island specialists prefer to call the grayfish. One of the people involved, Spiros Constantinides, told me that the strain on the clam supply could be eased if people simply utilized the available mussels and whelks as well. If the University of Rhode Island folks had their way, high-school productions of *Carousel* would probably include a song entitled "This Was a Real Nice Whelk Bake."

I like mussels myself, and I think that over the years I have done my share to see that they are not underutilized. In Nova Scotia, I often feel exceedingly virtuous when the girls and I go to a place that everyone else uses as a clam flat and gather mussels instead— and I feel even better when Alice transforms our haul into *moules marinière*. From Nova Scotia to Japan, I have done my level best to improve the reputation of the eel ("Not slimy at all. It's really not slimy. If I had to describe it in a word, 'slimy' is certainly not the word I'd use"). I suppose I would eat a whelk if anyone ever thought to offer me one. I regret that I cannot say the same for my daughters. I have spent so much time, mostly to no avail, trying to persuade Abigail and Sarah to utilize the overutilized species of fish that turning to the underutilized might seem like an act of folly. If talking Sarah into trying flounder required that much effort, what chance would I have with the ocean pout?

Virtuous as I am about downing mussels, I must still admit that I am partly responsible for the strain on the clam supply. I like clams. I like steamed clams and clams on the half shell—although the first time I saw one of those, when I was fresh from my own landlocked childhood, I assumed it was some sort of prank. I love fried clams. I like clam chowder so much that I have occasionally been willing to listen to Boston and New York fanciers argue about whether its base should be tomatoes or cream—the East Coast equivalent of the even drearier Southwestern argument about what belongs in chili—as long as I had a bowl of one type or the other in front of me during the discussion. In fact, almost as soon as I sat down for dinner at the Squantum—in a huge outbuilding called a bakehouse, which the members had the good sense to build on a patch of ground that people lacking their historical perspective might have used for a tennis court—I realized how the chowder theorists might symbolize the identity problem facing Providence as the large Northeastern coastal city that is neither Boston nor New York: some places around Providence, including the Squantum, make clam chowder with both cream and tomatoes, so that the bitter argument between red and white is avoided with an ambivalent pink.

The chowder had been preceded by clams on the half shell— served at the main clubhouse, a spectacular turn-of-the-century pile overlooking the bay—and clam broth and clam fritters. After some sausage and sweet potatoes and the baked clams themselves, the waitress brought around a dish of ice cream. I told Breed that the Squantum bake was a pretty good feed—considering that it was run by a gentlemen's club fancy enough to line up five forks at each place setting, and that many of those in attendance seemed of an age to exercise some moderation about what they ate in the six or eight hours before bedtime. Breed informed me that we were being served ice cream merely to cleanse the palate for the rest of the meal. Although I didn't remember any palate cleansing at the *Carousel* clambake, I followed the example of my host—and then followed it again as he downed some shad and a dish of coleslaw and more potatoes and a small lobster and some Indian pudding. The assembled club members consumed all this with routine dignity, as if they were eating prime ribs of beef *au jus* with potatoes *au gratin* and choice of one vegetable.

Breed was already talking about the bake to be held at Francis Farm a few days later. "Go easy on the clam cakes out there," he warned me.

"Aren't they any good?" I asked.

"Delicious," he said. "Small and very crisp. But they'll fill you up for the clams. You have to pace yourself."

•

"The chowder makes them expand in your stomach," one of the regulars at the Francis Farm public bake explained to me the following Sunday. He was warning me about the clam cakes, and he was popping some of them into his mouth as he gave the warning. I had brought the entire family to Francis Farm for the public bake, but I had also resigned myself to the fact that Abigail and Sarah were likely to be there as spectators rather than participants. Although I had assured them that they were not required to eat clams, Sarah was eyeing the fire with the sort of expression that might be seen on someone who had been told that it was being prepared for human sacrifices.

Like the Squantum, Francis Farm has been putting on clambakes for about a century, but unlike the Squantum, where only the clams are actually baked over the traditional wood coals and seaweed, Francis Farm is militantly anti-stove. Except for the substitution of iron ingots for large stones, the bake at Francis Farm is done the way it has always been done—starting with a four-foot-high hardwood fire. As the fire burns down, a troupe of college boys appears, like travelogue natives who have always known their role in the ritual. The coals and ingots are raked smooth, bags of rockweed are piled on, a screen is placed over the rockweed, just about everything anybody intends to eat is placed on the screen, and the entire pile is covered with canvases until the college boys return an hour later to "pull the bake." Francis Farm uses the traditional fire to bake clams, lobsters, sausage, fillet of pollack, onions, and even stuffing. George Taylor—who, along with his father-in-law, Frank Miller, bought the clambake operation from the Francis family in 1959—likes to say that everything is done "on the bake" except the chowder and the clam cakes, the watermelon, the coffee, and the condiments.

Most of the clambakes staged at Francis Farm are private— for a lodge gathering, say, or a company picnic or a high-school reunion. The grounds are arranged like back-to-back summer camps—summer camps where everyone is well fed and not homesick and allowed to drink beer without worrying about being spotted by a counselor—and there are two clambakes a day every day of the summer. A lot of the organizations come back the same day every year; the Red Man Lodge has thrown a clambake at Francis Farm on the first Saturday in August for more than sixty years. A true joiner, of course, can manage several cracks at the clams every summer. A bank officer named Tom Brady, for instance, told me he had come once that summer with the Rhode Island Commandery of the Military Order of Foreign Wars, once with the Sons of Irish Kings, and once with the bank he worked for. Apparently not having gotten his fill, he was back for a public bake.

Francis Farm holds nine public clambakes a summer—building up to a crowd of seven or eight hundred people by August— and even those bakes seem dominated by regulars. The man sitting across from me—Dick Lundgren, a sales engineer from Seekonk, Massachusetts—said he had been going to bakes off and on for forty years, ever since, as a child, he accompanied his father to the annual bake of the Seekonk Volunteer Fire Department. He told me that he attended most of the public bakes, and always sat at the same table with Len Estes, who ran boiler rooms for one enterprise or another before he retired in Newport, and Ed Gardner, a groundskeeper for the University of Rhode Island, in Kingston. The regulars called each other by their last names—perhaps because last names were written in marking pen on the paper tablecloth in front of each plate—and what they said tended to be something like "Pass the melted butter, Gardner" or "Are there any more clams over there, Estes?"

I was hungry, and I was feeling particularly virtuous, having dined the previous evening on broiled scup—a fish that sounds bad enough to be an underutilized species, although it happens to taste very good. For a while I seemed to be keeping up with Lundgren and Estes and Gardner, and so did Alice. She got so interested in eating clams that she forgot to tell me that I shouldn't feel compelled to eat as many as one of the regulars. I got so interested that I neglected my efforts to persuade the girls that they might like some of the food—efforts based on the contention that the pollack tasted like flounder and the sausage tasted like hot dogs and the potatoes tasted like, well, potatoes. Abigail had a few spoonfuls of chowder, and then they wandered off toward the bake fire, apparently curious about whether a missionary might be thrown in after all.

Then I started to pace myself to leave room for the dishes Breed had recommended highly—the clams and the onions and the pollack. The regulars next to me continued to hand out their own pacing advice, ignoring it all the while. Down the table, Breed seemed to be eating everything indiscriminately. Next to him, Tom Brady was eating in his own clambake style—pouring melted butter into a coffee cup and then tossing everything into it, like a Chinese eater constantly adding to a bowl of rice. ("Not everything," Brady told me later, in the tone of someone accused of using the wrong fork. "I never put in the stuffing.")

When I commented on the steady eating, I was informed by the regulars that the most serious eater among them, a Boston maintenance man named Bastow, had not shown up. At the final bake of the previous season, Bastow had apparently mentioned that he would be changing jobs, and some of the regulars surmised that he was no longer able to get away on Sundays. It sounded as if Bastow needed all of a Sunday to make it to the clambake, since he was said to take a train from Boston to Providence, a bus to Rehoboth, and, unless someone stopped to pick him up, a hike of two or three miles from Route 44 to the farm. "He's very skinny," Lundgren told me, "but he always has four bowls of chowder."

"He always heaps the last bowl high and covers it with a plate so it stays warm while he starts in on the clam cakes," one of the regulars said. "Then he takes a little walk, and comes back and finishes it off."

We were on the baked clams ourselves at the time. The waitress returned regularly to fill the platters, and Estes complained regularly about finding too many broken shells without clams. I was finding Breed's recommendations well considered. A clambake clam tastes like a steamer enhanced by a slight smoky flavor—and the same flavor works particularly well with fish and onions. "He's more than six feet tall," Estes said, talking of Bastow again.

"Completely bald," Lundgren added as he reached for more clams. "Doesn't drive a car."

"Mostly shells here," Estes said, picking around at the bowl of clams. "This must be the bottom of the barrel."

The waitress brought more clams and more onions and more brown bread and more sweet potatoes and more white potatoes. "Yes, sir," someone said. "He can eat four bowls of chowder, then go to the bar for a beer."

"He's six-foot-six and thin as a rail," Estes said. "He must be about a foot wide." Estes turned to Gardner. "Wouldn't you say about a foot wide?"

"Yeah, about a foot," Gardner said between bites of pollack.

The regulars were still talking about Bastow as they finished off their watermelon. Suddenly the meal was over, and they disappeared. A private clambake at Francis Farm usually lasts most of the day—there is ordinarily a break of a few hours for recreation between the clam-cake-and-chowder course and the time the bake is pulled—but some regulars at a public bake just show up to eat. I went to compliment George Taylor on the meal and to ask him if there really was a storied eater named Bastow.

"Oh, yeah—he looks like Silas Marner," said Taylor, who once was a high-school teacher. "I don't know what became of him today."

•

I still think about Bastow, particularly when I'm hungry for clams. I can see him rising early in the morning in Boston, carefully straightening his small room, and silently setting out for the long journey to Rehoboth. "It's Bastow," one of his neighbors says to another. "Off again—wherever he goes." At South Station he digs an old-fashioned coin purse out of his pocket and buys a round-trip ticket to Providence. He stares out of the window of the train, thinking of clam cakes. At the bus station in Providence the ticket agent just nods, and punches out a round trip to Rehoboth. "*Bon appétit*," the agent says. Bastow nods silently. He walks in from Route 44 toward Francis Farm—a steady pace, surprisingly graceful for a man who is six feet six inches tall and only a foot wide. Someone picks him up for the last mile or so—a fan, who says, "Four bowls today, Bastow?" Bastow smiles. Then they are at Francis Farm. The bake has been on for half an hour. Puffs of smoke escaping from under the canvas carry the smell of clams and onions. It is time for the chowder. Bastow sits down to eat.

(8)

Tasting

I MET PAULA ROME through Leo Braudy, her cheese-steak adviser. Braudy, who grew up in Philadelphia, is a cheese-steak authority of some renown who teaches English at Johns Hopkins on the side. It almost goes without saying that he is my kind of scholar. He analyzes what he often calls the "classic Philadelphia cheese-steak" with the sort of thoroughness he presumably expects his graduate students to use in dissecting *Paradise Lost*. He offers an essay on the essential crustiness of the roll. He uses literary allusions to comment on the steak itself—its tenderness, its crucial thinness. He cites research gathered from South Philadelphia to Swarthmore in discussing the way the steak blends with the cheese and the cheese blends with the onions. He footnotes, with a scholarly detachment that is compromised only by an almost imperceptible shudder, the preference of some cheese-steak eaters for mayonnaise rather than the traditional hint of ketchup. Braudy is hardly a one-subject scholar. He is also considered an authority on the Philadelphia hoagie. I have heard him compare the Philadelphia hoagie with what he considers the inferior foreign versions—submarines, grinders, heroes, po' boys. I have heard him compare one Philadelphia hoagie to another Philadelphia hoagie. I have even heard him compare Philadelphia hoagies to Philadelphia cheese-steaks—a critical tour de force that I believe a Hopkins graduate student might classify as "interdisciplinary."

When Braudy introduced me to Paula Rome, she had need of a cheese-steak adviser because she was employed as what amounted to a professional taster. She worked for the Rouse Company, which specializes in developing what it calls "marketplaces"—the best known of which is the collection of restored brick buildings on the Boston waterfront known as the Faneuil Hall Marketplace. Rouse had hired Paula Rome in connection with a similar project, called Harborplace, that it was then building on the inner harbor of Baltimore—the problem of Baltimore's lack of any old warehouses whose brick could be artistically exposed having been solved by beginning new buildings from scratch. One of them was due to contain almost nothing but food—a number of market stalls, a couple of full-service restaurants, and twenty-five fast-food booths. Mrs. Rome, whose experience included some restaurant reviewing in Baltimore, had been hired partly to help decide which twenty-five they should be. She had tasted the products of people who inquired about renting space. She had sniffed around the area for food discoveries—driving to Eldersburg, where she had a tip on a Mexican restaurant in a shopping center, for instance, or sampling the foodstuffs at a Frederick crafts fair, where she came upon a drink called Flying Fruit Fantasies. When I met her, she was involved in planning a bake-off among the nineteen separate enterprises that had approached Harborplace about a chocolate-chip-cookie stand. In other words, she had the job that a lot of people I know have been looking for.

I might as well admit that learning what Paula Rome did for a living set my own daydreams in the direction of professional tasting. I had already thought of myself as a devoted amateur. As I envisioned it, I would wander through the entire country looking for food to be included in a marketplace a block or so from my house—having easily solved the ostensibly insurmountable problems of geography and ingredients and logistics by reminding myself that it was all a fantasy anyway. In my thoughts, I spend a lot of time at Richard's, in Abbeville, Louisiana, carefully comparing their boiled crawfish and boiled shrimp to the fare served at the Guiding Star, in New Iberia. While I'm in the area, I do extensive boudin research, on the assumption that my design people will have no trouble simulating an authentic grocery-store parking lot. On the Lower East Side of Manhattan I lean on the counter at Moishe's, chewing on a pumpernickel bagel while discussing how many square feet would be required for a good marketplace bagel operation. I sample oyster loaves in New Orleans and Italian-beef sandwiches in Chicago and smoked mullet on the west coast of Florida. I compare the Cuban sandwich served on the West Side of Manhattan with the Cuban sandwich served in Union City and the Cuban sandwich served in Miami and, if I can persuade Fidel Castro that my quest is not political but humanitarian, the Cuban sandwich served in Cuba. I toss around questions of policy. Could there be a French-fries booth that includes both French fries from Arthur Bryant's Barbecue, in Kansas City—cooked in pure lard, with some of the skin left on here and there—and the *pommes frites* served in a chic Santa Monica restaurant called Michael's? How about a booth that sells both the *haute cuisine* version of *calzone* turned out by Alice Waters at Chez Panisse, in Berkeley and plain old lower-Manhattan-Italian-feast four-pound *calzone*? Would wandering around a marketplace that is filled with food booths—a particularly festive marketplace—be the equivalent of attending the sort of festival at which a stand-up sausage sandwich might be eaten? I sit at Maurice's Snack 'n Chat, in Los Angeles, sampling the spoon bread and discussing with Maurice, the proprietress, the question of whether the proper marketplace name for it would be spoon bread or *soufflé de maïs extraordinaire*. I start to tell Maurice about my plans to have a gelati stand and a stand selling *arancine*, those little fried rice balls they sell on the street in Sicily, but I have to cut the conversation short because I am on my way to the Zacatecas Café, in Riverside, to inquire about whether their Friday special of *nopales*—cactus and cracklings—could be turned into their Saturday-through-Thursday specialty as well. Then I am back at Bryant's Barbecue in Kansas City, in my professional capacity, trying to determine through carefully controlled testing whether Bryant's brisket would be suitable even for a marketplace shopper who insisted on eating four or five pounds of it at a sitting.

I had assumed that the central pleasure of being a taster in Baltimore would come from eating crabs on the job. The sort of

crabs served at a traditional Baltimore crab house—done in a peppery crab boil, served on butcher paper, and accompanied by a
small mallet—would be included in the marketplace of my dreams.
Unfortunately for Paula Rome, there had been no further need for
boiled-crab tasting by the time she joined the organization, a deal
having already been made with Philips Crab House of Ocean City
for one of the full-service restaurants in the food pavilion. She was,
therefore, off duty when she and her husband and Leo Braudy and
his wife and I spent a long evening at Gunning's, a crab house in
south Baltimore, eating a platterful of fifteens (crabs are customarily
ordered by how much they cost a dozen), accompanied by beer and
crab cakes and crab fluffs and soft-shell-crab sandwiches and coleslaw and French-fried onion rings and French-fried green-pepper
rings. Braudy said that Gunning's was the only place he had been
able to find green-pepper rings, even though he had spent a lot of
time exploring the crab houses of the area—apparently in an effort
to dispel the widespread notion that the perimeters of his gustatory
interests could be defined by the city limits of Philadelphia. In my
own marketplace the response to that news would be straightforward:
If Philips does not, in fact, serve equivalent French-fried green-
pepper rings, it will simply have to expand its repertoire or make
way for Gunning's.

Mrs. Rome made it clear that real-life tasting is not all that
simple. For instance, she said, it was conceivable that a cheese-
steak praised by Braudy as nearly adequate would not be appropriate
for Harborplace for a variety of reasons that had nothing at all to
do with its taste. In a project like Harborplace, agents have to
consider which cheese-steak man got there first and which cheese-
steak man helps the project's ethnic or racial balance and which
cheese-steak man seems most capable of running an operation that
can pay the rent and provide the sort of gross that the management,
which gets a percentage of it, finds appealing. Deciding among
nineteen chocolate-chip cookies might be the sort of task that fantasy
tasters love to think about, but the final selection in a real project
has to be made not just on how the cookie tastes but on how many
of them can be produced how quickly—a fact brought home to
Mrs. Rome when the cookie flogger at Faneuil Hall Marketplace

told her that he was turning out forty to sixty thousand cookies a day.

Mrs. Rome acknowledged that in the eight months she had served as a professional taster she had tasted a lot of good food in the line of duty, but she had also eaten a lot of food that she might have politely declined outside business hours. "For the first few weeks," she told me, "all the food seemed to be brown." When I met Paula Rome, she had, as a professional taster, sampled Chinese and Japanese and Polish dumplings, chopped barbecued pork, barbecued sausage, barbecued ribs, knockwurst, bratwurst, bauernwurst, a wurst whose name she didn't catch, moussaka, *stifado*, cheese pie, spinach pie, *golumbkas* (stuffed cabbage), *pirogen*, a meatball submarine, a hamburger submarine, a chopped-beef-and-cheese submarine, many cheese-steaks (none of which, in Leo Braudy's view, cried out for comparison with a Shakespeare sonnet), many hoagies, a roast-beef sandwich, several corned-beef sandwiches, a gyro sandwich, a sausage sandwich with onions and peppers, a sprout-and-alfalfa sandwich with cucumbers and mushrooms, many hamburgers, a Boursin-and-bacon burger, eleven varieties of fried chicken, *kang-pao* chicken, tandoori chicken, champagne chicken, twenty-five Buffalo chicken wings with celery and blue-cheese dressing (in her office, at ten-thirty in the morning, only a couple of hours after Judy Katz would have polished off some Santora's leftovers for breakfast), French-fried potatoes, cheese French fries (created by somebody's accidentally spilling cheese on the French-fried potatoes at a place called Brothers' Steak-n-Take), Western fries, baked potato stuffed with spinach and cheese, baked potato stuffed with sausage and vegetables, noodles with vegetables, tempura-fried vegetables, vegetable quiche, vegetable egg rolls, pork egg rolls, spring rolls, falafel, *tabbouleh*, tamales, fried dough, *calzone*, pâté, chopped liver, knishes, matzo balls, bagels, pizza bagels, pizza, midget pizza, Sicilian pizza, deep-dish pizza, Greek pizza, Mexican pizza, an enchilada and a burrito and a burrito supreme and several bowls of chili (all during the brown period), spinach with crab, crab soup, crab cakes, fried crab, fried oysters, seafood bisque, tofu-and-ginger seafood, fried fish, tandoori fish, avocado stuffed with shrimp, shrimp salad, tuna salad, a muffin stuffed with

tuna salad (creating what its inventor called a muffit), a spinach
muffit, a boeuf Bourguignon muffit, a ham-and-cheese muffit, a
ham-and-cheese crêpe, a frittata, onion soup, zucchini soup, beet
borscht, *souvlaki*, tandoori lamb, Hunan beef, moo shu pork, Jap-
anese-style steak, Polish sausage, beef kebab, baked ham, sautéed
goat, duck stew, peanut stew on rice, sweet-potato greens on rice,
stewed beef and rice, rice and beans, rice balls, broccoli-mushroom-
and-cheese casserole, macaroni and cheese, fried eggplant, sorrel
punch, lemon soda, lemonade, lemon cream, lemon chicken, turkey salad, salad Niçoise, Greek salad, Greek bread, French bread,
Indian bread, rye bread, pumpkin bread, fruit toast, *pain de raisin*,
brioches, croissants, blueberry muffins, banana-nut muffins, apple-
spice muffins, strawberry muffins, strudel in five varieties, a rum
bun, a sweet-potato square, baklava, assorted Polish pastry, assorted
Filipino pastry, gingerbread loaf, carrot cake, banana cake, apple-
caramel cake, an unnamed cake with green icing, strawberry cake,
cheesecake, amaretto cheesecake, chocolate cake, butter-cinnamon
cake, almond cake, dessert burrito filled with apples, walnut-honey
pie, peanut-butter *oritani* squares, Grand Marnier crêpe, miniature
doughnuts, full-size doughnuts, full-size honey-dipped doughnuts,
zeppole, brownies, pear tart, oatmeal cookies, Italian butter cookies,
chocolate-topped cookies, raspberry sherbet, grapefruit sherbet,
rum-raisin ice cream with fudge sauce, chocolate ice cream with
fudge sauce, Oreo ice cream with fudge sauce, peanut-butter ice
cream with fudge sauce, coffee-brickle ice cream with fudge sauce,
orange-chocolate ice cream with fudge sauce, five varieties of fudge
("I like fudge actually; it's not a hardship"), tutti-frutti ice cream
without fudge sauce, chocolate frozen yogurt, five varieties of soft
pretzels, homemade potato chips, caramel corn, cheese corn, choc-
olate-dipped glacé fruit, chocolate-covered ginger, orange-chocolate
wafers, coffee candies, rum cashew crispies, jelly beans, saltwater
taffy, chocolate-covered banana-flavored saltwater taffy on a stick,
and a lot of Tab—not to mention the nineteen varieties of chocolate-
chip cookies. She had gained nine pounds.

I was not surprised to hear that nineteen people had inquired
about setting up the chocolate-chip-cookie operation in Harborplace. When I wandered through the Lexington Market in Balti-

more—an old-fashioned city market that no one would ever think of calling a marketplace—I noticed that it had, among stalls advertising chitterlings and hog maws and cut-up chickens and pickles, a booth called Chippity-Doo-Dah. The chippers were obviously thick on the ground. I was surprised, though, to hear that the second-most inquiries had been received from purveyors of stuffed baked potatoes—seven outfits with names like Meal-in-a-Peel. My surprise was based partly on the fact that I had been completely unaware that the baked potato had become, as the saying goes, a meal in itself. I realized what must have happened. There was a time when Americans were accustomed to splitting their baked potatoes and inserting a wedge of butter. Then someone thought of sour cream. Then sour cream and chives. Then bacon bits. For some years, that seemed to be the extent of the potato-stuffing game. Then, without my knowledge, someone apparently broke the bacon-bit barrier. Mushroom sauce. Tuna fish. Sausage and onion. Suddenly, there were no limits: chicken à la king and Jell-O mold could be seen on the horizon. Fast food is fast. It is so fast, in fact, that Paula Rome had to concern herself with the possibility that even before Harborplace opened, the stuffed-potato game might proliferate into the ubiquitous franchise operations that the project was trying hard to avoid. The problems facing a professional taster are enough to put a devoted amateur off his feed.

Even before Paula Rome explained some of the complications of her job, though, my daydreams had started to take a dispiriting turn toward reality. In my thoughts, the design coordinator of the marketplace walked in, wearing designer blue jeans, and informed me that the folks at Richard's had refused to clear off crawfish shells in color-coordinated buckets instead of the galvanized ones they are accustomed to using—and that they might have replied to his request in an insulting manner, although their accent made it difficult for him to be certain. The security man informed me that it would be absolutely out of the question for Arthur Bryant to tend his barbecue pit all night, and that stacking hickory wood in front of the kite store "blocked egress." A delegation from an organization called Friends of the Desert began picketing the marketplace, claiming that the Zacatecas *nopales* "would inevitably lead to clear-cutting of cactus." The proprietor of Moishe's was threatening to pull out if Richard's did not agree to stop serving anything as overtly non-kosher as shellfish. Maurice, who had served three of the 257 customers lined up for her spoon bread, was complaining that turning out spoon bread at such a madcap rate might endanger quality. I walked back to her booth with her, hung out a sign saying CLOSED DUE TO HARASSMENT, asked for an order of spoon bread, and told her to take her time.

9

Fried-Chicken War

I SUPPOSE I ROMANTICIZED the fried-chicken war of Crawford County a bit. When it comes to fried chicken, I often get carried away. Word of a dispute between Chicken Annie's and Chicken Mary's, two regionally renowned fried-chicken emporiums in southeast Kansas, had reached me in New York, where fried-chicken deprivation can cause someone who was raised in the Midwest to go feverish with poultry nostalgia. In that condition, I took it for granted that the hostilities in Crawford County—hostilities that broke out when Chicken Annie's tried to have the county road that runs in front of both establishments named Chicken Annie's Road—would engage fried-chicken devotees from several counties in fearsome debate, characterized by completely bogus historical references and sneering remarks about the opposition's tendency to serve dried-out white meat. In my own hometown of Kansas City, after all, a peripatetic fried-chicken cook called Chicken Betty, who became well known some years after I had resigned myself to an Eastern life lacking in wishbones, inspired such fierce loyalty that droves of chicken eaters slavishly followed her from restaurant to restaurant, the way rich ladies might flock after a temperamental but brilliant hairdresser. On one trip home, I had caught up with Chicken Betty at a place called R.C.'s, in an annexed patch of the county people still call Martin City, and from that experience I knew that a movement to name a road after her would find me strongly opposed: whatever was named after Chicken Betty would have to be much more important than a road. Her fried chicken livers alone would merit a turnpike, and they're just a side dish. I would have long ago suggested that the airport be named after her—it still labors under the unfortunate and rather fanciful name of Kansas City International—if I hadn't been planning a campaign to have it named after Arthur Bryant, the city's premier barbecue man.

I realize that southeast Kansas is not the sort of place that strikes absolutely everybody as a dramatic setting. Kansas in general is not prime territory for a truly venomous conflict; folks try to get along. A lot of Crawford County looks like the peaceful Kansas where Dorothy and Aunt Em and Uncle Henry lived so contentedly before the cyclone hit, but the eastern part of the county, where Chicken Annie's and Chicken Mary's dispense their fried chicken, does have some of the elements that make for Old-World Drama. The settlement that set the tone for life in the southeast corner of Kansas— the section jammed in next to Missouri and Oklahoma, not far from Arkansas—was not a mid-nineteenth-century settlement of Ohio farmers looking for homestead land but an early-twentieth-century settlement of Europeans looking for work in the coal mines. A lot of people in eastern Crawford County are children or grand-children of people who came to Kansas straight from Sicily or Austria or Bohemia. Years ago, the area acquired a reputation for tumul-tuous politics and reliable home brew. It is still sometimes called the Little Balkans.

Annie Pichler, who became known as Chicken Annie through her skill in that most American of specialties, was born in a small village not far from Budapest. She began selling fried chicken— cooked in her own kitchen, in a big iron skillet—because her hus-band got hurt in the mines and she had three children to raise. That was in 1934, in a place called Thirteen Camp—the coal camp next to the No. 13 mine of the Western Coal Company. Working through the Depression, in a poor corner of Kansas where most of the deep mines were already played out, Anne Pichler gradually made a name for herself—although she resisted the name Chicken

Annie for a while because she thought it sounded "kind of raw." Then, in 1943, Mary Zerngast, whose husband had also had to give up work in the mines, opened a restaurant right where customers turned off the county road to get to Chicken Annie's. She served fried-chicken dinners. Mary Zerngast died in the late seventies, but when I went to Crawford County to investigate the chicken war I found Annie Pichler alive and well—a bouncy, friendly woman in her eighties—and though she told me, "I don't want to hold grudges to anyone," she left no doubt in my mind about which family might be the object of any grudges she permitted herself. "They used to come and eat all the time, and then all of a sudden they went ahead and built on the county road right at the corner, blocking the way," she told me the day I got to Crawford County. "They got me a little upset." A feud! A European feud! By Kansas standards, an ancient European feud! I was not unmindful of what happened some years ago in the other Balkans because of a feud that did not even concern fried chicken: the First World War.

•

By the time Chicken Annie's had moved into a new building out on the county road, in 1972, there wasn't much left of Thirteen Camp except the two fried-chicken restaurants, just a few hundred yards apart. Customers—as many as twelve hundred people at each place on a pleasant Saturday evening in the summer—drive in from somewhere else, and each restaurant has always tried to attract their attention by reaching around the competition with strategically placed signs. I figured that over the years, on some of those dark Balkan nights, signs for one place or the other might have blown over even when there wasn't much wind. "Oh, there was conflicts," Chicken Annie's daughter told me. "There was lots of conflicts."

The man who became proprietor of Chicken Annie's after Anne Pichler's retirement—her son-in-law, Louis Lipoglav—was convinced that most of Chicken Mary's customers were confused souls who thought they were at Chicken Annie's. The way Lipoglav figured it, hungry folks driving out from Pittsburg or Fort Scott or Coffeyville or Parsons could turn onto the county road from Highway 69 and stop at the first chicken restaurant they came to, even though he had attempted to clear up the confusion with a billboard at the turn and a huge sign next to Chicken Mary's parking lot informing chicken eaters that they only had to go another few hundred yards to reach the real article. When Lipoglav repainted his billboard one spring, he included a name for the road travelers were directed down—Chicken Annie's Road. Not long after that, without the matter's having gone before the county commission, an official county sign identified the road as Chicken Annie's Road for a couple of days—under circumstances about which both the Pichler-Lipoglavs and the Zerngasts were vague when I brought the subject up. Louis Lipoglav said, "Someone with the county put it up." Elizabeth Zerngast, Chicken Mary's daughter-in-law, said, "Someone tore it down."

After a decent interval, Lipoglav suggested that the county commission honor Anne Pichler by officially naming the road Chicken Annie's Road. The measure was introduced by Joe Saia, who had been on the commission since 1939 and whose experience in such matters extended to having had an entire overpass named after him. Elizabeth Zerngast complained that the name would advertise Lipoglav's restaurant rather than honor Mrs. Pichler, the commission tabled the matter, the local papers reported the outbreak of the chicken war, and I, deciding that authentic combat coverage demanded my presence on the scene, flew from the East to Crawford County, chickens dancing on pan-fried drumsticks in my head.

•

"We have never fought, really," Elizabeth Zerngast told me, as I sat in Chicken Mary's that afternoon. "It's more kind of like little digs all the time. Like good competitors. Competition kind of keeps you on your toes." Even though she had objected to naming the road in a way that would advertise her competitor, Elizabeth Zerngast told me, she had no objection at all to naming it Anne Pichler Road. "I know Anne Pichler and I like her," Mrs. Zerngast said.

"You do?" It occurred to me that the Pichler-Lipoglavs had also assured me that they had nothing personal against the Zerngasts, even as they mentioned some incidents that would try folks with less forgiving natures. Even more surprising, both families assured me that they had been pleased by the marriage some years before of Chicken Annie's grandson and Chicken Mary's granddaughter, who opened up a fried-chicken restaurant of their own just south of Pittsburg. It was as if the reaction of the Montagues and the Capulets to the romance of Romeo and Juliet had been to throw the young couple a big wedding bash and serve fried chicken. ("I prepared it, and they cooked it over at Chicken Annie's," Elizabeth Zerngast told me. "We had a real shindig.") Kansas people do tend to let bygones be bygones, but that's not an attitude I had associated with small villages near Budapest. Was it possible that the sun and the wind of rural Kansas caused European characteristics to evaporate faster than they might in a crowded Northeastern city? I had noticed that the only restaurant in Frontenac, a heavily Italian town just north of Pittsburg, specialized in steak and—what else?—fried chicken. Was it possible that I was witnessing the de-Balkanizing of Crawford County?

·

But where were the loyalists? I had assumed that the Crawford County fried-chicken war would include dramatic skirmishes between the Chicken Annie fancy and those who attended at Chicken Mary's. In Kansas City, where Arthur Bryant has an estimable rival in class barbecuing named Ollie Gates, I would take it for granted that a move to have the airport named after Bryant would face some resistance from hard-core Gatesites. During the Carter Administration, the Gates faction tried, unsuccessfully, to stop a proposed presidential visit to Bryant's by claiming that Mr. Bryant was a Republican—an accusation I discounted on the theory that Arthur Bryant has always been above politics. Could it be that there were no such loyalties in southeast Kansas? When I telephoned a serious eater I know in Fort Scott named Tom Eblen—a man who spent some years in Kansas City, most of them at Arthur Bryant's—he offered to meet me in Crawford County at either fried-chicken restaurant. This from a Bryantist who would no more suggest meeting at Gates's than he would suggest skipping lunch. If Eblen wasn't a loyalist, I figured, there couldn't be many loyalists.

As it turned out, some people eat only at Chicken Annie's or only at Chicken Mary's, but most people seem to patronize the two almost interchangeably. Even Commissioner Joe Saia, who is particular enough about food to turn out his own Sicilian salami, goes to both places, although he tends to speak of Annie's chicken as the standard he uses in rating the chicken he eats around the country at political conventions ("Colonel Sanders can't hold a light to it, and I've eaten a lot of the Colonel's, because he was a Democrat"). After eating at both places, I thought I understood the reason for the eerie tolerance people in the area show on the subject of fried chicken: although both Chicken Annie and Chicken Mary started out pan-frying chickens in huge iron skillets, they eventually turned to deep fryers. "People tell me it ain't the same," Chicken Annie told me, but nobody can pan-fry chicken fast enough to feed twelve hundred people a night. With a complete fried-chicken dinner for four people going for only about ten dollars, the Crawford County restaurants depend on volume. Chicken Annie's and Chicken Mary's do a good job of deep-frying chicken—they apply a non-Midwestern dose of garlic and they avoid the characteristic franchise batter that Chicken Betty has occasionally compared to a plaster cast—but a fried-chicken cook with a deep fryer is a sculptor working with mittens. I understood the practical, unromantic realities of running a large restaurant in a rural area that is not terribly prosperous, but the chickens that had danced in my head were dancing on pan-fried drumsticks. I decided that I might as well drop in on my hometown, as long as I was so close. Although Chicken Betty had gone into semiretirement since my previous trip to Kansas City, I had heard that she was still presiding over the restaurant at the Metro Auto Auction, in Lee's Summit, on Tuesdays. The next day was Tuesday.

•

The Metro Auto Auction is strictly to the trade. It attracts dealers from all over the Midwest who want to beef up their used-car inventory. Wholesalers collect used cars from dealers, clean them up, and take them to Metro—"same as you buy a skinny cow, feed it out, and take it to slaughter," one dealer told me. The place does have the look of a cattle auction. On three lanes, distinguished according to the age of the cars being sold, newly washed sedans and sports coupes and vans pull up in front of the auctioneer. While the auctioneer spews out his baffling chant—baffling, at least, to anyone not in the trade—the buyers stand around the cars being sold, occasionally peering under the hood or circling warily to observe the paint job or glancing in at the upholstery, until the auctioneer finally says "Sold to Gary" or "Sold to Max." When the buyers and sellers get hungry, they wander off the selling floor into what seems like a little coffee shop—a tiny place with a cafeteria line and no sign—and there whatever sins they may have committed on the used-car lot since the previous Tuesday are wondrously forgiven. Without even leaving the building, they are in the presence of Chicken Betty Lucas—the First Lady of Fried Chicken, whose recipes have been gathered for *The New York Times* by Mimi Sheraton, and who in a just world would have a bridge (major Missouri River crossing) named after her. There, on the stove, are her iron skillets. Using the restraint one learns in the East, I managed to wait until eleven o'clock to have lunch.

The chickens dancing in my head had in fact been chickens cooked by Chicken Betty—juicy chickens with a light, peppery batter. Once I had reassured myself on that point, I had a chat with Chicken Betty—a cheerful, red-haired woman who still had the no-nonsense manner of someone who had spent a good deal of her life as a waitress. As a waitress or a cook or a cashier or a bookkeeper, she moved when she felt the need to ("Life's too short to work where you're unhappy")—trailing, toward the end of her career, throngs of chicken eaters in her wake. By the time she got to the Metro Auto Auction—semiretired and with a pacemaker helping her heart—she was allowing someone else to stand behind the iron skillets, but there remained no doubt about whose standards were in force. When the Metro Auto Auction asked Chicken Betty to do twenty-four hundred pieces of chicken for the celebration of its first anniversary in Lee's Summit, Chicken Betty told me, "My chef said, 'I guess with that many we'll have to drop them in a French-fryer,' and I said, 'No, we won't.' "

It occurred to me that Chicken Betty, with her purist attachment to the iron skillet, had not ended up with an empire. The little coffee shop at the Metro Auto Auction was really the only restaurant she had run rather than worked in since she became renowned—although she owned a bar many years ago, and for a while she and her husband ran a tavern called Eddie's Lounge. The years at Eddie's Lounge did not give Chicken Betty a taste for management; she often got fed up with the help—particularly with slovenly waitresses—and with her husband, who "mostly sat on the end bar stool." Betty Lucas grew up on a farm sort of like the one Aunt Em and Uncle Henry ran—it was in Nebraska rather than Kansas—and she acquired strong notions about doing any job right. "We are talking here about the last of the great pan-fryers," I figured I would tell the bridge-naming subcommittee of the City Council. "The empire builders in our midst are not interviewed respectfully by Mimi Sheraton."

I asked Chicken Betty whether she would do anything different if she had it to do all over again.

"If I was doing this all over?" Chicken Betty said, taking out her towel to wipe away a mark I couldn't see on the table. She smiled. "If I was doing this all over," she said, "I would have franchised."

10

A Few Beers

with Suds and Dregs

FOR SEVERAL YEARS I had been looking for an opportunity to have a few beers with Suds Kroge and Dregs Donnigan, the authors of *A Beer Drinker's Guide to the Bars of Reading.* I like their style. It took a certain amount of flair, I always thought, for Suds and Dregs to spend a year investigating every single bar in Reading, Pennsylvania—a project that required stops at 132 bars, not counting return visits—and then dedicate the resulting book to their wives. I became familiar with *A Beer Drinker's Guide* when I ran across a copy for sale at Stanley's, a south-side neighborhood bar in Reading that had good reason to distribute it: Suds and Dregs gave Stanley's a 5B, or Five-Beer, rating, which is as high as they go. My purpose in buying the book was utilitarian. Like a lot of traveling people, I like to pause for a cold draught late in the afternoon, and I'm always happy to have the advice of any local who can warn me off the sort of joint where conversation is dominated by the host of *The New-lywed Game* or where, as Suds and Dregs once put it, the bartender has "the personality of a Handi-Wipe."

Leafing through *A Beer Drinker's Guide to the Bars of Reading,* I found that I liked the way Suds and Dregs approached the task at hand. The sentence or two they allowed themselves for summing up a place could be pointed ("It's like entering someone's living room—someone you don't know") or mysterious ("Pool table in

back room. Nervous barmaid") or absolute ("We'll never go back").
The excuse for meeting Suds and Dregs that I finally came up with
was prompted by a suggestion from a friend of mine that I take a
look at an Allentown bar called Chick's Hotel Grand, which my
friend described as the oldest stand-up bar in the country—the sort
of solid, beer drinkers' place that is increasingly hard to find now
that so many taverns have redecorated into the sort of place Suds
and Dregs have described as "disgustingly cocktail loungish." I figured I'd take Suds and Dregs along to Chick's as consultants. I also
figured we might have a few beers together in Reading, just to put
everything into perspective.

Reading is a beer drinker's town. In John Updike's novels, it's
the blue-collar town of Brewer, where Rabbit Angstrom and his
fellow printers used to stop in a neighborhood bar regularly for a
cold beer in the years before Rabbit fell in with that crowd of
suburban martini sippers. Around the turn of the century, Reading's
hosiery mills and railroad yards and packing plants drew Italian and
Polish and German and Ukrainian workers who had a strong attachment to the local taverns that even now seem to be the only
punctuation in block after block of row houses. The "Welcome to
Reading" greeting I found in my motel room from Suds and Dregs
was written, appropriately enough, on a brown paper bag. What
was in the brown paper bag was even more appropriate. Naturally
there was a package of locally made pretzels—Bill Spannuth's
Unique Pretzel Splits. The eighteenth-century settlers of Reading
and the surrounding hills and farmland of Berks County were Pennsylvania Dutch—fortunately for Suds and Dregs, mostly Pennsylvania Dutch of the fancy rather than plain variety, so that they
brought a taste for beer without the pietistic religion that would
severely limit its consumption—and the entire area has always been
known for its German pretzels. Until the middle seventies, when
Reading decided to adopt a motto that would reflect the presence
of dozens of factory-outlet stores in its abandoned mill buildings, it
was known as the Pretzel Capital of the World.

My gift paper bag also contained a large package of Dieffenbach's Old Fashion Potato Chips, which are made not far from
Reading, in Womelsdorf, Pennsylvania, in a small shed next to the

Dieffenbach family's house, and which carry on the package in large letters the warning DO NOT EXPOSE TO SUNSHINE. I learned later that Suds and Dregs both consider Dieffenbach's to be the Best Potato Chips in Berks County—an encomium that embodies the collateral distinction of the Best Potato Chips in the World. Dregs once read somewhere that some potato chips made in Hawaii were the best potato chips in the world, but he later had the opportunity to taste the Hawaiian chips; he speaks of the experience in the tone of voice he normally reserves for discussing cocktail lounges that are decorated in flocked wallpaper and do a steady business in Singapore Slings. Dieffenbach's potato chips, it almost goes without saying, are cooked in pure lard.

Rummaging around further in my paper bag, I found a hunk of Lebanon bologna and a hunk of local cheese—both of which would be found on the plate of assorted cold cuts that a lot of Reading bars serve under the name of Dutch Platter. At the bottom of the bag were two bottles of Lord Chesterfield ale and two cans of Yuengling's Premium—products of Yuengling Brewery, in Pottsville, the oldest brewery in the United States and a place that Suds and Dregs visit regularly in the spirit that Elvis freaks visit Graceland. I spread the contents of the gift bag on the dresser—beer, pretzels, potato chips, bologna, cheese. A Reading banquet! I figured it would brighten up the hour or so I had to wait until Suds and Dregs arrived for a bar tour. They cannot start visiting bars until after three in the afternoon: both Suds and Dregs are high-school teachers.

Suds Kroge and Dregs Donnigan are *noms de bière*. The authors of A *Beer Drinker's Guide to the Bars of Reading* figured that the school authorities might not like the idea of Berks County youth being placed in the care of people whose sideline required attendance at places like the Anthracite Cafe and Stew's Keg and Dot Bilski's Tavern ("Decor: Hope Rescue Mission"). Suds and Dregs had started out with the intention not of writing a book but simply of visiting every bar in the city—a project that seemed to grow naturally from an effort to find a suitable meeting spot for an organization of beer drinkers that Suds and Dregs usually refer to as "the lodge." ("A bunch of white-collar teachers playing blue-collar for a night now and then.") As it happened, though, the guidebook made Suds and Dregs local celebrities, and the school authorities turned out to be tolerant, or maybe even a bit proud. I can see why they might be. Suds and Dregs, after all, set the students a good example of persistence and thoroughness. They did not miss one bar. Their efforts before the idea of a guidebook emerged could even have been seen as pure research. Also, they were ambitious. After the success of the Reading book, they expanded into the entire county—visiting 238 bars for A Beer Drinker's Guide to the Bars of Berks. They have been referred to by their real names in the local press with no ill effect. Suds is really David Wardrop. Dregs's real name is Bob Weirich. I call them Suds and Dregs.

•

"This has it all," Suds said. "This is what it's all about." We were at the Grand Central Tap Room, in Fleetwood, a town more or less on the way to Allentown. In The Bars of Berks, the Grand Central got a 4½B rating, and Suds and Dregs were at a loss to explain what had led them to withhold the final half a beer that would have indicated perfection. They like everything about the Grand Central. The clientele is what Suds and Dregs tend to call "a good mix." Fleetwood is a blue-collar town best known for having produced the automobile bodies that gave the Fleetwood Cadillac its name, but there is also a large grain elevator that draws nearby farmers. Suds and Dregs dote on the Grand Central's French fries, which are listed on the menu board under Soups and Platters and which, it almost goes without saying, are cooked in pure lard. They love the decor—worn wooden floor, softball trophies, a long bar with "pie-plate" bar stools, a refrigerator for take-out six-packs with a television set on top of it, a checkerboard on one of the tables, a display of potato chips and pretzels and lighter fluid and razor blades and work gloves. They also like the prices. Suds and Dregs are conscious of what they always call "value." Dregs was still boycotting a beer called Prior Double Dark, because of a precipitous increase in its price several years before. We were drinking half-and-half— half Pabst draught and half Yuengling's porter. Porter is a dark beer that, according to the label on the bottle, is brewed by Yuengling "expressly for Tavern and Family Trade." We were too early to take advantage of an offer the Grand Central was making in honor of its centennial and reunion: after nine in the evening, three dollars bought a centennial beer glass that the management undertook to fill as often as necessary until eleven. Suds and Dregs believed the centennial offer to be particularly good value. "You get to keep the glass," Dregs reminded me.

We were at the Grand Central too early to take advantage of the centennial offer because Suds and Dregs had picked me up promptly after school, and we had headed nearly straight for Fleetwood—taking time only to have some draught Rolling Rocks at the Pricetown Hotel. Considering the amount of time Suds and Dregs have to spend in beer joints in the course of their research, they had struck me as remarkably trim and well spoken and neatly dressed—all in all, in fact, just the sort of young men to whose care you might be happy to entrust your high-school-age children. On the way to Pricetown, we had given a ride home to Suds's wife, Beth, who teaches home economics at the junior high next to the high school where Suds teaches graphics and printing and Dregs teaches English. I asked her if she had gone along to many of the bars being investigated for A Beer Drinker's Guide to the Bars of Reading.

"That was a different wife," Dregs said. "The first wife divorced him after the first book."

"Oh, that's a shame," I said, thinking partly, I'll admit, of the wasted dedication.

"I didn't think so," Beth said.

Suds had managed to hold on to his second wife straight through the research for A Beer Drinker's Guide to the Bars of Berks, although the suggestion that the dynamic duo follow up the county book by tackling the entire state of Pennsylvania did not fill her with enthusiasm. "Beth even guest-starred a number of times for the county book," Suds said proudly.

"Guest-starred?"

Someone who accompanies Suds and Dregs on their rounds, it was explained to me, is always referred to as a guest star. I was a guest star.

•

Because of a wrinkle in the liquor laws, a lot of Pennsylvania bars are called hotels, even though they often lack such hotel accoutrements as registration desks or lobbies or overnight guests. Chick's Hotel Grand turned out to be a corner bar that made a good first impression on both Suds and Dregs. "It looks like it has potential," Suds said as he walked up to the bar and ran his hand along a bar rail made of highly polished wood. Both the bar counter and the back bar—the shelves that bartenders normally use to display bottles of whiskey—were finely crafted of wood that had the look of decades of care. Under one end of the bar was a prizefight bell that the bartender could clang any time someone bought a round for the house. One wall of Chick's was devoted almost entirely to pictures of Babe Ruth. Attention had also been paid to Carmen Basilio. Suds and Dregs were impressed. They acknowledge a bias toward polished old wood and stamped-tin ceilings. Part of their interest in bars is obviously just an attachment to home ground. If they had lived in El Paso, I suspect, they would have done a book on every single Mexican restaurant in town, limiting their enthusiasm to the ones that serve *menudo* and allow only the mother of the family to preside over the kitchen. In Buffalo, they would be scholars of the chicken wing.

Suds and Dregs were less impressed by the Hotel Grand's clientele, two or three of whom looked as if a clang of the prizefight bell might find them unable to come out for the next round. One portly, gray-haired woman named Dorothy seemed particularly taken with Suds—she said he looked like a professor—and insisted on filling him in on what her life had been like in better days. She was drinking boilermakers. Just before we left, Dorothy pulled Suds aside for some intense conversation, and then started to weep—overcome with a sadness that seemed to have passed by the time we got to the door.

"A little too derelictish," Dregs said when we were back on the street.

"I'll say this for Dorothy," Suds said. "What started her crying was when she told me that a beer at the Hilton costs two dollars."

Dregs nodded in sympathy. "It's enough to drive anyone to tears," he said.

•

The next night, we finally got to Stanley's, a place Suds and Dregs revere as almost the model for 5B bars ("the kind of bars that make the world seem a whole lot better than it really is"). Stanley's appeal is not in the decor. A lot of brick buildings in Reading have glued-on façades of something called Perma-Stone—slabs of a dreary gray material whose appearance is made the more dispiriting by the implication in its name that it will be there forever. Stanley's has Perma-Stone on the *inside*. "At Stanley's, we rise above aesthetics," Suds told me. Although Stanley's is a Polish-run bar in a Polish neighborhood, its clientele is "a good mix," dominated by shift workers from a nearby box factory and meat-packing plant. The mix does not include women. Like a lot of Reading bars, Stanley's has what is still sometimes called a "side room"—a sort of family dining room accessible through a side entrance—and at Stanley's the side room has remained the only place where women and children are served. When Suds and Dregs drink at Stanley's, they tend to refer to their wives as "the little lady."

"One of the nice things about Stanley's is that if the little lady sends you out for groceries you can have a few beers at Stanley's and pick up some lunch meat and a dozen eggs before you leave," Suds told me. Although the barroom at Stanley's is small—there are maybe fifteen spots at the bar and three or four tables and a phone booth and a pinball machine—it seems to carry an inventory of goods comparable to a small K mart's. Naturally, Stanley's has takeout six-packs and lighter fluid and potato chips and work gloves and lottery tickets. But it also has groceries and kerosene space heaters. On the back bar, among the bottles of rye and bourbon, there were signs that said GENUINE ANTIQUE COIN NECKLACE $4.00 and MEN'S AND LADIES' WATCHES $10.00 and GAS-TEFLON APPLIANCE CONNECTOR $5.00 and PICNIC TABLE $10.00 and MODEL ROLLS-ROYCE $12.00. Suds and Dregs assume that Stanley, who was still behind the bar himself after forty or fifty years of owning the place, started selling model Rolls-Royces about the time he bought a full-size one for himself. Stanley's bar has always given good value—the draught prices listed on the back bar ranged from Piels at twenty cents to porter for thirty-five cents —and Suds and Dregs have concluded that the secret of Stanley's prosperity may be carried in the motto he once gave them: "I'd rather make a fast nickel than a slow dollar." In the side room there was an entire table of for-sale items—men's jackets and "ladies' designer sweaters" and assorted vases and ceramic pigs and plates with pictures of Jesus Christ on them and boxes of banana-creme cookies. A sign over the table said, PLEASE LORD—PARALYZE THE HAND THAT STEALS.

Suds and Dregs seemed to be settling in at Stanley's, and I was beginning to feel rather settled in myself. Stanley had made a lot of fast nickels on me, and before we arrived we had spent some time at Jimmy Kramer's Peanut Bar and a bar called the Shoboat Hotel—a place Suds and Dregs admire for its hunting trophies and always refer to as "the fur, fish, and game bar." I had come to believe that the evening was drawing to a close. Then Suds informed me that a friend of his from Berks Packing—a man who had just presented him with a ring bologna direct from the factory—had invited us back to the home of a colleague who was locally renowned for his homemade wine. That was going to put us behind schedule a bit, Dregs said, because we still had to go to the Paddock Bar and to a roadhouse in Reinholds, Pennsylvania, whose stamped-tin walls would knock me out. The evening, I realized, had just begun. The most bars Suds and Dregs ever visited in one evening while researching A Beer Drinker's Guide to the Bars of Reading was twenty-one. "And," Dregs said, "that was on a school night."

11

The Italian West Indies

I DAYDREAM OF the Italian West Indies. On bleak winter afternoons in New York, when the wind off the Hudson has driven
Alice to seek the warmth she always draws from reading the bro-
chures of ruinously expensive Caribbean resorts, I sometimes mum-
ble out loud, "The Italian West Indies." Alice gets cold in the
winter; I yearn for fettuccine all year round.

"There is no such thing as the Italian West Indies," Alice
always says.

"I know, I know," I say, shaking my head in resignation. "I
know."

But why? How did Italy manage to end up with no Caribbean
islands at all? The French have islands. The Dutch have islands.
Even the Danes had one for a while. The English have so many
Caribbean islands that they have been hard put to instill in every
single one of them the historic English gifts of parliamentary democracy and overcooked vegetables. The Italians have none. Christopher Columbus—a Genoan, as I remind my fellow citizens every
year when Thanksgiving approaches, and the man who taught Fer-
dinand and Isabella how to twirl spaghetti around their forks—took
the trouble to discover the Caribbean personally before the end of
the fifteenth century. Try to get a decent plate of spaghetti there
now. When I happen into one of those conversations about how

easily history might have taken some other course (What if the Pope had allowed Henry VIII's divorce? What if Jefferson had decided that the price being asked for the Louisiana Purchase was ridiculous even considering the inflation in North American real estate?), I find myself with a single speculation: What if the Italians, by trading some part of Ethiopia where it's not safe to eat the lettuce, had emerged from the colonial era with one small Caribbean island?

I dream of that island. I am sitting in one of those simple Italian beach restaurants, and I happen to be eating fettuccine. Not always; sometimes I am eating *spaghettini puttanesca*. Alice and I are both having salads made with tomatoes and fresh basil and imported Italian olive oil and the local mozzarella. That's right— the local mozzarella. The sea below us is a clear blue. The hills above us are green with garlic plants. The chef is singing as he grills our fresh *gamberos*. The waiter has just asked us the question that sums up for me what I treasure about the Italian approach to drinking wine: "You won raid or whyut?" I say "whyut," and lean back to contemplate our good fortune in being together, soaking up sunshine and olive oil, on my favorite Caribbean island, Santo Prosciutto. "Ah, Santo Prosciutto . . ." I found myself saying out loud one brutal winter day.

"You know very well there is no Santo Prosciutto," Alice said.

"The English obviously had a lot more islands than they could use," I said. "Aren't they the ones who are always going on about fair play?"

"Why don't we go to Capri this spring?" Alice said.

Capri! I looked more carefully at what she was reading. It wasn't a brochure about a Caribbean resort. It was the atlas that William Edgett Smith, the man with the Naugahyde palate, had given us as a wedding gift. It's a boxed, lavishly illustrated atlas that probably set Smith back forty or fifty dollars and has cost me thousands. Smith is a world traveler himself. He once spent a year or so in India and, as far as I can gather, lived entirely on the steak sandwiches served in the coffee shop of the Akbar Hotel in New Delhi—the only unreconstructed meat-and-potatoes man on the subcontinent.

"Capri!" I said. I could think of some closer places to get a plate of pasta myself. The only warm one I really longed for, though—Santo Prosciutto, I.W.I.—obviously didn't exist. We have not always been successful in looking for a non-Italian Caribbean stand-in. Once, we spent a week or ten days on the French islands of St. Martin and St. Barthélemy, having heard that they had become places where a tourist with a serious interest in marine life could find himself a serious bowl of bouillabaisse. As it happens, virtually nothing edible is grown or raised on the islands of St. Martin and St. Barts, meaning that the meat and produce and, I suspect, a lot of the fish is brought in from places like Miami and Puerto Rico—some of it looking more in need of reviving than the accompanying tourists do. It struck me at the time that the residents of Santo Prosciutto, descendants of peasants who had managed to coax already-stuffed eggplants from the cruel soil of Calabria, would scoff at the notion of having to import tomatoes from Miami. We were assured, though, that any number of imaginative chefs had been drawn to St. Martin and St. Barts to accept the challenge of running a French restaurant under conditions that required liberating the lamb from custom brokers in the San Juan airport. I realized after a few bites of salad during a St. Martin dinner by the sea that one of them must have been that woman who used to run the cafeteria at Southwest High School in Kansas City: I could recognize her touch with a grated carrot anywhere.

I don't mean that we had nothing good to eat during that trip. St. Martin has a noted resort called La Samanna, where a couple can while away a few days in casual luxury for the price of a smallish Steinway, and the management gets around the ingredient problems with gestures like flying in crawfish from Turkey. There's no question that St. Barts is a charming island—I was particularly charmed by the *soupe de poisson* at a place called L'Entrepôt—but I think I had been put off my feed a bit by a conversation that took place just before we had come over from St. Martin. I had asked a man who owns a restaurant for suggestions about eating on St. Barts— taking out my notebook to record his recommendations.

He considered my questions for a while. Then he said, "Stay away from the meat."

It was true that the trip we were planning for the spring was

in celebration of Alice's birthday. It was true that we wanted to go
someplace we had never been before—which ruled out Martinique,
the one Caribbean island whose food almost led me to forgive the
French for whatever chicanery they used to finagle it from its rightful
Roman owners. But Capri? Capri was the sort of place that appeared
in song titles. As it happens, though, Alice is a bit of a romantic
—even if the romance entailed in a search for the world's best
sausage has so far eluded her—and romantics actually like places
that appear in song titles. Alice does not simply like Paris, she likes
April in Paris. I think she is still itching to visit Capistrano, even
though I once explained to her, after a trip there, that the swallows
return to the old mission on the same day every year only in the
sense that the Easter Bunny comes to our house on a regular annual
basis, and that a photograph of the romantically historic old mission
before "restoration" shows it to be not easily distinguishable from a
low pile of stones. I suppose those observations identify me as a
nonromantic—someone whose reaction to seeing the sun set over
some South Pacific island is to wonder whether the local taxis have
a surcharge for travel after dark, or whether the maid back at the
Tiki Harbor Inn routinely turns the bed light on when she turns
back the covers and therefore attracts every mosquito between the
hotel and Calcutta, or, most often, whether the hotel dining room
will have run out of everything but the gray meat that was purchased
in large lots during the festivities surrounding an official visit by the
Duchess of Kent in 1957.

I suppose people who have a romantic in the house should
limit themselves to atlases in black and white. Alice said that Capri
was famous for its flowers and views—an island so staggeringly
beautiful that powerful people had built villas on its cliffs since the
Caesars. I said it was famous for its tour buses: a feature of song-
title sorts of places is the presence of hordes of people who have
heard the song. It occurred to me, though, that we could do a lot
worse than Capri. I had, after all, suggested that for Alice's birthday
we take a trip of an extravagance appropriate to the occasion. Even
nonromantics like to make a grand gesture now and then, preferably
at off-season rates. Was I the sort of husband who would start
humming "Moon over Miami" simply because a no-frills fare to

Florida might have gone back into effect? As Alice's birthday approached, was I going to search around for a revival of "Wish You Were Here" just on the chance that she might be inspired by "I'm Don José from Far Rockaway"? I made reservations for Capri.

·

The other passengers on the hydrofoil from Naples had the look of the vaguely decadent European rich an American traveler might associate with Capri—sleek-looking Italians with Milanese money and Florentine luggage. The men wore white pants and espadrilles and had finely knit sweaters thrown over their shoulders. The women looked as if they spent half their time at Gucci and the other half in the gym. Did these folks eat pasta? They weren't the sort of people I have always envisioned sitting at the beachside café in Santo Prosciutto, picking at the *gamberos* with their fingers and knocking back the sort of local Italian white that goes down so easily that it could probably be consumed through intense osmosis. It occurred to me that, given the clientele, the restaurants on Capri might resemble those fancy Northern Italian places on the East Side of Manhattan where the captain has taken bilingual sneering lessons from the maître d' at the French joint down the street and the waiter, whose father was born in Palermo, would deny under torture that tomato sauce has ever touched his lips.

My concern on that point was eased when we settled in for lunch at a simple-looking place overlooking the beach. *Spaghettini puttanesca* was on the menu. Roasted eggplant and grilled shrimp were on the menu. So was a salad made of tomato, fresh basil, olive oil, and mozzarella—a dish, it turns out, that is sometimes known as a Caprisian salad. The waiter approached us cheerfully and said, "You won raid or whyut?"

"I have to say this about Capri," I said to Alice after I had ordered a bottle of whyut, "the place has a certain amount of romance."

·

I thought for a while that the ice cream in Capri might distract Alice from the views. Alice likes ice cream. A person who spent a lot of time, say, comparing the various chocolate ice creams available in lower Manhattan would not be described by Alice as a food crazy. I think it's fair to say that Alice's interest in ice cream cuts across national boundaries, but she makes a particular specialty of Italian gelati. Her discussions of Rome tend to dwell on a café in the Piazza Navona whose *tartuffo* she finds sublime. When she is in a town that has a number of gelaterias, she can spend an evening going from place to place to inspect the merchandise, commenting from time to time on the richness of the vanilla or the smoothness of the hazelnut. Sometimes she will announce, almost to herself, "I've come to a decision: I'm not having gelati inside a brioche this evening"—which still leaves the decision of what kind of gelati to have not inside a brioche.

The ice cream did not distract Alice from the views. In a place like Capri, Alice is still gazing out to sea long after I have become what I believe the German intellectuals call Viewsodden. I suppose a high tolerance for views goes along with being a romantic. In a restaurant with a view, Alice always wants to sit where she can see out the window and I am equally interested in facing the dining room—keeping my eye on the waiters on the chance they might pass by with something worth coveting. She likes views from cliffs and promontories. Like the late John Foster Dulles, I have been to the brink many times, always with Alice. On Capri, she managed to combine her interests by looking at the view while eating a hazelnut ice-cream cone.

"Look at the castle!" she said one day, pointing to a huge stone castle on a far-off cliff. We were in a cab on our way to a village called Anacapri, where, Alice had heard, a marvelous view of the Bay of Naples was available to anyone who happened to be willing to dangle in a chair lift run by someone whose face seemed familiar from an Alfred Hitchcock movie. Alice has always been fond of castles. She likes to imagine someone like the seventeenth Baron of Provolone presiding over the estate while the lady of the house —once just an ordinary girl from some place like Harrison, New York—is waited on by hordes of liveried servants, every one of whom addresses her as *Principessa*. As it happens, I always address Alice as *Principessa* myself while we're traveling in Italy; I find it improves the service.

"Gerber's baby food," the driver said.

Alice and I looked at each other, puzzled. The driver explained that the castle was owned by someone whose fortune derived from Gerber's baby food. It was perfectly possible, of course, that such a person could be married to a *principessa*, having won her, perhaps, with promises of unlimited pureed lima beans. Alice sighed. Romantic notions of the high life on Capri are not easily kept intact. That very morning, an article in a magazine in our hotel room—an article about the sort of chic, sophisticated fun that jet-setters have on Capri every night after the day-trippers go home—had been ruined for Alice by a paragraph that began, "For many years, Mr. Hornstein (the Puss 'n Boots cat food heir), who owned Villa Capricorn on Via Tragera, was considered the top party giver."

"Well, babies have to eat," I said, trying to cheer Alice up. "So do cats."

Alice, though, likes her castles inhabited by people whose source of wealth has long faded into the history of their ancient principalities. In a place like Capri, she is even more interested in castles built by people who were powerful so long ago that no trace of family remains—Caesar Augustus and the Emperor Tiberius and that crowd. One morning, as we were being taken around the island in a small boat, she seemed particularly captivated by a high stone wall that had been built up one of Capri's sheer cliffs and laced with stairs that led to a huge villa at the top. It was the sort of wall that could conjure up in the mind of a song-title sort of person the picture of hundreds of North African slaves laboring to please the haughty but exceedingly tasteful Caesar who had chosen the most difficult perch on the island for the summer residence of his favorite concubine. Just then the boatman turned down the motor and came back to where we were sitting. "Estair Villy-yoom," he said.

"What?"

"Estair Villy-yoom," he repeated. When I continued to look puzzled, he pointed to the villa above the stone wall and went into an imitation of somebody doing the backstroke.

"Esther Williams," I said. "He says that villa belongs to Esther Williams."

"But not the wall," Alice said. "She didn't build the wall."

The boatman nodded his head knowingly. "Estair Villy-yoom," he said. "All Estair Villy-yoom."

•

When the cold wind began to blow the next winter, I tried to be realistic about the Caribbean. "How about Martinique?" I said to Alice. After all, we had liked Martinique. It not only has local ingredients but a lot of people who understand what to do with them—French Creole cooks who know that sea urchins were not put in the ocean merely to be stepped on. It even has some views, although when we were there I was too busy stuffing down stuffed crabs to spend much time looking at them.

"Too bad there's no gelati there," Alice said.

"Well, that would require an Italian island," I said. "Some-place like Santo Prosciutto."

"A little gelateria right in the piazza of the village," Alice said. "Specialists in hazelnut, although they would also do that chocolate-hazelnut combination. Nobody on a French island could understand about that chocolate-hazelnut combination."

"Ah, Santo Prosciutto," I said.

"Yes," Alice said. "Santo Prosciutto."

"Also, Alice, I was thinking," I said. "It would probably be the sort of place that couldn't really be harmed by being in a song title. Maybe something like 'A Plate of Pasta on Santo Prosciutto with You.' "

(12)

Noble Experiment

WHEN I HEARD THAT Lum Ellis was trying to put the entire city of Natchitoches, Louisiana, on the Pritikin Diet, I knew he was going to have his hands full. Any researcher of my interests, of course, would have had a sort of perverse curiosity about what Ellis was up to—the sort of curiosity that an historian who always specialized in military campaigns might have about a project to study the origins of pacifism. I thought I'd better go to Louisiana for a firsthand look, and Alice, to my surprise, seemed to agree. She may have been harboring the long-shot hope that, like some hard-nosed reporter who is sent to expose a cult of snake handlers and becomes a convert, I might find after three or four days with the Pritikin forces that I had an untapped obsession for Grape-Nuts and mung beans. I must admit that I was also drawn to Natchitoches by what researchers call a collateral field of inquiry. To many people, Natchitoches, a parish seat seventy miles south of Shreveport, was always known mainly as the oldest settlement in the Louisiana Purchase—a peaceful, rather charming old river town where a lot of people who live in nineteenth-century houses can tell you pre-cisely the year their house was built and how many generations of their family have lived in it. To me, it was always known mainly as the home of the Natchitoches meat pie.

In 1979, Edwin Edwards, who was then the governor of Louisiana, announced that the state would contribute forty thousand dollars toward an attempt to educate the citizens of one Louisiana town in the benefits of the high-fiber, low-fat diet advocated by Nathan Pritikin, whose Longevity Center in California is so expensive that it attracts the sort of people who are friendly with the governor of Louisiana. Edwards said he had chosen Natchitoches (pronounced, more or less, "NACK-i-tish") partly because it is a microcosm of the population of the state. It is true that in northern Louisiana, an area whose culture sometimes seems defined by a devotion to chicken-fried steak and a dread of the Pope, Natchitoches is a town where people are not shocked by exposure to either Roman Catholics or cayenne pepper—a northern Louisiana town with some southern Louisiana overtones. Although Natchitoches's celebration of its early French and Spanish settlers concentrates on their houses rather than their food, modern residents do eat, in addition to their share of chicken-fried steak, some food that a lot of people in northern Louisiana would consider foreign and maybe wicked—spicy meat pies, for instance, and dirty rice, and hot tamales, and even an occasional gumbo. Edwards—who, despite his Anglo name, is a Cajun from southern Louisiana—said that Pritikin would have found it easier to convert people in "other parts of the country where the food is no good anyway." On the other hand, he acknowledged that attempting such a project in Cajun country, where people's main interest in an old building tends to be what sort of food might be served in it, would be "too much of a test." I can still brighten up a gray winter afternoon by picturing the scene of Nathan Pritikin trying to explain his diet plans for Opelousas to the law firm of Sandoz, Sandoz & Schiff.

At the kick-off banquet for the Natchitoches project, held in the Student Union of Northwestern State University, Edwards, apparently attempting to reconcile his role as the host and his reputation as an unreconstructed Cajun, was quoted as saying, "A Cajun raised on gumbo and crawfish would just as soon die ten years earlier as eat this stuff, but it's a noble experiment." Lum Ellis thought that was an unfortunate remark, although not as unfortunate as a comment by one diner that seemed to make all the wire-service stories—the comment that the broccoli bisque, prepared with Pritikin-approved ingredients, tasted like "boiled cigarettes." Right from the start, Lum Ellis knew very well that he was going to have his hands full.

Those of us who struggle valiantly against the perils of cynicism find ourselves sorely tested by a project that uses state money in Louisiana to demonstrate a health theory developed in Southern California. My view of any project in Louisiana has been formed partly by a conversation in New Orleans some years ago in which a man I know in the French Quarter listened to several people theorize about how the Louisiana Superdome might affect the tone and the economy and the morale of the city, and then said, "What you have to understand about the Superdome is that after the financing the rest is commentary." According to one school of thought in Louisiana, the only significant question to ask about any state project is "Who's writing the insurance?"

Even though he has been caught wearing a necktie, Nathan Pritikin, who claims that he can reverse cardiovascular disease through diet and exercise, has many of the other characteristics associated with what students of the Freelance Cure might categorize as the Southern California School—no formal training in the field, cure claims that are questioned by the medical establishment, a horde of satisfied and sometimes even zealous customers, and a book that has been on the best-seller list in both hardback and paper. Of course, it is always possible, I have to keep reminding myself, that when the Deity finally decides to reveal The Truth to the human race—not simply the truth about what sort of food we should eat but The Truth—He may choose as His messenger a Southern California health guru who has a how-to book in the top ten and has managed to recruit both John Travolta and Barbra Streisand as disciples. It has been written, after all, that God works in strange and mysterious ways. If He wanted to tell The Truth, why would He be so obvious as to put it in the mouth of a Nobel Prize–winning Harvard biochemist and father of four? The man from California would say, without qualification, that he had The Truth ("Really, Merv, I'm not putting you on—this is The Truth"), and the cynics would all say, very slowly, "Uh-huh, I'll bet, sure, right." Perhaps the messenger would decide to demonstrate The Truth through a state-government-funded project in Louisiana. The insurance would be handled through open competitive bidding. I tried to keep that possibility in mind when I went down to Natchitoches to see how Lum Ellis was getting along on his project—Project LIFE, as he had decided to call it—and try a meat pie or two, as long as I was in the area.

•

Lum Ellis is a sociologist, but saying that doesn't describe him, even if you know that he was once the president of the Natchitoches Chamber of Commerce. In addition to running the Pritikin project, he and his wife—the co-director of Project LIFE—were running a tour business on the side. He drove a Lincoln Continental. At one time Ellis was a Baptist minister in Jonesboro—the sort of Baptist minister who was also named Jonesboro's Young Man of the Year. For a while he was the host of a radio talk show in Natchitoches. While working as an assistant to the president of Northwestern State University, he ran, unsuccessfully, for state superintendent of education. By the time the campaign was over, the president he had assisted for eight years had moved on. Lum Ellis was faced with going back to the classroom—a prospect that didn't strike him the way it might strike, say, Mr. Chips. Along came Project LIFE—a one-year project with forty thousand dollars of state money and some more from the Pritikin Research Foundation. It beat Introduction to Sociology 104.

When Ellis spoke of his involvement with Project LIFE, he reminded me of a familiar character in old Hollywood movies— the male lead who tries to make the heiress understand that even though it's true he was secretly hired by her parents to bring some romance into her life before she succumbed to the rare and fatal illness, he had grown to love her truly. Not many months before I met him, Lum Ellis had known nothing about the Pritikin Diet except that the project to bring it to Natchitoches needed a director. The first time he saw Pritikin, he was unimpressed: the founder was wearing sandals with socks and carrying a small bag of fruit, and Lum Ellis thought he looked like "a German refugee." But eventually, Ellis told me, he became a "lead-pipe believer." He lost weight. He announced that he was through with salt and fats forever. ("I wouldn't mess up the taste of grits or corn with salt and butter.") He told me that the only contact he maintained with his former way of eating was an occasional burst of "intelligent sinning"—a Baptist preacher's way of describing a system that my friend Fats Goldberg, the New York pizza baron, calls "controlled cheating."

In Natchitoches, Ellis, as affable and chatty as any old talk-show host who had also been a preacher and a Chamber of Commerce president, played the role of the cheerful missionary—a "Hiya, honey" here and a "How ya doin', darlin'?" there, a cable-television show on the benefits of making gravy with cornstarch and making milkshakes with dry skim milk, a Project LIFE column every week in the *Natchitoches Times* ("It's sure good to be home . . . where we can make our fat-free strawberry milkshake in our blender"), a sprinkling of diet-cooking classes and exercise rallies and Happy Heart Month programs, an occasional expression of good-humored exasperation at the daunting task he had taken on ("They say they want to eat something that sticks to their ribs. You know what that means? Hard to digest").

"Sometimes," Ellis told me, "people come up to me and say, 'Lum, I ate an egg this morning and damned if I didn't think of you and feel guilty.' " Sometimes someone who was asked if he was eating a lot of fiber replied, as the director of the cable-television show replied one night, "I eat anything that doesn't eat me." For a while there was some talk that as many as a couple of thousand of the sixteen thousand people in Natchitoches might be following the strict regimen of the Pritikin Diet, but after a time even Ellis didn't claim that many people in Natchitoches were lead-pipe believers—willing, say, to follow his example of carrying along Grape-Nuts and dry skim milk and a bowl and a spoon on business trips in order to avoid having to eat a sinful breakfast. What he did claim was that a significant number of Natchitoches residents— more than a third, according to a survey he had taken—had been led to change their eating habits in some way by the program. The survey was part of the research component of Project LIFE, the announced idea being to test the death and illness rates in Natchitoches during the year of the study against a control city. Although

Ellis sometimes described Project LIFE as a "multiple-risk inter-
vention study," he did not claim that its methodology was ever likely
to be studied by public-health schools as a model. "In a little old
project like this, we can't draw definite conclusions," he told one
interviewer, in one of his rare understatements, "but we can add
to the general body of knowledge."

While I was in Natchitoches, I went to a Kiwanis luncheon,
and some of the Kiwanians, speaking from behind small mountains
of food they had collected at the Holiday Inn buffet table (Salisbury
steak, liver with onions, shrimp Creole, rice, broccoli with cheese
sauce, candied yams, black-eyed peas, bread pudding), told me that
a lot of people in Natchitoches had cut down on salt and sugar. A
manager at one supermarket said that people might have been asking
for slightly leaner cuts of meat, although the demand for chopped
pork to make meat pies had not been affected. The manager of
Brookshire's Supermarket, a large man named Lonnie Casey, told
me that the store was selling a bit more whole-wheat flour and an
occasional package of Pritikin-approved sapsago cheese—the cheese
Casey had been referring to a few months before when he told a
visiting reporter from Houston, "God, I couldn't swallow that mess."

Brookshire's Supermarket was also baking a special Pritikin
bread, and selling about a hundred loaves of it a week. "Do you
eat it yourself?" I asked the man who baked it.

"Nope," he said.

"Have you ever tasted it?"

"Yes."

"What does it taste like?"

"Cardboard."

I took a bite. Cardboard with a slight aftertaste. It occurred to
me that if Lum Ellis was willing to make a steady diet out of such
things in the name of research he was a true man of science, Lincoln
Continental or no Lincoln Continental.

•

Although one doctor in Natchitoches criticized Project LIFE on
both medical and ethical grounds—he called it a publicly funded
advertising campaign that happened to be advertising a diet that

might not even be advisable for the general population—most people seemed to approve of any effort that called attention to the need for exercise and nutrition, even if they expressed that approval between bites of pork cutlet with gravy. The claims of Nathan Pritikin for his longevity clinic aside, after all, the belief that Americans would do well to heed his advice about cutting down on salt and sugar and meat is widespread—although not so widespread as to include the members of the Natchitoches Parish Cattlemen's Association. They went to Baton Rouge to try to block Lum Ellis's appropriation. What was worrying Ed Hunter, the president of the association, was that the Pritikin forces would figure out a way to dredge up from the murky statistics some way to confirm their diet's wonders, even though Hunter told me he was convinced that "if you shook all the bushes here hard you couldn't find a hundred people on that diet." In Hunter's view, Project LIFE was just an ad campaign that the citizens of Louisiana, including the beef farmers, were paying for. "It's going to benefit nobody but Nathan Pritikin," he told me. I pointed out that there was one other certain winner—James Lasyone, the proprietor of Lasyone's Meat Pie Kitchen & Restaurant.

Lasyone turned out to be a rotund, enthusiastic man who works in the kitchen of his place rather than in the dining room. After twenty-five years as a butcher in a Natchitoches grocery store, he began in the early seventies to see if he could start a commercial enterprise based on the meat pie that people in Natchitoches have always eaten at home. A Natchitoches meat pie is a half-moon pastry that has been filled with chopped pork and chopped beef and spices and then fried in deep fat—emerging as something close to an empanada. When there is a festival in Natchitoches—the annual Christmas-light celebration, say, or the old-home tour—meat pies are sold from stands. When there is a party, the hostess often orders them from one of the women around town known for the specialty. Years ago, a book on Natchitoches recalls, they were sold on the street by black children, who chanted "Hot-ta-meat pies. Red-d-d hot!"

Lasyone sold meat pies from his butcher counter for a couple of years and then opened up a restaurant next door with meat pies as the premier dish—served with a generous portion of dirty rice. Several years after the restaurant opened, a writer from *House Beautiful*, apparently in town to admire the old houses and the brick street that runs along the river, happened into Lasyone's, and the result was an article that Lasyone came to think of as "the break of a lifetime." Lasyone's began to show up in restaurant guides. Eventually, the tourists who came to Natchitoches Parish were looking not just for plantation houses but for a genuine Natchitoches meat pie. A meat-pie recipe was included with the brochure on historic sites. After a while it became common to see a huge tour bus parked in front of Lasyone's Meat Pie Kitchen & Restaurant.

If Nathan Pritikin wanted to distribute a list of foods to be avoided at all cost, he could simply hand out the menu of Lasyone's Meat Pie Kitchen & Restaurant. Lasyone's daily special is likely to be something like smothered calves' liver. His dessert specialty is Cane River Cream Pie—a sort of cake with vanilla filling, chocolate syrup, and whipped topping. Lasyone does have vegetables, but when he serves okra he takes the trouble to fry it.

When Project LIFE began, Lasyone was somewhat concerned that tourists might get the idea he had switched from meat pies to mung beans and the sort of cheese that just about did in Lonnie Casey at Brookshire's Supermarket. Lasyone's concern had been provoked by a phone call from the American Express Travel Service asking about his involvement with the Pritikin Diet. "I told them I had nothing to do with it," he told me, "and then they booked two buses."

As it turned out, of course, Project LIFE worked to Lasyone's advantage. How could a television crew assigned to poke around in the eating habits of Natchitoches resist a cheery antithesis to the Pritikin thesis? Lasyone's Meat Pie Kitchen & Restaurant became more famous than ever. Lasyone told me that the year of Project LIFE was the best year his restaurant ever had.

Even Lasyone was quick to say that he has nothing against people trying to eat healthful food—although he does believe that efforts to change people's eating habits are doomed to failure. When the subject came up, he tended to look serious and responsible. "Lum Ellis is a fine fellow," he told me. "He's trying to make a living trying to get people on a diet, and I'm trying to make a living trying to get them off." He went on to explain how he makes the roux for the beef stew whose gravy he pours over the chicken-fried steak. "The only way to make a good roux is to start with pure hog lard," he said.

"Just the sort of thing Mr. Pritikin goes for," I said.

James Lasyone began to giggle.

A Stag Oyster Eat

Below the Canal

I BECAME AWARE OF THE Georgetown Volunteer Fire Company's annual stag oyster eat and dance while reading the premier issue of *Shellfish Digest*. I try to keep up with the scholarly journals. All-male dancing under the auspices of volunteer firemen was a new subject for me altogether, but then I could say that about a lot of what was in that first issue. What I took to be the lead article discussed the Quik Pik, a machine developed by the Sea Savory Company to shake the meat right out of crab bodies. The fragile-looking body of a Maryland blue crab is quite capable of withstanding the sort of treatment the Quik Pik deals out, the article reported, unless the shell is already damaged—in which case the crab flies apart as if it had exploded. ("However, these fragments can be easily discarded.") The process requires such ferocious shaking that the first models of the machine lumbered right across the floor. When I feel myself in need of cheer and I can't seem to conjure up the picture of Nathan Pritikin presenting his diet plans to the law firm of Sandoz, Sandoz & Schiff, I try to imagine a couple of crab pickers being pursued across the shed by an aroused Quik Pik.

I had picked up the first issue of *Shellfish Digest*—which was then called *Shellfish News* and also appeared in the form of a newsletter called *Chowder* and eventually, like a crab growing a hard shell, evolved into a series of books on shellfish—while I was still under the illusion that all oyster knives were pretty much alike; none of them, after all, has any purpose beyond opening oysters. That issue, though, discussed at least sixteen different models, all of which it offered for sale. As one of those rare publications that combine elements of the literary magazine and the mail-order catalogue, the *Shellfish Digest* offered its readers the opportunity to send in for almost anything it wrote about—not including the Quik Pik, which weighs fifteen thousand pounds. Someone who thought he had simply ordered a mussel cookbook by mail could pick up *Shellfish Digest* and discover that he had actually written a letter to the editor. "Enclosed—my check and order for two knives and a subscription" was not an unusual beginning for a contribution to the *Shellfish Digest* letters column, and neither was "Very interesting magazine—please do not print order blank on reverse side of drawing." (Once, as it happens, an entire issue of *Chowder* was printed on the back of a place mat.) The editor's own book, *The Craft of Dismantling a Crab*—one edition of which he had the foresight to publish on stain-resistant paper—was offered for sale in that first issue, as was the clam knife described in a piece he wrote called "Editor Designs Sharp Dagger and Lives to Tell about It."

The editor, Robert H. Robinson, had by then sold some fourteen thousand copies of *The Craft of Dismantling a Crab*, which, being crustaceously ecumenical, also offers illustrated advice on dismantling clams, lobsters, mussels, oysters, and even whelks: "Discard the orange viscera (A) and the horny black operculum (B), which is like a trapdoor." I learned the sales figures while Robinson was taking me for a sightseeing tour of Georgetown—a pretty town of two thousand people which serves as the county seat of Sussex County, Delaware. I was there for the annual Georgetown Volunteer Fire Company Oyster Eat.

•

Sussex County is what people in Delaware sometimes call "below the canal." The Chesapeake and Delaware Canal slices right across the top of the state from east to west; most of what is urban and industrial lies above it. Wilmington is above the canal. Above the canal, there are people who live right next to Pennsylvania or just across the river from New Jersey. Sussex is the southernmost and most rural of the state's three counties—culturally as well as geographically as far below the canal as you can get. It is well down the peninsula that below-the-canal Delaware shares with the Eastern Shore of Maryland and an unlikely detached tail of Virginia—a peninsula that has the Atlantic Ocean on the east and not many years ago was accessible from the south and west only by ferry. Below the canal, change comes slowly. While I was in Georgetown, one of the law firms was renovating an old building near the courthouse for its offices, and the local legal fraternity was of mixed opinion about whether the firm was taking some risk by installing some of its lawyers on the second floor. In Sussex County, lawyers have always been on the ground floor. I was informed of this situation by Robinson's wife, Battle Robinson, who happens to be a lawyer herself. "People will walk upstairs to see a dentist," she said. "But nobody's sure if they'll walk upstairs to see a lawyer."

On the second day after any important election, Georgetown still celebrates Return Day, as it has for at least a hundred and fifty years—bringing together the winning and losing politicians to shake hands, march together in a parade, and help consume an ox or two. For years, it was customary in some parts of Sussex County to mark the opening of the oyster season with Big Thursday celebrations, which included dancing right on the dock or on a dancing board made out of a barn door. It seems to have been a predominantly male form of dance. Describing one of the most famous dancers of the early part of the century, a county paper wrote in the thirties: "Even when he was seventy-five years old he could dance for two or three hours along with his son 'Matt,' who survives him and is known throughout lower Delaware for his power of endurance on a dancing board." The Big Thursday celebrations eventually died out, perhaps because there came a time when fewer places along the Sussex County shore could count on having a celebratory oyster catch. A man who wants to do some stomping on a board while a fiddle plays, though, can still count on one opportunity a year—the Georgetown Volunteer Fire Company Oyster Eat. For the price of admission—seven dollars the year I went —he also gets all the oysters and beer and egg-salad sandwiches and hard-boiled eggs he wants. And he doesn't have to worry about behaving the way his mother told him to behave when there are ladies present. When I arrived in Georgetown, Robinson informed me that the fire company had managed to maintain the tradition of the oyster eat for forty-four years—even though the previous year the oysters had to be hauled up from Louisiana.

•

Georgetown, which is eighteen miles from the ocean, is not a place where everyone eats oysters routinely. There may not be such a place. Oyster eating is not geographically predictable. I once met somebody whose eating memories of a childhood in Iowa are dominated by a barrel of oysters kept in the cellar. In New York, some friends of ours who are South Dakota expatriates annually have people in for a Christmas Eve feast of oyster stew as a reminder of their home state. I suspect that oysters have been a traditional dish in parts of the upper Midwest because, compared with other seafood, they tend to keep—although I remain skeptical of an old newspaper item quoted in *Shellfish Digest* about an oyster that was eighty-six years of age when it attacked a fish dealer's tomcat. ("The octogenarian clung to the cat's tail," the fish dealer was quoted as saying. "I never saw the cat or the oyster again.") They don't keep that well.

I don't remember any oysters in the part of the Midwest I grew up in, but I have been trying to make up for their absence ever since I left. Since I have publicly identified myself as the person who once nominated Mrs. Lisa Mosca, of Mosca's restaurant in Wagaman, Louisiana, for the Nobel Prize because of the perfection of her baked oysters, it almost goes without saying that I have a strong appreciation for the oyster. I like oysters on the half shell. I think the New Orleans oyster loaf is a concept so brilliant that I look forward to an extensive research project someday investigating its origins. I love oyster stew. When our South Dakota friends canceled their Christmas Eve oyster-stew bash one year simply because they had an opportunity to go to Egypt, I was outraged; Alice had to restrain me from picketing their apartment building.

Even near the shore, though, there are a lot of people who won't eat oysters. Battle Robinson, who ate oyster stew as a child in the interior of North Carolina, told me that she seemed to meet a lot of people in Georgetown who claim some sort of allergy when the subject of oysters comes up. Oysters, like the wicked witch in some fairy tales, are ugly inside and out. On the half shell, they are eaten alive. Plenty of the regulars at the Georgetown oyster eat can't imagine why anyone would eat an oyster. According to Robinson, a notoriously gullible member of the Georgetown Fire Company who does not happen to be an oyster eater was told once that a member who is widely known for his foolhardiness can, on occasion, eat an oyster through his nose. To a non-oyster eater, apparently, that did not sound much more unlikely than downing one in the conventional manner, and it is thought that the gullible fireman might have believed the story even without the deft touches of verisimilitude that went with it—that the oyster had to be small, of course, and that the eater had to leave off sauce "else he'd sneeze."

•

Robinson and I walked to the oyster eat from his house. He had furnished me with an oyster knife and an International Harvester baseball cap, in the manner of an English country gentleman handing his guest a walking stick before the evening's stroll. (He later sent me a photograph of the two of us in our oyster-eat costumes; on the bottom of it he had taped the caption "You can either help these two continue their Vo-Tech education in fender repair or you can turn the page.") The oyster knife had been picked with some care in Robinson's office. Robinson runs a county weekly that was founded by his grandfather, but he seems to treat it as more or less of a sideline—the way I imagine Leo Braudy treats English literature when he's in the heat of one of his cheese-steak research projects. The office file drawers had titles like "Crabs" or "Shrimp."

"What I would recommend to you is this Virginia Breaker," Robinson had said, hefting a nasty-looking little knife.

"Well," I said.

"No, this Murphy Gulf would be good," he said, rummaging around in another box.

"The Murphy Gulf would be fine," I said, realizing that with fourteen or fifteen other oyster knives available for consideration we might never get to the oysters. My favorite oyster bar in New Orleans, the Acme, used to close early, and I think the disappointment of arriving there several times only to find the door locked may have left me with a permanent anxiety about missing out on oysters; it comes over me as the sun falls.

I had been impressed by the careful selection of knives, but I had not found it encouraging that just before we left for the oyster eat Battle Robinson served a full dinner. I can't imagine a hostess in Providence sending people along to a Squantum club clambake after serving them a full dinner. The oyster eat has a reputation for raucousness, and I was getting the impression that some residents of Georgetown did not think of it as a serious eating event. Also, in this era of liberation and sexual equality, I naturally felt a bit awkward that Robinson and I were in the position of pushing back from the table, thanking the little woman for dinner, and wandering off for a bit of jollity at the fire hall. When I mentioned this to the little woman in question, though, she seemed unconcerned—more or less as if I had taken it upon myself to apologize for the fact that males had a stranglehold on the outdoor jobs of the Sussex County Sanitation Department.

When we arrived at the fire hall—a huge one-story building constructed of cinder blocks and painted pale green—I realized that Robinson, wise in the ways of life below the canal, had provided me with the appropriate costume. I had never seen a greater variety of baseball caps. Within a few minutes, I noticed caps that advertised Adams Oil Company, Hitchens Bros. Construction, Delaware Blue Hens, West Virginia University Mountaineers, Perdue Chicken, Paramount Chicken, Sussex County Country Club, Valiant Plant Food, Milford Sure-Crop Fertilizer, Magnolia Volunteer Fire Department, Joy Dog Food, Tull's Farm & Home Center, Enforce Air Shocker, and Firemen Are Always in Heat. The floor of the fire hall was instep-deep in sawdust. The fire trucks had been removed for the evening. There were a couple of trash barrels around, but I took them to be tokens. Six or eight tables had been set up for oysters steamed in the shell—tables with holes in the middle for shells and with raised central shelves for condiments. The oyster eaters stood around the tables opening or eating or having a beer while they awaited new supplies. All of them had their own knives, and a lot of them wore gloves. ("Oysters are the hardest and riskiest of all shellfish to open," Robinson has written. "Still, style is very important. As in dismantling a lobster, you are rated by performance and you can easily lower your rating by slipping and sending the blade of your oyster knife through your hand.") In one corner, somebody opened and served raw oysters. In another part of the hall, egg-salad sandwiches and hard-boiled eggs were being handed out. There were hundreds of men in the fire hall, practically none of them without a glass of beer in his hand.

In one corner, next to a bandstand where a hard-bluegrass band was playing, eight sheets of plywood had been arranged in a square to form a dance floor. Half a dozen men were stomping away, with a crowd around them furnishing encouragement with yelps and whoops. There are sometimes people at the oyster eat who become sufficiently inspired by the good fellowship and the drink at hand to make an inexpert stab at a few jig steps late in the evening (I might be put in that category myself; Robinson had the wit to stay off the boards), but most of the dancing at the oyster eat is done by a small group of people who come there to dance. The dance they do is sometimes called "flatfooting." Sometimes it resembles a jig, or what people in Tennessee call "clog dancing"—with hands in the pockets or behind the back. Sometimes it requires some serious stomping on the plywood. Some of the dancers danced alone, but most of them faced partners. Most of them seemed to be people whose families had always danced. "The old man taught us boys. He's been flatfootin' since he was eleven or twelve years old," I was told by Lawrence Coverdale, a young machinist from Milford, who danced mainly with his brother Jim. "We were raised up on it." There aren't many flatfoot dancers left in Sussex County, but because a few families took the trouble to raise some up, a number of them are young. I suspect that the oyster eat is in no more danger of running out of dancers than it is of running out of oysters. If it does, it can just haul some up from Tennessee.

Among the rest of the crowd milling around the fire hall—farmers and politicians and car dealers and swampers and first-floor lawyers—the main activity seemed to be talking and drinking beer.

In fact, late in the evening I realized that, with talking and watching the dancers and having a few beers and trying out a few jig steps, I had not put much time in with my Murphy Gulf. I was not surprised the next day when I heard someone at a secondhand store asked if he had been to the oyster eat and he said, "Naw, I quit drinking." Battle Robinson may be from North Carolina instead of below the canal, but she knows enough to give people dinner before they go to an oyster eat.

(1 4)

Hong Kong Dream

I CAN'T COUNT THE NUMBER of hours I have spent in China-town dreaming of Hong Kong. The spell usually comes over me after dinner, as I stroll down Mott Street, ostensibly engaged in what passes for after-dinner conversations on those outings—a sort of postgame analysis of the stuffed bean curd, maybe, or some mild disagreement over whether the pan-fried flounder was really as good as last time. Alice is always there, and often the girls. Sometimes, William Edgett Smith, the man with the Naugahyde palate, is walking down Mott Street with us, pretending to be in a sulk because nobody would let him order egg foo yung. We are usually walking toward the amusement arcade, on Mott Street near the Bowery, where it is possible to finish off an evening in Chinatown by playing ticktacktoe with a live chicken. A bag of fortune cookies awaits anyone who beats the chicken, but as far as I know, nobody ever has. The chicken gets to go first—a sign on the outside of the cage lights up "Bird's Turn" as soon as the coins are dropped—and that advantage seems to be enough to carry the day. Some people think the chicken always wins because it is being coached by a computer telling it where to peck by means of light bulbs that can't quite be seen from the outside of the cage. Some people think the chicken always wins because it happens to be one smart chicken. Sometimes during that after-dinner stroll—when we are discussing the pan-fried flounder, or when our best ticktacktoe player is being wiped out by a chicken, or when Alice and I are negotiating with Abigail and Sarah over whether it would be appropriate to compensate for our failure to win the fortune cookies by asking the Häagen-Dazs store and the David's Cookies store next to it to join forces for a chocolate-chocolate-chip-ice-cream sandwich on chocolate-chunk cookies, or when I drop into the supermarket across from the arcade to replenish my supply of fried dried peas—I am often heard to murmur, "I'd really like to go to Hong Kong."

"Don't you mean China?" I'm sometimes asked, if there's someone along who hasn't been with us before when I say "I'd really like to go to Hong Kong" as I'm strolling down Mott Street.

No, not China. I'll admit that the coverage of those banquets thrown during Richard Nixon's first visit revived in me what had been a flagging interest in superpower relations. For those of us who spend a lot of our evenings on Mott Street discussing stuffed bean curd, it was difficult to look at pictures of Nixon sitting at the banquet table—sitting there with a look that suggested he was longing for a simple dish of cottage cheese at his desk or for dinner at one of those Southern California restaurants where salad with Green Goddess dressing is set before you with the menu—and restrain ourselves from thinking, Why him? The opening of China to tourists did present a temptation. In New York there are people—some of them members of my own family—who find it odd that someone wants to eat four or five Chinese meals in a row; in China, I often remind them, there are a billion or so people who find nothing odd about it at all. Soon, though, reports began to drift back from Chinatown denizens who had visited the People's Republic, enduring tours of primary schools and irrigation projects just to get a crack at the restaurants: the non-presidential food was disappointing. The Chinese, I was given to believe, had other priorities—getting on with the revolution and that sort of thing. Fine. I'd wait. Meanwhile, I dreamed of Hong Kong.

For years, while China watchers gathered in Hong Kong to interpret and reinterpret every bit of news from Peking, I remained in New York—a Hong Kong watcher. From thousands of miles away, I analyzed news from the colony in terms of how it might affect my vision. When there were reports that another few hundred thousand people had been permitted to leave China for Hong Kong, I could see gifted chefs from Shanghai and Peking and Chiu Chow and Hunan—people who had chafed for years at having to read *The Little Red Book* when they wanted to be reading recipes—rushing over the border, ready to knock themselves out for the running dogs of Yankee imperialism. In Hong Kong, I figured, people who felt the need to skip from one cuisine to another at every meal, like a fickle debutante who can't permit herself to dance with the same boy twice in a row, could simply say something like "We just had Cantonese last night; why don't we go to a Peking place for lunch?" When I read that the Chinese businessmen of Hong Kong had far outstripped the English bankers who once dominated the economy of the colony—partly because real estate, traditionally controlled by the Chinese, grew to be much more valuable than whatever business was conducted on it—I could envision managers of the most expensive dining spots gratefully crossing Yorkshire pudding off their menus and beginning to compete ferociously for the hottest refugee chef. (But would rising real-estate values force rents too high for restaurants that concentrated on food rather than on flashy surroundings? We Hong Kong watchers had a seminar on that one, over salt-baked chicken and dried Chinese mushrooms with bean curd.) When I read of Hong Kong's importance to the People's Republic of China as a source of foreign exchange, I could envision the political détente of my dreams—ingredients from the heartland of Communist China flowing into a place where capitalistic Chinese eaters were only too happy to pay for them. When the turmoil of the Cultural Revolution spilled over into Hong Kong, reviving talk of how easily China could take over the colony, some Hong Kong watchers thought the dream had been shattered, but I was not among them. "Can't you see?" I would say, during one of our *dim sum* symposia. "Now they'll be eating like there's no tomorrow."

My dream of Hong Kong was not a criticism of Chinatown. I love Chinatown. I love the outdoor market that has grown up along Canal Street, and I love the food stores where I can't ever seem to get anyone to tell me what anything is in English. I'm even fond of the chicken who plays ticktacktoe; I've never been a sore loser. I count myself fortunate to live a bike ride away from a neighborhood that is always mentioned—along with Hong Kong and Taiwan and Tokyo—whenever serious eaters of Chinese food talk of the world's great concentrations of Chinese restaurants. Still, Hong Kong is always mentioned first. There are weekend mountain climbers who take great joy in hauling themselves around the Adirondacks, but they dream of Nepal. Eventually, if they're lucky, they get to Nepal. Eventually, I got to Hong Kong.

•

We were sitting in a restaurant called Orchid Garden, in the Wanchai district, beginning our first meal in Hong Kong, and I had just sampled something called fish-brain soup. I was about to comment. Alice was looking a bit anxious. She was concerned, I think, that over the years I might have created a vision of Hong Kong in my mind that could not be matched by the reality—like some harried businessman who finally arrives in what he has pictured as the remote, otherworldly peace of a Tahiti beach only to be hustled by a couple of hip beach-umbrella salesmen wearing "Souvenir of Fort Lauderdale" T-shirts. Even before we had a meal, she must have noticed my surprise at discovering that most of the other visitors in Hong Kong seemed to be there for purposes other than eating. That's the sort of thing that can put a visionary off his stride. How would the obsessed mountain climber feel if he arrived in Nepal after years of fantasizing about a clamber up the Himalayas, and found that most of the other tourists had come to observe the jute harvest? It appeared that just about everyone else had come to Hong Kong to shop.

Hong Kong has dozens of vast shopping malls—floor after floor of shops run by cheerfully competitive merchants who knock off 10 percent at the hint of a frown and have never heard of sales tax. There are restaurants in some of the shopping malls, but most of the visitors seemed too busy shopping to eat. It was obvious that they would have come to Hong Kong even if it had been one of those British colonies where the natives have been taught to observe the queen's birthday by boiling Brussels sprouts for an extra month. That very morning, in the lobby of a hotel, we had noticed a couple in late middle age suddenly drawing close to share some whispered intimacy in what Alice, the romantic, took to be a scene of enduring affection until one of the softly spoken phrases reached her ears—"customs declaration."

The sight of all those shoppers racing around, their shopping bags bulging and their minds feverish with schemes for flimflamming the customs man, had not really disturbed me. Hong Kong is the sort of place that can provide more than one vision. There must be people, for instance, who see it as a symbol of flat-out free enterprise prospering next to the cheerless regimentation of the world's largest Communist society, and there must be people who see it as a hideous example of capitalist materialism next to an inspiring land of collective sacrifice—although either vision would be blurred by a visit to the People's Republic department stores in Hong Kong, which accept American Express, Diners Club, Visa, and MasterCard. What can the struggle of the two great forces for the domination of the world mean if the Reds are on Diners? My own vision could be similarly blurred, Alice knew, if the fish-brain soup turned out to be only marginally superior to the bird's-nest soup or hot-and-sour soup routinely ladled out in Chinatown—the sort of first course that would be mentioned briefly on the after-dinner stroll as a lead-in to the subject of whether we should try the fried dumplings next time. I hadn't even bothered to claim to Alice that my principal interest in a trip to Hong Kong was the opportunity it presented to expand some research I had been doing on the varieties of scallion pancakes; she knew I was on a pilgrimage. I had another spoonful of fish-brain soup. "To quote Brigham Young, a man who never ate a shrimp," I said, " 'This is the place.' "

I'm tempted to say that I never doubted for a moment that it would be, but of course I had my doubts. Even before our first meal, though, my confidence was being shored up. Like so many other visitors, I had rushed out on my first morning to make a purchase—in my case a guide to Hong Kong restaurants—and I was rewarded by learning that the discussions in Hong Kong about what the colony's future will be after the British lease on the New

Territories expires in 1997 are rivaled in intensity by the discussions about which restaurant serves the best Peking duck. My vision of Hong Kong was built on the belief that it would be not simply a place where the fish-brain soup dazzled but also a place where people took it for granted that a normal response to hearing a visitor ask "What's Macau like?" would be to offer an opinion on which Macanese restaurant offers the most succulent prawns—a place, in other words, where priorities had been established. Within a couple of days, I felt like a China watcher who, after having spent years spinning out generalizations about China based on the flimsiest perusal of monitored radio broadcasts and fanciful refugee accounts, is finally permitted to make an extended visit to the mainland and finds, to his astonishment, that he was right all along.

At the precise moment that this feeling came over me we had just finished dinner at a businessmen's club called the Shanghai Fraternity Association. We had eaten smoked fish and drunken-chicken and something resembling bok choy and shark's fin soup and mixed vegetables and fried pork and river shrimp and Shanghai dumplings and a sort of sesame fritter. What I had to keep reminding myself was that we were consuming the Hong Kong version of club food. One of our dining companions, an ore trader of Shanghainese background, had spent part of his afternoon consulting with the club management about precisely what should be served. That, I was told, is routine among Hong Kong businessmen who entertain. I tried to imagine an English or an American businessman giving over part of his afternoon to planning a meal at his club. Even if it occurred to him to do it, what would he say? "Let's be sure to have some of those tasteless canned vegetables, Emile. And what sort of spongy gray meat is good this time of year? And a dinner salad of iceberg lettuce would be nice, I think. With Green Goddess dressing."

•

It was the rain that drove me into the Central Market of Hong Kong. I stayed only a couple of minutes. I have a weakness for markets, but when it comes to Chinese food I have always operated under the policy that the less known about the preparation the better. Even in Chinatown, it seems to me, a wise diner who is invited to visit the kitchen replies by saying, as politely as possible, that he has a pressing engagement elsewhere. That policy of selective ignorance should obviously be followed in Hong Kong, where old hands are often heard to mutter, "The Cantonese will eat anything." What astounded me about the Central Market—in the short time I had for observation before I decided that I preferred the rain—was not simply that it was a place where a moderately energetic public-health inspector could write his year's quota of citations in fifteen or twenty minutes. I was even more amazed by the fact that, even though the same purveyors presumably operated out of the market routinely day after day, there was something impromptu about it. People squatted on the floor here and there, between a basket of squid and a couple of discarded cattle heads, as if they had merely wandered by to say hello to a fishmonger friend who said, "Listen, Joe, as long as you're here, why don't you just sit yourself down on the floor over there and peel this pile of shrimp?"

Even after I started giving the Central Market a wide berth, I found unwelcome knowledge creeping through my defenses. In Chinatown, for instance, I had always taken it for granted that the "bird's nest" in bird's-nest soup was a direct translation of some evocative Chinese phrase describing some sort of vegetable that grows only in certain districts of certain provinces. It wasn't until I wandered into some Hong Kong shops that specialize in selling them that I realized that a bird's nest is a bird's nest—a swallow's nest, to be exact, usually imported from Thailand. What did that say about fish-brain soup?

Whatever it was, I resolved not to listen to it. "It's all a matter of mind-set," I informed Alice. "What we're talking about here is a vision, a ceremony. A person taking Communion doesn't need to know where the wafers came from." Fortunately, the rain got worse; even strolling along Hong Kong streets became difficult. I suppose there were visitors to Hong Kong who fretted about being prevented from taking in the countryside of the New Territories and observing the culture of the inhabitants. The shoppers must have been irritated, considering how easily a sodden shopping bag can break through at the bottom. I remained cheerful. Between meals,

I sat in the hotel room, going over lists of restaurants, protected from markets and shops—from everything but the final results.

•

Duck better than any duck I had tasted in Chinatown. Fried seaweed better than the fried seaweed we used to eat in Peking restaurants in London. Shad brought to the table sizzling on an iron plate. Yak fondue. *Dim sum*. More *dim sum*. Duck tongues (undoubtedly, I told myself, some colorful Chinese phrase for a particularly conventional cut of beef). Minced abalone and pork wrapped in lettuce leaves. I was reeling. I wondered what happened to some of those mountain climbers when they finally got to Nepal. Did they get up there on one Himalaya or another, in that thin air, and decide that they could never return to a place where mountain climbing meant schlepping to foothills on the weekend? Did they just stay in Nepal, eking out a living as consultants to the jute marketing board?

The question was in my mind one evening when we were having dinner in what appeared to be a rather ordinary Hong Kong restaurant—it was a last-minute substitution after the place my research had dredged up turned out to be closed—and noticed on the menu some of the same dishes served by one of our favorite restaurants in Chinatown. We ordered two of them—roast pigeon and fried fresh milk with crabmeat. The pigeon was a lot better than the Chinatown version. The fried fresh milk with crabmeat was so much better that it tasted like a different dish.

"We haven't tried the pepper and salty shrimp," Alice said.

We had both noticed it on the menu. As it happens, the Chinatown restaurant's finest dish—even better than the pigeon or the fried fresh milk with crabmeat—is by far the best version of pepper and salty shrimp I have ever eaten.

I thought about ordering pepper and salty shrimp. I suspected it would be better than the Chinatown version, but I wasn't sure I wanted to find out. The minced abalone and pork wrapped in lettuce leaves that we had eaten in Hong Kong was superior to the version we sometimes eat in a Chinatown restaurant, but something about finding that out had seemed almost disloyal: Abigail and I are so fond of the Chinatown version that our definition of a truly special treat is for the two of us to sneak down there on a school holiday and make a lunch out of however many orders of it are required to fill us up. I live only a bike ride away from Chinatown, after all. I miss it when I'm out of the city, even when I'm in Hong Kong. I miss the stroll down Mott Street toward the amusement arcade. I almost miss the chicken. It occurred to me that even people interested in knowledge for its own sake have to set some limits to how much they want to know.

"I think I'm kind of full," I said to Alice. "Maybe we should save it for next time."

Just Try It

WHAT I DECIDED TO TELL Sarah about catfish was that it tastes like flounder. She eats flounder, although I can't say she's an enthusiast. When it comes to food, her enthusiasm runs toward chocolate—her favorite dish (if that's the word) being a chocolate-chocolate-chip-ice-cream cone with chocolate sprinkles. She once went in the Village Halloween Parade as a chocolate-chocolate-chip-ice-cream cone with chocolate sprinkles—the ultimate tribute. I can't remember what I told her flounder tastes like. Whatever it was must have been mentioned in a speech of considerable eloquence. There is general agreement in our family that my speeches on how closely Chinese fried dumplings resemble ravioli were as persuasive as any I have delivered—Sarah happens to love ravioli; I wouldn't be at all surprised to see her suit up as a ravioli some Halloween—but four years of such speeches were required before Sarah agreed to take one microbite of one dumpling. Trying to persuade Sarah to taste something is not a struggle that is undertaken in the expectation that success will be rewarded with the opportunity to see her yelp with joy as she cleans her plate. She's not likely to be crazy about it. Once, Alice used a food processor and creamed cheese and absolutely fresh spinach and considerable imagination to turn out a spinach dish one bite of which would have probably caused Paul Bocuse and maybe even Herman Perrodin to ask about the possibility of apprenticing for a while in Alice's kitchen. Sarah tasted the spinach and, displaying a certain sensitivity toward the feelings of the chef, said, "It's better than a carrot." I must admit that the chef and I have found that phrase useful ever since. As we walk out of a movie, one of us sometimes says, "Well, it was better than a carrot" or, occasionally, "That one was not quite as good as a carrot."

The notion that Sarah might be persuaded to taste catfish was based on my observation that she might have been growing slightly more adventuresome about non-chocolate foodstuffs. The days are past when she refused to go to Chinatown unless she was carrying a bagel ("just in case"), and even though she still doesn't eat salad, she is too old to repeat her grand preschool gesture of refusing to return to a summer-recreation program because those in charge had the gall to serve her salad at snack time. Slowly, arbitrarily, she has expanded to half a dozen or so the exotic dishes she enjoys in apparent contradiction to her entire policy on eating—so that she will casually down, for instance, a Chinese dish called beef with baby clam sauce, like a teetotaler who happens to make an exception for slivovitz or south Georgia busthead. Still, I often hear myself making the sort of appeal I can imagine thousands of parents making to thousands of ten-year-olds at the same time: "Just try it. Would I lie to you about something as important to me as fried dumplings? If you don't like it, you don't have to eat it. Just try it."

There are, of course, a lot of grownups who won't try catfish. Some people think catfish are ugly. To be perfectly honest about it, just about everybody thinks catfish are ugly. I have run into people willing to defend the looks of hyenas and wild boars, but I have never heard anyone say, "The catfish, in its own way, is really quite beautiful." A catfish has whiskers that might look all right if attached to some completely different animal—although an appropriate animal does not come immediately to mind. The best thing that can be said of a catfish's skin is that it is removed before eating. At a fish plant, anyone who cleans catfish is ordinarily called a catfish skinner; part of the process is to pull off the skin with the kind of pliers that are used by other people to snip the heads off roofing nails. People who are particularly conscious of the tendency of catfish to feed along muddy river bottoms think of cleaning a catfish as a process that has ultimate failure built right into it; they avoid catfish precisely because they believe that there is no such thing as a clean catfish. Some people avoid catfish because they believe that no catfish—even one whose bones have been removed by a boner with the skill of a surgeon—is harboring fewer than seven small bones somewhere within it. There are also people who wouldn't think of trying a fish that in some parts of the country is thought to be eaten mainly by poor folks. In the South, where most catfish is consumed, even the way restaurants customarily advertise it implies that they are offering a bargain rather than a delicacy— CATFISH AND HUSH PUPPIES, ALL YOU CAN EAT: $3.25. Writing in *The New York Times* once about the place of catfish in his Mississippi boyhood, Craig Claiborne did describe the pleasure of eating it on summer picnics that included ladies carrying parasols, but he also left the impression that catfish was eaten on picnics because his mother wouldn't allow it inside her house.

With catfish farming now a considerable industry in Mississippi and Arkansas and Alabama, there has been some effort in recent years to make catfish a respectable national dish, rather than a slightly disreputable regional specialty, but seeing it on the menu of the sort of eclectic Manhattan restaurant that also serves salmon mousse and fettuccine with wild mushrooms still leaves the impression of having run into a stock-car racer at a croquet match. I preferred to think, of course, that the class implications of catfish eating would have no effect on Sarah's willingness to try it out— we have tried to raise her to believe that honest pan-fried chicken is in no way inferior to pâté—but it is impossible to predict such things; she happens to love particularly expensive cuts of smoked salmon, and the first wild-card dish she doted on in Chinatown was roast squab.

Naturally, I am interested in any opportunity to nudge Sarah's eating habits in a democratic direction, and that was one reason I chose the Fourth Annual St. Johns River Catfish Festival in Crescent City, Florida, as the destination for a little trip we were planning to take together while the rest of the family was occupied elsewhere. The other reason was that I happen to love catfish. I even love hush puppies. Sarah was enthusiastic about going to Florida, although I must admit that the first question she asked was how far Crescent City is from Disney World. Then she narrowed her eyes and said, "Catfish?"

"It tastes like flounder," I said. "You can just try it."

"Okay," she said, in the voice she uses for acknowledging the necessity of wearing gloves on cold days. "Maybe."

"Their other specialty is alligator tail," I said. "And for all I know alligator tail may taste like flounder, too."

Sarah didn't bother to reply to that one.

•

"I might try some catfish," Sarah said on the day before the festival, as we were discussing preparations with its founder, Ronnie Hughes. "It depends on how it looks."

"If you don't have any before the catfish-skinning contest, I suspect you won't have any after," Hughes said.

It was clear by then that the people in Crescent City, a pleasant little north Florida town below Jacksonville, were not among those trying to tidy up the reputation of the catfish. When Hughes, the publisher of the Crescent City Courier-Journal and Trading Post Shopper, persuaded the Rotary Club to sponsor a catfish festival, it was partly with the idea of celebrating the local commercial cat-fishing industry, but there has never been any claim that what the fishermen catch is anything other than an ugly beast with more bones than any fish has need of. "It's not something that's going to grace a table," Hughes said. Among the articles in his newspaper's Catfish Festival supplement was one that investigated the various styles of trying to eat a catfish—styles that divided catfish eaters into pickers, peelers, chompers, suckers, spitters, and animals—and con-cluded that all of them were more or less unsuccessful. In other parts of the South, boosters of the domestic catfish industry may argue for wider acceptance of their product on the ground that farm-raised catfish do not have a muddy taste; a resident of Crescent City tends to say he prefers the wild catfish caught in the nearby St. Johns River precisely because they do taste muddy. People around Crescent City take the catfish on its own terms.

"We don't mind if you refer to Crescent City and southern Putnam County as 'the sticks' or 'red-neck country,' " the brochure that the Rotary put out for the Catfish Festival said. "We're a down-home community." In north Florida, it is common to hear people speak of their part of the state as "the real Florida"—meaning that it is the part still not dominated by tourists or retired Yankees or Cubans or anybody else except people who like to refer to themselves as crackers. "This here's a natural Florida cracker here" is the way Buck Buckles, the man who always presides over the preparation of the festival's swamp cabbage, was introduced to Sarah and me. The celebration of crackers in southern Putnam County is for qualities pretty much like those attached to the catfish—being ornery and plain and uncouth and unconcerned about offending the pompous ("He don't care," Gamble Rogers, a country storyteller who performed at the festival, said of a cracker fisherman in one of his stories who rams the boats of tourists. "He flat do not care") and basically lovable.

Being down-home, people in Crescent City would not think of calling swamp cabbage by its other name—hearts of palm. They sometimes refer to another local specialty, soft-shelled turtle, as "cooter." Buck Buckles, whose crew helps him gather four hundred Sabal palm trees every year from an area scheduled for clear-cutting, is aware that some people serve hearts of palm fresh in salad, but for the Catfish Festival he cooks swamp cabbage for a day or so with noodles and salted bacon.

"How did you happen to learn how to do all that?" I asked Buckles, a friendly man in his sixties who has worked most of his life as a heavy-equipment contractor.

"Ever hear of Hoover?" Buckles said. There wasn't much money around southern Putnam County in the thirties, he told me, and anyone who wanted something to eat often had to "catch it, tree it, cut it out of a palm, or scratch it out of a hole."

Sarah was impressed with the process of preparing swamp cabbage—cutting the trunk of the palm into logs and then using machetes to strip away one layer after another in order to reach the heart. She announced, though, that she wasn't going to try any. I hadn't expected her to. The name "swamp cabbage" didn't seem to bother her, but she never eats anything that might ever be part of a salad—just to be on the safe side.

I also hadn't expected her to try the sort of exotic meats that Satsuma Gardens, a restaurant ten miles up the road from Crescent City, includes in what its menu lists as a "Swamp Critter Special"—frogs' legs, soft-shelled turtle, and gator tail. I was eager to taste gator tail myself—partly because it is the only exotic meat I have ever run across that nobody seems to describe as tasting like chicken. I suppose I harbored some faint hope that somebody might interest Sarah by saying that it tastes a bit like roast squab—as it turned out, most people in Putnam County compare gator tail to pork chops—but after we had a talk about alligators with John Norris, one of the proprietors of the St. Johns Crab Company, that hope evaporated. The St. Johns Crab Company is a few miles from Satsuma, in Welaka, where there are a number of fish plants that buy the crabs and catfish that the same families have been hauling out of the St. Johns for generations. The company provides a lot of the catfish eaten at the festival, although the impossibility of diverting four tons of small catfish—the kind Southerners like to eat—from regular customers once a year means that the festival supply is quietly supplemented by some farm-raised catfish from Mississippi, with the hope that festivalgoers will not be able to detect that telltale lack of mud.

"They don't just take a whole alligator tail and serve it like that," Norris said, in a reassuring way. "They cut out the muscle—"

"Well," I said, in the tone of someone who has been reassured, "once they dispose of that, then—"

"That's the part you eat," Norris said.

As it turned out, I liked gator tail—at least the way it was prepared by Jack Ketter at Satsuma Gardens, a friendly little roadside restaurant that is decorated with a beer-can collection and signs with sayings like "A Woman with Horse Sense Never Becomes a Nag." The first time I tasted alligator—at a vast, crowded restaurant where the meal reminded me once again that any time you're called to your table over a loudspeaker, what you are served there is likely to be disappointing—I found it rather, well, muscular. Ketter, though, serves a first-rate gator tail—cut into thin slices, pounded, and lightly fried. In fact, he caters the gator-tail booth at the festival, since alligator can be served only by a restaurant proprietor licensed to buy meat from the supply acquired by the shooting of "nuisance gators" that have been declared an exception to the alligator-protection law because of a tendency to frighten golfers or snack on Airedales. "It tastes like veal scallopini," I said to Sarah during our second meal at Satsuma Gardens. The remark did not inspire Sarah to pick up her fork for a taste. She doesn't eat veal scallopini.

"I might have tried alligator if that man hadn't told us about the muscle," she said, glancing at my dinner of alligator, catfish, soft-shell crab, fried mushrooms, fried okra, and coleslaw. As it was, she was having a hamburger—which is what she had eaten for lunch at Satsuma Gardens the previous day. "This place actually has very good hamburgers," she said. "In fact, excellent." At our first Satsuma Gardens meal, the waitress who brought Sarah a sack of potato chips as a side dish (if that's the word) opened the sack as she placed it on the table, and I, remembering that some particularly sophisticated people trace their worldliness to having been taken as children to restaurants by fathers who advised them on selecting the wine and dealing with the captain, looked at the open sack and said, "That's the way you can tell a classy joint."

•

The Fourth Annual St. Johns River Catfish Festival was held in the Crescent City town park—a long, square block in an area dominated by huge live oaks with Spanish moss. Sarah liked it. She liked the arts-and-crafts booths, particularly the booth that displayed a talking parrot. She liked the parade, which featured a series of Shriners driving by in every conceivable sort of vehicle that a grown man could look silly driving. She was impressed by Geetsie Crosby, the lady who always presides over the catfish chowder at the festival: Mrs. Crosby told Sarah that her own daughter would eat nothing but canned tuna for most of her childhood, and managed to grow up to be a very fine doctor.

"Maybe one of these years we can find a canned-tuna festival," I said. I had the feeling that Sarah wasn't going to eat much catfish.

She had seemed to be preparing me for that on the way to the festival when she said she wasn't really all that hungry. When lunchtime came, I got one catfish dinner instead of two, and offered her a bite.

"I don't really think I want any, thanks," Sarah said.

"But it tastes like flounder," I said.

"Does it taste like chocolate?" she said.

I didn't think I could make a very good case for its tasting like chocolate. I hadn't really expected the question. "Well, at least that leaves us free to go over and watch the catfish-skinning contest," I said. "As soon as I finish eating."